An Example for All the Land

An Example for All the Land

EMANCIPATION AND THE STRUGGLE OVER

EQUALITY IN WASHINGTON, D.C.

KATE MASUR

The University of North Carolina Press

Chapel Hill

The paper in this book meets the guidelines for permanence and durability
of the Committee on Production Guidelines for Book Longevity of the
Council on Library Resources.

The University of North Carolina Press has been a
member of the Green Press Initiative since 2003.

Library of Congress Cataloging-in-Publication Data
Masur, Kate.
An example for all the land : emancipation and
the struggle over equality in Washington, D.C. / Kate Masur. — 1st ed.
p. cm.
Includes bibliographical references and index.
ISBN 978-0-8078-3414-5 (cloth : alk. paper)
ISBN 978-0-8078-7266-6 (pbk. : alk. paper)
1. African Americans—Washington (D.C.)—History—19th century.
2. African Americans—Washington (D.C.)—Politics and government—19th century.
3. African Americans—Civil rights—Washington (D.C.)—History—19th century.
4. African Americans—Suffrage—Washington (D.C.)—History—19th century.
5. Washington (D.C.)—Politics and government—19th century. I. Title.
F205.N4M37 2010
323.11960730753—DC22
2010006643

Portions of the text have been published elsewhere: "The African American
Delegation to Abraham Lincoln: A Reappraisal," *Civil War History* 56, no. 2
(June 2010); and "Civil, Political, and Social Equality after Lincoln: A Paradigm and a
Problematic," *Marquette Law Review* 93, no. 4 (2010). Used by permission.

cloth   14 13 12 11 10   5 4 3 2 1
paper   16 15 14 13 12   5 4 3 2 1

for Eva

Contents

Figures and Maps

FIGURES

MAPS

An Example for All the Land

Introduction

As a new congressional session opened at the end of 1874, residents of the District of Columbia looked ahead to a debate of great significance. The nation's legislators would consider a bill to establish for the capital a government run by three commissioners appointed by the U.S. president. The legislation proposed to end permanently not only local self-government but also a brief period in which black men and white men alike had cast ballots and held elective offices and the Republican Party had been dominant in local affairs. "Have we come to the point where we find it necessary to undo what we have done; to tear down the house we have built?" asked the editors of Washington's *National Republican* newspaper. Many found it remarkable that residents of the capital of a nation founded on the principle of local self-government might soon be denied the right to choose their own officials. It was even more surprising to consider that such disfranchisement might come at the hands of a Congress dominated by the Republican Party, the nation's preeminent force in securing African American men's right to vote.

Since the Civil War, Republicans in Congress had repeatedly used the nation's capital as a laboratory for experiments with democracy and racial equality. It was, Senator Charles Sumner said, "an example for all the land." The Constitution, which restrained Congress's power in the states, gave the nation's legislators virtually unchallengeable authority over the roughly seventy square miles of territory that was home not only to federal workers but also to long-standing local residents and thousands of newly arrived freedpeople. Republican-controlled Congresses had abolished slavery, established schools for black children, banned discrimination on streetcars and railroads, enfranchised black men, and forbidden racial discrimination in office holding and jury service. "It was in this District that the experiment of enlarging the elective franchise was first made," the *National Republican* reminded readers. "It was here that in other days . . . the Republican party entered upon the policy of equal rights for all men, and avowed it to the world."[1]

Yet, in 1874, Republicans were divided among themselves about how the capital should be governed, and their internecine disagreements were magnified by Democrats eager to declare the Republican experiment in universal manhood suffrage a failure. That spring, Congress had taken the dramatic step of placing the District of Columbia under the temporary control of three commissioners appointed by the president. Now, in December, Republican senator Lot Morrill of Maine, long a congressional leader in District affairs, proposed making the commission form of government permanent. Morrill claimed the bill was "in the interest of honest government" and would "relieve this District from the oppressions and the difficulties under which it has been struggling."[2] His Democratic colleague, Thomas F. Bayard of Delaware, was more specific: "I believe that negro suffrage in the District of Columbia has been the largest contributing cause to the present debt and the bad government of this community." He challenged congressional Republicans to decide whether to continue supporting biracial suffrage in the capital or "get themselves out of it" by disfranchising black and white men alike.[3] The nation's legislators got themselves out of it in 1878 when they made the commission government permanent. It would be almost 100 years before local sovereignty returned to the nation's capital.

The disfranchisement of District of Columbia residents was the final act of a drama that began during the Civil War, when Americans began to contemplate the implications of abolishing slavery. It was relatively straightforward to decree that human beings could no longer be considered property and that no one could enjoy the benefits of others' uncompensated labor. Much more complicated was the question of postemancipation equality. In the Northeast, slavery's abolition in the early nineteenth century had led not to a regime of racial equality, but rather to a society in which both customary and legal discrimination were commonplace. As southern slavery ended, Americans asked crucial questions about whether and how to eliminate the features of slavery that might remain in law and public life even after abolition. Would the nation tolerate local and state black codes, which explicitly restricted free African Americans' opportunities to engage in business, hold meetings, purchase property, and even settle in certain places? In what areas of life should people interact as equals, and where should inequalities be preserved? Which aspects of the problem of inequality were matters of policy and which were best left untouched by government? These were some of the greatest questions of the postwar era. This book tells how Washingtonians, including congressmen, presidents, former slaves, longtime free black residents, and black migrants from the North, tried to answer them.[4]

I began work on this book focused not on the concept of equality but on citizenship. Amid scholars' growing interest in linking social history with the history of politics and public life, I thought an exploration of debates about citizenship in post–Civil War Washington would yield new insights into how contemporaries understood which people had which rights in which places.[5] I wanted to use citizenship not as an amorphous category of belonging but as a formal, legal concept. Yet I soon realized that the capital's special status as a dominion of Congress made the study of legal citizenship there virtually impossible. Because post–Civil War citizenship in large part concerned the relationship of the federal government to the states, the capital—not being a state—was a terrible place to study it.

What I found, however, was that congressional debates, presidential policy, and the tumult on the streets of the city had produced an unusually unadulterated debate about the meanings of equality. When federal officials debated Reconstruction policies for the states of the former Confederacy—including the crucial question of how they would define racial equality before the law—they confronted constitutional limits on federal power. By contrast, Congress's exclusive jurisdiction in the District cut away much of the chaff, exposing the core of their disagreements about the rights to which all people were entitled and the measures that were necessary to secure them. African American leaders understood that the District of Columbia could be a laboratory for egalitarian policy and pressed Congress to pass local laws that reflected their expansive aspirations. Woman suffragists watched with interest as Congress experimented with racial equality in the capital, and they lobbied intensely for a parallel experiment in woman's enfranchisement. If Washington was a bad place to study citizenship, it was the perfect place to study struggles over equality.

Equality is a crucial concept in American history, but it has received comparatively little attention from historians of Reconstruction. In recent decades, the concept of freedom has been far more favored. As Eric Foner and others have demonstrated, one of the central questions the nation faced after emancipation was how former slaves' freedom would be defined. In the United States and other postemancipation societies, freedpeople sought to escape the oversight of whites, form families and communities, and cultivate the land as they chose. But in pursuing their goals, freedpeople often came into conflict with people who viewed freedom simply as the absence of bondage and pushed them to work for wages, under close supervision, while denying them access to land of their own. Historians have shown how meanings of freedom differed not only between blacks and whites and between northerners and southerners, but also among African Americans, across lines of sex, class, and region of origin. The meanings of freedom were myriad, and it mattered immensely whose definitions won out. But the focus on freedom has left other important concepts relatively unexplored. Equality is one of them.[6]

This study of debates over equality during Reconstruction demonstrates the importance of two separate but interconnected threads of American thought on the subject. First, as we do now, nineteenth-century Americans traced a tradition of individual equal rights from ancient Greece, through the Enlightenment, to the American Revolution and, in particular, to the declaration that "all men are created equal" and "endowed by their Creator with certain inalienable Rights." In the late eighteenth century, Enlightenment ideas of natural rights and human equality became available not only to creole revolutionaries but also to enslaved people, who drew on them and on their own indigenous views of justice and community to demand rights in the societies being born from revolution. In the first half of the nineteenth century, white men successfully used the equal rights tradition to argue for white manhood suffrage, while abolitionists and woman's rights activists demanded, with less success, even more sweeping interpretations of universal rights.[7]

Whereas the concept of freedom almost always implied liberty—or people's ability to act as they chose, unconstrained by government or by other private persons—the concept of equality had everything to do with policy. When people demanded equal rights, they were in essence asking for government measures that would ensure that individuals who were in some ways unequal would be treated equally or offered equal opportunities. But the questions of what measures to take and which inequities to attempt to remedy were extraordinarily difficult to settle.

Historical scholarship on how such questions were debated during Reconstruction has been hampered by historians' tendency to impose on the past contemporary ideas about the proper scope of equality, rather than to look at how people in the nineteenth century understood the concept. Thus historians have sometimes implied that during Reconstruction a bundle of civil rights existed and that the central issue was who would be allowed to claim them. Recent legal historians have begun to complicate that view, however. They have shown that nineteenth-century conceptions of who had which rights, in which places, were shaped by multiple legal regimes. They have demonstrated, for example, that common carriers such as streetcars and railroads were governed by different principles of accommodation from public schools. Departing from the field's traditional focus on courts and constitutions, they have also illuminated relationships among legal and political institutions and between elite decisions and popular struggles. Such scholarship has begun to demonstrate that it is not sufficient to argue simply that some Americans sought equality and others fought against it. We must now ask, what kinds of equality? And where?[8]

The equal rights tradition represented by the Declaration of Independence was extremely important during Reconstruction, but so, too, was another thread of thinking that focused more on inequality than on equality, and more on status and privileges than on individual rights. For much longer than historians have often recognized, Americans adhered to a vision of a corporate social order in which people were understood less as individuals than as members of different and overlapping groups, differentiated by such attributes as race, sex, age, economic status, and length of residence in the community. In antebellum America, the social group to which a person belonged (whether one was black or white, male or female, wealthy or poor) had a great deal to do with what rights and privileges one enjoyed. So did reputation. A poor person known in the community to be honest and responsible had more public credibility than one known as a drunkard. Membership and leadership in churches, benevolent societies, and other ostensibly private clubs and associations could also enhance one's public status and therefore one's ability to claim prerogatives in the community.[9]

The manifestly inegalitarian worldview inherent in such practices was nowhere more clear than in structures and conventions of local citizenship. Citizenship did not become a national, constitutional status until the Fourteenth Amendment was ratified in 1868. Before the Civil War, Americans most often viewed citizenship as a local status tied to a person's standing in the community. Moreover, as recent historians have pointed out, antebellum citizenship was more closely connected with corporate and associational privileges and immunities than with rights. Full citizenship was often associated with the vote, but voting was considered less an individual right than a privilege to which only those with certain kinds of elevated status—property holders or white men, for example—were entitled. Citizens enjoyed benefits, but they also had obligations to the community, such as serving in the militia, paying taxes, and contributing to charities. The concept of citizenship implied stewardship and a vision of reciprocity in which the fulfillment of obligations was rewarded with the privilege of high standing. The citizenship status of antebellum white women was thus particularly vexed. Indeed, members of a vibrant movement for women's equality insisted that sex should not preclude women from either fulfilling the obligations or enjoying the privileges granted to men of their stature.[10]

Because northern precedents were of great relevance during the era of Republican dominance that followed the Civil War, it is particularly useful to understand how hierarchical understandings of citizenship and civic culture shaped the lives of free blacks in the antebellum North. Laws in most northern states made no racial distinctions in basic civil rights to enter into contracts, sue in court, and move from place to place. But some laws did discriminate. For example, all states reserved the duty of militia service for white men only; some prohibited black settlement; some permitted only white men to vote, and others imposed more stringent voter qualifications on black men than on white. Discriminatory practices were rampant in public life even where laws did not require them. African Americans often faced segregation and exclusion in quasi-public places such as railroads, streetcars, and hotels. Northern states, unlike their southern counterparts, had no black codes restricting African Americans' ability to convene meetings or walk the streets at night. But whites nonetheless subjected black churches, schools, and other associations to special scrutiny and, in times of heightened racial tensions, violently attacked them. Some black and white northerners condemned all these practices, but most nineteenth-century white Americans saw everyday inequities as manifestations of a social order in which different groups of people naturally occupied different, and hierarchically organized, places in the community.[11]

The cataclysm of the Civil War and the abolition of slavery exploded much of the received wisdom about American public life and provided an opportunity for reconstituting the nation along more egalitarian lines. Even before the war, theories of individual rights and contract were replacing local traditions that stressed standing and collectivity. The rise of the Republican vision of free labor ideology, the Union victory, and the raft of federal legislation and constitutional amendments that followed the war all magnified this trend. Indeed, it is a commonplace that postwar legal changes at the federal level laid the groundwork for the modern state and for a new vision of individual rights.[12] Yet the focus on federal legislation and constitutional change has kept our range of vision narrow, drawing attention to individual rights and away from older but still important convictions about group identities and the privileges of local citizenship. Moreover, we still know relatively little about how people disputed equality on the local level during Reconstruction. This book focuses simultaneously on federal, municipal, and street-level politics, and it pays particular attention to how people on all sides of the debate invoked both the Enlightenment tradition of individual rights and more culturally embedded ideas about local standing and membership. It is at once a reinterpretation of Washington's Reconstruction history and a meditation on the meanings of equality at a pivotal moment in American history.

Washington became an example for all the land not only because Congress experimented with policy there, but also because local residents saw slavery's end as an opportunity to transform the city. Beginning during the Civil War, black Washingtonians insisted on a remarkably expansive interpretation of racial equality. The black population was anything but homogeneous. Existing black residents, the majority of whom had been free before the war, were joined by thousands of fugitives from slavery and by migrants from the North who came in search of work, education, and opportunities for political activism. In their private lives, African Americans observed distinctions in wealth, education, and place of origin. When it came to making demands in public, however, they were strikingly allied across classes in the pursuit of a broad definition of equality. Using a variety of tactics, including written petitions, individual protests, and mass demonstrations, black Washingtonians demanded much more than basic equality in legal proceedings. They sought recognition as members of the civic body and full and equal access to streetcars, theaters, public schools, and the proceedings of Congress. They demanded fair treatment by the police and a fair share of public works employment, equal access to trade unions, and official recognition of their militia organizations.[13]

Time and again, black Washingtonians demanded rights and privileges ahead of legislation. I call the claims they made in advance of the law "upstart claims," to emphasize that these were not claims to existing rights, nor were they supported by existing policies. Black Washingtonians made upstart claims using, and sometimes merging, visions of individual rights and traditions of privileges and standing. For example, black soldiers were the first to demand equal access to Washington's streetcars, and they invoked their elevated status as soldiers to validate their claims. Congress, in turn, passed legislation that translated those demands into a positive right to ride the streetcars. After that, African Americans demanded enforcement of the law, not only as a right but also as a privilege accorded to men and women who displayed respectable comportment. As this example suggests, African Americans' upstart claims could be translated from one idiom to another. Such translations usually went in one direction—from status to rights—as advocates of expansive visions of equality found theoretical support in the universalism of the rights tradition and practical support from Republicans in Congress.

Black Washingtonians did not always orient their claims toward getting a law implemented or enforced, nor were their attacks on inequality in public life always demands for assimilation into the broader, white-dominated community. To the contrary, they also demanded recognition of their own, autonomous institutions, both as a perquisite of freedom and as confirmation of their equal civic stature. As emancipation dawned, they brought their churches, mutual aid societies, and other associations into the streets of the city, demonstrating to one another and to the white public their worthiness of participation in the civic life of the community and, by extension, their insistence on recognition as citizens. More than any other institution, African American churches mediated between the relatively autonomous world of black Washington that had developed under the strictures of slavery and the white-dominated world of official politics. Before black men's enfranchisement, black Washingtonians used churches to host citywide discussions about public affairs, and afterward the churches became centers of Republican Party organizing, even as they retained their crucial role as independent black organizations.

It was precisely because the world of churches, families, and other ostensibly private institutions was inseparable from that of public policy that it was nearly impossible to reach a consensus on the meaning of one of the most important concepts in Republican politics: racial equality before the law. In one of his 1858 debates with Stephen Douglas, Abraham Lincoln had argued, "There is no reason in the world why the negro is not entitled to all the natural rights enumerated in the Declaration of Independence, the right to life, liberty, and the pursuit of happiness." Yet the future president also added that he had "no purpose to introduce political and social equality between the white and the black races." Lincoln thus parsed equality into three separate conceptual categories: natural, political, and social. In his support for equal "natural rights"—which were often known as "civil rights" when translated into law and policy—and his opposition to political and social equality, Lincoln was in the broad mainstream of the antebellum Republican Party. Yet the categories of civil, political, and social rights and equality were malleable and unstable, not separate and clear-cut as Lincoln's blunt statement suggested.[14]

In the wake of the war, there was a broad agreement, at least among Republicans, that African Americans should enjoy civic equality with whites. This usually meant that laws themselves must not discriminate and that there must be no racial discrimination in access to legal proceedings. In the capital and elsewhere, Republicans' preferred mode of creating civil equality was to eliminate any laws that applied only to African Americans and to eliminate the word "white" from statutes, making privileges and rights heretofore available only to whites unrestricted by race. African American activists and some white radical Republicans, however, demanded a far broader vision of basic civil equality, insisting that the principle of racial equality before the law required equal access to all institutions that were chartered or regulated by government, including public schools, common carriers (such as streetcars, railroads, and steamers), and other public accommodations.

If Republicans were divided on the outer limits of civil equality, they were even more conflicted on the question of political equality. Political equality conventionally referred to the vote, but it could also allude to office holding and jury service. All three were traditionally considered privileges associated with elevated status, and because so many northerners doubted that freedmen were capable of making sound judgments, Republicans were divided on whether to seek policies that would make African American men politically equal to white men. African Americans and white radicals often rejected the separation between civil equality and political equality, arguing instead that the vote was a fundamental civil right whose origins, like the origins of other civil rights, were in natural law. But Democrats and moderate Republicans demanded recognition of a clear line between the two categories, a move that allowed them a measure of precision about which forms of equality they supported and which they did not.

Still more ambiguous was the category called "social equality." Unlike the other two terms, social equality had no concrete existence. Rather, people used the concept of social equality as a container for everything they considered anathema. Thus, for example, when black Washingtonians sought a law prohibiting discrimination on the District's streetcars, conservative senators insisted that this was a "social" matter and not an appropriate subject of legislation. Later, Democrats and some moderate Republicans insisted that public school integration was a "social equality" measure that would usurp the authority of parents to determine the company their children kept. Supporters of African Americans' equal access to streetcars and public schools claimed that what they sought was not undue government intervention in the private realm but, rather, appropriate government regulation of essentially public institutions. But their opponents, who sought to constrain the scope of legal equality, portrayed "the social" as vast and inviolable. The social equality shibboleth allowed people who were moderate and conservative on racial matters to move the conversation onto ostensibly private terrain where, they argued, taste and custom should reign and the government should have no say.[15]

Although there was little agreement about the limits of legal equality, Republicans' insistence on removing discriminatory language from laws, itself, made a forceful statement. After the Republicans came to power in Washington's city government, for example, the publisher of the city directory stopped placing a "c" next to the names of "colored" residents. Yet if talk of race was now off-limits in some contexts, plenty of other categories of distinction and hierarchy were still available for those hoping to slow the galloping pace of change. As wealthy white Washingtonians, Democrats and Republicans alike, mobilized to end radical Republicanism in the capital, they constituted themselves as "citizens" and "taxpayers" and complained not about the enfranchisement of black men as such but about the electorate's ignorance and lack of civilization. The white elite's use of these complex and freighted terms, I argue, reveals the interpenetration of their concerns about racial and class upheaval and shows how they adapted their arguments to the requirements of the moment. Instead of making a frontal attack on the new world of racial equality before the law, Washington's municipal reformers launched an extremely effective flanking maneuver.[16]

Amid a growing reaction against popular government in both northern and southern cities, Congress disfranchised residents of the capital in two stages. First, in 1871, it moved to diminish voters' power by structuring the capital as territory similar to federal territories in the U.S. West. Then, three years later, it abolished elected government altogether. The city that for more than a decade had stood as an example of biracial democracy thus became a model of precisely the opposite. Throughout the country, suffrage reformers searching for ways to curtail the power of objectionable voters observed this transformation with interest and often with admiration. In the end, northerners turned not to outright disfranchisement but to a sustained movement for municipal government reform. Southerners, by the 1890s, adopted direct disfranchisement, not based on race or color—for that would violate the Fifteenth Amendment—but based on literacy, taxpayer status, and other nonracial markers of low status. Just as the capital's economic elite had preferred to disfranchise the entire community, black and white, rather than allow black men's suffrage to continue, so too did later southern disfranchisers embrace a racialized vision of elite rule in which some poor whites were swept, alongside African Americans, into a growing category of people who were proscribed from formal politics. The late-nineteenth-century assault on popular government confirmed the prediction of Senator George E. Spencer, a white carpetbagger from Alabama, who in 1877 argued that the termination of self-government in the capital was part of "a crusade against the suffrage and against the exercise of other popular rights . . . which bids fair to shake the foundations of American freedom."[17]

The narrative that follows is arranged roughly chronologically. The first three chapters trace African Americans' upstart claims in the years before black men's enfranchisement. Chapter 1 focuses on the Civil War, when thousands of fugitive migrants entered the capital and Congress took its first steps to end slavery and its legacies. It shows how black Washingtonians used church-based organizations as hubs for political and civic organizing. It also reveals how black Washingtonians galvanized to stop the rendition of fugitive slaves to their owners, and how black soldiers, once enlisted, pressed for unprecedented rights and privileges. Chapter 2 explores the moral uplift programs implemented by Freedmen's Bureau agents, missionaries, and teachers, who sought to impart lessons of civilization to freedpeople and thus prepare them to claim equality. It also shows how freedpeople availed themselves of the aid such people offered but, in the process, made demands of their own and sometimes forced changes in policy. Chapter 3 emphasizes struggles to define equality in public and quasi-public spaces, including African Americans' insistence on attending debates in the Capitol, riding the streetcars as equals, and organizing militias. Collectively these chapters demonstrate that by the winter of 1867, when Congress passed legislation enfranchising black men, the capital was already a crucible of conflict over national Reconstruction policy and host to rich local debates about the meanings of racial equality.

The subsequent three chapters focus more intensively on the meanings and implications of the vote. Chapter 4 shows how, after black men were enfranchised, a newly energized local Republican Party, led by black and white men, briefly dominated Washington politics and developed policies that favored laborers, municipal development, and an expansive vision of racial equality before the law. Chapter 5 examines woman suffragists' demands for women's voting rights in the capital and reveals how the local movement fractured over whether to support or condemn black men's enfranchisement. It also shows how a powerful bipartisan movement of businessmen coalesced in favor of reforming the District's governing structures. That movement persuaded Congress to consolidate the three separate municipalities within the District of Columbia—the cities of Washington and Georgetown and rural Washington County—into a single government and to significantly diminish the power of voters. As Chapter 6 demonstrates, the resulting territorial government, led by businessman Alexander Shepherd, jolted the capital into urban modernity. But it also ran roughshod over democracy and eventually alienated wealthy property owners, laborers, and black activists alike. Endeavoring to dismantle the territorial government—and consistent with the sense, increasingly shared by elites across the nation, that urban democracy needed to be curtailed—Congress in 1874 placed the capital under control of a presidentially appointed commission.

The irony that for the next ninety-nine years residents of the U.S. capital were not permitted to choose their own local government is inseparable from the larger American paradox that a nation founded on the principle that "all men are created equal" also permitted and promoted the enslavement of people of African descent. The black Washingtonians and their white allies who demanded expansive government action to eliminate slavery's vestiges in Washington were the first of many generations to attack the problem of postemancipation equality. Their ideas and tactics resonate into the present, as do the strategies of those who ultimately defeated them.

1

Everywhere Is Freedom and Everybody Free

THE CAPITAL TRANSFORMED

On Thursday, August 14, 1862, an extraordinary meeting convened in Washington's Union Bethel African Methodist Episcopal Church in downtown Washington. The previous Sunday, President Abraham Lincoln, through a representative, had put out word that he wanted to meet with a small group of black Washingtonians. Amid great excitement and curiosity about the purpose of the meeting, African American church congregations selected delegations to convene at Union Bethel days later. Going into the meeting, attendees were unsure what the president wished to discuss or even whether he would be present.

Lincoln was not in Union Bethel that day. It fell to his representative, James Mitchell, a white minister from Indiana, to inform the group that the president wanted to discuss African American emigration out of the United States. Like many other Americans, Lincoln was pessimistic that black and white people could live together peacefully under conditions of equality, and he had long seen black emigration as a potential solution to that problem. In the preceding months, the federal government had begun to lean toward colonization as policy. Congress had placed $600,000 at Lincoln's disposal for settling newly freed African Americans outside the United States, of which $100,000 was earmarked for residents of the capital. James Mitchell's announcement in Union Bethel suggested that the president was ready to begin spending that money.

The historic implications of the invitation itself were clear. In the midst of a civil war capable of destroying slavery, Lincoln's request implicitly recognized African Americans as a part of the American public to be consulted, not simply acted upon. Yet those who assembled in Union Bethel had grave doubts about the president's purposes, and many were reluctant to comply with his request. First, they were skeptical about the government's turn to colonization

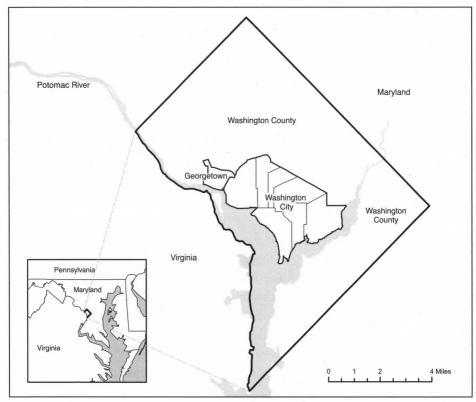

Potomac River

Maryland

Washington County

Georgetown

Washington City

Washington County

Virginia

Pennsylvania

Maryland

Virginia

0   1   2   4 Miles

MAP I. THE DISTRICT OF COLUMBIA

as policy. They questioned the origins and credibility of Lincoln's proposal "to a great length." Was this the "voluntary action of the President, or forced upon his consideration by the selfish interest of non-resident parties?" they wondered. Some were also uncomfortable at the prospect of a small delegation being asked to represent the views of all the black residents of the capital, or perhaps even the nation. One attendee "did not feel authorized to commit our people to any measure of colonization."[1]

Mitchell attempted to reassure, and after much debate the assembled group decided to send a delegation to Lincoln. First, however, Edward M. Thomas and John F. Cook Jr. proposed two resolutions that would register the group's objections. The first declared it "inexpedient, inauspicious, and impolitic" to advocate emigration out of the United States and suggested "that time, the great arbiter of events and movements, will adjust the matter." In other words, with the war on, they thought it best to wait and see what would happen. The second resolution questioned the propriety of a small group of people presuming to represent all black Americans, stating that it was "unauthorized and unjust for us to compromise the interests of over four-and-a-half millions of our race by precipitate action on our part."[2] The Union Bethel meeting adopted the resolutions. Thus having rejected the very premises of the conversation Lincoln hoped to initiate, the five-man delegation, which included Cook and Thomas, left with Mitchell for the Executive Mansion.

Abraham Lincoln's August 1862 meeting with a delegation of African American men is well known to students of the Civil War, but the broader local context for that meeting has been largely forgotten. Historical literature on the capital during the war has focused on military defense and intrigue in the federal government but has paid little attention to the unfolding of emancipation and to the debates about racial equality that also occupied local residents, congressmen, and the president of the United States.[3] In fact, by the summer of 1862, when Lincoln invited the black delegation to meet with him, the debate about racial equality in the national capital was already well under way. That spring, Congress had passed legislation, beginning with an Emancipation Act for the District of Columbia, to implement the Republican vision of basic racial equality before the law. Yet black Washingtonians were pushing the struggle for equality further than Congress originally intended to go.

As policy makers debated whether a war for union should become a war for emancipation, thousands of fugitives from slavery migrated into the city in search of freedom, safety, and employment. Crowds gathered in the streets and at the courthouse to insist that officials cease to enforce fugitive slave laws in the Union capital. Members of the long-standing black elite mobilized to aid and uplift the destitute and to shape the public debate, which in 1862 was centrally concerned with whether to emigrate out of the United States rather than risk an uncertain future at home. Local African American debate about emigration, which began before the Lincoln delegation and persisted after it, revealed divisions among black Washingtonians not only about emigration itself but also about who could represent whom and whether it was important for African Americans to be united on the crucial issues of the day.

By 1863, however, the federal government's turn toward a policy of emancipation provided an impetus for bolder demands at home. Black soldiers, enlisted late that spring, rejected conventions of racial deference and demanded, instead, to be respected on the streets and to ride the city's newly established streetcars as equals to white men. By the summer, African Americans were insisting, through public demonstrations by the citywide Sabbath school movement and benevolent associations, that freedom must mean full citizenship in

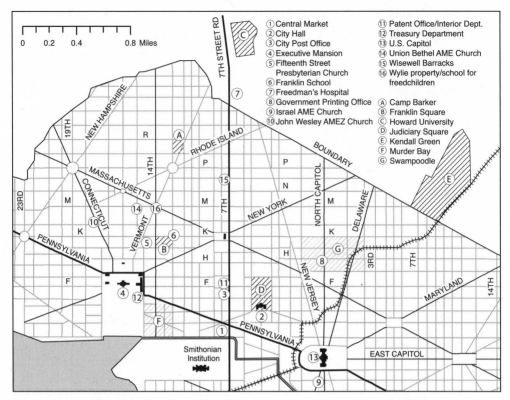

① Central Market
② City Hall
③ City Post Office
④ Executive Mansion
⑤ Fifteenth Street
   Presbyterian Church
⑥ Franklin School
⑦ Freedman's Hospital
⑧ Government Printing Office
⑨ Israel AME Church
⑩ John Wesley AMEZ Church
⑪ Patent Office/Interior Dept.
⑫ Treasury Department
⑬ U.S. Capitol
⑭ Union Bethel AME Church
⑮ Wisewell Barracks
⑯ Wylie property/school for
   freedchildren

Ⓐ Camp Barker
Ⓑ Franklin Square
Ⓒ Howard University
Ⓓ Judiciary Square
Ⓔ Kendall Green
Ⓕ Murder Bay
Ⓖ Swampoodle

MAP 2. LANDMARKS IN CENTRAL AND NORTHWEST WASHINGTON CITY

the community. African Americans combated inequality not only by demanding rights but also by insisting on equal privileges and equal status in local life. Their agenda, the willingness of some in Congress to take up their cause, and white Washingtonians' almost unmitigated hostility, all laid the groundwork for the protracted struggles of Reconstruction.

The Combination Yet Wanting

When Charles Dickens visited Washington in 1842, he called the capital "the City of Magnificent Intentions" and ridiculed its "spacious avenues, that begin in nothing, and lead nowhere." Beginning with its emergence from the Constitutional Convention of 1787, the nation's capital was a contradictory mix of planning and spontaneity, grandiose dreams and more mundane realities. Delegates to the convention purposely gave the capital its own territory, apart from the states, to avoid fueling jealousies among states or subjecting the federal government to the influence of a single state. And the capital, not being a state, had no representatives in Congress. The first Congress determined in 1790 that the new capital city would be located on the banks of the Potomac River, and, while president, George Washington sited the city where the river forked just below the Great Falls of the Potomac. Washington City thus joined the existing towns of Georgetown and Alexandria within the confines of a federal district carved from land donated by Virginia and Maryland. The rural area surrounding the three cities was designated Washington County. The federal government began moving to the unfinished city in June 1800, and Congress first convened there that fall.[4]

President Washington and his engineers envisioned a regal capital of wide boulevards and imposing public architecture that would become a commercial hub and a civic beacon. Yet, in a new nation where many people held a deep suspicion of centralized government, ideological predispositions and conflicts over spending priorities meant that federal authorities never appropriated enough money to build the monumental capital that its planners had envisioned. Nor did the capital become the commercial center that George Washington had imagined. It lagged behind the vibrant port city of Baltimore, fifty miles away, and did not become a gateway to the West as its boosters had hoped.[5] In the midst of the Civil War, the poet Walt Whitman described the ironies and unevenness of the capital's development as a metaphor for the nation as a whole: "The city, the spaces, buildings, &c make no unfit emblem of our country, so far, so broadly planned, every thing in plenty, money & materials staggering with plenty, but the fruit of the plans, the knit, the combination yet wanting."[6]

The contradictions of quotidian life in the antebellum capital were nowhere clearer than on the busy strip of Pennsylvania Avenue between the Executive Mansion and the Capitol. Designed as a grand artery and the symbolic link between the executive and legislative branches of the federal government, "the Avenue" was wide and regal, and from early on Washington's socially conscious made it a place to see and be seen. Yet even on the Avenue, tawdriness converged with grandiosity. Well-dressed women and men mingled with shoe shiners and newspaper boys, fancy carriages shared the street with decrepit hacks, and expensive boutiques stood near the city's cacophonous central market. The south side of the street hosted a hodgepodge of businesses and residences, many of them considered disreputable. That side also ran close to the city's putrid canal, essentially an open sewer running through the heart of the city. The adjacent slum was known as Murder Bay. Ever conscious of

FIGURE 1.1. This photograph of Abraham Lincoln's funeral procession shows the scale and style of buildings on the north side of Pennsylvania Avenue. Courtesy Library of Congress, LC-DIG-cwpb-00593.

the implications of spatial mingling and contamination—perhaps both literal and figurative—the promenading elite shunned the south side of the Avenue, confining its self-conscious rituals to the north side.[7]

The capital's governing structures mingled federal authority with municipal regulation. The Constitution gave Congress power "to exercise exclusive Legislation" in the District, but from almost the beginning Congress delegated some governing responsibilities to municipal governments within the capital. Washington's original charter provided only for a mayor appointed by Congress, but an 1820 charter established a bicameral legislature (a board of aldermen and a common council) and a popularly elected mayor. At first, the privilege of voting was limited to white men with $100 or more of property, but in 1848 the property requirement was dropped. Congress also granted Georgetown a municipal charter, and Washington County was governed by an appointed body called the Levy Court. Congress returned Alexandria and the Virginia portion of the capital to the state of Virginia in 1846, and from then on the District of Columbia contained three separate local jurisdictions— Washington City, Georgetown, and Washington County—over all of which Congress had ultimate power.[8]

Despite its uniqueness as the nation's capital, however, Washington was in many respects similar to other midsize cities of its era. This was a period of rapid urbanization throughout the nation, and Washington shared in that trend. As in other cities, boosters and businessmen advocated grading and paving of streets and turnpikes, improved railroad links with other cities, drainage of polluted waterways, and better policing. And as elsewhere, the municipal government sought to raise money by taxing real estate and other property and by issuing bonds. In Washington, improvements did not keep pace with the needs of the growing population, but the same was true in cities throughout the country, which also struggled to finance basic infrastructure. Still, improvement-minded residents of the capital were quick to blame the federal government itself for holding the city back. The government paid no taxes on property, and the nation's legislators took little interest in local urban development, except to the extent that it improved their own lives. Indeed, in the antebellum years, the federal government extended the Capitol, built a water supply system (oriented toward federal offices, not District residents), and paved the Avenue.[9]

Slavery and its legal and cultural trappings were integral to the antebellum capital. Free and enslaved black workers worked alongside white men in building such national monuments as the Capitol and the Executive Mansion, and black laborers filled myriad positions typical of the urban South: domestic workers, skilled craftsmen, laundresses, and day laborers.[10] During the antebellum years, Washington's black population grew steadily, while the proportion of slaves to free blacks diminished. In 1860, 78 percent of the local black population was free, up from 73 percent ten years earlier. Yet, even as increasing numbers of black Washingtonians enjoyed nominal freedom, the threat of sale hung over everyone. The decline of slavery in the Chesapeake region generated a thriving business of selling slaves to the booming Southwest. Enslaved people were always at risk of being sold away, while their free counterparts were threatened with kidnapping. As historian Stanley Harrold put it, slavery in antebellum Washington was "both weak and vicious."[11]

Federal and local officials worked together to secure both slavery and the racist legal order that supported it. During the 1830s, for example, proslavery congressmen countered abolitionists' demand for emancipation in the capital with a gag rule that prohibited Congress from receiving antislavery petitions. In the Compromise of 1850, antislavery legislators managed to ban the slave trade in the District, yet slavery itself continued on, protected by the good graces of Congress.[12] Meanwhile, Congress gradually augmented the powers of the Washington city government, and the city government in turn passed black codes designed to circumscribe the activities of free blacks. In 1820, the municipal government enacted laws requiring free blacks to obtain signatures and peace bonds from prominent whites who vouched for their continued good behavior. Later laws established curfews for African Americans, banned them from certain lines of work, and forbade them from holding meetings without a permit from city officials. In a sign of the intent to reduce the presence of black people in Washington's official public spaces, Congress in 1828 instructed the federal commissioner of public buildings to bar African Americans from the Capitol grounds except when there on "business."[13] Some of the black codes were enforced sporadically, but the threat of enforcement always loomed, particularly in times of heightened racial tension. After an 1848 attempt by dozens of slaves to escape on the schooner *Pearl*, for example, Georgetown and Washington officials petitioned Congress for broadened police powers to prevent slave escapes and to tighten controls over free blacks. Washington City soon more than doubled its police force and created a requirement that free blacks purchase $50.00 certificates of their free status and carry them at all times.[14]

Free black Washingtonians faced not only legal restrictions on their lives and livelihoods but also discrimination in the labor market and by white laborers and trade unions. Growing numbers of European immigrants put pressure on the labor market for both skilled and unskilled jobs, intensifying racial tensions among laboring people. For instance, in 1852 a group of 250 white laborers petitioned Congress to reduce the federal government's employment of African Americans, insisting that since white men offered "support of the country in time of war or civil commotion" they were entitled to be hired before black men. Irish immigrants were the largest national immigrant group in antebellum Washington, and their relationship to African Americans was—and would remain—complex. Irish men, often unskilled laborers themselves, were the most intense white competitors for jobs usually done by African American men.[15] At the same time, however, the poverty and low status of both groups would create opportunities for political alliance in coming years.

Despite the pressures of black codes and quotidian white hostility, antebellum black Washingtonians managed to develop a robust associational life, much of which was rooted in churches. Decades before the Civil War, African Americans founded independent Methodist and Baptist churches, and the more centralized African Methodist Episcopal (AME) Church sent talented pastors from other parts of the country to build the denomination in the capital. In 1841, John F. Cook Sr., a prominent AME minister, founded 15th Street Presbyterian Church, which became one of the capital's most elite and politically active churches. Many church leaders were also educators, and the capital's private schools for African American children were widely seen as remarkably developed, particularly for a slaveholding city. Black private schools and their teachers often faced harassment and arson, but the schools flourished nevertheless, their graduates and teachers a source of pride for black Washingtonians.[16]

Among those who established themselves as leading figures in the community was Cook's son, John F. Cook Jr., who was one of the delegates to Abraham Lincoln and who would later become the first African American elected to citywide office. Born in 1833, Cook attended a school run by his father before moving on to New York's Central College and Oberlin College in Ohio. Returning to the capital, Cook taught school and was an active Freemason.[17] Cook became unusually successful in business and politics, but his life story was similar to those of other local black men and women, many of them born enslaved or just one generation away from slavery, who also managed to obtain a measure of formal education, develop marketable skills, and sometimes purchase property. Such people were almost never wealthy by white standards, but they had exceptional financial and cultural resources compared with most other African Americans, and they were well positioned to assume leadership positions in politics and civil society as emancipation dawned.[18]

Black Washingtonians developed impressive religious and civic organizations in the antebellum era, but their associations and opportunities were always circumscribed by the strictures of slavery and the black codes. City authorities and white residents kept black organizations under special scrutiny, using the black codes and police authority to force many African American institutions to the margins of public life.[19] The restrictions black codes placed on African American civic life were not only an inconvenience and a humiliation. They were also a marker of free African Americans' marginal status in the larger community. One of the central privileges of local citizenship was the prerogative to form and cultivate associations. Indeed, most contemporaries assumed that when white people formed churches, mutual aid societies, and clubs, they were contributing to the collective good.[20] Although white Washingtonians did not (and probably could not) prohibit African Americans from forming such associations, the black codes and their enforcement proclaimed that African Americans, by dint of race and nothing more, did not have the same civic privileges as their white counterparts.

FIGURE 1.2. "The Civil War in America: Drumming Out a Soldier of the Federal Army through the Streets of Washington." Military men are at the center of this picture, but the artist juxtaposed the white soldiers with black civilians—men, women, and children—suggesting that the fates of the two groups were intertwined, both on the streets of Washington and in the war itself. *London Illustrated News*, December 28, 1861, 666. Courtesy Library of Congress.

The Politics of Emancipation

Witnessing throngs of uniformed military men in the capital of the republic in 1862, one reporter noted "that the government, for the nonce at least, is one of naked force."[21] What struck many people about the onset of the Civil War in Washington was the transformation of a civilian city into a military garrison. The army enforced martial law, soldiers encamped in the Capitol building itself and on the outskirts of the city, and laborers worked to complete a series of sixty-eight forts to ring the capital. The city suddenly became home to thousands of mules, hogs, and cattle, and the drivers and teamsters who managed them. Prices of food and lodging skyrocketed. Wounded soldiers filled the city as the battlefront approached, then receded, and then drew closer again. The capital was the heart of the Union's war effort, and its fortunes would rise or fall with those of the entire nation.[22]

As dramatic as the militarization of the capital was, however, it was the political and social upheavals that began during the war that would have the most enduring consequences. The secession of eleven slaveholding states cleared the way for a new legislative agenda in Congress, and radical Republicans quickly sought to transform the capital from a citadel of slavery into a symbol of the far-reaching possibilities of both emancipation and equality before the law.[23] Policy changes, combined with the dramatic migration of thousands of fugitives from slavery into the capital, opened unprecedented possibilities for African Americans to express visions of equality that sometimes converged with, but often exceeded, those of radicals in Congress. Black Washingtonians took to the streets to demand an end to enforcement of fugitive slave laws, newly enlisted black soldiers insisted on equal access to the city streetcars, and black Washingtonians demanded that their civic institutions be accorded the respect conventionally granted to their white counterparts. Masses of new arrivals to the city and long-standing black residents alike thus made upstart claims across a variety of arenas, attacking racial inequality not just before the law but also in quasi-public places like streetcars and in the realm of associational life, where status and group identity took precedence over individual rights.

The enormous political changes in store for the capital were suggested early on, when the 1861 inauguration of a Republican administration (and the departure of so many Confederate sympathizers) allowed northerners unprecedented influence in local affairs. From the Executive Mansion to the lowliest cogs in the party's patronage machine, Republicans changed the tenor of public life in the capital. Philadelphia editor John W. Forney began publishing the *Daily Chronicle*, whose orientation was more radical than the other daily Republican organ, the *National Republican*. Republicans also arranged to bring abolitionist speakers to the Smithsonian's prestigious lecture series. One attendee at those lectures was Sayles J. Bowen, a New Yorker who had been in the capital since the 1840s. Bowen was delighted "that such sentiments could be uttered in Washington, before a crowded audience, without even a dissent being expressed." Marking the rapidly changing climate, he wrote, "Every man who lectured there would have lost his head if he had dared utter the same sentiments in Washington only one year before."[24]

Congress quickly turned its attention to the growing paradox of slavery in the Union capital. The question took on enormous practical urgency as growing numbers of fugitives from slavery in Maryland and Virginia poured into the city. As Union troops passed through Maryland en route to Washington and the opposing armies faced off in nearby Virginia, enslaved people left farms and plantations and sought respite in the capital. The U.S. government soon signaled that human property claimed by secessionists would not be returned, giving Virginia fugitives in the capital reason to hope that their owners

FIGURE 1.3. "Secrets of the Prison-House—The Black Hole of Washington." *Frank Leslie's Illustrated Newspaper*, December 28, 1861, 88–89. Courtesy Library of Congress, cph 3c03911, cph 3c03912.

would not come after them. Fugitives from Maryland faced an entirely different situation, however. Federal fugitive slave laws were still in effect, and Lincoln's administration was committed to upholding them, not least out of determination to cultivate Unionism among that state's slaveholders.

In the winter of 1861–62, the question of what would become of escaped slaves drew increasing attention from both local and federal officials. Local police and the federal marshal for the District of Columbia, Ward Lamon, imprisoned scores of fugitive men, women, and children. Antislavery congressmen, in turn, used the incarceration of fugitives to agitate for an emancipation bill for the capital.[25] Massachusetts senator Henry Wilson and other antislavery legislators publicly investigated the D.C. jail and scrutinized Lamon's role in imprisoning the fugitives. The notion that slave catchers were abetted in the shadow of the Capitol was scandal enough for the editors of *Frank Leslie's Illustrated Newspaper*, who published a two-page spread on the inhumane conditions under which black women and children, whose only crime was attempting to escape slavery, were imprisoned in the U.S. capital.[26]

Following the jail controversy, Wilson would play a leading role in passing the District of Columbia Emancipation Act. But the proposal to end slavery in the capital met strenuous opposition. Border state senators insisted that District of Columbia residents (white ones) be allowed to weigh in on the matter, and they argued that the proposed legislation forecast congressional Republicans' broader emancipation agenda. Meanwhile, the Maryland state legislature unanimously condemned the emancipation bill, and a group of "loyal union men" in Rockville, about twelve miles from the District, charged that emancipation in the District was "an entering wedge to a scheme of general emancipation."[27] The Washington city council passed an antiemancipation resolution, arguing that "a large majority of the people of this District is adverse to the unqualified abolition of slavery" and encouraging Congress to prevent the city from becoming "an asylum for free negroes—a population undesirable in every American community."[28]

Proponents prevailed, however, and on April 16, 1862, Lincoln signed the District of Columbia Emancipation Act into law. In its final version, the law had two especially notable features. First, it appropriated $100,000 for the voluntary colonization of African Americans living in the capital, a nod to those, including Lincoln, who doubted that black and white people could peacefully coexist in the United States once slavery was over. The appropriation made the capital the national center of debate about black emigration, as proponents of colonization lobbied Congress with proposals in hand and sought prospective emigrants from among Washington's growing black population.[29] Second, the District of Columbia Emancipation Act provided for compensation to slaveowners who could prove Union loyalty, a measure that helped Congress avoid the charge of unconstitutionally depriving citizens of their property. The law established a board of three presidential appointees to hear each slaveholder's request for compensation and pass judgment on the loyalty of each owner and the value of each slave. Anticipating Congress's subsequent push for formal legal equality in the capital, the Emancipation Act required the emancipation commissioners to receive testimony "without the exclusion of any witness on account of color."[30]

As that clause suggested, Henry Wilson and other abolitionist legislators believed that slavery's abolition must be accompanied by measures designed to secure equal treatment for African Americans once they were free. Immediately after passage of the Emancipation Act, Wilson introduced legislation to establish public schools for African American children in the capital. Wilson's home state, Massachusetts, was famous for its common schools and educational reformers, and the move might have seemed an obvious one to him. People newly freed from bondage would, like any poor population, require basic reading and math skills in order to make their way in a competitive and urbanizing world. But public education in any form was in its infancy in the capital, and the mandate for black schools was enormously controversial. Local law required that 10 percent of property and real estate taxes be allocated to a public school fund. African American taxpayers contributed to that fund just as whites did, but they saw no benefit, since the public schools supported by the fund were for white children only. In 1858 and again in 1860, the city's white school leaders had asked Congress to help support local public education. Conservatives in Congress were willing, but antislavery legislators had attached a rider demanding that the city stop using taxes paid by African Americans to fund the white schools and, instead, establish a separate fund for black public schools. Proslavery congressmen had killed the bill rather than create a fund to serve black children.[31]

By 1862, much had changed. With Republicans in power, Congress that spring passed legislation instructing the governments of Washington and Georgetown to use the school taxes paid by African Americans to fund "a system of primary schools" for black children in the two cities. On witnessing local politicians' adamant opposition to this modest beginning for black public schools, Congress quickly passed an additional law that placed the black schools under a Board of Trustees of Colored Schools, whose members would be appointed by the secretary of the interior. This legislation would have far-reaching implications. In the short term, the Department of Interior's oversight kept the nascent black public schools out of the hands of hostile city governments. In the longer term, the independent administrative structure of the black public schools would allow African American educators and administrators to develop a school system in which they had considerable autonomy.[32]

As Congress set up a scaffolding for black public schools in the capital, it also continued its assault on legalized racial inequality by overturning the racially discriminatory black codes that had long circumscribed the lives of local free blacks. Left in place, those laws would have applied to all black residents of the capital, since all were now free. But most Republicans in Congress had no intention of allowing racially discriminatory legal structures to persist. Since the black codes were local statutes passed by the Washington city council, congressional Republicans first attempted to persuade the city council itself to overturn the laws. When the council refused, Congress went over its head. Wilson placed a clause in the first school bill that repealed all racially discriminatory laws within the District. It established that "all persons of color . . . shall be subject and amendable to the same laws and ordinances to which free white persons are." After that broad preface, it specified that black people could not be tried for different crimes, or subjected to different punishments, than white people. Congress went even further in July, when it added to a law whose main purpose was clarification of the procedures of the emancipation commission a final clause decreeing "that in all judicial proceedings in the District of Columbia there shall be no exclusion of any witness on account of color."[33] The repeal of Washington's black codes and the prohibition of racial discrimination in witness testimony established in the capital a regime of formal legal equality common in the Northeast on the eve of war. Indeed, the apparent lack of debate about these measures in Congress reflected a general consensus among Republicans that the same laws should apply to everyone, regardless of race. Yet this would not be the final word on racial equality before the law. In the coming months and years, many African Americans and white Republicans would ask whether it was enough to eliminate racially discriminatory language from laws, or whether creating an egalitarian legal order demanded laws that explicitly banned racial discrimination. Some would also insist that the domain of legal equality was much broader than simply the laws themselves, and that private associations that received government charters were subject to antidiscrimination principles as well.

Meanwhile, the thousands of fugitives who were migrating to the wartime capital provided popular momentum to continue dismantling slavery and the legal and cultural structures that upheld it. The influx began somewhat slowly, but by the summer of 1862 it had grown to significant proportions. Across the region, individuals, small clusters of families and friends, and even large phalanxes were making calculated decisions in the face of the crisis. Among the larger groups, some fifty to seventy-five Marylanders escaped nearby Anne Arundel County and Prince George's County, skirmishing with armed slave patrols on their way into the capital. Several hundred African Americans fled Fredericksburg, Virginia, in June 1862, in anticipation of a Union military maneuver there. Many of them were members of Fredericksburg's Shiloh Baptist Church, and soon after their arrival in Washington they began working to reorganize the church, join the local federation of Baptists, and begin a school.[34] Such developments thrilled black residents of Washington, who, according to one correspondent, "rejoice more over one poor downtrodden soul escaped from chains, than over the taking of ninety and nine cities."[35]

The migration was evident in broad population shifts both in the capital and across the region. Historian Allan Johnston's county-level census research showed that African Americans from Maryland and eastern Virginia migrated into urban areas from Norfolk to Baltimore, and places in between. From 1860 to 1870, Washington's black population grew more than any other city's, in both relative and absolute terms. During that decade, about 29,000 new black residents moved to the capital. Not merely a temporary wartime bulge, the population continued to grow after 1870, though at a slower rate. The ratio of African Americans to whites also changed considerably. In 1860, the black population was at a historic low of 19 percent. Just ten years later, it had grown to 33 percent, a ratio that remained constant until the 1910s, when the proportion of African Americans began to decline.[36]

The fate of the thousands of fugitives arriving in the capital remained uncertain. The Emancipation Act provided for the liberation of slaves owned in the capital, but it made no mention of the status of fugitives from elsewhere. The Confiscation Act, passed in the summer of 1861, allowed military authorities to retain slaves fleeing from service in the Confederacy, but there was nothing to prevent ostensibly loyal Maryland slaveowners from reclaiming fugitives who escaped into the capital. In fact, most legal authorities believed federal fugitive slave laws were still in force in the capital, and in 1862 the Circuit Court of the District of Columbia appointed fugitive slave commissioners to adjudicate the demands of slaveowners who sought human property that had escaped into the federal district.[37] One of those commissioners was Walter S. Cox, son of an eminent Washington lawyer and an 1847 graduate of Harvard Law School. Cox and the other commissioners took seriously their mandate to render the escapees to their owners, even to the point of declaring—contrary to the emerging principle that only Unionists could claim runaway slaves— that they had no obligation to investigate the loyalty of the claimants.[38]

For much of 1862, however, those who sought to enforce federal fugitive slave laws came into open conflict with the District's military governor, James S. Wadsworth. Wadsworth was a New Yorker whose antislavery sentiments were well known. During his tenure as military governor, from March through October 1862, Wadsworth frequently attempted to override decisions by the Circuit Court and the fugitive slave commissioners. Under his direction, the provost marshal's department provided passes and protection to fugitives at its discretion. Yet civil law often prevailed, despite his efforts and those of a cadre of antislavery lawyers.[39]

The influx of fugitive slaves and the disputes at the highest levels of law enforcement provided an opening for black Washingtonians, who publicly demanded an end to fugitive slave renditions. Particularly in the weeks before and immediately after passage of the Emancipation Act, black Washingtonians surrounded would-be slave catchers on the streets, drawing attention to their efforts to reenslave those who had sought freedom in the capital.[40] Crowds composed primarily of African Americans pursued slave catchers to City Hall and filled the courtroom for hearings before Cox and the other commissioners. So great was the popular interest among African Americans that even an arrest of two black women for fighting drew a great crowd. Thinking the women were being apprehended as fugitives, the crowd brought "rocks, sticks, and every imaginable missile" but then desisted upon discovering the real reason for the arrests. "Had it been a slave-catcher, sad would have been his condition," remarked a correspondent for the AME *Christian Recorder*, a weekly newspaper based in Philadelphia. Members of the antebellum black elite offered highly visible support by arranging to post bond, sometimes as much as $1,000, for the release of arrested fugitives. They also organized to present a decorative cane to a white lawyer who doggedly represented fugitives in court.[41]

By many accounts, the crowd actions succeeded in discrediting the fugitive slave commissioners and the laws themselves. Antislavery editors recognized the political effectiveness of the crowds. "It has become manifest," the *National Republican* editorialized in May 1862, "that the Fugitive Slave Act cannot be enforced here without excitements and collisions, which will be lamentable, and may even be dangerous to the public peace." The public conflicts the renditions engendered—"between the slave and slave-catcher; between the slaveholder and the people; between the civil and the military authorities"—disgraced both the city and the nation, opined the *National Anti-Slavery Standard*. As these accounts suggest, the crowds' effectiveness stemmed from their publicness. Crowds of African Americans turned the rendition cases into political theater, dramatizing the continuing vulnerability of fugitives from slavery and, by their very presence, repudiating the old order. Proscribed from expressing their views through channels such as voting or lobbying, black Washingtonians found a way of establishing a civic voice and, not incidentally, helped make the fugitive slave laws a dead letter in the District.[42]

The pivotal legal decision concerning fugitive slaves came in the spring of 1863, in the case of Andrew Hall, a nineteen-year-old fugitive who had fled the estate of his owner, George W. Duvall, of Prince George's County, Maryland. Hall had been working in the capital for several months when, in April 1863, Duvall demanded the arrest under federal fugitive slave laws of Hall and the two other men with whom he had escaped. Ward Lamon, the federal marshal, apprehended Hall in the city market, and Hall's lawyers filed a writ of habeas corpus, requiring that their client be brought to court for a hearing.[43]

Hall's case had special significance because it was the first fugitive slave case heard since Congress had reorganized the upper reaches of the District of Columbia's court system. In March 1863, Congress had terminated the long-standing Circuit Court and, against vehement protests from local lawyers and city officials, created the District of Columbia Supreme Court, whose justices were to be appointed by the president. Lincoln's Emancipation Proclamation had gone into effect months earlier, but the newly organized court retained Cox as fugitive slave commissioner, an indication that it planned to enforce the 1850 Fugitive Slave Act. Observers thus watched the Hall case closely to see what course the new justices would pursue.[44]

The case was heard in a courtroom filled with black and white spectators. After extensive testimony and considerable deliberation, the four new justices remained divided on the merits of the argument, made by Hall's lawyers, that fugitive slave laws applied only to the states and not to the federal district. Finally, in a split decision, the court affirmed that it must uphold fugitive slave laws, provided would-be owners could prove Union loyalty.[45] Since Duvall had affirmed his support for the Union, the decision implied that Hall must return to his owner's custody. But Hall's lawyers immediately asked military authorities to intervene to secure his freedom. A melee ensued at the court-house, as Duvall tried to grab Hall while onlookers sought to protect him. Military authorities took custody of Hall, and Duvall's lawyers, in turn, attempted to bring charges against Hall's attorney. But Duvall was powerless as provost marshal officials escorted Hall away. Hall later enlisted in the black regiment then being organized in the capital, and the next winter the court dismissed Duvall's lawsuit.[46]

Fugitive slave laws technically remained in force in the capital and through-out the nation until June 1864, when Congress voided them. Long before then, however, an informal coalition of freedpeople, members of the black elite, sympathetic white lawyers, and military officials had sought to nullify them, using both popular and legal means. Wadsworth and other military officials offered fugitives piecemeal protection, but the crowds of black Washingtonians who drew attention to the renditions addressed not only slave catchers but also the broader public. As a result, as newspaper editorialists acknowledged, fugitive slave laws became unenforceable long before they were repealed. Masses of black Washingtonians had insisted by their actions that they were members of the community and entitled to a voice in public proceedings. Their freedom still insecure, they protested the policies of the federal and local governments, insisting that emancipation must be accompanied by a far more robust vision of civic equality than most white people could imagine.

Bone of Our Bone and Flesh of Our Flesh

The influx of fugitive slaves created new opportunities for the city's long-standing black residents, but it also introduced new dilemmas. The capital's black churches had been at the center of antebellum community life, and they continued to anchor black public life during and after the war. Churches were accustomed to raising money and providing for needy people. In wartime, church organizations extended these missions, mobilizing to feed, clothe, and shelter freedpeople. Black Washingtonians' strenuous and self-sacrificing efforts on behalf of freedpeople complicate the argument, often made by historians of Washington, that members of the black elite were far more concerned with advancing themselves than with the fate of the freedpeople.[47] Yet the war and the new migrants themselves also challenged black Washingtonians' existing structures of organization and leadership. As a controversy over the fate of the Lincoln delegation demonstrates, black Washingtonians not only disagreed about emigration itself; they also argued over who had the authority to represent whom and what it meant for a small group of people to represent a much larger mass. Indeed, while some black leaders wanted to discipline African Americans' nascent political voice into a harmonious choir, others called forth a raucous cacophony.

As the scale of black migration into the capital became clear, ministers and lay leaders sought to organize congregations to offer food, shelter, and support to freedpeople. Bishop Daniel Payne, formerly a minister at Washington's Israel AME Church but now based in Baltimore as an AME bishop, returned to Washington to preach at Ebenezer Chapel in Georgetown, urging his congregants to invite the fugitives, who had "ransomed" themselves from slavery, into their homes, churches, schools, and social circles.[48] Henry McNeal Turner, the minister at Israel Church, used his dispatches to the *Christian Recorder* to represent freedpeople as hard workers who were anxious to support themselves. Reversing stereotypes of "contrabands" as lazy and dependent on others' largesse, Turner commended the migrants for their "enterprise." Hundreds never even went to the "contraband camps" established by the government, he reported, but instead sought "immediate employment." Yet he also recognized that circumstances might prevent refugees from immediately establishing economic independence: "Hundreds are compelled to remain at the camps," he wrote, "because it is impossible to procure a house or room in which to stop." Turner sought to elevate a sense of shared racial destiny among African Americans over the differences in education or economic standing that might divide them. Local blacks, he insisted, must "extend a hand of mercy *to bone of our bone and flesh of our flesh*."[49]

Lay leaders of churches took up the challenge. Men and women who were active in church-based societies and auxiliaries already knew how to organize meetings and raise money, and they poured themselves into the project of aiding freedpeople. Many African American Protestant congregations and Catholic groups organized freedmen's relief societies, the best documented of which are those associated with Union Bethel AME Church and 15th Street Presbyterian. The Union Relief Association, organized in the basement of Union Bethel, was originally composed of fifty-three men and women. John Simms, who was involved, recalled that the group assembled "to collect provisions and clothing to be distributed among the freedmen who were then coming in to the city in large numbers." Their suffering, he wrote, "moved us to provide some means by which they might be relieved." The group raised substantial donations, and its meetings drew large crowds of "ladies and gentlemen, of all grades and classes."[50] A group of some forty women affiliated with 15th Street Presbyterian Church and led by White House seamstress Elizabeth Keckly organized the Contraband Relief Association in the summer of 1862. The women combined practical and spiritual goals, hoping to provide freedpeople with "shelter, food, clothing, medicine and nourishments" and to "alleviate their sufferings, and help them on towards a higher plane of civilization." Keckly traveled north to solicit contributions, and the group became a conduit for clothing and funds raised there as well.[51]

As the composition of Keckly's organization suggests, black women were centrally involved in freedmen's relief efforts. Israel Church also had a women's freedmen's relief organization; women in southwest Washington organized a mutual aid society; and women associated with an AME Zion church created a society to provide support to black soldiers and their families. As Turner acknowledged in an address to the "ladies" of Israel Lyceum, a literary society associated with his church, "It is female assistance which has given impetus to all reforming enterprises, and redeeming deeds."[52] Like organizationally minded white women of this era, black women in Washington had long been involved in church-based fund-raising and teaching efforts. But black women's activism was shaped not only by a belief in women's special role in institution building but also by the race-based solidarity that had long tied elite black women such as Keckly to the less fortunate, regardless of the great differences in status and life experiences that might have separated them.[53]

Tapping into traditions of church-based organizing across neighborhoods and denominations, in November 1862 representatives of the various freedmen's relief societies met at Union Bethel to organize a collective "plan by which the contrabands in our city could be cared for" and decided to continue meeting weekly.[54] Groups cosponsored benefits in Washington and Georgetown, and the organizations combined to hold a "thanksgiving" feast later that month. Such coordination of action earned praise from some quarters. An *Anglo-African* correspondent reported that black Washingtonians were "soaring above all petty jealousies" and were "more united, than they are in any other town."[55] In the meantime, some black residents of Washington offered whatever space they had to shelter the newly arrived freedpeople. Turner reported that "many" had "thrown open their finest parlors, given up their kitchens, garrets, and even closets to shelter these escaping sons of humanity." And a correspondent to the Democratic *New York World* noted that "the city has literally a substratum of negroes living in cellars and basements, from Georgetown to the Navy Yard."[56]

Black Washingtonians' mobilization to support freedpeople was accompanied by an efflorescence of activity in African American cultural institutions. Black northerners who had heretofore feared or refused to travel to Washington now visited, and many delivered lectures to attentive audiences. Events combined entertainment, education, and preparation for fuller participation in civic and political life. One black literary association hosted Robert Smalls, the former slave from South Carolina who had commandeered a Confederate ship in Charleston harbor. In church-based literary societies, lecture topics ranged from geology to matrimony to "The Equality and Inequality of Man." The goal of civic education was especially clear in a mock court session in which members of Israel Lyceum dramatized a jury trial before a rapt audience. "It was certainly productive of good, and materially enlightened the minds of our people," Turner reported, "for many had never been engaged in a lawsuit, nor seen one conducted." New kinds of entertainment were also possible. One northern speaker sought to "test the freedom of the capitol" by bringing his show about John Brown to the city. The popularity of his exhibition and its peaceful run squelched "doubts" about "the safety of a colored man exhibiting the hero of Harper's Ferry, south of Mason and Dixon's line."[57]

Yet black leaders were also aware of the limited resources their institutions commanded, and they worked to extend help to freedpeople without undermining the organizations they had worked so hard to build. Pastor J. P. Hamer of John Wesley AME Zion Church carefully portrayed that dilemma as he kept readers of the *Christian Recorder* apprised of his church's efforts to help freedpeople infected by smallpox. The church had closed in October 1862 "on account of sickness among the contrabands" living in the church's basement. The escapees, Hamer related, had begun their residence when a church trustee permitted "a group of them . . . to stay one night." By the time the smallpox outbreak began, almost one hundred people were staying in the church. The congregation allowed the refugees to remain and raised money to support them before closing the church to stem the outbreak. At great expense, the congregation repaired damage to the building and contributed to burials for those who died. After the refugees had weathered the worst of winter in the church, Hamer explained, the congregation decided to reopen the church for worship and evicted the families.[58] The congregation had done as much as it could, Hamer felt, and needed to continue with its regular business.

Departing from church-based organizational structures and explicitly seeking a voice in contemporary political debates, some of the capital's elite black men organized a nondenominational association whose purpose was to "improve our condition by use of all proper means calculated to exalt our people." Washington's Social, Civil, and Statistical Association (SCSA) counted among its members many of the best-educated and wealthiest black men in Washington. They were teachers, businessmen, and employees of the federal government, and many were also active in church-based organizations and secret societies. Some were associated with 15th Street Presbyterian Church, the city's most prestigious black congregation. Among the SCSA's members were John F. Cook Jr. and Edward M. Thomas. Its president was William Slade, the lead servant in the Lincoln White House.[59]

Internal records of the association have not been located, and many details about its goals and procedures remain unknown. Yet it is clear that members saw the association not just as a mutual aid society but also as an organization that would shepherd black Washington through the upheavals of the Civil War. In the spring of 1862, members of the SCSA collected statistics about the number of black private schools in the capital and the amount of real estate owned by black individuals and churches, information that could be used to demonstrate African Americans' ability to thrive in freedom. The SCSA's orientation toward claiming citizenship in the local community helps explain why members of the

EVERYWHERE IS FREEDOM AND EVERYBODY FREE

association took dramatic action against emigration agents in late July and why in August some became members of the delegation to President Lincoln.[60]

To the dismay of members of the SCSA, colonization promoters were enjoying a good deal of success in the capital. Men representing schemes to send African Americans to Haiti, Liberia, and Central America converged in Washington after passage of the District of Columbia Emancipation Act. They discovered considerable interest among fugitive slaves, for whom life as refugees in the capital offered little comfort or security. Historian Steven Hahn found that across the South newly freed African Americans often considered emigration as "one of several strategies designed to create or reconstitute freed communities on a stable foundation—and at arm's length from whites." The phenomenon Hahn called "grassroots emigrationism" was as vibrant in the capital as it was elsewhere in the South.[61]

At the same time, emigrationism also made headway in more elite black circles. Joseph Williams, an African American man who was promoting emigration to Central America, won support from Henry McNeal Turner, the AME minister, and he mobilized Turner and other local African Americans to sign petitions asking Congress to allocate colonization funds for settlements in Central America.[62] Williams's success drew scorn from Frederick Douglass, who argued in his newspaper that "whether many or few" had signed the petitions, "their proceeding in this case has no other effect and can have no other effect than to inflict an injury on the cause of the colored people at large." Even a small number of people volunteering to leave would make the wrong impression, he wrote. "The action of the few," he argued, "will be taken as representing the wishes of the many" and thus would inadvertently aid the cause of white colonizationists "who have made the ridding of the country of negroes, the object of long years of unwearied but vain exertion."[63]

Members of the SCSA probably already had similar concerns when they heard about controversial statements made by an agent of the Liberian government and decided to take action against colonization agents in their midst. The Liberian representative, John D. Johnson, had allegedly told a Republican congressman that "contrabands . . . should be sent out of the country whether they are willing to go or not," and that escaping slaves were "mere children in capacity" and "needed the control of the superior race."[64] The comments attributed to Johnson represented much that African Americans despised in the traditions of white-led emigration efforts with which Liberia was associated. Black northerners had long feared that white supporters of emigration to Liberia sought to forcibly deport African Americans and not simply offer them the option of leaving the United States. Moreover, they had long suspected that the Liberian enterprise was driven more by racist sensibilities than by assessments of African Americans' best interests. Members of the scsa thus found Johnson's comments offensive in the extreme.[65]

The scsa quickly convened and sent a delegation to confront Johnson and demand that he leave town immediately. In a tense verbal confrontation, Johnson was defiant. Later that day, two members of the scsa returned to the boardinghouse where Johnson was staying, challenged him again, then knocked him down and (likely) hit and kicked him several times.[66] A groundswell of local opposition to colonization agents followed. Rumors circulated that action would be taken against promoters of emigration to Haiti, and a group of young men gave "a severe beating" to Joseph E. Williams, the advocate of Central American emigration. In a report to the *Anglo-African*, an scsa representative crowed, "The colored people are now aroused, and unless these men leave the city, it is feared that a general outbreak will follow."[67]

Less than two weeks later, in this extremely fraught climate, James Mitchell appeared in Union Bethel Church to recruit a delegation of black men to meet with President Lincoln. After attendeess at the meeting reluctantly decided to send a delegation to the president, they chose as their representatives men who were likely to oppose Lincoln's proposal. Three of the five, including delegation chair Edward M. Thomas, were members of the scsa. At the famous meeting in the Executive Mansion, Lincoln reminded the delegates that "you and we are different races" and that it was "better for us both . . . to be separated." The president hoped the Chiriquí region of what is now Panama would be a suitable destination for African Americans. He acknowledged that the "intelligent colored men" before him might feel little inclination to leave the United States. But he urged them to think of impoverished freedpeople and "to do something to help those who are not so fortunate as yourselves." The delegates pledged to "hold a consultation and in a short time give an answer," and Lincoln told them to take all the time they needed.[68]

Northern African Americans and the abolitionist press erupted in indignation, charging Lincoln with racism and insisting that African Americans should demand rights and equality in the nation of their birth. If members of the scsa had hoped that the delegation to Lincoln would join the chorus of condemnation, however, they were sorely disappointed. Two days after the meeting, Thomas informed Lincoln that the members of the delegation had entered the meeting "entirely hostile" but had changed their minds after "all the advantages were so ably brought to our views by you." Thomas proposed that two delegates visit Philadelphia, New York, and Boston to discuss the proposal "with our leading friends," predicting that it would take only two weeks for such meetings to generate ample support for the president's plan.[69] Although Thomas used the pronoun "we," as if the entire delegation was in agreement, he was the letter's only signer.

Meanwhile, Thomas and at least two of the other delegates decided to report back to the SCSA, not to the coalition of church representatives who had selected them at Union Bethel. When Thomas and his allies on the delegation failed to appear at a meeting at Union Bethel Church, where committees from the city's black churches expected to hear a report, many in attendance were outraged.[70] But Thomas, who had announced that he personally planned to go on the Chiriquí expedition, was also in bad graces with the SCSA. The organization refused to accept his report, arguing that it was not the body that had originally sent the delegates. The SCSA proceeded to put Thomas on trial, essentially for his support of the Chiriquí proposal. In the end, members were divided on how to deal with Thomas and decided not to expel him from the organization. Regardless of the trial's outcome, those in the SCSA who had hoped the delegation would yield a unified expression of opposition to Lincoln's proposal likely saw the entire affair as a fiasco.[71]

Because of developments entirely outside their control, however, the SCSA and other African Americans who opposed emigration had less to worry about than they initially feared. Lincoln's colonization project collapsed before even one ship had departed for Chiriquí. Thousands of black Washingtonians had volunteered to emigrate under government sponsorship, but Central American governments opposed the plan, making it impossible for the U.S. government to go forward.[72] The proposal's failure left many would-be emigrants in dire straits. Hoping that the government might yet procure a ship, a group of anonymous petitioners informed Lincoln of the human costs of his failed gambit. "Many of us have sold our furniture, have given up our little homes to go on the first voyage," they explained. "Poverty in a still worse form than has yet met us may be our winter prospect." The stranded migrants professed disbelief that Lincoln would "create hopes within us, and stimulate us to struggle for national independence and respectable equality," only to abandon them. Still looking for a new destination, Lincoln—through an assistant—asked for their forbearance.[73]

Thomas's leadership of the Lincoln delegation was a dismal failure, but the issues of public leadership raised by Lincoln's request to meet with a black delegation were much more significant than one man's choice of tactics. The scsa, with its elite members and connections to powerful white people, seemed determined to be an arbiter of debate in black Washington and a liaison between African Americans and the newly interested federal government. In the service of such goals, the scsa continued to try to limit the scope of debate and to downplay disagreements among African Americans. Indeed, after attempting to banish colonization agents and ostracizing Edward Thomas, the organization published, in both black and white newspapers, a series of resolutions advising local black institutions to be selective in the lecturers they hosted. Black organizations should invite only "such orators and teachers in the cause of religion, morality, literature and science as may be disposed to benefit us" and avoid "mock lecturers and political agitators" who, out of "speculative and individual motives," attempted to stir controversy, the scsa advised.[74]

The scsa's impulses to manage the debate over emigration were driven, at least in part, by a desire to protect freedpeople from those who would exploit them. The organization had accused John D. Johnson, the Liberian commissioner, of attempting to take "heartless and unprincipled advantage of men . . . whom a condition of cruel bondage has denied all means of knowledge." Freedpeople, the organization insisted, must be shielded from those who "[held] out to them inducements to emigrate to Africa . . . which we know with their limited knowledge in the matter, they are unable intelligently to accept."[75] In a similar vein, Frederick Douglass, who complained bitterly about black Washingtonians' support for emigration, insisted that additional "intelligent colored men" must join Edward Thomas on the trip to Chiriquí, with "the purpose of counselling the emigrants, and aiding in the direction of their future movements."[76]

But many black Washingtonians were uncomfortable with a largely self-selected group of leaders proposing to represent the interests of an enormous and diverse group of people. Turner believed the Lincoln meeting gave African Americans an unprecedented chance "to speak to the civilized world."[77] But many also saw troubling implications in this opportunity for a few local residents to command so much attention. Some at the original Union Bethel meeting had questioned how a small group of black men chosen there could represent all the people of African descent in the United States. Following the Lincoln meeting, when Thomas and other delegates failed to return to Union Bethel, a pseudonymous correspondent to the *Christian Recorder* charged that the delegation was a "*bogus* committee." "Cerebus" wondered "*who* gave *that committee* authority to act for us, the *fifteen thousand* residents of color in this

District—and who requested them to represent the interests of the *two hundred and ten thousand* inhabitants of color in the Free States."[78] The men who met with Lincoln, he argued, had no constituency and represented no one besides themselves.

Turner saw the delegation quite differently. In a published response to Cerebus, Turner defended the process by which the delegation had been selected and meditated more generally on the problem of political representation for African Americans. The delegation was not a political body, he wrote. "Mr. Cerebus talks as though the President had called a congress of colored representatives, and that they had been in session, and had cast the destinies of the colored man." The reality, Turner argued, was that Lincoln had "called for a committee of ministers, or a committee of intelligent colored gentlemen, and not for a representative." "Colored people have no representative yet in a political point of view," Turner insisted. With his emphasis on "yet" and on the "political point of view," he sought to distinguish between the proto-politics in which they were now engaged and electoral politics, with its ostensibly clear rules for choosing representatives. Yet he went still further, questioning how any small group of people could "represent" the interests of a much larger group. In fact, he said, "every man and woman is his or her own representative, and has the right of representing themselves."[79]

As he cast doubt on the founding principles of representative government, Turner also insisted that all individuals were capable of making their own decisions and advocating for their own interests. Indeed, here and elsewhere, Turner's writing revealed little of the concern, shown by people like Frederick Douglass and the members of the scsa, about the ability of freedpeople to make decisions about their own lives. In the waning days of 1862, as people waited to see whether Lincoln would follow through on his promised proclamation of emancipation, Turner announced, "We have all the world before us." "We are going *just where we please*; going to church, going to stay here, going away, going to Africa, Hayti, Central America, England, France, Egypt, and Jerusalem; and then we are going to the jail, gallows, penitentiary, whipping-post, to the grave, heaven and hell. But we do not intend to be sent to either place unless we choose."[80] Freedom, Turner seemed to argue, was the opportunity to make one's own choices, whatever they might be and wherever they might lead.

In the end, the scsa proved unable to silence debate about emigration or to control whom black Washingtonians listened to or whom they chose to represent them. But the matter of government-sponsored emigration itself became virtually obsolete, as federal policy shifted. In the fall of 1862, the U.S. attor-

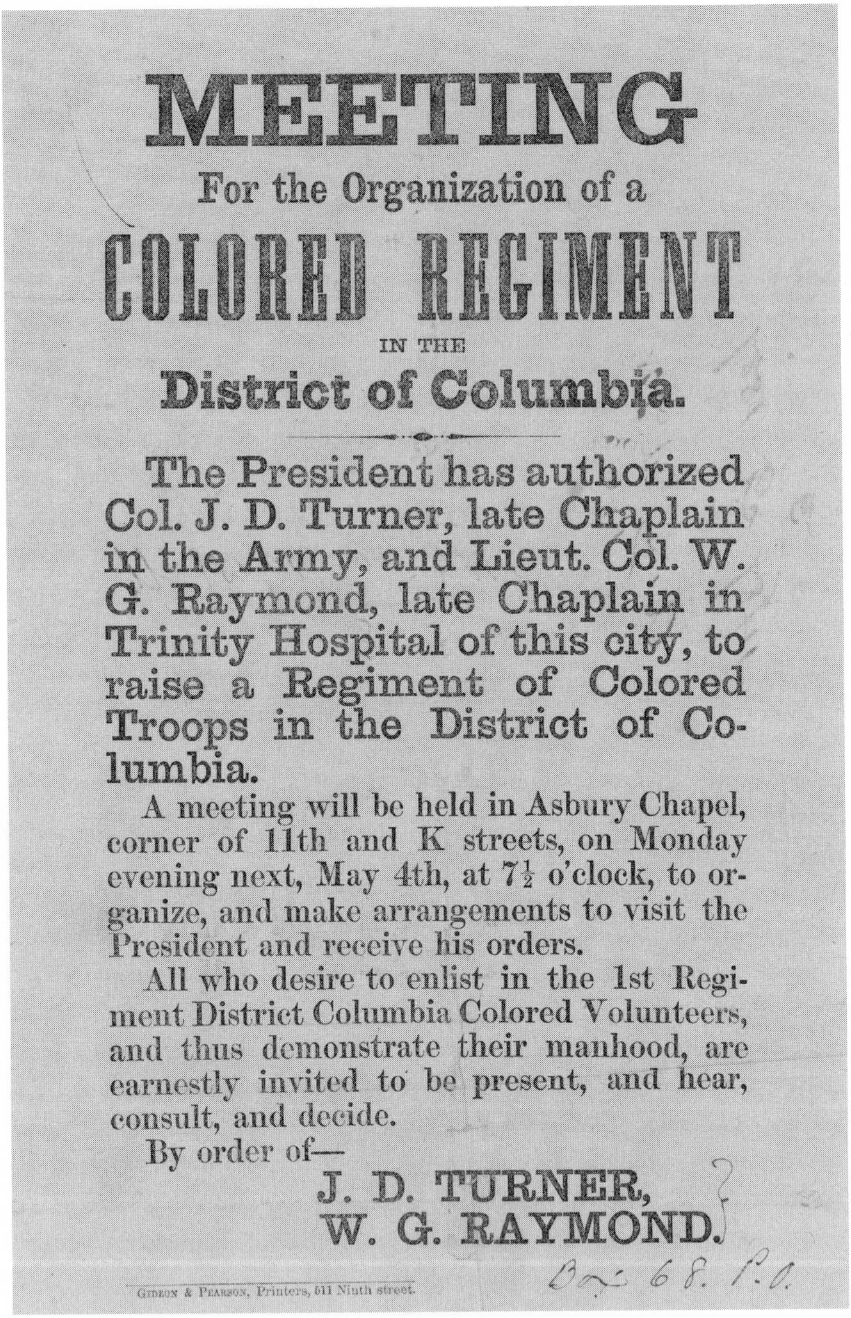

MEETING

For the Organization of a

COLORED REGIMENT

IN THE

District of Columbia.

The President has authorized Col. J. D. Turner, late Chaplain in the Army, and Lieut. Col. W. G. Raymond, late Chaplain in Trinity Hospital of this city, to raise a Regiment of Colored Troops in the District of Columbia.

A meeting will be held in Asbury Chapel, corner of 11th and K streets, on Monday evening next, May 4th, at 7½ o'clock, to organize, and make arrangements to visit the President and receive his orders.

All who desire to enlist in the 1st Regiment District Columbia Colored Volunteers, and thus demonstrate their manhood, are earnestly invited to be present, and hear, consult, and decide.

By order of—

J. D. TURNER,
W. G. RAYMOND.

GIDEON & PEARSON, Printers, 511 Ninth street.

FIGURE 1.4. This broadside announced the first recruitment meeting for the 1ST USCT. The meeting was held in Asbury Chapel, a Methodist church with a large and active African American congregation. Black men were invited to "demonstrate their manhood" by enlisting. Courtesy U.S. National Archives and Records Administration.

ney general issued an opinion stating that citizenship was a national status that adhered to all people born in the United States, a direct refutation of the 1857 U.S. Supreme Court decision in *Dred Scott v. Sandford* and an affirmation that race did not pose a barrier to citizenship. Lincoln's Emancipation Proclamation, promised in September, took effect on January 1, 1863, making emancipation federal policy and clearing the way for black men's enlistment in the Union army.[81]

Attacking the Features of Slavery

Black Washingtonians celebrated the Emancipation Proclamation quite differently from how they had celebrated the District of Columbia Emancipation Act the previous April. In April, church leaders had issued public messages urging calm and deliberation, and people rejoiced inside their homes, not sure that public displays of ebullience would be well received.[82] By January 1, 1863, however, such reticence had given way to mass celebrations in public. At Camp Barker, the military-run camp for freedpeople, multitudes gathered to wait for the stroke of midnight, offering prayers and songs in celebration. On New Year's Day, throngs convened around Israel Church to hear the reading of the Emancipation Proclamation from the afternoon newspaper. As Henry McNeal Turner recalled, cannons were fired and "men squealed, women fainted, dogs barked, white and colored people shook hands, songs were sung." Celebrations resounded throughout the city.[83]

Amid the jubilation, however, racial tension was rising. As the strictures of slavery and legal discrimination were toppled, white Washingtonians proved increasingly inclined to smash church windows, set fire to buildings, and attack African Americans on the streets.[84] Turner informed readers of the *Christian Recorder* that "rude young men" had disrupted a District-wide meeting of freedmen's relief organizations and that when a church trustee had tried to quiet the rowdies, they "beat him unmercifully." Local whites also threatened teachers of black schools. "They call me negro and negro-teacher as I pass along," Emma Brown, an African American teacher, wrote to a friend. "When I leave my house I usually leave my *feelings* there for I expect to be meddled with in the street. I wonder why the Creator gave feelings to some folks." She lamented that the police offered little recourse, even when the damage was more visible. "I sent for an officer not long ago to arrest some vile boys who threw stones into the school-room," she wrote. "The officer refused to come—my next appeal will be to the mayor."[85]

FIGURE 1.5. The African American soldiers in this photograph, which was taken at Fort Lincoln on the northeast edge of the District of Columbia, displayed the arms and uniforms that rankled so many white Washingtonians. This is Company E of the 4th U.S. Colored Infantry. The photo was likely taken soon after the war ended. Courtesy Library of Congress, LC-DIG-cwpb-04294.

Facing constant insults and police indifference, African Americans seem to have been emboldened by the promise of military enlistment. Reflecting a growing militancy, in early January 1863 congregants poured out of Israel Church and gave chase to rowdies who stoned the windows during a meeting to plan a celebration of emancipation. A *Christian Recorder* correspondent reported that, had the assailants been found, "they never would have disturbed any one else, for the colored people would have laid them down as cool as ice."[86] Assertive attitudes became more pronounced that May and June, as the army began recruiting a regiment of black soldiers in the District. This was the moment many black leaders had been waiting for since the war began. Men like Turner and local recruiter Thomas H. C. Hinton, a New York native, believed the opportunity to soldier for the Union would allow black men to prove they could rise to the highest challenge expected of men in a republic. Soldier status would provide a platform from which black men could demand full citizenship once the war ended. After all, activists asked, how could the nation continue to marginalize men who had offered to lay down their lives for its preservation?[87]

When the soldiers of the 1st United States Colored Troops (USCT) began drilling on Pennsylvania Avenue, Washingtonians recognized that they were witnessing a momentous event. The black soldiers "presented a fine appearance, and elicited the attention of quite a crowd of citizens, who applauded them while passing the streets," noted the *National Republican*. A correspondent for the *Christian Recorder* acknowledged that "instead of being snarled at and hissed as some expected," soldiers drilling on Pennsylvania Avenue "were applauded and saluted by officers in high command." President Lincoln, Secretary of State William Seward, and Lincoln's secretary, William O. Stoddard, stood among the onlookers on Pennsylvania Avenue. Stoddard later recalled, "They were really a fine looking body of men, and marched well for such new recruits. It was indeed a curious and deeply interesting sight, seen for the first time." Observing the black soldiers on parade caused Stoddard to reflect years later: "It seems strange now that so many of us, even of those opposed to slavery, found it hard to approve of what was doubtless so wise, so necessary a policy as the arming of slaves." Even within Lincoln's closest circle, black enlistment had seemed "a somewhat doubtful experiment."[88]

The regiment's first public parade ended at Israel Church on Capitol Hill, where spectators—most of them black, but with "a sprinkling of white"—assembled on the grounds. Some men of fighting age expressed doubts about whether the army would grant them equal pay and similar lodgings to white enlistees.[89] Despite such concerns, however, about 200 recruits enrolled that day, filling two companies. Among the officers assessing volunteers' fitness for service was Alexander Augusta, a black physician who had recently accepted a commission as a major in the army medical corps. Already publicly known for protesting racial discrimination at the Baltimore railroad depot, Augusta would remain a visible and committed activist for racial equality in Washington and would be among the founding faculty of Howard University Medical School.[90] The day's activities culminated in a mass meeting inside the church, at which speakers blended humor with gravity as they exhorted black men to continue enlisting to fight for their collective freedom.[91]

If the atmosphere at Israel Church was joyful and righteous, however, the mood on the street was more perilous. Public tensions among whites and blacks had increased when recruiting for the 1st USCT began. At the initial recruitment meeting, the *National Republican* reported, the army stationed ten white soldiers outside Asbury Chapel to "prevent any unfavorable demonstration by the negro-hating, rowdy Copperheads who might be disposed to obstruct or defeat the objects of the meeting."[92] The *National Republican* had its political biases, but the ubiquity of white violence during the recruitment suggests that the threat was real. As recruiting continued, edgy whites made frequent attacks on black civilians and soldiers. In broad daylight at the busy corner of 14th Street and Pennsylvania Avenue, a conflict between a black hackman and a white laborer grew into a broader racial melee in which combatants used bricks as weapons. A group of African Americans returning from a day of picnicking outside the city "came into collision" with white teamsters in the working-class neighborhood of Swampoodle, and a "general fight ensued." Days later, several African Americans leaving church "were attacked by a crowd of white men" who threw rocks, knocking some of the black men to the ground.[93]

Recruitment coincided, as well, with a municipal political campaign and election. Emancipation and the founding of black public schools were very much on people's minds as Republicans, backed by Forney's *Chronicle*, squared off against Unconditional Unionists (largely Democrats at pains to demonstrate their loyalty to the Lincoln administration and the war effort). The June 1 election resulted in a sweeping victory for the Unconditional Unionists.[94] That success evidently gave rowdy elements a sense of license, for that night and the next white laborers launched organized attacks on African Americans and their property on the west side of Washington. Armed with "shot guns, pistols, slingshots, &c.," they raided numerous homes before military guards managed to stop them. Military authorities foiled plans by white teamsters to attack Camp Barker, but not before several African Americans were severely injured.[95] A week later, emboldened Democrats launched a new publication, the *Daily Constitutional Union*, which professed Union loyalty while at the same time contributing prolifically to antiblack, anti–U.S. government discourse in the capital.[96]

White hostility notwithstanding, uniformed and armed black soldiers began using their elevated status to undermine some of the vestiges of slavery in the city. In particular, they identified the city's streets and streetcars as places where they were entitled to equal access and respectful treatment. Streets and streetcars were not public spaces, controlled or operated by the government. Yet neither were they private, like a home or even a church. Rather, they were the kind of quasi-public places consistently at issue as Americans sought to define the boundaries of equality in the era of emancipation. In making an issue of their treatment on the streets and in streetcars, black soldiers changed Washington and helped set an agenda for the future.

The capital's streetcars were a wartime innovation. Washington businessmen had discussed building streetcar lines in the late 1850s, but it was not until 1862 that Congress chartered the District's first streetcar company. When the horse-drawn cars began running that fall, conductors excluded black passengers or forced them to ride on the open platform in front, following conventions long used on the city's omnibuses, the mode of public transportation that streetcars would soon replace. Now, amid the widening debate about the implications of abolition, many African Americans condemned such practices as remnants of slavery. At least one black minister spoke out immediately against racial discrimination on the streetcars, and at an April 1863 Emancipation Day celebration, recruiter Thomas Hinton denounced discrimination on the streetcars as "one of the features of slavery that exists in our midst."[97]

The men of the 1st USCT had streetcars on their agenda from the outset. At an early recruitment meeting, a white recruiting officer condemned discrimination on the cars, and George Hatton, an enlistee and a leading light among local black men, announced that "he would not ride in the cars until he had his rights and could sit inside." Days later, a correspondent to the *Christian Recorder* reported: "The soldiers all ride the street cars or any other cars they want to ride in; and you might just as well declare war against them as to declare that they can't ride there because they are colored."[98] By the end of 1863, the District's single streetcar company had begun running separate cars for "Colored Persons."[99]

Such grudging acceptance, however, did not satisfy black soldiers' demand for the same unqualified access and respect that white soldiers were accorded. A New York correspondent to the *Anglo-African* noted the special humiliation black soldiers felt when confronted by signs that read "colored persons may ride in this car." Even for soldiers, access remained "a privilege and not a right," the correspondent observed.[100] The soldiers of the 1st USCT did not wait for lawmakers to recognize or create their "right" to ride the streetcars. To the contrary, they sought to create that right themselves by demanding equal access to the streetcars while wearing soldiers' uniforms that publicly declared them to be worthy of respect and even deference. Black soldiers forced streetcar conductors and the riding public to consider how it was possible that men who risked death for their country could be treated like pariahs in public. They surely hoped Congress would codify in law their right to ride, but neither their demands nor streetcar companies' responses depended on new legislation.

Whites' disapproving and often violent reactions to black soldiers' demands for public respect on the streets of Washington reveal just how disruptive their claims to standing were. Observing black soldiers who often walked around the city in small groups looking for entertainment and perhaps for opportunities to display their newfound status, the *Constitutional Union* complained of their "exhibiting the swagger and air of hauteurs, so characteristic of their race when the regimentals have been donned." Whites who attacked "swaggering" black soldiers were fully justified, the paper argued. "If any of the negro soldiers are maltreated, it is generally their own fault; many of them are puffed up with vanity on account of their new profession as soldiers, and . . . thinking themselves better than white men, are insolent and overbearing." Elsewhere the paper sneeringly commented, "It would appear . . . that among the newly-claimed *rights* of negroes, is one of roaming at will, armed with muskets and bayonets."[101] Angered by watching African Americans reject deferential conventions in favor of the privileges of soldiers, conservatives not only ridiculed the soldiers but also incited violence against them.

Among whites' numerous attacks on black soldiers that summer, an incident involving a black noncommissioned officer, Corporal John Ross, received the most attention. As in many other racially charged conflicts, this one began as a problem among a few individuals but spiraled into a broader conflagration involving a mob of hostile whites. Ross, wearing an army uniform decorated with chevrons indicating that he was a corporal, was walking past the Northern Market, an area where a number of assaults on black soldiers had already occurred, when several white men assaulted him. A threatening crowd developed, and two policemen arrived. The policemen's intentions are not clear, but it seems that Ross resisted arrest but offered to accompany the police to the army's central guardhouse. Surrounded by an angry crowd, at least one policeman struck Ross with his baton, and someone tore the chevrons from Ross's jacket. According to an eyewitness account published in the *Christian Recorder*, Ross and the policemen walked to the army's central guardhouse, "amidst the clamoring of the mob, their yells and shouts of 'kill the black —— —— ——,' &c., &c., &c."[102] Military officials arrested the offending policeman and held a hearing on the case. Conflicting accounts were aired. Ross claimed the policeman tore off his chevrons, while the policeman claimed to have no recollection of doing so; some witnesses asserted that Ross was drunk, while others denied it. Ross found a measure of vindication, however, when the military official holding the hearing concluded "that the negro had been shamefully and inhumanely treated; that, whatever might be the private opinion of any one, the Government having authorized it, they [black men] should be treated as soldiers."[103]

The Ross incident demonstrated that U.S. military officials could be a powerful force in defense of black soldiers' claims to dignity and respect. This is not to say that military officials built an entirely supportive relationship with black soldiers or with black Washingtonians more generally. Black Washingtonians trusted the military hierarchy only tentatively. In one case, when unfamiliar men suddenly replaced the original recruiting officers of the 1st USCT, African American men simply ceased volunteering. African Americans also complained bitterly of discriminatory treatment in the provost marshal's office, and the soldiers of the 1st USCT protested when they discovered that their pay was unequal to that of white enlisted men. Nonetheless, white officers and black soldiers alike evidently realized that once black soldiers were enlisted they could not easily be abandoned.[104]

In the volatile summer of 1863, however, even military officials proved unable to protect black soldiers and residents of the city from white-led violence. By late June, attacks had become frequent enough to prompt officers of black troops to meet to discuss "cases of assaults, attacks, &c., on colored soldiers." It was "said that there are enough cases already before them to keep them steadily engaged for some weeks."[105] The next month, the supervisor of Camp Barker became concerned upon hearing about the New York City draft riots, in which whites immersed that city in nearly a week of violence, much of it directed against African Americans. Fearing a similar uprising in Washington, and in particular an attack on Camp Barker, the supervisor asked that a company from the 1st USCT be deployed as guards and requested "a hundred and fifty muskets with ammunition to place in the hands of our laboring men . . . so that in case of riot we may be able to defend ourselves."[106]

Among African Americans, threats and attacks did not diminish excitement at the prospect that black men's military service would provide a platform for collectively demanding citizenship. Thomas Hinton, the military recruiter, reported to the *Christian Recorder* that when a group of black soldiers visited a Washington church "the excitement of the colored ladies knew no bounds, each trying to get a peep at these *true Americans*."[107] And when the 1st USCT went on dress parade one Sunday afternoon in June, a correspondent described the various comments of satisfied black onlookers. "The soldiers executed the different drill manoeuvres so exceedingly well, that all sort of pridish remarks were made by our people, such as: —'Don't they do it? Look at the coons, will you?' 'Now don't them darkies know it's against the law to do that?' 'What do you reckon Mr. White Man thinks of that?' 'Ah! boys, go it, can't be better employed;' 'Ha, ha, ha, look yonder at that fellow, don't he hold his head high; take care old fellow, Jeff. will get you, he will limber that neck.'"[108] As the proud and ironic commentary revealed, it was becoming clear that the Civil War might result not only in the abolition of slavery but also in new opportunities for black men to claim full status in the body politic.

The assertive and celebratory mood swept into civilian life that summer as black civic organizations took to the streets in parades and public demonstrations that would have been forbidden just eighteen months earlier. In July, the District's Sabbath School Union converted its annual meeting into a citywide spectacle. Thousands of students and their teachers marched from 15th Street Presbyterian Church, past the White House, down Pennsylvania Avenue, and past the Capitol, before gathering at Turner's Israel Church to hear exhortatory speeches. "The proslavery citizens could hardly believe their own eyes," crowed one participant.[109] The same month, Georgetown's black Freemasons marched through the streets displaying a "very beautiful banner" that they had "dared not" show in public "during the Dark Ages."[110] In the fall, the Grand United Order of Odd Fellows held its national convention in Washington. "This was one of the sights which many of us never expected to witness in this city, or anywhere south of Mason and Dixon's line," commented an *Anglo-African* correspondent.[111]

African Americans' newfound ability to display their civic organizations in public was of no small importance. Participation in civic associations, though not necessarily considered a right in need of protection, had long been linked with status in communities. While white Washingtonians had tolerated some black civic associations in antebellum Washington, the black codes had severely restricted them and, in so doing, reinforced the racially unequal privileges of membership in the local community. Thus, when black Sabbath school teachers and students, Freemasons, or Odd Fellows orchestrated public displays in the streets of the capital they were demanding and also enacting a form of civic equality long denied to them. By taking to the streets with banners and regalia, black associations asserted civic standing, showing themselves and other onlookers that their associations, too, were valued and legitimate parts of the broader civic fabric.

By the middle of 1863, black Washingtonians had revealed their determination to attack and discredit the "features of slavery" that continued in their midst. The abolition of slavery, the end of the black codes, and the nullification of fugitive slave laws had begun the process. But to transcend slavery and build a society based on principles of equality it would be necessary to knock down all racial barriers in public or quasi-public places. What black Washingtonians sought was not just access, but equality. Black men did not want to enlist without assurance that they would be treated the same as white soldiers, and black soldiers refused to perform the rituals of public deference long required of blacks only. Black secret societies insisted on taking to the streets with their banners and insignias, just as white societies had always done. Forging racial equality required claims to individual rights, but it also demanded that all privileges commonly granted to white organizations be granted to black ones as well.

The nation's capital was a crucible of equality during the Civil War. The convergence of the local and the national and the changes wrought at both levels were clear on February 12, 1865, when Henry Highland Garnet delivered an address in the chamber of the U.S. House of Representatives. Garnet, a nationally known African American minister and activist who had moved to Washington to become the pastor of 15th Street Presbyterian Church, spoke from the desk of the Speaker of the House to an overflowing crowd that mixed "whites and blacks, soldiers and citizens." In his speech, Garnet denounced the crime of slavery, heralded the Thirteenth Amendment, and called for black men's enfranchisement.[112]

More than the speech, however, it was the event itself, and the crowd in the gallery, that attracted national attention. Although occasional black spectators had attended sessions in the Capitol prior to Garnet's address, this was evidently the first time black people gathered en masse. "Up to that date . . . no man of color was allowed to set his foot inside the National Halls of Legislature," wrote James McCune Smith, a black abolitionist. "The high places where his chains were forged were hidden behind the veil, and from his sight, by express enactment: the evil doers rightly hid from their victims the scene of their evil deeds."[113] For those in attendance, Smith suggested, Garnet's address demystified the Capitol itself, the space where power was brokered and laws were made. The speech represented not only the elevation of one prominent black man into the halls of American power, but also the entrance of masses of black people into the Capitol as would-be constituents. Still prohibited from voting, black spectators nevertheless made themselves stakeholders in national politics. Far from Washington, newspaper readers who considered the mixed crowd and the African American speaker knew that great changes were at hand.

The impact of African Americans' wartime claims to equality in the capital was clear to James McKim, a white abolitionist who, in a fund-raising letter to a women's organization in Edinburgh, Scotland, compared the Washington of late 1864 to the slaveholding citadel it had been just four years earlier. "Now, what do I see to-day? Freedom, Freedom, Freedom everywhere! In the Presidential mansion, in both houses of Congress, in the Supreme Court . . . in the hotels, in the public parks, on the streets, everywhere is freedom and everybody free! Not nominally and abstractly, but really and actually."[114] McKim recognized that freedom was not simply the absence of bonded labor but was, instead, something that must be contested in a range of spaces in the city. Each site of freedom seemed worth mentioning in its own right because different spaces had difference valences and African Americans' access to each one had different meanings.

Yet McKim was overly hasty in pronouncing freedom a reality. Advocates of expansive visions of racial equality still faced widespread convictions, held even by many Republicans, that the perquisites of citizenship must be earned and that African Americans must now prove themselves worthy of the equality they sought. Many observers believed former slaves, in particular, faced overwhelming odds in this pursuit. Many white people who rejected the idea that people of African descent were biologically inferior to those of European origin (in other words, those who were not racists in the scientific sense) nonetheless saw freedpeople as severely damaged and believed they would require a great deal of tutelage if they were to merit equal rights and full citizenship. The struggle over equality encompassed not only the world of public life but also the more private realms of housekeeping, childrearing, and sexual morality.

2

They Feel It Is Their Right

FREEDPEOPLE, REFORMERS, AND
THE DEMANDS OF CITIZENSHIP

In 1867, several months after the Freedmen's Bureau named John Kimball superintendent of freedpeople's marriages, freedwoman Caroline Grice came to see him about her daughter, Hannah. Hannah had recently given birth to a "white child," and Caroline informed the bureau agent that the infant's father was a guard at the Freedmen's Bureau barracks where she and her daughter lived. This report was not simply a point of information, however. It was a claim to redress. As Kimball knew, District of Columbia law provided that unwed "free women" could claim from their child's father $30.00 per year for the first seven years of the child's life. With the financial stakes of the case in mind, Kimball instructed a subordinate to investigate the allegation.

When questioned by a bureau agent, the alleged father, Silas S. Chamberlain, refused to acknowledge paternity and described Hannah Grice as "a girl of lewd habits and notorious character." Several witnesses (all recommended by Chamberlain) stated that Hannah Grice had sexual relationships with many men, and some said she had talked of taking money for sex. Two witnesses said Grice had "criminal connection" with a white former watchman at the barracks, the timing of which implied that he might be the child's father. A lawyer for the Freedmen's Bureau concluded that the testimony, particularly that concerning Grice's alleged relationship with the watchman, cast doubt on Chamberlain's paternity and, more broadly, "that the character of said Hannah Grice has been very bad—that she is unworthy of belief."

Bureau agents believed that the witnesses' testimony exonerated Chamberlain, but they were chagrined nonetheless. In setting up barracks housing for freedpeople in the capital, they had hoped to promote what they considered good moral values among freedpeople by renting only to married couples, widows, or soldiers' wives, and by teaching hygiene, household management, and virtuous labor. Yet how could such programs succeed if employees of the bureau were, themselves, complicit in promoting freedpeople's immoral behavior? The public suggestion that at least one of the bureau's own employees was embroiled in a scandalous relationship with a freedwoman diminished the bureau's credibility as an agent of moral reform. Kimball, a New Englander who had been a chaplain in the Union army, called it a "miserable affair" and requested that Chamberlain be transferred, regardless of the outcome of the investigation. Another bureau agent noted that Grice should not have been allowed to live in the barracks in the first place. "Permitting a female of 'lewd habits and notorious character' to remain," he reminded a superior, was "a direct violation of one of the rules."[1]

The barracks where Chamberlain worked and the Grices lived were one of four constellations of housing run by the Freedmen's Bureau in Washington. Such housing was designed to provide clean and affordable domiciles for migrant freedpeople. Yet, as the scandal about Hannah Grice's pregnancy made clear, material aid was not the bureau's only goal. Indeed, Freedmen's Bureau agents and affiliated agents of private relief societies, most of them from the North, offered freedpeople clothing, firewood, and food rations, as well as housing. But such largesse was always accompanied by the insistence that freedpeople reform and improve themselves, throwing off the bad habits they had supposedly learned in slavery and conforming to what many northerners considered the norms of civilization. Likewise, bureau agents' attempts to find paid labor for former slaves were driven not just by practical concerns but also by their conviction that such labor would uplift a population that did not, because of past experience, understand the intrinsic moral value of working for wages.

Bureau agents and other northerners sometimes expressed their views using what historian George Fredrickson called "romantic racialism," or the idea that different races of people had different innate character traits. Yet, among bureau agents and missionaries in Washington and also among African Americans involved in freedmen's relief, theories of innate racial difference were far less important than their convictions about the barbarism of slavery and the need to "civilize" freedpeople. They believed slavery had created a world in which labor was degraded, parental authority devalued, monogamy disregarded, and violence ubiquitous. These reformers' objective was to mitigate the harmful cultural legacies of slavery and to lift benighted freedpeople out of the depths of degradation.[2]

Programs to improve freedpeople's comportment—whether in barracks housing, through home visits, or through the education of young people and adults—were designed to lay the groundwork for freedpeople's incorporation into civil society and perhaps into the polity. Bureau agents and their allies connected freedpeople's personal habits to their nascent claims to rights and equality, believing that uplift and civilization at home would lead to higher status in the community. Freedpeople required more tutelage than other poor people, they thought, because of the damage done them by slavery if not because of their supposed racial difference. Only improved habits in the most intimate realms—in housekeeping, child rearing, and sexual relations—would prove them worthy of the public respect that, many Americans believed, was a prerequisite to citizenship and claims to rights. Such expectations were clear in the hope of Andrew K. Browne, a defense lawyer for the Freedmen's Bureau, that discrimination against freedpeople would dissolve when they demonstrated their "elevation in the scale of respectability."[3]

Such attitudes are important not only in their own right but also for what happened later. In the period of Republican dominance that followed the Civil War, the Republicans' ostensibly nonracial vision of freedpeople's civilizational deficiencies became a tool for Republicans and Democrats who sought to undermine the egalitarian impulses of Reconstruction while avoiding using explicitly racial justifications. Where Republicans dominated—in states and, in particular, in the federal government—explicit allusions to racial inferiority became objectionable, but arguments resting on the supposed cultural deficiencies of freedpeople or of African Americans in general remained far more acceptable. Thus, as later chapters will show, moderate Republicans and conservatives seeking to discredit popular government in the capital and elsewhere in the South drew on long-standing doubts about freedpeople's moral and political capacities to justify racially discriminatory policies without making recourse to biological race or to blatant racism.

For all the importance of rhetorical strategies, however, it is also critical to recognize the dynamic processes that took place when bureau agents and their allies attempted to put their ideals into practice. As the case of Hannah Grice suggests, actual practices in the barracks—and in other uplift institutions—often challenged reformers' expectations. The bureau did not, in fact, evict Hannah Grice for her supposedly "lewd habits." And, in fact, bureau officials were forced to confront the reality that the behavior of Silas Chamberlain made a mockery of the bureau's demands of sexual propriety from freedwomen. Time and again, bureau agents and other reformers found themselves unable to fully impose their visions of personal reform on freedpeople. They encountered clients whose actual lives challenged their received assumptions, and they often retooled their policies as a result. Thus, a full accounting of the relationship between the Freedmen's Bureau and freedpeople requires an examination of both the bureau's rhetoric about such issues as marriage and parenting and the realities of how freedpeople and bureau agents interacted on the ground.

Schools for African American children fit this pattern well. This chapter places the establishment and cultivation of freedmen's schools, first under the bureau and missionary teachers and then in a public school system, in the larger context of tutelary efforts by northerners interested in uplifting freedpeople for citizenship.[4] Bureau agents and missionary teachers saw schools as ideal places for teaching freedchildren the habits of personal comportment that were the foundation of civic standing. Following their logic of civilizational uplift, bureau administrators believed that the schooling of freedchildren required special efforts, since freedchildren suffered special disabilities. Bureau agents and other federal officials particularly treasured the capital's schools for freedchildren and used black children's successes in the Washington schools to trumpet their argument that, under proper tutelage, black children learned just as fast and as well as white ones.

Yet the development of education for African Americans in the capital was not simply a top-down matter. The postwar schools were literally built atop the myriad private schools established by black educators before the Civil War, and black Washingtonians drew on the tradition of independent black schools—and on the argument that African Americans were the ones best suited to administer and teach in schools for black children—to demand continuing autonomy for the black public schools in the postwar period. Many African American educators shared with white missionaries a vision of freedpeople's education as civilizational uplift, and yet they also experienced discrimination by white educators and knew that black public schools could become important employers of black teachers. In the end, Congress's establishment of separate black public schools in the capital both created a Jim Crow system of education and made it easier for black educators to make those schools their own and build a school system of which they were justly proud.

The Politics of Neighborhood

In order to understand the challenges migrant freedpeople faced in the capital and the roles of the Freedmen's Bureau and of northern relief institutions, it is useful first to examine how municipal authorities, Democrats, and wealthy white residents responded to the influx. Essentially, these parties insisted that freed migrants were not citizens of the city and were entitled to few privileges or rights. From the earliest wartime discussions of emancipation, city officials and white citizens had opposed any measure that would result in a large population of free African Americans in the capital. The city councils had feared that emancipation would make the District an "asylum for free negroes." Expressing white residents' widespread desire that freedpeople be pushed to the margins of the city, the Democratic *Constitutional Union* had demanded that the city's "contraband camp" be moved "to some backwoods." And, in 1866, the paper complained of the "degraded contrabands" who "now fester this city like a mighty sore."[5] Indeed, the term "contraband" itself, used prolifically by city and federal officials alike, helped identify escapees as outsiders to the city and therefore lacking the prerogatives even long-term free black residents might claim.[6] The city government and most wealthy local whites saw freedpeople as a social and financial burden and feared they would become a source of disorder and, relatedly, declining commerce and property values.

The local government continued to deny that it had any responsibility to the new migrants and to obfuscate when federal officials sought its cooperation. For instance, Mayor Richard Wallach grudgingly agreed to offer space at the almshouse to "the colored poor who are permanent residents of the city," but he rejected entreaties to serve the migrant refugees, insisting they were the federal government's responsibility.[7] The Washington city government also denied a federal request that a brick building on Judiciary Square be used as an "Industrial School, Employment office, and Store House for the Freedpeople of this city." The building, which before the war was used as a school for white children, had been a military hospital during the war. Now Mayor Wallach fired off angry letters to the secretary of interior, and the city council officially protested "placing any building on any part of Judiciary Square, or using any building already there for the purposes of a House of Refuge, or any similar institution," arguing that the square was "in the very heart of the City, in close proximity to the City Hall, and also to one of the female Public Schools of the City."[8] An institution for freedpeople did not belong in the "heart" of the city, and the council's invocation of the girls' school was a reminder that many whites already perceived African Americans as a threat to the purity of white girls and women. Assessing the local government's consistent hostility to freedpeople, an agent of the Freedmen's Bureau reported that the "municipal

authorities . . . had fallen in with many of the inhabitants in their unjust discriminations and prejudices against the negro—as free."[9]

As the agent's report suggested, it was not only the local government that
sought to keep freedpeople at the margins of Washington life. Influential private citizens also attempted to keep freedpeople at arm's length. Andrew Wylie,
a Lincoln appointee to the District of Columbia Supreme Court, raised a vehement protest to Congress and the Department of Interior when the army
began to convert the freedmen's hospital near his house into a school for freedchildren. Wylie argued that the children's presence would decrease the value
of his property, which he had bought "for a large price hoping to secure a
quiet and comfortable home."[10] Wylie lived on the northern edge of Washington's densely settled downtown, and he hoped the value of his property would
rise as urban development engulfed his neighborhood. He anticipated that the
small public park in front of his land would soon be "inclosed and adorned,"
and he was especially fearful that a school nearby—"whether for white or
black children"—would lower the value of an investment on which he expected
significant returns. Wylie's concern was probably heightened by the fact that
significant numbers of freedpeople had already moved into the neighborhood,
looking for opportunities to squat on uninhabited squares.[11] Although Wylie
claimed that "every respectable family" in the area opposed the establishment
of the school, other neighbors informed federal officials that they did not support Wylie's campaign. Federal officials remained unmoved by Wylie's protest, and the group of black schools near his house flourished.

Wealthy property owners like Wylie were used to having their way in Washington. From the earliest days of American cities, municipal governments were
structured as instruments of property owners and taxpayers. Whereas state and
federal governments were designed to represent the interests of "the people,"
the thinking went, city governments—whose most important powers concerned
taxing and investment—should be in the control of those who would bear the
brunt of taxation. Indeed, the prerogatives of the wealthy were so entrenched
in cities that as states dropped taxpayer and property-holding requirements
for voting during the 1830s and 1840s, municipal governments often retained
them. By the 1850s, states had asserted the authority to determine franchise
requirements in their cities. Yet municipal governments still made no pretense
that goods such as street paving, lighting, and waste removal would be distributed democratically. Most often, improvements were funded through special assessments on the owners of land adjacent to the projected improvement.
This meant that neighborhoods where people were poor, or rented land, were

less likely to enjoy basic services than those where landholders were able (and willing) to put up their share of the money. William Novak has shown that when municipal governments conflicted with private property owners, antebellum courts largely ruled in favor of expansive prerogatives for "the public," as represented by city government. But in nineteenth-century cities, members of the economic elite increasingly managed to define the public interest as that which promoted commercial development and rising property values.[12] This context helps explain why Justice Wylie believed he could make a case for removal of the black school near his house by reference to the tenuous value of his own property.

Given municipal government's mission to stabilize and promote property values and commerce, it is not surprising that the capital's Metropolitan Police, whose charge was the protection of property, sought help from the federal government in containing what they saw as the threatening, and literally contagious, aspects of freedpeople's existence in Washington. In the spring of 1866, amid fears that a cholera epidemic would strike the city as the weather warmed, the police board instructed A. C. Richards, the police superintendent, to investigate the houses and streets of the neighborhoods where "contrabands" resided.[13] Richards explored several dense neighborhoods, and one, known as "Murder Bay," became a focal point. Located on the route between the Capitol and the Executive Mansion, Murder Bay was adjacent to the National Mall. Even before the war, the area was known for its concentration of gambling venues and houses of prostitution. As the city's population grew during the conflict, its inexpensive housing and empty spaces attracted a large population of poor whites and African Americans. Contemporaries often described the area as an eyesore, a health hazard, and a den of crime and corruption.[14] To city officials, Murder Bay was of surpassing importance because of its central location. Whereas poor housing conditions on the fringes of the city seemed less threatening, both to public health and to the value of property, such blight in the city's center was a matter of great concern to the police and no doubt to those who hoped to prosper from Washington's wartime growth.[15]

Having investigated the housing of poor African Americans in a variety of locales, Superintendent Richards wrote up a report that described the housing of freedpeople in Murder Bay in dramatic language. "Here crime, filth, and poverty seem to vie with each other in a career of degradation and death," he wrote in a letter that quickly became a staple in local political rhetoric.[16] He described families crammed together in shanties that virtually lacked roofs. With special concern for ventilation and "miasmatic effluvia" from the nearby canal, he called the indoor atmosphere "stifling and sickening in the extreme." He reported slightly better housing on an adjacent block, where the houses had small backyards. But the yards were situated on low ground, and "with the advent of warm weather, the seeds of disease must spread among and destroy these wretched people."[17] Openings between the buildings led "in so devious a course that one with difficulty finds his way out again." Adding to his disorientation and disapproval was the fact that multiple families lived crowded together in a building that also contained a restaurant and a boardinghouse and, on the second floor, "a large dance hall, where these people nightly congregate for amusement." Richards mingled his concerns about contagion and disease with worries about freedpeople's leisure activities and family structures—in other words, about their moral well-being.

The Richards report proved effective in prompting federal action against the dilapidated housing in which many freedpeople lived. In the Senate, the chair of the District of Columbia Committee, Lot Morrill, used the report to press for a special appropriation for "destitute colored people" in the District.[18] Some legislators who were generally unsympathetic to the Freedmen's Bureau and to the cause of freedmen's aid supported the appropriation. Presumably swayed by the Richards report and by their own observations of conditions in the city, many realized that the crowded and impoverished situation of the District's freedpeople might lead to the spread of cholera and other epidemic diseases. The problem, a West Virginia senator put it, "affects ourselves." But Willard Saulsbury of Delaware opposed the proposal, insisting that it was unfair to poor whites that the money should be designated only for African Americans. Other senators countered that slavery and sudden emancipation had made freedpeople as a group especially needy, and that the local government provided for relief of the white poor but did nothing for poor African Americans. The senators finally compromised by designating the $25,000 appropriation for the destitute of the District, without specification of the "race" of the recipients, a move that conformed with many Republicans' commitment to race-neutral language and that paralleled Congress's decision, the previous year, to mandate that the newly created Freedmen's Bureau serve white "refugees" as well as freedmen.[19]

The appropriation secured, Freedmen's Bureau officials sought cooperation from the Metropolitan Police in efforts to clean, whitewash, drain, and raze the worst housing in the central city, beginning with Murder Bay. Although the two agencies shared an interest in cleaning up freedpeople's housing, the collaboration was far from seamless. William F. Spurgin, the Freedmen's Bureau official overseeing the effort, found the police unwilling to offer much assistance. Spurgin believed that freedpeople were being unfairly singled out for living in squalid conditions, and his reports often highlighted the abysmal circumstances in which white people also lived. "While the premises occupied by the freedmen . . . are filthy in the extreme," he noted in one case, "the same is true without a single exception of the premises occupied by white persons." "It would be well were a corresponding endeavor made to cleanse other portions of the city *not* occupied by Freedmen," he advised in another. Drawing attention to the multifarious sources of filth in the city, he cited commercial laundry establishments and a brewery, offering consistent rebukes to the original police mandate to investigate only the living conditions of "contrabands." The *Constitutional Union* took note of Spurgin's tactic and denounced it. Its editors smirked: "We hope he . . . is more than ever convinced of the superiority of the dirty contraband."[20]

Despite their tensions, representatives of both the Freedmen's Bureau and the police agreed that dramatic measures were required to clean up freedpeople's housing, even to the point of demolishing buildings and leaving their denizens homeless. Indeed, when bureau officials deemed edifices so damaged that no amount of cleaning would improve them, they recommended tearing them down and "scattering the occupants."[21] In 1868, the police board reported that "quite a number" of the "small tenement houses occupied by the poorer class of colored people" had "disappeared from the more thickly populated parts of Washington." The police were encouraged by "steps . . . now being taken by certain benevolent individuals to erect comfortable frame dwellings in the suburbs of Washington to be rented at a low price to this class of people."[22] Compared with more organized housing reform efforts at the end of the century, attempts of the late 1860s to sanitize and segregate Washington were relatively haphazard. The impulses were similar, however. Municipal officials and, to a lesser extent, agents of the Freedmen's Bureau saw freedpeople as an urban problem to be resolved. And because freedpeople had neither high status in the community nor a right to participate in the selection of public officials, they were buffeted by policies over which they had no influence.[23]

To Provide and Subject: The Bureau and Domestic Uplift

The whitewashing campaign run by William Spurgin was one small component of the Freedmen's Bureau's multifaceted work in the postwar capital. In the hope of helping freedpeople earn an adequate living and elevating them out of the barbarism of slavery, bureau agents encouraged freedpeople to leave the capital for places where work was more plentiful, helped them find employment in the capital, distributed outdoor relief, offered housing in military barracks, and contributed to the creation of schools. Bureau agents and their acolytes saw all these projects as materially important, but their endeavors also fit within a broader ethos of civilizational uplift. Like religious and moral reformers engaged in other causes, they believed reform began at home, with altering habits of housekeeping, child rearing, and family relations. Yet their agenda was not simply about private uplift. To the contrary, bureau agents and their associates also believed that by helping freedpeople substitute civilization for degradation, they were preparing former slaves to claim both individual rights and the privileges of citizenship in the local community.

The Freedmen's Bureau is best known as the federal government's first foray into large-scale domestic social policy. Established in the spring of 1865, the bureau was run through the War Department and staffed largely by Union veterans. An assistant commissioner oversaw bureau operations in each state, and the assistant commissioner for the District of Columbia was responsible for both the capital and Maryland. The first local assistant commissioner was John Eaton, a New Englander who had run a wartime free labor experiment at Davis Bend, Mississippi. The second was Charles H. Howard, the brother of the bureau's commissioner, Oliver O. Howard.[24] Many agents were necessary to carry out the work both assistant commissioners envisioned, and bureau agents in the capital received help from scores of northerners who traveled there to distribute relief on behalf of northern aid societies, to teach, and to otherwise help freedpeople. Indeed, the District of Columbia became a focal point for the freedmen's aid movement during the war, and it continued to be so afterward. The capital offered easy access from the Northeast, a large population of freedpeople who seemed in dire need of relief and uplift, and the possibility of attention from federal officials.

From the outset, the local assistant commissioners made visits to freedpeople's homes a centerpiece of their efforts. When he took charge, John Eaton resolved that bureau agents would call on every family of freedpeople in Washington and Georgetown. When Charles Howard succeeded Eaton in 1866, he expanded and systematized that work. Bureau agents divided the capital into relief districts in order to make management easier, with visiting agents and physicians assigned to monitor the conditions of housing, poverty, and disease throughout the capital. Following practices of outdoor relief that were developed in cities before the war, bureau employees and volunteer agents

THEY FEEL IT IS THEIR RIGHT

sought to determine who was "truly" needy. They assessed whether members of impoverished households were capable of working for wages, or whether they were too young, too old, or too sick to support themselves.[25]

Visiting agents assessed freedpeople's home lives not just to determine how much material relief to offer but also to deliver lessons in moral uplift. Visiting agent Lucy Colman, for example, recalled that freedpeople needed no instruction in religious observance, but that the "requirements of civilization were not so familiar to them, such as cleanliness, and prudence, sobriety and independence." White abolitionist Julia Wilbur, also a visiting agent, reported giving "severe lectures" in disorderly homes and that "one family were so filthy that I did not think it right to help them." John L. Roberts, a minister who later supervised the rental of barracks housing, declared that "much of the misery and apparent bad conditions of the tenements result from the shiftlessness of their occupants" and recommended that the bureau's visitors try to "enforce cleanliness in person, equipage, & appurtenants."[26]

Amid what they saw as freedpeople's flagrant disregard for morals and hygiene, agents sometimes noted homes that measured up to their standards. One agent made the connections among cleanliness, thrift, and morality especially clear when he wrote, "Some of these people are found living in a very filthy, miserable, demoralized condition, . . . wicked, poor and lazy, while others have made themselves homes, own wagons and horses, and are doing well."[27] A pair of visiting agents was "glad to find a goodly number of families of colored people who have either been freed for many years or were born free living in their own houses very comfortably and some, quite genteely," a situation that "convinces us more and more, that these people can be educated to take care of themselves."[28] Evidence of African Americans' prosperity and gentility helped assuage nagging doubts that "these people," by virtue of their race, could ever be elevated to an acceptable level of civilization.

African Americans involved in freedmen's relief work also scrutinized the personal habits of freedpeople and aspired to teach housekeeping, thrift, and other domestic habits. The women of the Contraband Relief Association, for example, felt it was their "duty" to "assist [freedpeople] towards a higher plane of civilization." Sojourner Truth, who worked with freedpeople near the capital, found freedwomen "very ignorant in relation to house-keeping, as most of them were instructed in field labor, but not in household duties." "They all . . . want to learn the way we live in the North," she added. Tennessee-born educator Rufus Perry sought to teach children the value of independence and reported that his students were "beginning . . . to have a very clear idea of the

FIGURE 2.1. "Glimpses at the Freedmen's Bureau—Issuing Rations to the Old and Sick." In addition to visiting freedpeople at home, Freedmen's Bureau agents distributed food, clothing, and fuel from depots in the city. In this image, a freedwoman hands the bureau agent a ticket she may have received during a home visit. Bureau agents and other visitors handed out such vouchers to those whom they judged deserving of aid. This sketch was made in Richmond, but similar facilities operated in Washington. *Frank Leslie's Illustrated Newspaper*, September 22, 1866, 5. Courtesy Library of Congress.

personal responsibilities attending their new relation to society, and fully to understand that the state of freedom is the state of self-reliance." As in the case of their white counterparts, the uplift these black reformers promoted, with its strong demands for what historians have broadly called "respectability," was about more than imposing class-specific ideas about proper behavior on poor ex-slaves. It was also about attempting to usher freedpeople into the civic body and, concomitantly, preventing them from becoming pariahs marginalized by the heritage of slavery or race.[29]

Bureau agents' ultimate hope was that freedpeople would find paying work, become self-supporting, and discover the moral value of working for wages. Consistent with the "free labor ideology" that had become central to Republican politics and culture in the antebellum years, bureau agents and missionaries viewed waged labor as a civilizing force for men and women, and they often assumed that freedpeople did not understand the intrinsic value of work because of their experiences as captive laborers. Yet the large population of freedwomen in the city, especially those with dependent children, posed challenges for those who believed freedwomen must work for wages. Sayles Bowen, head of the locally organized National Freedmen's Relief Association, noted that freedwomen cared for their children with "a selfsacrifice and energy rarely if ever met with in the history of mankind," but he lamented that they must "lock up their little ones for the day, with half a breakfast and no fire, and after a days work of sewing, partake of their first and only scanty meal." Another relief worker explained how the tension between waged work and child care contributed to freedwomen's periodic need for government support. "As soon as they or their children are sick, their labor ceases; they suffer proper food." It was best to aid such women for the few weeks a year they needed it, that person argued, rather than to send them to a government-run camp, for "it does not seem right that a woman who has a feeling of independence, and wishes to support her own family, should be forced into dependence all the time."[30]

Responding to the particular employment problems women faced, the Freedmen's Bureau, in conjunction with northern relief associations, established several "industrial schools" to promote freedwomen's financial independence. Some industrial schools provided instruction in hand and machine sewing, while others were basically large-scale laundries where women washed and ironed. During 1866, the bureau reported, the seven industrial schools in the District offered "employment and instruction to some 369 women," who "made, repaired, and distributed a large amount of clothing."[31] Sometimes the products of the women's labor were sold at a discount back to the federal government, with women receiving compensation (often nominally) for their work. Bureau officials expressed some anxiety about whether industrial schools would create a form of unhealthy dependency on government relief, but proponents of such schools argued that their purpose was "not so much to furnish employment and do a large quantity of work" as to "*help the freedwomen help themselves.*"[32]

As in so many reformer-supported endeavors related to freedpeople, economic and moral purposes came together in the industrial schools. One white woman reported that the freedwomen at the industrial school she supervised showed "marked improvement" in personal cleanliness and were learning to obey the laws of government and society, "receiving and adapting such instruction with an evident wish to become good citizens." On visiting an indus-

FIGURE 2.2. Freedmen's relief workers believed that "industrial schools" such as this one in Richmond, Virginia, would teach freedwomen marketable skills and inculcate them with a proper appreciation for waged labor, thus preparing them for citizenship. *Frank Leslie's Illustrated Newspaper*, September 22, 1866, 5. Courtesy Library of Congress, cph 3a33775.

trial school in Washington, another white woman remarked, "It was almost as thrilling a sight to me to see these earnest women together at work with their needles, as it was to see the first colored soldier in the Union blue."[33] If the comparison between women sewing and men soldiering evoked two separate, gendered visions of racial uplift, it was also clear that reformers believed that freedwomen and freedmen alike must learn to become proper members of the civic body. Industrial schools aspired to teach not just concrete and marketable sewing skills but also the more abstract attributes of conformity and discipline that were considered markers of civilization and belonging.

Yet industrial schools for women did not resolve the problem of what small children would do while women were at work, nor did they spare freedwomen from the widespread view that they were insufficiently prepared for motherhood. Indeed, with so much reformist focus on the home, assessments of freedwomen's capacity for appropriate mothering assumed great importance. John Eaton, the first assistant commissioner in Washington, praised freedwomen's

THEY FEEL IT IS THEIR RIGHT

"almost superhuman efforts to regain their children" but warned that helping them required "wisdom," for sometimes "the mother was not sufficiently emancipated from the brutal ideas of her bondage to understand the duties of a Christian parent."[34] Such indictments of freedwomen as mothers did not require allusions to intrinsic "racial" traits of people of African descent. To the contrary, some of the most potent abolitionist imagery—of slave owners' sexual dominion over enslaved women, of the sale of children away from their parents, and of owners' usurpation of slave parents' authority—had implicitly cast doubt on the parenting capacities of people emerging from slavery. Observers saw much evidence of loving, committed mothering as they witnessed freedwomen's determination to reunite families after emancipation. But the conviction that freedpeople were backward in familial relationships was potent.

Northerners' movement to establish schools for freedpeople was part of their broader commitment to civilizational uplift and reflected their concerns about the deficiency of moral instruction in freedpeople's homes. As was typical elsewhere in the South, in Washington northern missionary societies provided teachers for freedmen's schools, and the bureau paid teachers' transportation costs and provided buildings—often barracks and other edifices no longer needed by the army—in which schools could be housed. Northern societies founded and staffed dozens of schools in Washington during the war, joining the efforts of locals organized in the largely white National Freedmen's Relief Association and of existing African American teachers.[35] Most of the newly arrived missionaries and teachers were white, but some were African American, reflecting the ongoing attraction of the capital to black northerners interested in reform and politics, as well as its proximity to hubs of northern black life such as Philadelphia and New York City.

Results were soon manifest in schools that opened across the city. By the end of 1865, one newspaper estimated, the capital was home to fifty-three schools in which 5,618 black children were studying, as well as an array of night schools for adults and industrial schools for women. Schools convened, one bureau agent reported, "in the bodies of churches with their inconvenient pews . . . in gloomy and damp basement rooms, . . . old stables, and roughly built shanties where wind and rain could beat through the many openings."[36] Scholars and teachers used available spaces continuously, with daytime classes for children and nighttime and weekend ones for both adults and youth. Attempting to give the enterprise some order, Freedmen's Bureau officials organized the District of Columbia Educational Association, which convened teachers in the "colored" schools for monthly presentations and discussions of pedagogy.[37]

Federal officials soon began using the capital's flourishing schools for freed-people as exhibits in the service of the argument that freedchildren were just as intellectually capable as white children. Secretary of State William Seward, for example, frequently brought visiting diplomats to the school at Freedman's Village, across the Potomac River, to demonstrate "the native powers of the negro in his most untutored condition."[38] In 1867, John W. Alvord, the Freed-men's Bureau's national commissioner of schools, reported approvingly, "The past year's experience has fully settled the question of the natural ability of the colored people to become educated and intelligent. Hundreds have visited the schools in this city (Washington) and gone away with their doubts removed and their prejudices much abated."[39]

Alvord himself believed that schooling for freedchildren had different ob-jectives from schooling for even the poorest white children. Not surprisingly, those differences revolved around personal habits. Schools should educate freedpeople to be equal citizens, Alvord maintained, "with rights and interests to be respected in common with those of other citizens; poor and dependent indeed, but no longer in any sense a servile caste." Yet, Alvord maintained, the education of freedpeople should not follow "the precise routine of culture given to white children." "In fact," he stated, "we are dealing with a people to be *untaught* in habits of thinking, feeling, and acting."[40] Alvord believed freedchildren needed special instruction in manners and morals. In the case of freedchildren, he wrote, "the various affairs and economies of every-day life should be taught; cleanliness, dress, home habits, social properties, uses of furniture, preparation of food, and tasteful construction of dwellings, though with rustic material; also industry, with individual self-reliance; labor, produc-tive of support and thrift; habits of saving, with right use of what is saved."[41] Unlike white children, Alvord argued, freedchildren required instruction in the personal habits that were the foundation of civilized life.

Nor did Alvord completely avoid allusions to the intrinsic abilities of people of African descent; he sometimes noted that "the negro" had particular—and static—racial traits. It was "not in the nature of the negro to roam Indian-like as wild men, and resist culture," he suggested in one report. "He loves to congregate in families, in groups, in villages. This was his habit originally in Africa, and the plantation always had some *social* features which, in a measure, alleviated the negro's bondage."[42] Alvord recognized that even in slavery Afri-can Americans had managed to build relationships and institutions, but he at-tributed those successes not to broad, human characteristics but to their nature and, in particular, their African heritage. Like many of his colleagues, Alvord drew on both essentialist ideas about racial characteristics and on more liberal theories of uplift as he speculated on freedpeople's educability.

If anyone represented the racialized, civilizing spirit of freedmen's education from the top down, it was bureau commissioner O. O. Howard. Well known as a pious man, Howard spoke and wrote often about the importance of freedmen's education and did not hesitate to place it in the context of Christian missionary efforts to supposedly barbaric people. Urging a friend to solicit donations from antislavery activists in England in 1866, Howard likened what he hoped would be the English attitude toward freedmen's education to American missionaries' work abroad. "The same spirit that stimulated us to plant schools and churches in Asia, Africa, or the Islands of the Ocean," he argued, "will doubtless animate the christian people of England in their missionary efforts among our freedpeople." He concluded that until the government established a working "system" of public education, "every friend of civilization, of humanity, and of religion" must use private channels to improve "those sections of the country where prejudice and ignorance are dominant."[43]

At their most optimistic, the men and women who undertook freedmen's relief work were sure their charges would rise to the civilizational challenges they faced. In one particularly happy (and self-congratulatory) report—at the end of 1867—John Alvord summarized the dramatic results of the bureau's work in the nation's capital: "Extreme ignorance among that multitude of colored people who flocked to this great centre . . . has been exchanged for comparative intelligence. Their former servile spirit has largely given place to self-respect. The marriage relation is now stamped with sacredness. Home life with its blessings begins to appear. The rising generation are taught to commence with high aims, and multitudes of these children have acquired a vast amount of elementary knowledge."[44]

Alvord expressed confidence in freedpeople's abilities to overcome the obstacles they faced, but he also delineated a daunting range of arenas in which freedpeople were deemed deficient. Indeed, if one interpretation of his remarks was that freedpeople were progressing in all areas, another, more pessimistic view was that the challenges they faced were virtually insurmountable and that it would be years, or even decades, before freedpeople and their descendants were sufficiently educated to merit inclusion, on an equal basis, in the life of the community. Freedmen's relief workers and bureau agents accomplished much that was valuable and, indeed, probably saved many people from dying of starvation and exposure. Yet the vision of freedpeople's civilizational deficiency that motivated their work was adaptable and would soon be turned to far less egalitarian political purposes.

They Feel It Is Their Right

Visions of moral uplift shaped the goals that Freedmen's Bureau agents and northern missionaries set for themselves and the methods they established to achieve them. And yet looking only at reformers' ideas obscures freedpeople's own goals and the clashes and compromises that resulted when freedpeople and bureau agents came into contact. Freedpeople were not the blank slates many outsiders imagined them to be, and they greeted efforts to uplift and improve them with mixed responses. Some aspects of reformers' pedagogical program meshed with freedpeople's own goals and needs. Many suffered from exposure and starvation in the city, and the shelter and food provided by the bureau and its allies met basic bodily demands. Freedpeople everywhere embraced literacy and sought to reunite families, and in Washington too they welcomed schools established by northern missionary societies and went to the bureau for help locating family members and rescuing children from apprenticeships.

Yet the relationship between freedpeople and bureau agents did not simply go in one direction, with freedpeople accepting the overtures and mandates of those seeking to help and uplift them. To the contrary, freedpeople resisted policies that they disliked or that did not conform to their priorities. Bureau agents often expressed frustration with freedpeople's unwillingness to cooperate with their initiatives. But they also proved willing to adapt their policies to fit more closely with the conditions of freedpeople's lives. Thus, in some instances freedpeople found that they faced not a hard wall of official policy but, rather, pliable rules that agents could ignore or change. Some bureau agents who worked closely with freedpeople also came to understand that, despite the abolition of slavery and the formal codification of equality before the law, racial inequality remained deeply entrenched in public life. In response, they began to develop new categories of unassailable rights to which freedpeople should be entitled.

The Freedmen's Bureau began its work in the capital with ambitious hopes for moving thousands of people out of the city, either by sending them back to where they had come from or by shipping them north to find work. In the fall of 1866, assistant commissioner Charles Howard saw in northern migration "the surest means . . . of relieving the Government of the future support of

many of these people," a policy that would "give them all the benefits of independence and vastly improve the condition of such as may remain."[45] Bureau
agents quickly found, however, that encouraging migration, and even paying
for the transportation, did little to alleviate crowding and unemployment in the
city. Thousands of people did depart the capital under the bureau's auspices,
but thousands more continued to arrive, including some of those who had accepted transportation from the bureau but later returned.[46] Meanwhile, bureau
agents and their helpers were struck by how little freedpeople seemed to trust
the government and how strenuously many of them resisted the prospect of
leaving the capital. In fact, many had come from the surrounding region and
had no desire to set out for unfamiliar territory. They also knew that however
bad conditions might be in the city, in the countryside they could well be worse,
as employers frequently broke labor contracts, farms were doing poorly, and
whites were prone to violent attacks on African Americans.[47]

Bureau agents realized that despite their efforts to encourage migration,
overcrowding and a lack of decent housing would remain a problem, and
they turned their attention to ameliorating the conditions of those freedpeople
who stayed. As the capital's population swelled—the result not only of freedpeople's migration but also of the expansion of the federal government and
its requirements for labor at all levels—real estate owners constructed rudi-
mentary shacks on unimproved land and charged extortionate rents for the
most decrepit accommodations.[48] Many longtime black residents opened their
doors to migrants, and freedpeople inhabited every conceivable place in black
Washingtonians' homes. Still, the sheer numbers of migrants far exceeded the
capacity of local African Americans to take them in.[49]

Hoping to provide freedpeople with an alternative to the exploitative conditions created by private landlords—and at the same time relishing the chances
for domestic uplift public housing would provide—bureau agents opened their
first rental apartments to freedpeople in October 1865, in a former military hospital at the north end of Seventh Street. By the winter of 1866, the bureau was
renting apartments in three different barracks (on Capitol Hill, at 7th and O
Streets, and at Kendall Green, on the northeast edge of the city, site of present-
day Gallaudet University), as well as at the hospital, which became known
as Freedman's Hospital. The enterprise would continue into 1868, when the
bureau embarked on plans to build new tenements and tear down the old ones,
even as it gradually shut down its other operations.[50] The majority of barracks
residents were women and children, reflecting the gender imbalance of the
black population in Washington and the special problems of poverty women

and children faced.[51] Some barracks residents may have been families of soldiers stationed far away, but in many cases, family members remained closely
connected. In late fall of 1866 and early 1867, barracks superintendents noted
a sudden rise in the number of residents, as relatives of renters returned to the
city after the harvest.[52]

In most respects, residents of the Freedmen's Bureau barracks carried on
their lives as they might have in private housing. There were limited opportunities for people to work around the barracks, cleaning and improving the
properties, and bureau agents at the barracks ran employment offices to help
people find paid work.[53] Other than that, renters were on their own. They pursued livelihoods in the city as best they could, and they even had to furnish their
own stovepipes if they wanted to heat their rooms. One man used his room in
the barracks to store oysters, which he sold on the street. Many women worked
as laundresses and seamstresses, sometimes in industrial schools organized at
the barracks themselves, while some residents scavenged for rags, paper, bones,
and other items to resell for small sums. Such work afforded opportunities for
additional entrepreneurship; at least one barracks resident bought salvaged
items from others to resell in bulk.[54] As the Hannah Grice paternity case suggested, barracks residents cultivated social and sometimes sexual relationships
with bureau employees. Rivalries, communities, and alliances likely developed
as they would in any densely settled neighborhood. By 1869, ward-based Republican Party associations held meetings in the barracks, a sign that residents
had become part of local political culture and that the buildings themselves
were considered important institutions in the broader community.

The barracks represented a good alternative to private landlords, at least as
far as rent was concerned. Private landlords often charged between $6.00 and
$10.00 per month for a single room, while residents of the bureau-run barracks
typically paid $2.00 or $2.50 monthly and could not be evicted for inability to
pay rent.[55] It is less clear that the quality of the housing provided by the bureau
was better than that offered by private landlords, although it seems likely. The
barracks were of relatively recent construction, and the descriptions of private housing penned by bureau agents, private relief workers, and policemen
were quite lurid. At least the bureau-run barracks had official inspectors who
reported fire hazards, disgusting privies, stagnant water, and leaking roofs.[56]
And the bureau's assistant commissioner, Charles H. Howard, seems to have
responded to such reports. For instance, when an inspector complained that
roofs at East Capitol Street Barracks needed immediate repair, Howard gave
orders that estimates be obtained and the work be done.[57]

Barracks housing also afforded bureau agents and volunteers a captive audience for their efforts at domestic uplift. Under the supervision of John L. Roberts, the East Capitol Street Barracks offered schools for children and adults, including an industrial school for women. Children, Roberts explained, were "taught to be neat, instructed in manners, in sewing, braiding straw &c."[58] Roberts was evidently a true believer in the pedagogy of citizenship. In a report to Charles Howard, he claimed, "The effect of opening these and other Barracks for the accommodation of these people, has been not only to provide for them comfortable homes, but it has subjected them to the observance of disciplinary rules which have had a tendency to elevate them . . . and now these people, or many of them, have become industrious and self-supporting."[59] As Howard himself described the barracks housing program late in 1867: "Strict sanitary regulations are enforced, and the adult people are in this way brought together in a community accessible to education at night, industrial and sabbath schools."[60] The pedagogical aspects of tenement housing were clear.

Those who rented apartments in the barracks faced more surveillance than renters of private tenements, but bureau agents also tried to accommodate some of the choices freedpeople made and the conditions in which they lived. The man who stored oysters in his room was "ordered to vacate it or discontinue its use for that purpose," and able-bodied men perceived to be lounging around were forced to go look for employment. Barracks residents were forbidden to keep pigs or poultry, and bureau agents enforced sanitary rules of all kinds, down to forbidding public urination.[61] Yet bureau agents evidently ignored the rule against housing women of "lewd habits and notorious character" in the case of Hannah Grice. And when residents of one building made clear that their main source of income was collecting rags for resale, bureau agents created a special room where the rags could be stored without becoming a fire hazard.[62] Bureau agents also charged lower rents than they had planned. The first idea had been to charge $3.00 per month, but actual charges were more often about $2.00.[63]

A similar willingness to accommodate freedpeople's needs and desires was also evident in bureau agents' attitudes about marriage. From the outset of the barracks housing program, in the fall of 1865, bureau officials had linked access to housing with reform of freedpeople's marital relations, hoping to use their leverage as landlords to force freedpeople to conduct their private lives along lines the agents favored. On opening the bureau's tenements, the local assistant commissioner instructed the tenement superintendent that the apartments were designed for "those worthy people least able to pay the exorbitant rents demanded in town." The superintendent was to give preference "to those poor, industrious men" who have "large families" as well as to "widows, and soldiers wives," and to "become acquainted with the case of each applicant." "No rooms," he instructed, "will be rented except on your recommendation."[64] Such instructions are not surprising given the bureau's interest, throughout the South, in promoting marriage and nuclear family units among freedpeople. Bureau agents saw marriage as an institution that fostered both moral and economic goals. On the moral side, bureau agents thought they were undoing the work of slavery by pushing freedpeople to adopt conventions of coupling that seemed Christian and civilized (in contrast to circumstances under slavery, which were characterized by owners' disregard for the sexual purity of enslaved women and the patriarchal prerogatives of enslaved men). On the economic side, bureau agents frequently complained that without the bond of marriage, men were more likely to become involved with new women, leaving their former partners with small children and few resources. Thus they hoped formal marriage would establish proper relations of dependency, making women and children dependent on their husbands and fathers and in the process reducing the burden on the state.[65]

Considering the bureau's intense interest in marriage, it is particularly striking that when faced with freedpeople's actual choices and experiences it abandoned its marriage requirement in the barracks. Charles Howard informed a congressman in the summer of 1866 that bureau officials had realized that "few of those most needy" were able to "show evidence of lawful marriage." In addition, "They are reluctant to be married *de novo*, saying this makes their former children illegitimate, besides they cannot well meet the expense of a license."[66] Because state laws had never recognized slaves' marriages, the legal status of relationships between freedmen and freedwomen was ambiguous. Howard acknowledged that this situation, along with freedpeople's resistance to marrying "under the flag" and the cost of a marriage license, had rendered impractical the bureau's policy of only renting to people who could prove that they had been legally married and that their children were legitimate.

In the same letter, Howard cast freedpeople's desire that relationships formed in slavery be recognized as marriage as a right to which they were entitled. Referring to a bill, then pending before Congress, that would accept as marriage a variety of existing relationships among freedpeople, Howard concluded, "In general I may say *they feel that it is their right* to have a law removing the disabilities in this matter, arising from slavery and clearing the way for a complete reformation."[67] Here, Howard recognized that for freedpeople, legal equality in fact required not simply the end of racially discriminatory laws, but also positive legislation fitted to freedpeople's particular circumstances as former slaves. As the next chapters will discuss, radical Republicans often made such arguments, but resistance to them was fierce, as even Republican moderates tended to insist that any law that recognized the distinctive status or requirements of freedpeople, or of African Americans more generally, violated the principle of racial equality before the law.

In passing the District of Columbia marriage law that Howard advocated, Congress in fact acknowledged freedpeople's view that relationships they had formed in slavery should count as marriage. The District of Columbia marriage law bestowed all the "rights and privileges"—and expected all the "duties and obligations"—of "all colored persons in the District of Columbia" who before emancipation had "occup[ied] the relation to each other of husband and wife" and who were then living together "or in any way recognizing the relation as still existing." The District of Columbia law represented, at once, the government's hope of regularizing marital relations among freedpeople and freedpeople's demand for flexibility in institutionalizing relationships they had forged in slavery.[68]

Although Howard did not explicitly acknowledge it in his letter lobbying for the marriage statute, superintendents at the Freedmen's Bureau barracks had abandoned their original marriage policy well before the new law passed. Whereas in the fall of 1865 a barracks superintendent had been instructed to rent to "*worthy* people least able to pay the exorbitant rents demanded in town," that winter the superintendent for the newly opened barracks on East Capitol Street was instructed to rent to "such freedpeople as are least able to pay." And whereas in the fall of 1865 instructions had been to favor "poor, industrious men who have large families," in the winter of 1866 instructions made no mention of men or family structure.[69] In a report filed four months after the new marriage law passed, an inspector reported that rooms in all the barracks were rented to "such Freedmen as apply," and tabular monthly reports filed by barracks superintendents made little mention of the marital status of the renters, either before or after the law's passage. In those reports, superintendents filled in the name of each head of household, the number of people in the household, the household head's occupation, the amount of rent paid, and a few other details. One superintendent assiduously noted that each woman household head was a widow, implying that a marriage had existed and that the children were viewed as "legitimate." But other superintendents did not bother with such notes, suggesting that they felt no obligation to account for the familial relations of the renters.[70]

Still, Howard was correct in believing that the new marriage law could help resolve some of the problems that freedpeople's varied family situations posed to bureau agents hoping to encourage official marriages and male-headed households. In effect, the law made it easy for any woman and man to claim to be married, reinforcing the more flexible policy that bureau agents had already begun to implement. The new law also helped let the bureau off its own hook, since any adult applying for barracks housing could claim to be married and, therefore, all children could be considered legitimate. The new legislation may have translated into a smoother experience for freedpeople seeking housing in the barracks, particularly for women who came to the city with children but without a man.

This is not to say that the bureau gave up on its mission to instill in freed-people its own norms about sex and marriage. In a late 1866 report from East Capitol Street Barracks, John Roberts lamented that among the residents "there still exists an habitual looseness with reference to the marriage relation."[71] In the summer of 1867, bureau superintendent of marriages John Kimball vigor-ously publicized the new marriage law and hired a deputy to go door-to-door, investigating whether couples qualified for the retroactive marriage provided by Congress, marrying people who did not, and informing all that "this rela-tion" should continue until "death do us sever." To all whose coupling was deemed legal, the deputy "solemnly" distributed marriage certificates, which would "be important evidence hereafter."[72] To Kimball's frustration, however, some couples refused his efforts. He was particularly troubled by those who had begun living together since emancipation but declined to marry. To him, such couples were illegally cohabiting and their children were illegitimate. This state of affairs seemed to Kimball to require additional legislation by Congress and showed "a sad and alarming state of morals and crime."[73]

To secure what bureau officials considered appropriate familial relation-ships among freedpeople, bureau agents also sought to reunify parents and children separated by slavery or the war. Here, too, bureau agents ended up responding to freedpeople's plight by delineating new rights. Throughout the South, freedpeople placed urgent importance on reuniting with children and other family members, and they were willing to use any means available—including not only the bureau, but travel, word of mouth, and advertising in newspapers—to accomplish those ends. Their goals were many. Parents and

THEY FEEL IT IS THEIR RIGHT

other relations sought to regenerate ties of love and support and to ensure that children had opportunities to attend school. Moreover, children, particularly older ones, could make important economic contributions to free households, and some adults sought custody of children in order to secure their labor or even to bind them out as apprentices.[74]

Yet parents were often stymied by former slaveowners who insisted on holding freedchildren as apprentices. The problem was particularly acute in Maryland. When Maryland abolished slavery, through a new state constitution adopted on November 1, 1864, former slaveowners rushed to secure the labor of freedchildren, taking advantage of racially discriminatory state laws that allowed for the involuntary apprenticeship of free black children. They brought children into court and requested a judge to bind them as apprentices, often using flimsy pretexts about parents who could not take care of their children or who were not present that day. Although such procedures were contrary to the spirit of emancipation, they were technically legal in the state of Maryland until the 1866 Civil Rights Act made racially discriminatory statutes illegal. And illegal apprenticeship of black children continued even after the federal law passed. With bureau agents scarce in Maryland, freedpeople often traveled to Washington to file complaints.[75]

Freedmen's Bureau agents in Washington were inclined to help the scores of freedpeople who sought support for wresting their children away from apprenticeships to which they had not consented. Bureau officials saw slaveowners' patriarchal power over slaves' families as an anachronism of the slavery era, and they saw the reunification of freed families as part of the project of civilizational uplift. Indeed, by encouraging supposedly natural ties among blood relations, agents were seeking to remedy the damage of slavery and to help reform slaves into citizens whose gender conventions and familial relations approximated those that they, bureau agents, considered normative. By helping freedpeople create self-sustaining families composed of adult wage earners and dependents, bureau agents also hoped to ensure that children and infirm adults would not become dependent on the state. As in the case of promoting marriage, the Freedmen's Bureau's support for parents' claims served both economic and ideological ends.[76]

In family reunification, as in tenement housing, bureau agents offered a service that coincided with freedpeople's own goals. In both instances, however, the bureau offered help in exchange for pledges that recipients of aid would adhere to the values bureau agents believed important in transforming slaves into citizens. In a fairly typical case, freedwoman Eliza Low asked the bureau to help her claim her fourteen-year-old daughter, Harriet, who was being held by Low's former owner in Fredericksburg, Virginia. As part of her request, Eliza assured bureau agents that she and her husband were employed and could support their daughter. That statement, which echoed a sort of script many freedpeople used in similar situations, was intended as a guarantee that once Harriet arrived in Washington, she could depend on her parents for support and would not become a public burden. The bureau, in turn, furnished Eliza Low and others in her position with letters reminding recalcitrant whites that slavery was over and instructing military personnel stationed nearby to help parents get custody of their children.[77] To obtain federal assistance in recuperating her daughter, Eliza Low had to represent her own situation as conforming to bureau agents' ideas of family relations and economic independence. But the bureau's demand for conformity probably seemed a small price to pay, if it seemed a price at all, to get her daughter back.[78]

Meanwhile, in the process of helping freedpeople reclaim family members from slavery, bureau agents developed a language of parents' *rights* to their children. Since family relations were rarely translated into the liberal discourse of rights, a positive "right of the family" did not exist in formal law. Certainly freedpeople had no official right to families in Maryland in 1865, where racially discriminatory apprenticeships were entirely legal. Yet when Sophia Howard set out for Cedar Grove, Maryland, to wrest her daughter away from the white man who held her, she carried a form letter from the bureau explaining parents' prerogatives. "The wishes of the parent and child are both to be considered before those of any third party and all the *rights of the family* must be recognized and respected among these people the same as among the whites."[79] The federal agent had translated a freedwoman's claim to her daughter into a right that did not yet exist in any formal sense, just as Charles Howard had done when he argued for freedpeople's right to an accommodating marriage law. In both instances, bureau agents translated freedpeople's insistence on the integrity of their familial bonds into an idiom of positive rights.

Interactions between freedpeople and bureau agents were generative, not static. The volume of correspondence of Freedmen's Bureau agents—typically statements of policies, reports, and the like—may make it difficult to see how freedpeople's claims could push bureau agents to adjust their operations. Yet a close reading of the sources reveals that the relationship was a dynamic one. When bureau agents saw how difficult it was to eke out a living in the capital, the lengths to which former owners would go to keep children in bondage, and the challenges men and women faced in having their relationships recognized as legitimate, they sometimes altered their course. Freedpeople's demands challenged agents' tidy visions of civilizational uplift in the barracks, and freedpeople's insistence upon respect for their families and their circumstances yielded new and expansive claims about the range of rights to which all free people were entitled.

The Children to Be Taught in These Schools Are Our Children

One area of uplift work in which African Americans consistently and powerfully demanded a voice was schools. From the early nineteenth century, black educators in Washington had cultivated private schools for black children, often withstanding harassment and arson. During and immediately after the war, missionary schools served the capital's growing black population. But missionary societies gradually reduced their efforts, leaving the capital's nascent black public school system to preside over the education of freedchildren. Congress had given administrative authority over the black public schools to the Interior Department, and black Washingtonians had established a dynamic relationship with a series of interior secretaries. African American church and civic groups organized petitions for the appointment of particular candidates to the Board of Trustees of Colored Schools, often disagreeing among themselves about whom the interior secretary should select, and they also voiced concerns about the management of the schools. Building on a history of independent black education, which reached back many decades, black Washingtonians insisted that African American teachers should staff the schools and that black administrators should run them. Although black Washingtonians welcomed the black public schools as opportunities for advancement and as evidence that African Americans were nascent citizens entitled to education, they were also loath to part with the racial autonomy and self-help that the private schools had long represented.

During and immediately after the Civil War, public education in Washington remained something of a novelty. In the North during the 1830s and 1840s, reformers had begun to advocate taxpayer-funded "common schools" as part of a broader project of building a mass democracy. They connected access to common schools with the future of government, arguing that the poorest Americans must learn at least the rudiments of literacy and numeracy to prosper and to fulfill the responsibilities of citizenship. As in the domestic uplift efforts of the Freedmen's Bureau, there was often a tenor of ethnic and class condescension in school reformers' vision of the uplifting influences of public schools. The school reformers, themselves largely Protestants, self-consciously directed their reforms at immigrant children, particularly Catholics, and they viewed the schools as agents of assimilation into middle-class, Protestant values. Slaveholding states lagged behind free ones in establishing common schools. Indeed, abolitionists frequently cited the lack of public investment in education as yet another manifestation of slavery's depressing impact on the South.[80]

In keeping with regional patterns, Washington City's antebellum public schools for white students were meager. Congress had given the city governments of Washington and Georgetown power to tax residents to support public schools for white children, but school development always lagged. Public schools were stigmatized as "pauper schools," and, to the frustration of local educators, Congress never contributed financially. According to an 1867 report, the city's antebellum public and private schools combined never served more than one-quarter of white school-age children.[81]

The war and the ascent of Republicans in Congress and local life helped bring something of a renaissance to the white schools, but city fathers continued their adamant opposition to public schools for black children. On July 4, 1864, Washingtonians inaugurated the city's first modern public school building (for white students only) with great pomp and circumstance. James Patterson, a congressman from New Hampshire and a member of the House of Representatives' District of Columbia Committee, gave the keynote address. Voicing views typical of New England school reformers, Patterson argued that public schools were agents of peace and upward mobility in a diverse nation. Free schools were "necessary in view of the mingling of races, ideas, and prejudices in our origin and growth," he claimed. They allowed "heterogeneous and discordant elements" to be "fused into one, and the whole population pervaded and actuated by an intense spirit of nationality."[82] Such sentiments did not apply to African Americans, however. Indeed, although the wartime mayor, Richard Wallach, had led the effort to expand white public education, he staunchly opposed the same opportunities for black children. In 1864, Congress overturned its initial requirement that only taxes paid by African Americans would be used toward African Americans' schools. Now, school tax money would be allocated to the white and "colored" school systems according to the proportion of white and black school-age children in the capital. Many local whites saw the new policy as an affront to white taxpayers, who paid more per capita in taxes than black residents did. Wallach, for his part, simply refused to turn over the required funds to the Trustees of Colored Schools. Local black leaders protested, the Trustees of Colored Schools filed a lawsuit, and Congress passed new legislation. Still, Wallach insisted on grossly underestimating the number of black children who lived in Washington.[83]

The situation began to change in 1867, when the District of Columbia Supreme Court demanded that the city government pay the colored schools the tax funds it owed and the interest accrued during the period of obfuscation. Congress also commissioned a special census to determine how many black and white children lived in the capital, in part to combat Wallach's insistence on making recourse to the 1860 census, which showed African Americans at about 20 percent of the population. According to the new census, African American children now made up 32 percent of the District's school-age children (ages six to eighteen).[84] The city began to remit the funds, and the trustees were finally able to purchase property on which to erect schoolhouses, hire additional teachers, and open new schools.[85]

The new schools did not start from scratch, however. Rather, the black public school system stood on the foundation created by black educators in the capital's antebellum private schools. Unlike in Virginia and many other parts of the South, no antebellum laws had forbade formal education for African Americans in the capital. Whites often expressed hostility to schools for black children and attacked them when tensions over slavery ran high. Yet black educators in Washington had persisted in their efforts, forming tuition-based primary schools and more advanced "institutes" and seminaries. On the eve of the war, it was estimated, between 1,000 and 1,400 children attended the capital's private schools for black students.[86]

How antebellum schools and educators became the foundation of the postwar public schools is clear in the case of Charlotte Carroll's school. Charlotte was born a slave in Alexandria, Virginia, but she attended private school as a child. She was later manumitted in Washington, and she began a successful teaching career after her first husband died. In 1860, she married David Carroll, an elder in the prestigious 15th Street Presbyterian Church. The couple moved to the evacuated farmhouse of one of the capital's leading Confederates, Cornelius T. Boyle, located in the southeast section of Washington County. They began holding classes and religious services for African Americans in the neighborhood. Whites in the area protested, but the Carrolls received support from local black clergymen and Union troops stationed nearby. At length they established a church and a school on the Boyle property. As fugitives from slavery surged into the capital, Charlotte Carroll's school accommodated some one hundred students. Carroll and her daughter taught in the school until 1865, when David Carroll died and the women moved back to the city.[87]

Yet the school continued under public auspices. The superintendent of the black public schools appointed a white northern teacher, who was paid by a northern relief association. The Trustees of Colored Schools then purchased a lot from a local black property owner, perhaps the same man who had originally allowed the school to operate there, and they paid for the construction of a school building.[88] The incorporation of Charlotte Carroll's school into the nascent black public school system gave the school a more permanent footing, but it also required local residents to relinquish a measure of control over both the disposition of the land and the choice of teacher.

Black educators and parents were well aware of the trade-offs and compromises attendant to the expansion of the public school system. Indeed, as the black public schools gradually overtook both missionary schools and the long-standing private schools, black Washingtonians raised questions about who would control the schools, who would be hired to teach in them, and how transparent their administration would be. At the outset, the interior secretary named white antislavery activists such as Sayles Bowen and his friend Daniel Breed to the three-member Board of Trustees of Colored Schools, which was charged with hiring teachers and otherwise distributing funds. Soon, black religious and secular leaders demanded a say in the interior secretary's decisions about whom to appoint. In an early controversy over the trustees in the spring of 1866, a group of "colored citizens" petitioned Interior Secretary James Harlan for the resignation of trustees Breed and Charles King. "Dr. Daniel Breed . . . has not taken the interest in our schools as he ought to have done, and has rendered himself by expressions and otherwise obnoxious to our people," they claimed. King "is an entire stranger to us, nor has he sought to make himself acquainted, so far as we are informed, with our people." Harlan duly obtained resignations from the two men and within months appointed two others recommended by the petitioners.[89]

African Americans soon challenged the Interior Department's practice of favoring white men as appointees to the three-man school board. In 1867, the year black men were enfranchised, the interior secretary appointed the first black man, businessman Alfred Jones, to the board. The next year, a group of local African American luminaries—including two Baptist pastors and several leaders in business, education, and politics—petitioned Congress to expand the role of African Americans in school administration. They explained that as the public schools "must eventually put out of existence our private schools," they wanted to "be thoroughly acquainted with the management and work-ings of those schools, and those who are to be entrusted with the education of our children." Therefore, they requested "a colored committee, or board of supervisors to be composed of intelligent resident citizens of Washington, and tax payers to act in concert with the commission already appointed." The petitioners clarified their view that a special sense of mutual obligation bound African Americans together and separated them from whites. "The children to be taught in these schools are our children," they explained, "and we must nat-urally feel a deeper interest in their proper management and ultimate success than others possibly can, who have no personal identity with them, however well they may be disposed."[90] The sense of collectivity in the letter was strik-ing. Without diminishing the efforts of white educators, the petitioners argued that their "personal identity" with the students would ensure that they would take good care of the schools. Congress did not comply with the request for a separate "colored committee." However, from 1868 until the schools were placed under control of the municipal government in 1873, the board consis-tently comprised two black men and one white.[91]

African American petitioners might have generally shared the view that black oversight was best for the black schools, but they frequently disagreed about who, in particular, should be chosen for the school board. Petitions in the files of the Interior Department reflect divisions among African Americans about the appropriate qualifications for school board members, as well as a measure of what appears to be personal factionalism. One nominee might be too much of an outsider; another might not have enough formal education. Almost all the petitioners were men, but in 1870 a group of women teach-ers joined the discussion by submitting a petition for their favored candidate. Although their petition was made a "laughing-stock" by some male Interior Department employees, the teachers wanted the secretary of interior to know that teachers "are brought into immediate and intimate business relations with [the] trustees," and that they could only "perform our duties with ease and sat-isfaction" if board members were cooperative and professional.[92] The consid-erable wrangling over appointments to the board reflected real differences of opinion and political factions among black Washingtonians. But it also demon-strated the importance of the schools in black public life and black Washingto-nians' sense of entitlement to a voice in the schools' administration. Complete autonomy was impossible, given that the secretary of interior appointed the members of the board. Yet a succession of interior secretaries seems to have attempted to make sense of the divergent requests, to appoint men who had broad support, and to remove those whom locals distrusted.

Consistent with their hope for relative autonomy, African American educators and administrators generally sought black teachers for the black public schools. Many thought black teachers would be better role models and would care more for the students. As Harriet Jacobs wrote from Freedman's Village in 1864, "I do not object to white teachers but I think it has a good effect upon these people to convince them their own race can do something for their elevation. It inspires them with confidence to help each other." William J. Wilson, a newly arrived teacher from Brooklyn, also preferred black teachers. "As long as the dominant class are to fill among us the first places," he wrote, "& we to be regarded as minors and recipients of favors we shall be but the same helpless & dependent people, slaves."[93]

Ensuring that schools for black children hired black teachers was also important for the teachers themselves. Teaching was one of the few professional occupations open to African Americans, particularly women, and black educators believed it was important to protect and expand those opportunities. As the missionary schools had grown under the auspices of the Freedmen's Bureau, black teachers had experienced discrimination by teachers and administrators alike. Emma V. Brown, an African American teacher and a native of Georgetown, abhorred the attitudes of newly arrived white teachers and of John Kimball, the Freedmen's Bureau's local superintendent of education. Brown, who had attended a private school in Washington and Oberlin College, believed both Kimball and the missionary associations preferred white teachers to black ones.[94] She derisively referred to the monthly meetings for teachers in the black schools as "N.T." meetings—for "Negro Teacher," or still more insultingly, "Nigger Teacher." She was especially dismayed when Kimball asked a group of black and white teachers to state whether they thought black children could "learn as well as white children." The white teachers offered responses to the question, while the black teachers "as though they had known of this ridiculous performance beforehand . . . declined taking any part in the debate." By the end of the meeting, she wrote facetiously to a friend, "I wished I had remained in school teaching my children to be as honest as white folks."[95]

The Trustees of Colored Schools in the capital sought to give preference to black teachers in cases where applicants otherwise seemed equal. They phrased the policy in terms of both equality and difference, stating, "While we think it right to give preference in our schools to colored teachers, *their qualifications being equal*, yet we deem it a violation of our official oath to employ inferior teachers when superior ones can be had for the same money." Not surprisingly, the trustees found many highly qualified black teachers, from the District and from elsewhere. In 1869, the superintendent of the black schools reported that of 63 teachers working for the public schools, 40 were black and 23 were white—a stark contrast to a report from two years earlier that the District's teaching corps comprised 109 white teachers and 26 black ones.[96] Most schoolteachers were women, some of whom were new arrivals in Washington and some—such as Emma Brown and Charlotte Carroll—were natives of the region and graduates of the antebellum private schools for black children.

The capital's constellation of strong public schools, normal schools, and Howard University increasingly made Washington a hub for the black elite and a center for the training of teachers. A high school was inaugurated as early as 1864, and in 1870 a preparatory high school became part of the public school system. Black educators were justly proud of that school, since preparatory high schools for African Americans were virtually unheard of in the South, where urban public school districts under white control showed little concern for advanced education for black students.[97] Meanwhile, Congress chartered Howard University in March 1867 as a private institution of higher education, designed for "both sexes and all colors." Organizers, most of them northern Congregationalists, immediately established a preparatory school and a normal school for teacher education. By 1869, the university had installed its namesake, O. O. Howard, as president and had opened a medical school and a classics course. The law school opened soon after.[98] The university gradually established a strong presence on the land its trustees had purchased just north of Boundary Street (now Florida Avenue) and east of Seventh Avenue, an area already home to settlements of freedpeople and near the bureau-run Freedman's Hospital. In keeping with their vision of the nation's capital as a hub of all things progressive in freedpeople's education, its founders hoped Howard University would, as John Alvord put it, "stand at the head of the entire system of freedmen's schools."[99]

Notwithstanding all the positive aspects of the capital's educational institutions for black students, however, the black public schools were unable to serve the majority of eligible children. By the end of 1868, only a few missionary-run schools remained, leaving behind an embryonic public school system that could accommodate far fewer students than the missionary schools had in their heyday.[100] At the height of the missionary schools, more than 6,300 black children attended school. By 1870, only half that number attended, and the

Trustees of Colored Schools reported that they were serving only one-third of the eligible population.[101] Meanwhile, the trustees focused intensively on providing schools for small children, claiming that resources did not permit them to maintain night schools. This made it impossible for laborers—many of them adolescents—to continue the education many had begun in missionary schools. Alvord lamented in 1869 that many people, "especially young men employed during the day, but able to study evenings, have complained bitterly of this neglect."[102] The quality of education provided by the District's black public schools and the possibilities for advancing to high school and beyond made the capital's schools for black children and youth a source of great pride to black Washingtonians. Yet, even as the schools became renowned across the nation, they remained plagued by overcrowding and underfunding far into the future.

As African Americans' opportunities for claiming new forms of equality advanced in the late 1860s, some black Washingtonians, along with white allies, demanded an end to the exclusion of black children from the municipal public schools. The question of whether to press for school integration—or, more precisely, for African American children's access to the "white" schools—was a complex one. Demanding access to the white schools might suggest a diminished commitment to the black schools, themselves prized community institutions. Integrated schools might jeopardize the jobs of black teachers and administrators, whose authority to supervise white children would be questioned. Moreover, it was unclear how much African Americans would benefit from abandoning their relationship to the interior secretaries who oversaw the black schools, in favor of oversight by a municipal government historically unsympathetic to black education. Indeed, some believed that the black schools, operating under federal auspices, offered children a better education than the struggling white schools.

Yet the schools were also a logical place to advance the struggle for an expansive interpretation of racial equality before the law. That fight had officially begun in antebellum Boston, where public school regulations had provided that children could not be excluded from neighborhood common schools without legitimate reason. In practice, black children were excluded from the neighborhood schools, while the Boston school board operated one separate school, ostensibly to accommodate them. In the 1848–49 case of *Roberts v. City of Boston*, black parents, a black lawyer named Robert Morris, and white lawyer (and future senator) Charles Sumner had argued that race was an invalid criterion for denying black children admission to neighborhood schools. They lost the case when the Massachusetts Supreme Court ruled that as long as black children were provided with a public school their race-based exclusion from white schools was legitimate. The case was a landmark, both because Sumner and the black parents made an expansive argument against racial discrimination in public schools and because of the court's claim that racial segregation of schools did not violate the state's avowed principle that all persons were "equal before the law."[103] The argument was destined to be rehashed in post–Civil War Washington, where black activists, some of whom had been involved in antebellum school integration struggles in the North, brought forward similar arguments. Advocates of school integration in the capital found limited but vocal support in Congress, particularly from Senator Sumner. Indeed, as Chapter 4 will discuss, from mid-1868 until the consolidation of local governance under conservative rule in the mid-1870s, the question of integrated schooling in the capital engaged African American voters, church organizations, local politicians, and Congress itself.

Bureau officials and missionaries began the work of schooling, housing, and visiting freedpeople, imagining their charges as victims of a barbaric institution who needed instruction and civilization. What they found, however, was much more complex. They encountered people who had their own ideas about what they wanted: locals who believed schools must answer to the community, ragpickers who refused to take their business out of the barracks, former slaves who would not make their marital relations conform to reformers' ideals. Freedpeople and the capital's black leaders demanded recognition of their experiences and their priorities. All these claims formed part of a broadening conversation about the meanings of racial equality and the measures required to erase the legacies of slavery. New institutions—including the Freedmen's Bureau and the nascent black public schools—provided platforms from which black Washingtonians launched claims that policy makers might never have forecast. And although those institutions were certainly not infinitely malleable, administrators did find their way toward responding to African Americans' demands for recognition of the particular challenges they faced and the priorities they valued.

It is not quite adequate, I have argued, to characterize the Freedmen's Bureau and its allies as agents of race-blind free labor ideology, or of social control, or of a relatively just legal order of "equal rights." Besides offering immediate, material relief to those most in need, bureau agents and their allies sought to lift freedpeople out of the misery imposed by slavery and into the civic body, to prepare them for citizenship. The rubric of civilizational improvement and progress best captures their reformist outlook. Without mobilizing explicitly racial ideologies of biological destiny (though they sometimes did that, too), bureau agents, freedmen's aid workers, teachers, and administrators were able to argue that freedpeople were entitled to an array of basic rights and that in order to embrace those rights freedpeople must be "untaught" what they had learned in slavery about morals, manners, housekeeping, and child rearing. The connection was particularly clear in bureau education superintendent Alvord's comment that the "right to a higher status" would follow from freedpeople's "quick transition to faithful industry, to economy, thrift, self-support, and to almost invariable good behavior."[104] The myriad tutelary projects of the bureau and its allies—home visits, barracks housing, industrial schools, and common schools themselves—all furthered the project of better outfitting freedpeople for rights and equal citizenship.

The demand that freedpeople show themselves to be worthy of new rights offered up ambiguous opportunities for freedpeople and other black activists. Many African Americans publicly engaged with the visions of respectability propounded by white and black educators. They deliberately cultivated a public image of themselves as worthy of respect and standing in the local community. Indeed, they used conventions of respectability to claim rights never heretofore granted to black people or, in some cases, never explicitly granted to anyone. But they also drew on natural rights traditions to insist, both explicitly and implicitly, that it did not matter whether one was well clothed, or polite, or a taxpayer, when claiming a part in public life. In mass demonstrations and individual actions, African Americans claimed new privileges and demanded new rights, always cognizant of the different meanings of different kinds of space in the city.

3

Someone Must Lead the Way

CREATING AND CLAIMING CIVIL RIGHTS

At two o'clock in the afternoon on a late February day in 1868, Kate Brown, an employee in the Senate, left work in the U.S. Capitol and boarded a train for Alexandria, Virginia. She planned to visit a relative and return to work about an hour later. Brown chose a seat in the car reserved for white "ladies" and their white male traveling companions. But Brown, who was by most contemporary descriptions "mulatto," had no illusions about whom the "ladies' car" was meant for. As she later put it, she had boarded "what they call the white people's car."[1] The alternative was the car designated for African Americans and white men not in the company of ladies. Often known as the smoking car, that car was a more promiscuous space in which people mingled in an environment with no pretensions of refinement or protectiveness. Tobacco chewing and smoking, activities from which proper ladies were supposed to be sheltered, were permitted in this general car. Brown did not care to mingle with the unruly public in the smoking car, and she believed she was entitled to ride in the ladies' car if she chose. A man standing on the Washington platform advised her to change cars, but Brown remained in her seat and had no further trouble.[2]

Brown also had every intention of returning to Washington in the ladies' car. But when she boarded the train at the Alexandria depot a short time later, a special policeman (likely a security guard hired by the railroad) indicated that she must leave the ladies' car. She refused. As she later testified: "I told him I came down in that car, and in that car I intended to return; that I had my ticket, a return ticket, which I had bought in Washington, and I was going back in the same car; he said I could not go; I asked him why, as I had paid my fare and had come down in the same car; he said that car was for ladies; I told him then that was the very car I wanted to go in."[3] Not interested in debating, the policeman grabbed Brown and tried to pull her from the car. She held fast to the inside of the door and braced her foot against the seat. According to Brown, when the policeman demanded, "Ain't you coming out of this car?" she replied, "Never; I bought my ticket to go to Washington in this car, and I am going in it; before I leave this car I will suffer death." When the policeman threatened to beat her, she told him he could go ahead: "I had made up my mind not to leave the car, unless they brought me off dead," she averred.[4] The policeman pounded Brown's knuckles, twisted her arms, and grabbed her collar. He was soon joined by a man who called himself a "sheriff," who held her by the neck and, with the policeman's help, succeeded in dragging her out of the car and onto the platform. Brown estimated that the struggle on the Alexandria platform had lasted about eleven minutes, and she believed several white men had watched the entire incident. She later testified: "I declare they could not have treated a dog worse than they tried to treat me. It was nothing but 'damned nigger,' and cursing and swearing all the time."[5]

The assault on Kate Brown at the Alexandria railroad depot became something of a local cause célèbre. The radical Republican *Daily Chronicle* called the incident "a dastardly outrage" and a "disgrace to this age of civilization." The newspaper contrasted Brown's impeccable comportment with the barbarism of the "several representatives of the 'chivalry' of the South" who had attacked her. Julia Wilbur, a white abolitionist from New York, visited Brown during her recovery and was "much shocked to see her condition." She felt only "scorn & contempt" for Brown's attackers, "wretches . . . so infinitely beneath [Brown] in every respect."[6] Radical Republicans in the Senate, who knew Brown as an employee, brought the incident to the attention of the entire Senate and argued that it demonstrated the inadequacy of existing civil rights laws. The Senate committee on the District of Columbia investigated the matter and took Brown's own testimony, as well as statements from elite black Washingtonians who knew her, including physician Alexander Augusta and caterer George T. Downing. Brown also filed suit against the railroad company for damages, a move one unsympathetic federal official considered "a purposely got up case for the sake of a judicial row between the colors."[7]

Kate Brown's refusal to leave the ladies' car and the steps she and others took in search of redress are particularly dramatic examples of a broader culture of protest that developed in the national capital during the 1860s.[8] During the war and immediately afterward, black Washingtonians demanded access to a remarkable range of arenas previously understood as the domain of white people only. Black men and women made upstart claims—in advance of any law or other policy—at the U.S. Capitol, on the grounds of the Executive

Mansion, and on the city's streetcars. These were not meek or quiet gestures. Rather, black Washingtonians demanded that white locals and federal officials consider their claims and respond to them. Black leaders solicited government officials' support for an Emancipation Day parade in 1866 and then routed the parade past the Executive Mansion and the Capitol. And black veterans who sought to form peacetime militias insisted on recognition of their legitimacy from federal and local officials.

Black Washingtonians made those demands in a legal climate that was, itself, in flux. Historians have often seen postemancipation upheavals in southern cities as reflections of an old order turned upside down or of a radically unsettled "public sphere" that was entirely separate from the world of law and government. But quotidian unrest during Reconstruction also revealed an on-the-ground struggle to define a new regime of legal equality.[9] Immediately after the Civil War, no one knew what kinds of laws and customs would replace the vanquished world of slavery and the black codes. Even among northerners, there was widespread disagreement about the meaning of civil rights and the domain of equality before the law. Most Republicans agreed that there should be no racial restrictions on a set of basic "civil" rights, including an individual's right to enter into contracts, purchase property, and move from one place to another, nor should there be racial discrimination in legal proceedings. That consensus vision of racial equality was manifest in Congress's 1862 eradication of the District's black codes. Yet those advances nonetheless left many urgent questions unanswered. As black Washingtonians quickly surmised, the abolition of the black codes had no bearing on a range of arenas in which racial equality was up for debate, including voting rights, streetcars and other public accommodations, and public schools. Nor did the formal codification of "equality before the law" guarantee that police would put that principle into practice.

Disparate legal regimes, customs, and values governed the array of public and quasi-public places to which African Americans demanded equal access in postwar Washington. The Capitol and the Executive Mansion, for example, were one kind of public space, since they were the domain of the federal government. Streetcars, owned by private companies but chartered by Congress, were quite another. Neither public nor private, streetcars, inns, and restaurants were considered "public accommodations" under the common law. Their particular legal status—and the customs that went along with it—gave distinct qualities to African Americans' struggle for access to them. Finally, the city's streets had different qualities altogether. Supervised by the Metropolitan Police, whose charge was to enforce the law and keep the peace, the streets were often unruly places where the violence inherent in slavery and war burst forth unabated. Yet the climate on the streets varied depending on who lived and worked there and how they were policed.

If different arenas had distinct legal statuses and customary expectations, they also shared some common characteristics. In most public places (excluding "low" places such as houses of prostitution or venues devoted to drinking or gambling), respectable comportment was considered the basis for claims to rights. Basic manners were important not only in high society or among middle-class social groups but also in public and quasi-public places, where people's claims to access were considered more legitimate if they could demonstrate that they were clean, self-controlled, and well-mannered. People with middle-class sensibilities may have enforced these norms, but the norms themselves were derived from centuries-old common law conventions that required inoffensive behaviors from would-be members of the traveling "public."[10] As black Washingtonians claimed access to spaces from which they had previously been excluded, they attempted to fit themselves into these widely recognized ideals of public comportment. Indeed, widespread ideas about African Americans' lack of civilization or racial inferiority placed a special burden on them to demonstrate that they were worthy of inclusion in the public.

African Americans in cities throughout the South, like black Washingtonians, demanded new rights and inclusion in the civic body. Yet the situation in the capital was unique because of the close ties between the local community and the federal government. The District of Columbia remained, as it had been during the war, a site for Republican legislative experimentation. When it came to the capital, legislators could put aside constitutional concerns about the limits of federal power and debate the relationship between equality and the law on its own terms. Thus, the congressional debate about African Americans' access to the city's streetcars involved enduring questions about the extent of basic civil rights and the role of legislation in protecting such rights. At the same time, newly arrived freedpeople and black northerners, as well as long-standing residents, in myriad realms and using divergent tactics, pressed the government to define civil equality as broadly as possible. The combination of black activism and Republican experimentation placed the capital at the vanguard of the Reconstruction experiment with racial equality.

Black Washingtonians recognized the Capitol and the Executive Mansion as gateways to full citizenship. Although transparency of government and citizen participation were often considered hallmarks of republican government, these Washington institutions had historically been open to a "public" composed of white people only. At the same time, although both were federal government institutions, they had particular significance to local people. Washingtonians did not have to travel from out of town to attend Congress or pay a call on the president. Until now, however, only white residents had exercised those privileges. With the destruction of slavery, African Americans, long proscribed from those places, made clear that they would demand access to them and, by implication, recognition of their status as citizens of the nation.

African Americans viewed access to the Capitol and to Congress as a particularly important measure of their equal civil status, since Congress was the branch of government most identified with "the people." As James McCune Smith had remarked when Henry Highland Garnet spoke in the House of Representatives in February 1865, the exclusion of "the man of color" from the Capitol had kept "the high places where his chains were forged . . . hidden behind the veil." During the war, black men and women began to lift that veil by attending congressional debates. At the outset, the climate was hostile. According to one account, in 1861, "the negro who then had dared to show himself at the door of one of the galleries would have been regarded as crazy" and hustled out.[11] But people kept coming. In the spring of 1862, minister Henry McNeal Turner attended debates about the confiscation of Confederates' property (debates that pertained directly to slavery as well as other property relations). In the fall of 1863, Henry Johnson, a minister from Ithaca, New York, toured the Capitol building and then observed Congress in session. That spring, when the Senate voted to pass the Thirteenth Amendment, which abolished slavery, numerous African Americans were in attendance, including Frederick Douglass's son, Charles, who wrote his father, "I wish that you could have been here. . . . Such rejoicing I never before witnessed." Indeed, by the end of that session, it was not unusual for African Americans to attend congressional debates, particularly in the Senate. When the second session of the Thirty-eighth Congress convened in December 1864, it was the first time African Americans were a visible presence on an opening day. "This revolution . . . will not go backward," wrote one approving observer. "Hereafter color will not be a qualification for admission to all parts of the Capitol."[12]

FIGURE 3.1. "Scene at the Pennsylvania Avenue Entrance to the Capitol Grounds at Washington on the Daily Adjournment of Congress." White women feature prominently in this sketch of the busy atmosphere in front of the Capitol building. *Harper's Weekly*, April 28, 1866, 268. Courtesy *HarpWeek*.

What congressmen or employees of the Capitol did to change the policy is not as clear as the fact that their policy did shift. The subject of whom to admit to the galleries was not a question of legislation but rather one of discretion by officials of each house of Congress. The two houses of Congress do not seem to have kept records on the matter, but some of the changes are discernable from press reports, especially in the case of the Senate. During Lincoln's first administration, Vice President Hannibal Hamlin was responsible for instructing Senate Sergeant at Arms George T. Brown about whom to admit and where they might be seated. According to one account, when the Senate resumed in December 1862 Brown told subordinates to admit black people to Senate galleries "whenever they applied." The same 1864 account related that House Speaker Galusha Grow had informally admitted African Americans to the galleries in the first years of the Civil War, but that definite orders were given only when Schuyler Colfax became Speaker, in December 1863.[13]

By the end of the war, a combination of black activism and Republican control of Congress had opened the galleries of both houses to African Americans. Small groups of African American spectators yielded to a tide of popular interest, manifested by the crowd at Henry Highland Garnet's sermon in the House of Representatives in February 1865. When the matter of voting rights for black men in the District of Columbia came before the House in January 1866, African American women and men turned out in force. The day the bill passed, the scene was remarkable: "The gallery was full of the disfranchised class," wrote Frances Gage, a white abolitionist, "fully one thousand dark faces looking down upon those makers of law, that have so often by their acts declared that black men 'have no rights which white men are bound to respect.'" At the end of a long day and multiple votes, the bill passed, and "the colored people rose *en masse*, and with one wild shout made that spacious gallery echo and re-echo their joy." Congressmen too rose to their feet, and the chamber was filled with the shouts of "black and white, women and men." A racist diarist named William Owner interpreted the scene quite differently. The galleries were "crowded with the niggers and at the announcement of the vote the niggers stamped and shouted and the white niggers on the floor joined in chorus." He concluded, "A more humiliating scene was never witnessed."[14]

African Americans' attendance in Congress raised questions about gender and respectability that reverberated in all discussions of race, rights, and space in Reconstruction Washington. When the Senate built a new spectators' gallery in 1859, it had created a separate "ladies'" section where proper women could be sheltered from the masculine culture of politics that surrounded them. That masculine climate was clear to white abolitionist Julia Wilbur, who on attending Congress was disgusted to find "public *snuff boxes*" in the Senate chamber for senators' use.[15] The establishment of separate ladies' accommodations in the Capitol mirrored a common practice, developed in the antebellum period on railroads and ferries, of providing ladies' accommodations in which proper women and the men who accompanied them could ride, cordoned off from the masses of ticket holders. Once segregation by sex had been established and ratified under the common law, it was not a stretch to argue for the legitimacy of racial segregation.[16] The two issues were not merely parallel; they were intertwined. It was one thing for African American men and women to seek admission to the areas of train cars where the masses of men rode without particular comfort or respectability, but it was quite another for black women to

FIGURES 3.2 a, b. These illustrations, from the same issue of *Harper's Weekly*, depict African American men participating in two very different kinds of political activity at the Capitol. In a scene captioned "Outside of the Galleries of the House of Representatives during the Passage of the Civil Rights Bill," black men in modest dress are shown celebrating with Union veterans and black children. In another scene, captioned "The Lobby of the House of Representatives at Washington during the Passage of the Civil Rights Bill," a well-dressed black man is shown, center right, "lobbying" a congressman. As Reconstruction dawned, black men and women of various classes and social positions demanded a place in public life at the Capitol. *Harper's Weekly*, April 28, 1866, 264–65, 269. Courtesy Library of Congress and *HarpWeek*.

seek admission to ladies' cars or, especially, for black men to seek to ride in ladies' cars as women's companions. The relationship between sex segregation and race segregation would be critical to the debate over streetcar ridership in Washington, and it was also important to how people understood the beginning of African Americans' attendance in Congress.

White observers noticed not just the presence of black people in Congress, but also where they sat. In 1862, Kentucky senator Garrett Davis commented on "several negroes thronging the open door listening to the debate" on emancipation in the District, suggesting that, early on, black visitors to the Capitol did not feel comfortable actually entering and being seated. Taking stock of the rapid changes at hand, Davis predicted that in "a few months they will be crowding white ladies out of these galleries."[17] The concern that African Americans would soon try to sit in the Senate ladies' gallery was manifold. People objected not just to their assertion of a right to membership in the public, but also to the idea that black women would make pretenses of being "ladies"—that is, of having the pure, proper status typically reserved only for middle-class and upper-class white women.[18] They also feared that if black women sat in the ladies' galleries their black male companions might also wish to sit there, placing them in overly close proximity to the white "ladies" for whom the gallery had been designed.

African Americans of course understood these white preoccupations and knew that attempting to sit in the Senate ladies' gallery was a more dramatic incursion than seeking access to the general seating area. Minister Henry Johnson alluded to such race/sex preoccupations when he expressed his surprise and satisfaction that, on meeting Secretary of State William H. Seward at a reception, Seward "took me by the hand and introduced me to his daughter and the ladies present." "These privileges," he informed readers of the *Anglo-African*, "were granted me without molestation or insult."[19] White conservatives would have perverted such a gesture into evidence that Johnson was interested in sexual liaisons with the women of Seward's family, but Johnson himself saw the interaction as a political ritual that proved it was possible for a black man to be received in the company of the nation's most elite politicians.

An 1868 article in *Frank Leslie's Illustrated Newspaper* asserted that black women showed little interest in attending the Senate, but other evidence indicates that black women attended both houses of Congress and did take seats in the almost sanctified space of the Senate ladies' gallery. Journalist Lois Bryan Adams noticed three black women and three black men watching the Senate pass the Thirteenth Amendment in the spring of 1864. In December 1865, William Owner complained that "nigger prostitutes filled up the entire front seat of the 'Ladies' gallery" and imagined that "bachelor" senator Charles Sumner enjoyed "throwing 'Sheeps eyes' at his favorites."[20] Owner, who made a habit of attending Congress, was certainly clear that he had seen black women at the front of the Senate ladies' gallery, though his conviction that they were prostitutes undoubtedly had less to do with reality than with his own feverish imagination. It seems that black women's attendance in the Senate ladies' gallery was not commonplace, however. Even in 1869, white abolitionist Julia Wilbur described helping a black woman "find her way into the gallery," presumably the ladies' gallery. "I had her occupy a front seat by my side," Wilbur wrote in her diary, suggesting that it was still a statement for a black woman to sit in such a place.[21]

Some white observers were bothered by far more than the presence of African Americans in the Senate ladies' gallery. Indeed, many white contemporaries believed it was inappropriate for African Americans to take an interest in politics, holding that they were not yet ready to assume such privileges and should leave matters of legislation to those who were more qualified. One senator suggested that black men turned out for political debates to avoid work. He criticized the "young, hale, stout negro men" who seemed to be there "day after day, week after week, and month after month," "when there are hundreds and thousands of poor young white men in this country who cannot afford to take one single day to listen to your debates."[22] In 1868, *Frank Leslie's Illustrated Newspaper* published a picture showing black men in the Senate's "gentlemen's gallery" looking disheveled and inattentive. Text accompanying the image emphasized the political illiteracy of such observers, stating that they were there because they considered it a "duty" and a "privilege," but that they understood little and soon fell asleep, "regardless of appearances or the possible consequences."[23] Whether or not black spectators ever dozed off during the proceedings, the account used sleeping and other breaches of respectability to support the widespread assumption that black men were not capable of making the political judgments required of citizens.[24]

The pressure on African American upstart claimants to conform to expectations of proper comportment was intense. Any misstep could undermine their insistence that they were worthy of the new privileges and rights they demanded. The virulence of the opposition, and its targeting of varieties of improper behavior—the idea that black women were "prostitutes" or that black men fell asleep in the galleries—reflects the intensity of that pressure. Those who defended African Americans' claims also reflected that climate. For

FIGURE 3.3. "The Gentlemen's Gallery in the Senate Chamber, Washington, D.C." The senator holding his glasses is Charles Sumner. *Frank Leslie's Illustrated Newspaper*, February 1, 1868, 312. Courtesy Library of Congress.

instance, white journalist Lois Bryan Adams was always careful to note the propriety and good behavior African Americans displayed when they asserted new prerogatives in public. In her rendering, black visitors to the Capitol sat "quietly," were "handsomely and neatly dressed," and "the best behaved people in the gallery."[25] Such descriptions were commonplace among those who touted the readiness of black people (or at least certain black people) for citizenship.

The African Americans who attended congressional debates added a layer to the already complex dynamics of race and power within the Capitol. Slaves had performed much of the construction work on the building itself, and free and enslaved black people had always worked there as common laborers, laundresses, watchmen, and handymen. The best-paid and most prestigious work, that of messengers and caterers, for example, involved working with the (white) public or with congressmen directly. Among the prestigious service positions at the Capitol was that of attendant to the ladies' retiring room outside the Senate ladies' gallery. Since the position involved interacting with the proper white "ladies" who visited the Senate, the black woman hired for the position would have needed to display considerable decorum herself, to have full knowledge of social conventions among elite white people, and also to understand the racialized conventions of service to that class.

Kate Brown began working as the ladies' retiring room attendant at the end of 1861. Earlier that year, she had been hired as a laundress for the Senate, a job that entailed washing curtains, towels, and other linens at her home. She was quickly promoted to supervisor of the ladies' retiring room, where she likely distributed towels and otherwise helped enhance the comfort of white women visitors to the Senate. The sources that document Brown's employment in the Senate tell her job titles, the dates of her employment, and her salary, but they do not offer details about what it was like to be a black woman working in the Senate during this tumultuous period. We do know that Brown worked in the Senate during the years that black men and women began to attend sessions of Congress; that she was acquainted with black Washingtonians like Downing and Augusta, who were prominent professionals and advocates for racial equality; and that her immediate boss was Senate sergeant at arms George T. Brown, who was a Lincoln ally from Illinois.[26] Perhaps Kate Brown and other black Senate employees pushed George T. Brown to admit African Americans to the Senate galleries. Perhaps Brown's experiences serving white ladies in the Senate helped persuade her that she, too, could demand the privileges of ladyhood. We cannot know for certain, but the fragmentary evidence is surely suggestive.[27]

At the train depot in Alexandria, Brown risked her physical safety to demand treatment as a lady. The personal consequences were enormous, for she was seriously injured by the two men who forced her from the train. Her left shoulder and elbow were sprained, and for weeks after the incident she coughed up blood as a result of internal injuries.[28] Too ill to get out of bed, Brown received the Senate investigating committee in her home. More than four months after the assault, one of her acquaintances reported, "She is some better, but will never get well." Fortunately for her, the Senate sergeant at arms continued to employ her; she remained on the Senate payroll throughout her ordeal and only ceased working there in 1880, when Democrats, newly in power, saw fit to fire her.[29]

African Americans made significant demands for equality in other official federal spaces besides the Capitol. Sometimes, as in the early days of African American spectatorship at Congress, such assertions were only made by an elite few who were willing to risk rejection, humiliation, and assault. Black physician

Alexander Augusta drew public attention for trying to observe Supreme Court proceedings in 1864, and in February 1865 Massachusetts lawyer John S. Rock sought and received admission to the Supreme Court bar.[30] Other times, African Americans joined en masse to attend events and ceremonies from which they would previously have been excluded. For example, when Lincoln's body lay in state inside the Executive Mansion, African Americans paid their respects alongside whites. When the president's casket was conveyed up Pennsylvania Avenue, the city's black residents participated in the formal procession and, by one estimate, made up two-thirds of the spectators who lined the street.[31]

Meanwhile, African American organizations and associations began to seek access to explicitly national spaces in the city. In 1864, a group of black Catholics sought and received permission from President Lincoln to host a fund-raiser for Catholic Sabbath schools on the grounds of the Executive Mansion. The event garnered considerable press coverage and was deemed a social and financial success.[32] The next summer, a group composed of eminent black northerners and members of the local black elite received President Andrew Johnson's permission to hold a massive July 4 celebration on the president's grounds. Its organizers called it "the first time that the colored people have attempted any celebration of a national character." The daylong celebration drew thousands, most of whom were Sabbath school students bearing "banners, flags, mottoes, and devices."[33] Speakers recognized the symbolic significance of meeting on the president's lawn. William Howard Day, a black New Yorker, opened his speech by saying, "We come to the National Capital—our Capital—with new hopes, new prospects, new joys, in view of the future and past of our people."[34] Republican newspaper editor John Forney, editor of the *Daily Chronicle*, recognized that the meeting on the "grounds of the Presidential Mansion, with the free consent of the Chief Magistrate of the republic," was "a fitting *finale* of the great struggle" and proof that the "Capital is no longer the rendezvous or the citadel of slavery."[35]

When African Americans, in masses or as individuals, attended Congress or held celebrations in the federal spaces of Washington, they were in effect staking claims to national belonging. They converted scraps of approbation— such as permission from the president to celebrate on the grounds, or simply not being thrown out of the Senate gallery—into opportunities to make upstart claims to membership in civil society and, even beyond that, to a voice in politics. In other southern cities as well, African Americans created occasions and spectacles through which they constituted themselves as people with a stake in civil and political proceedings. Only in the nation's capital, however, could local people insist on respect and recognition from congressmen, senators, and the president himself.

The Common Law of Common Carriers and the Positive Affirmation of Rights

The public character of government properties such as the galleries of the Capitol or the presidential grounds was quite different from that of streetcars, railroads, and steamboats. Common carriers such as these were part of a broader category of institutions known as public accommodations, which also included inns, hotels, theaters, and restaurants. These were services run by private individuals or corporations for the public benefit. In common law, proprietors of public accommodations had a duty to serve the public and could not deny service arbitrarily. Their policies must conform to the principle of "reasonable regulation," which allowed them to establish rules to preserve the peace, protect travelers, and cultivate the business itself. Thus, for example, proprietors could refuse to serve people who were drunk or ill, as their conditions might negatively affect other patrons or be disruptive to business. Whether proprietors could refuse accommodation to African Americans, or insist that they use segregated services, simply because of their "race" or skin color was very much in question. Some argued that such discrimination was arbitrary and therefore impermissible; others insisted that racial discrimination was a form of reasonable regulation that business owners could use to protect their business and the public peace.[36]

Access to streetcars and other common carriers had long been litigated under the common law, but the law of common carriers was itself a moving target. As historian A. K. Sandoval-Strausz has argued, the common law of common carriers was traditionally concerned with the duties of innkeepers and common carriers to the public or the common good—not with their rights or even with the rights, as such, of individual riders or patrons. That orientation began to shift in the antebellum period, however, as courts increasingly recognized proprietors' rights as owners of private property over their duties as servants to the public. As the discourse of individual rights merged into the law of common carriers, riders and proprietors alike stood to claim new rights.[37] In fact, the struggle to create civil rights over the next one hundred years was in some measure a struggle to wrench individual rights out of the increasingly submerged common law tradition of duties and obligations.

In Washington and other postwar cities, streetcars became a focal point in the debate over African Americans'access to public accommodations. Unlike other public accommodations that were also under debate, including restaurants and fancy theaters, streetcars were not meant as accommodations for the elite or even the bourgeoisie. Tickets were relatively inexpensive, and although the very poorest residents could not have afforded it, streetcar travel was within reach for many working people. Moreover, because streetcars were single cars drawn by a team of horses, they offered fewer options for segregated seating than railroads or steamboats. Streetcar companies did not sell first-class tickets or operate separate ladies' accommodations. The interiors of streetcars were typically mixed-class spaces, where laborers and middle-class people, men and women, congressmen and laborers shared a single car. In this, streetcars were distinctly urban institutions, characteristic of life in the country's increasingly dense, populous, and diverse cities.[38]

Black Washingtonians began demanding equal access to streetcars during the Civil War. When black soldiers protested exclusion as they were being recruited during the summer of 1863, the capital's one streetcar line inaugurated separate cars for black riders. The New York–based *Anglo-African* at first applauded the separate cars as a mark of progress, but the paper soon complained that the cars were inadequate to meet the growing demand by black riders.[39] That winter, army surgeon Alexander Augusta made a high-profile protest after being refused a seat on a streetcar while traveling on official business. Declaring Augusta's expulsion an "outrage," the *Anglo-African* predicted that the event could "turn out to be a great good for our people, as both the military and congressional authorities have taken the matter in hand."[40] Augusta outlined the incident in a letter to the military judge advocate and forwarded a copy to Senator Charles Sumner.

Augusta's protest and the broader turmoil over discrimination on the city's streetcars coincided with the effort of a group of businessmen to charter a second streetcar company in the District, the Metropolitan Railroad Company. The first streetcar company's charter, created in 1862, had been silent on the matter of racial discrimination. Meanwhile, Congress's willingness to act against racial discrimination on common carriers in the capital became clear in 1863, when the charter of the Washington and Alexandria Railroad was renewed with a provision—offered by Sumner and adopted with little debate—requiring that "no person shall be excluded from the cars on account of color."[41] Then, in the 1864 discussion of the Metropolitan Railroad Company's charter, Sumner introduced a clause prohibiting "exclusion of colored persons from the equal enjoyment of *all* railroad privileges in the District of

FIGURE 3.4. A Washington streetcar (detail from figure 3.1 above). Until 1865, African Americans were either excluded entirely or forced to ride on the platform in front of the car, where they faced exposure, rain, dust, and mud. Note that a well-dressed woman is trying to board while the car is moving.

Columbia."[42] His wording marked an advance from the Alexandria and Washington Railroad's charter, since by prohibiting "exclusion . . . from equal enjoyment" the provision implied that separate accommodations for black people would not suffice and the cars must be integrated. Sumner read Augusta's complaint in the Senate and insisted that more be done to safeguard the rights of African Americans to ride the city's streetcars. The cars for black people only came "now and then, once in a long interval of time," he argued, creating particularly severe hardships for women. It was a "disgrace to this city" and a "disgrace to this Government."[43]

The matter was assigned to the committee on the District of Columbia, which returned with an opinion that relied heavily on common law conventions and the assumption that African Americans who felt aggrieved could make recourse to the courts. Nothing further needed to be done to ensure the rights of black people on the streetcars, the committee argued, because the company's accommodation of African Americans on separate cars fulfilled its duty to serve the public. Beyond that, African Americans who believed they were being treated unjustly could sue a streetcar company in court. "The law is as open to a colored person as it is to a white person," committee chair Waitman T. Willey of West Virginia insisted.[44]

Sumner would not let the matter drop, however. He withdrew his proposal to prohibit racial discrimination on *all* District of Columbia railroads and proposed, instead, that on the Metropolitan Railroad alone "there shall be no regulations excluding any persons from any car on account of color," another clear demand for integration, not just accommodation.[45] An acrimonious debate ensued, as senators plumbed the complex legal questions at issue. There was something of a consensus that the common law forbade carriers from excluding passengers without good reason. But the common law had allowed for a variety of kinds of segregation: separate accommodations for ladies, for example, or for first-class travelers. Now senators argued over whether the principles that governed access to public accommodations permitted racially separate facilities as well.

Opponents of integration made perhaps their strongest case by citing railroad companies' widespread practice of running separate cars for separate classes of travel. Railroads often ran ladies' cars to which men could be denied access, as well as smoking cars and refreshment cars, all of which were understood to be permitted under the common law principle of reasonable regulation. As Wisconsin senator James R. Doolittle explained, "Public carriers" must "furnish a seat to every man who purchases a ticket and asks for a seat . . . and they are bound to furnish it in a reasonable time and in a reasonable manner . . . and that is all they are bound to do." Proprietors had "rights and privileges" when it came to operating their business for the comfort and safety of their riders. If company managers decided the public was best served, and the peace best administered, by providing separate cars for black people and white people, such was their prerogative. In a community equally divided between white and "colored" people, Doolittle argued, it might be "for the convenience of the traveling public that cars should be separated, and seats for colored persons provided in one car and seats for white persons in another."[46]

Others, however, argued that race and color were not varieties of difference that could be used in making distinctions among paying customers. Maryland senator Reverdy Johnson, a widely respected legal thinker, argued that common carriers had a "right . . . to establish . . . different classes of cars and charge different sums to the passengers in those respective cars," but they did not have "the right to establish a distinction between black men and white men, both of whom are anxious to travel upon the particular car." There was no doubt that companies were allowed to preserve order within the cars, Johnson acknowledged, but that prerogative did not mean they could make distinctions among law-abiding men.[47] Nonetheless, Johnson, a conservative on matters related to emancipation and racial equality, opposed additional legislation to outlaw racial discrimination, insisting that such legislation was redundant. The common law, he argued, already implied that distinctions based on race were inappropriate. By way of explanation, Johnson developed an analogy that conflated the quasi-public spaces of streetcars with the definitively public space of the Executive Mansion. It would be ridiculous, he argued, for Congress to pass a law mandating that black men and women have "the same right to visit the presidential mansion on public occasions as the white men and the white women." Public functions at the president's house were already open to anyone who wanted to attend, and it was the president's "business . . . to see the public when it does not interfere with his other duties." In that hypothetical case, as in the case of the District's streetcars, laws that positively banned racial discrimination would "guard by special provision this particular class of citizens."[48] Such "special provisions," he argued, took unnecessary cognizance of race when universal access was already protected by the common law. Not only that, they were dangerous, as they would tend to invite "a certain class or certain parties to bring about difficulties which the peace of society requires should be avoided, if possible."[49]

Johnson's analogy between the Executive Mansion and streetcars ignored the legal and cultural distinctions between common carriers, which were private entities, and the more definitively public spaces of the Executive Mansion or the Capitol.[50] Moreover, Johnson's analogy failed to take stock of the difficulties African Americans even of Frederick Douglass's stature continued to encounter when attempting to attend certain kinds of "public occasions" at Lincoln's house. The president had proven willing to meet with African Americans on political business, but he evidently did not take a strong stand for admitting them to more "social" occasions, such as public receptions, New Year's Day levees, or the second inaugural ball. For instance, Lincoln was happy to meet with Sojourner Truth in her role as a black diplomat, but when she sought admission to a social reception, she was turned away. The Republican *Chronicle* lauded Lincoln for inviting people "of every creed, clime, color and sex" to the annual presidential reception on New Year's Day, 1865, but a correspondent for the abolitionist *Liberator* reported that black people were denied entry by armed security guards.[51] When a controversy arose over whether African Americans would attend Lincoln's second inaugural ball, the Republican *Chronicle* defended the refusal to sell tickets to black men by saying that "the ball is a private affair, in which the parties concerned have a perfect right to invite whom they please and exclude whom they please."[52] And, in fact, African Americans were not welcome at the postinauguration reception. Frederick Douglass knew that "no colored persons had ever ventured to present themselves on such occasions" and decided to attend. But policemen at the door denied him admission, "for their directions were to admit no persons of my color." Douglass was finally admitted after sending word to Lincoln himself that "Frederick Douglass is detained by officers at the door."[53] This incident is often cited as evidence of Lincoln and Douglass's friendly rapport, but it also suggests that Douglass was able to attend the party not because African Americans were welcome, but because he had a special relationship with the president. Indeed, Lincoln's staff and perhaps Lincoln himself seem to have observed a distinction between admitting African Americans on political business and admitting them on more social occasions. Contrary to Reverdy Johnson, then, a formal announcement that racial discrimination was prohibited at the Executive Mansion would not have been redundant.

Charles Sumner and his allies in the Senate insisted that recourse to the common law was not sufficient to the challenges African Americans faced. "It is an undeniable fact that the spirit of the old law and the old practices still lingers," argued Massachusetts senator Henry Wilson. Citing an allegation that the local government discriminated against black men in the distribution of business licenses, Wilson argued that locals must "be made to understand that there is no inequality in law in this District, and that these people have their rights."[54] Whereas opponents insisted that most African Americans were content with the situation as it stood (and that Alexander Augusta was merely a rabble-rouser), Sumner said people brought examples of injustice on the streetcars to his attention "almost daily." To the argument that those who felt injured had recourse to the courts, Sumner replied that poor people could not afford lawsuits and that legislation explicitly outlawing discrimination would push streetcar companies to admit African Americans on an equal basis and therefore make legal action less necessary. Citing legal authorities, Sumner argued that "declaratory acts" were appropriate in cases in which "there is a doubt as to the meaning of a statute or of the common law." "The positive words which I propose leave no loop-house for doubt," he argued. In instances such as this, Congress's obligation was to declare "what the law of the land is."[55]

The debate brought disagreements over slavery and the future of African Americans to the surface, giving it a highly emotional and sectional tinge that may ultimately have pushed a few Republican moderates into Sumner's camp. Delaware senator Willard Saulsbury, not content with close legal reasoning on the common law, argued that attempts to "equalize with ourselves an inferior race" were "insane." White people who refused to ride streetcars with African Americans showed "good sense and good taste," he claimed, before lambasting the North as the source of every awful "'ism' of the modern day": "Woman's rightsism, spiritualism, and every other ism, together with abolitionism."[56] Such arguments grated on Republican moderate Lot Morrill of Maine, who joined Sumner in arguing for the antidiscrimination language, not because he considered it legally necessary but because he interpreted the border state senators as defending the system of racial domination that had underpinned slavery. What was truly at issue, Morrill pointed out, was not the proximity of white and black people on the streetcars, but the new terms of that proximity. Saulsbury and his ilk had no problem riding with "colored men and women," provided they wore upon themselves "the badge of bondage and servitude." "It is in good taste to do that!" Morrill exclaimed sarcastically.[57] Republicans did not agree on the lengths to which the federal government could go to ameliorate problems resulting from slavery, but they did agree on the imperative of ending slavery itself. Morrill had reframed the measure as one that would help eliminate slavery, and this may have helped secure the Senate votes necessary to pass the Metropolitan Railroad incorporation act with Sumner's clause included. The House at first rejected the antidiscrimination provision, but a conference committee worked out the details, and the Metropolitan Railroad was finally incorporated with an antidiscrimination clause on July 1, 1864.[58]

Congress's codification of African Americans' right to ride the District's streetcars was a significant innovation, not just because it represented a willingness to undertake progressive policy experiments in the capital but also because the concept of an individual right to ride was, itself, very new. In the 1840s, Massachusetts had abolished segregation on railroads not by legislative enactment but through the voluntary cooperation of the railroad companies. Indeed, it was not until 1865 that any state affirmatively banned discrimination based on color or race on common carriers and in other public accommodations. (Again, that state was Massachusetts.)[59] African Americans had insisted that, once free, they must be entitled to full membership in the traveling public and to the privilege of using ladies' or first-class accommodations if they so desired and could afford it. Their claims had pushed Congress to discuss the meaning of common law principles and the necessity for declaratory legislation where the common law was violated, and Congress had created a "right" to ride as a result. Questions about the boundary between public and private, and about the legitimacy of various kinds of discrimination, would remain crucial as Americans continued to debate the question of where—literally in what spaces—people's "civil rights" began and ended.

The Streetcar Struggle of 1865

At least for the moment, political tides were turning in the direction of Sumner's wing of the Republican Party, and in the spring of 1865 Congress passed legislation (introduced by Sumner) extending the antidiscrimination provision in the Metropolitan Railroad charter to "every other railroad in the District of Columbia."[60] Yet declaring the intention of the common law did not make it so. Days after the law passed, a black Union army sergeant boarded a streetcar and asked a white man whether he could sit beside him. The man responded that "he once owned a number of colored persons and was not ashamed of the race," but when the soldier sat down four white men attacked him. Police arrested two of the assailants and took them before a police magistrate, who held them for a court appearance.[61] For the rest of the year, streetcars were at the heart of the local debate about equality. As African Americans demanded enforcement of their new right to ride, white soldiers and riders, as well as streetcar conductors, reacted with hostility and sometimes violence.[62]

One very visible participant in the struggle was Sojourner Truth, who used the public nature of the city streets and her own status as something of a celebrity to stage several protests against continuing racial discrimination on the cars. Truth had come to the capital in late 1864 to help distribute food, clothing, medicine, and advice to freedpeople. An antebellum abolitionist with extensive connections in activist circles, she held a variety of positions. Working for the government, Truth offered freedpeople instruction in housekeeping at Freedmen's Village, on Mason's Island, and later at Freedman's Hospital. She participated in the public life of black Washington, giving lectures and joining local African Americans in raising money for the Colored Soldiers' Aid Society of the 15th Street Presbyterian Church. She also collaborated with Josephine Griffing, a white woman with whom she had worked in the abolitionist movement, in promoting freedpeople's emigration out of the capital.[63]

In her biography of Truth, Olive Gilbert, who was a close friend, related several incidents in which Truth publicly protested when Washington streetcars refused to stop to pick her up. According to Gilbert, Truth once stood on a corner, after being passed by two different cars, and yelled, "I want to ride! I want to ride!! I want to ride!!!" A sympathetic crowd forced the next streetcar to stop so Truth could board and then cheered when she did so.[64] In another account from Gilbert's narrative, Truth and a black female companion were confronted inside a streetcar by a pair of white women, one of whom asked the conductor, "Does niggers ride in these cars?" The conductor answered in the affirmative, and Truth added, "Of course colored people ride in the cars. Street cars are designed for poor white, and colored, folks." Truth gestured to private carriages outside the window and suggested the white women pay to ride those if they sought more select company. The women, Truth recounted, hastily exited the car.[65]

Truth's series of protests culminated in late September 1865, in a confrontation that left her injured and prompted her to sue the streetcar company. Truth was traveling with Laura Haviland, a white abolitionist who was visiting the city, when the two women decided to board a streetcar, a decision they knew would be provocative. Gilbert quoted Truth's account of the story: "I stepped [to] one side as if to continue my walk and when [the car] stopped I ran and jumped aboard." Gesturing to Haviland, the conductor ordered Truth to make way for the "lady." Truth countered, "I am a lady too." When the two women changed streetcar lines, they were confronted again. A conductor attempted to force Truth off the car, but she clung to the railing with both hands. Haviland sought to intervene, and the conductor impudently inquired whether Haviland was Truth's owner. Haviland replied, "She belongs to humanity."[66]

Truth's shoulder had been injured in the incident, and she filed suit. Police arrested the offending conductor, one John C. Weeden, and the Freedmen's Bureau furnished Truth with a lawyer. At a police court hearing, which was briefly noted in local newspapers, Haviland and a Freedmen's Bureau doctor were called to testify. Defense witnesses claimed Weeden was merely trying to keep Truth out of the car while passengers exited. The police magistrate decided to hold Weeden for a court appearance, suggesting he took the matter seriously enough. The criminal court's grand jury dismissed the case, however. Truth later reported that the whole incident "created a great sensation" and the conductor "lost his situation." She also took sole responsibility for having ended racial discrimination on the Washington streetcars, telling Gilbert that soon after the incident, conductors were welcoming black women into the streetcars with the respectful address: "Walk in, ladies."[67] Although Truth was one among many black Washingtonians who insisted that their right to ride be respected, her very public protests undoubtedly raised awareness of the issue, and her lawsuit may have pushed conductors to enforce the law more faithfully. Around the time Truth was thrown off the car, a visitor from Pennsylvania described "perfect equality pervading between the colored and white street-car travellers, street cars jam full—black and white passengers forming a complete checker-board."[68]

Lois Bryan Adams, a Washington-based correspondent for a Michigan newspaper, used a parable about Washington's streetcars to describe the enormous changes afoot in the postemancipation South. In Adams's story, a character named Mrs. Airy Stocracy boarded a Washington streetcar, struggling to keep her giant crinoline under control. The car was crowded, and, befitting the respectable decorum expected inside a streetcar, "a gentleman rose" to let her sit. Soon, however, Mrs. Stocracy noticed a mulatto woman ("Southern miscegenation illustrated") "touching her sacred skirts." She "drew in her drapery" and summarily instructed the woman, "Go out on the platform, where you belong!" But Mrs. Stocracy, with her excessive clothing and outdated manners, found no allies within the car. "Everybody" knew that the law now forbade discrimination on the cars, and no one volunteered to support Mrs. Stocracy's cause. "Go along, I tell you! Why don't you go out on the platform where you belong?" Mrs. Stocracy repeated. As the other passengers smiled quietly, the character Missy Genation, "evidently aware of the rights of her situation," turned calmly to face her adversary and replied, "'Cause I don't want to." Humiliated, Mrs. Stocracy descended from the car onto the rainy street, "a wetter and perhaps a wiser woman."[69]

In late December, the *Chronicle* reported a confrontation between two men that mirrored the fictional story Adams had offered months earlier. When a white man attempted to force a black man off a streetcar at gunpoint, the black man stood his ground until the white man left the car, "muttering a hardy imprecation upon the black race." The Republican newspaper expressed outrage that the conductor had not stopped the car and called the police.[70] Indeed, by the end of 1865, violent incidents on the streetcars were ebbing. After several years of struggle, both in the streets and in Congress, African Americans had secured a right to ride on the capital's streetcars.

African Americans' successful campaign to ride the streetcars as equals to whites shaped an ongoing discussion of proper comportment on the cars. In streetcars, men and women of all stations might brush against one another's bodies, converse, and even steal illicit glances. Some people welcomed such mingling as a symbol of expanding democracy; others disdained it as evidence of a growing proximity among diverse groups that threatened to undermine a social order founded on entrenched hierarchies of race, sex, and class.[71] As African Americans began riding the cars, Cincinnati journalist Whitelaw Reid observed that "the most aristocratic ladies sat beside well dressed Negroes without a shudder," as they discovered "that worth has as much as color to do with what is respectable and what is not."[72] The white "ladies" were evidently surprised to find that racial integration of the streetcars did not bring with it a diminution of respectability. Yet the proper atmosphere on streetcars could easily become compromised. Shortly after the March 1865 antidiscrimination law went into effect, the *Chronicle* denounced "several evils" among passengers and drivers. Drivers, it complained, were "grossly profane, and seem to be as regardless of the presence of ladies as of any other class, upon whose ears their profane language grates harshly." It also criticized women in the habit of "spreading their crinoline so as to occupy the space designated for two persons," suggesting that if women were going to take up two seats, they should pay two fares. The writer did not link concerns about comportment with the recent passage of the antidiscrimination law, but another newspaper described a white woman draping her crinoline over the seat beside her to discourage a black man from sitting there.[73]

Some opponents confronted integration not with crinoline-shifting gentility but with animus toward the new law and toward African Americans themselves. The Democratic *Constitutional Union* described whites' revulsion at sharing the cars with black riders who reeked of a "peculiar odor" on a hot summer day.[74] The newspaper also published a sympathetic account of a streetcar conductor who insisted that he was powerless to eject a rancid smelling black man "from the very fact of his being a negro." The conductor alleged that "if a filthy white man was to get on my car, I would drive him off at once." "The difference is," the newspaper concluded, "that the negroes have more latitude than the whites, and the white must give way before the black."[75] Those who complained that certain African Americans smelled bad or were disorderly cleverly avoided outright racism by suggesting that their objections were not to the race or color of black riders as such but, rather, to their comportment. The conductor and the newspaper also marshaled the popular argument (also made by Senator Reverdy Johnson) that positive laws against discrimination actually gave blacks *more* rights than whites and somehow prevented companies from enforcing conventional "reasonable regulations" on black riders. The antidiscrimination law said no such thing. In their purposeful misreading, however, conservatives concealed their own racism behind the veneer of the common law and sought to cast themselves as defenders of racial equality against those who supposedly sought special favors for African Americans.

Since social interactions on streetcars were so volatile, and since whites so often questioned African Americans' capacity for respectable behavior, black passengers considered proper comportment on streetcars particularly important. As historians have shown, the tradition of "ladies'" accommodations created an opening in which black women who could present themselves as reputable could claim access. Indeed, in keeping with conventions of gender and respectable ridership, sympathetic accounts of black women attempting to ride Washington's streetcars usually made prominent reference to their proper bearing. In August 1865, for example, an army officer described a freedwoman who had been assaulted after attempting to ride a streetcar as "cleanly-well dressed," saying she had "conducted herself in a respectful manner notwithstanding the abuse received by vile language, and personal violence from these white citizens."[76]

Black men faced distinct and in some ways more difficult obstacles to claiming respectable ridership. Courts in the antebellum North had held that black men could not be completely excluded from public conveyances, but they usually affirmed that accommodation alone was sufficient, and therefore that black men must accept dirty, humiliating, or otherwise inadequate conditions.[77] Yet beginning in 1863, some black men could draw on their elevated status as soldiers to claim the privilege of ridership, as groups of black soldiers and army surgeon Alexander Augusta had done in 1863 and 1864. Soldiers' claims were difficult to refute in the midst of war, when uniformed men were being asked to sacrifice their lives for the nation. But even after military demobilization, black men in civilian dress continued to protest segregation and exclusion, and supportive observers described them, too, as well dressed and respectful, directly rebutting those inclined to resort to common law conventions of reasonable regulation to justify discrimination.[78]

The black men and women who emphasized dignified comportment on the streetcars implicitly built their case for access on long-standing common law conventions that prohibited common carriers from turning customers away without good reason. Their public displays of respectability also had purchase in the world of individual rights that was gradually surpassing the common law vision of obligations and duties. Indeed, as Chapter 2 emphasized, many contemporaries—even those sympathetic to African Americans' claims to racial equality—did not believe rights inhered in individuals but thought instead that rights must be earned through demonstrations of proper comportment and morality. By dressing neatly (if not expensively) and conducting themselves with dignity and reserve, black riders sought to make an unassailable case that they were worthy of the rights they sought to claim.[79]

African Americans' demands for equal access to streetcars in the urban South are a little-appreciated but important aspect of a broader national debate about the meanings of civil equality after slavery. In other cities in the postwar South, African Americans made concerted demands for access to streetcars after the passage of the 1866 Civil Rights Act and, particularly, after the 1867 federal Reconstruction Acts mandated black men's voting rights and promised, in many places, vast changes in the political balance of power.[80] The national capital was ahead of the curve, in large part because some congressional Republicans were willing to listen to the demands of black locals and to experiment with legislation. The prohibition on racial discrimination in common carriers in the District of Columbia transcended the widely agreed-upon vision of "equality before the law" because it applied not to legal apparatuses but to private associations that were regulated by law. Black Washingtonians would continue pressing for that more expansive definition of legal equality, seeking municipal ordinances that would guarantee African Americans' access to an array of other public accommodations, including hotels, ice cream parlors, and theaters. On the federal side, Senator Sumner remained a prime mover, advocating for expansive equality before the law both in the District and, even more controversially, in the states themselves.

Policing and Resistance in the Streets

Streetcars were not the only places where passage of antidiscrimination laws did not mean antidiscrimination in practice. In 1862, Congress had overturned the antebellum black codes and specified that criminal laws must be enforced in a nondiscriminatory way. Yet black Washingtonians continued to face quotidian violence and harassment by local whites, and they could not expect fair treatment by police and other law enforcement officials. In response, black Washingtonians adopted a variety of tactics, ranging from legal appeals to spontaneous public denunciations. In demanding fair treatment from the police and others, African Americans rejected the idea that there could be an intermediate status between slave and citizen. They insisted, through both words and actions, that slavery would end only once they were granted the full range of rights and privileges to which white people were accustomed.

It was the task of the Metropolitan Police to maintain a semblance of order in the crowded and disorderly capital city. The police board and members of the force felt overwhelmed by the influx of strangers and unable to address crime problems generated by the growing and unruly population. Beggars, petty thieves, and vagrants overcrowded the jail and the workhouse. Facilities for incarceration and trial were inadequate, and the jail building was so fragile that prisoners often escaped. The poor conditions of police work fostered corruption and lack of discipline, and policemen were frequently dismissed for drunkenness and other offenses. One historian who studied police personnel records for the 1860s and 1870s found that the Metropolitan Police "had a chronic discipline problem in the postwar period."[81]

The police superintendent from 1864 to 1878 was A. C. Richards, an Ohio native who had come to the capital in 1851 to teach high school. Richards, a Republican, seems to have done what he could with the underfunded force, attempting to reduce the staff's twelve-hour shifts and surveying other cities to discover ways to improve training and working conditions. His efforts to run the police department garnered considerable respect among white Washingtonians, and he remained on the job through the Johnson and Grant administrations, ultimately retiring in 1878.[82] Yet, although Richards pushed the police force to protect African Americans' rights at critical moments—for example, in the first election in which black men voted—the force on the whole was ambivalent, at best, about the mandate to enforce the basic legal equality of African Americans.

Some regions on the periphery of urbanized Washington and Georgetown were particularly tumultuous. For instance, the area called Swampoodle, located along North Capitol Street and in northeast Washington, was known as a working-class Irish neighborhood and was also the site of a number of federal installations, including the Government Printing Office, the headquarters of the Quartermaster of the Military Department of Washington, and (further east) Kendall Green, where military barracks had been converted into tenements for freedpeople. North Capitol Street was a major artery leading from the U.S. Capitol to the northern suburbs, and military convoys frequently used it for transporting supplies during the war. Federal installations made Swampoodle the home and workplace of many African Americans, but the area's substantial white working-class population resented the growing black presence and often lashed out violently, particularly at black laborers. Irish-born laborers no doubt felt considerable pressure from emancipation and black migration into the city. According to the U.S. census, between 1860 and 1870 the District's Irish-born population increased by just under 1,000, while the African American population grew by 29,088.[83]

Swampoodle was particularly explosive during 1865, as the federal government gradually ceded authority over the city to the Metropolitan Police.[84] That fall, Republican newspapers and federal officials pointed out that attacks on African Americans were rampant in the neighborhood.[85] Officials from the quartermaster's department complained that white people attacked black teamsters traveling along H Street, Northeast, almost daily. The *National Republican* indicated that although Irish "toughs" perpetrated the offenses, "old Washingtonians" sanctioned them.[86] The superintendent of the Government Printing Office reported to the Freedmen's Bureau "outrages" on "unoffending colored persons" by keepers of Irish saloons near his office, charging that "police officers stationed in that part of the city do not use proper exertions to maintain the peace." Black printing office employees "dare[d] not cross the street" for fear of being attacked.[87] The problems in Swampoodle were evidently beyond the ken of the police. As September ended, Freedmen's Bureau agents gave up on local law enforcement and requested military guards for the area, while the quartermaster requested a military patrol to protect his black laborers. Finally, the army established a special patrol for the area.[88] The neighborhood nevertheless retained its rough reputation. Decades later, veterans of the police force would remember Swampoodle as one of the city's most challenging neighborhoods.[89]

In contrast to the marginal Swampoodle neighborhood, the Seventh Street corridor, running north from the National Mall to Boundary Street and beyond, was at the center of city life. Seventh Street linked the central city with the surrounding rural areas of Washington County and Maryland that lay to the north, and it was a major thoroughfare for both federal and local Washington. Approaching the city on Seventh Street Road, a visitor would have encountered a settlement of freedpeople around Freedman's Hospital. Nearby, the trustees of Howard University in 1867 purchased land and began building their institution.[90] Proceeding south, Seventh Street was lined by federal buildings. At Seventh and O Streets stood Wisewell Barracks, where the Freedmen's Bureau supervised housing for freedpeople. Next came the Patent Office and Department of Interior, followed by the city Post Office. And at the intersection of Seventh Street and Pennsylvania Avenue stood the city's Central Market, about half-way between the Executive Mansion and the Capitol and not far from the infamous Murder Bay neighborhood. The market saw a great deal of the city's retail business. One observer remarked in 1868 that German merchants worked inside the building, while African Americans "who have driven in from the Seventh Street suburbs" worked outside.[91]

Seventh Street—with its market traffic, freedpeople's housing, and federal buildings—could be combustible. In the summer of 1865, a Freedmen's Bu-

FIGURE 3.5. Illustration of African American women selling flowers outdoors at Washington's Central Market. *Harper's Weekly*, June 4, 1870, 365. Courtesy Library of Congress.

reau agent reported that it was "not uncommon" for whites to commit violent assaults on African Americans on the Seventh Street streetcar line.[92] The hostile sentiments of local white residents and the police were particularly clear in the summer of 1866, when white men repeatedly attacked black men along Seventh Street while the police largely stood by or helped the whites. One particularly tumultuous day witnessed a "pitched battle" between black residents of Wisewell Barracks and white locals who had challenged them to a fight. Guards at the barracks struggled to keep a crowd of some 300 people at bay: "Stones were freely used," and two pistol shots were fired. A Freedmen's Bureau official summoned the police, but by the time a patrolman arrived tensions had diminished and the crowd had dispersed.[93] The bureau agent who reported the incident was particularly troubled by the white denizens of the area. Although not all were aggressive toward freedpeople, he wrote, there were "many who seem to take every opportunity to get up a disturbance with colored men." The agent recommended a stronger police presence in the neighborhood, but he also expressed doubt about the police force's commitment to enforcing the law and maintaining the peace. "It is stated that a policeman was with the white men and urged them on," he reported.[94]

Washington's police and municipal judges did not need a black code in order to discriminate against blacks. A view prevailed in some quarters of white Washington that African Americans were a source of crime and disease in the city and that they were entitled to few rights. Law enforcement officials did not hesitate to translate such ideas into practice. For instance, although the District had no racist vagrancy statutes (unlike many southern states in the early postwar years), one freedmen's relief worker reported that police "locked up" freedmen and boys "for sleeping in the markets and other public buildings, for wandering about the streets at late hours of the night, for being [of] suspicious character &c &c." Once arrested, African Americans faced other kinds of discrimination. When freedpeople's larceny cases came before police magistrates, plaintiffs and witnesses often exaggerated the value of the supposedly stolen property in order to obtain the most stringent possible sentence. As one African American activist put it, "The law is simply for the white man and not for the black."[95]

Knowing that the principle of racial equality before the law meant little if African Americans had no legal representation in court, the Freedmen's Bureau began a legal defense program in the summer of 1866. The leading bureau lawyer was Andrew K. Browne, a white New York native who had arrived in Washington during the war.[96] In 1866, he and other lawyers working for the Freedmen's Bureau made themselves available to people who walked into their office on Pennsylvania Avenue, and they visited the jail and police stations in search of people who needed legal representation. The bulk of their work related to enforcement of labor contracts and rental agreements, but they also sought justice for freedpeople involved in criminal cases. During one thirteen-month period, Browne estimated that attorneys in his office had made 683 visits to the jail and worked on 291 criminal cases, as well as almost 600 civil ones.[97] But the lawyers were swamped during the roughly two years the office existed, and they likely served only a fraction of the freedpeople who would have benefited from legal representation.

Largely deprived of such aid, African Americans sought other ways of combating discrimination by law enforcement officials. One obvious strategy was to avoid contact with the police. Another option was to use their voices—in conjunction with the publicness of the city's streets and tribunals—to make a case for fair treatment. For instance, after two white men forced her off the ladies' car in Alexandria, Kate Brown publicly challenged them to go find some real criminals. "What are you going to arrest me for?" she demanded. "What have I done? Have I committed robbery? Have I murdered anyone?"[98] In another instance, Richard Clements, a black man who had been arrested after he and some friends were assaulted by Irish rowdies, challenged a police court magistrate to justify the fine he was about to impose. Angered by Clements's defiance, the judge ordered him back to the jail cell where he had spent the night, along with his friend Charles Simon. Later, Clements paid the fine. As the two men were leaving, the following colloquy ensued.

JUDGE: the next time you come here with your impudence
  I will fine you five dollars, do you hear that?
SIMON: yes sir I heard it.
JUDGE: I suppose you don't take any heed to it do you?
SIMON: I heard it.[99]

The judge acknowledged that Simon was unlikely to "heed" his authority, and Simon, for his part, refused to participate in an outdated ritual of racial deference.

Acting defiant may have been a satisfying way to express outrage at the injustice that continued to saturate local legal proceedings, but it had its limits as a strategy. Talking back was unlikely to change outcomes; it entailed significant risks; and it did nothing to shift the overall balance of power in the city. Indeed, many black leaders believed a more powerful and organized response was required to mitigate legal and physical violence against African Americans on the streets. Black men needed the right to vote. "Without the right of suffrage, we are without protection, and liable to combinations of outrage," a group of black leaders explained in an 1865 petition. "The petty officers of the law respecting the source of power, will naturally defer to the one having a vote: and the partiality shown in this respect operates greatly to the disadvantage of the colored citizen."[100] Poor people of all kinds tended to suffer at the hands of city police, who were charged, essentially, with safeguarding private property. But the plight of African Americans was unique for there was no pretense that black men could vote out officials whose policies and appointees they disliked.

Ambiguities of Civil Rights

As black Washingtonians demanded that law enforcement officials respect their basic rights and insisted on access to streetcars and other common carriers, a national debate was under way about the meaning of civil equality and the limits of civil rights. During 1866, a simmering conflict between congressional Republicans and President Andrew Johnson boiled over, as it became clear that Johnson favored leniency toward former Confederates and opposed even moderate protections for southern African Americans. Johnson's intransigence helped unify congressional Republicans in support of a Reconstruction program that would attempt to secure citizenship and basic rights for African Americans. Yet Republicans did not agree on precisely which rights the U.S. government would now guarantee. Moderates insisted on separating what they considered civil equality—racially equal access to the legal system and the absence of discriminatory laws—from so-called political equality, or the rights to vote and hold office. Nor did legislators themselves specify what constituted civil rights. Thus even as the 1866 Civil Rights Act made citizens of African Americans, it left the people and the courts to define the rights of citizenship.

Meanwhile, black Washingtonians continued to push for an extremely expansive definition of civil rights. They enlisted federal officials' support of their citywide celebration of emancipation in April 1866, and they asked the Freedmen's Bureau commissioner and the secretary of war to approve and arm a black militia regiment. Like their demands for equal access to the capital's streetcars, black Washingtonians' insistence on recognition of their nascent civic equality and, in particular, of their right to organize militia were upstart claims that challenged officials to think about the broadest implications of slavery's abolition.

Residents of the nation's capital both observed and participated in the showdown between Johnson and the congressional Republicans. In mid-February 1866, Johnson vetoed a bill to renew the Freedmen's Bureau and issued a sweeping indictment of the entire congressional Reconstruction effort. Democrats exulted at Johnson's pluck in defying Congress, but it soon became clear that the president's course actually served to unite the congressional Republicans in opposition.[101] Tensions mounted on the streets, as Democrats applauded Johnson's course and African Americans rallied behind the congressional Republicans. Johnson helped inflame the situation on the night of February 22, when he gave a speech to supporters in which he likened his congressional opponents to Confederate traitors and compared himself to Jesus Christ. As Democrats rejoiced, many of Johnson's moderate Republican allies were appalled. Julia Wilbur, a white abolitionist doing freedmen's aid work in Washington, hung an American flag draped in black to show her dismay and alluded to the celebrants as "old secesh citizens, returned rebels, copperheads, & the rabble generally." Days later, when someone shot at Frederick Douglass during a visit to Baltimore, Wilbur declared the region "on the brink of a rebellion" and concluded, "Things cannot remain as they are."[102]

They did not. The spring and summer of 1866 brought decisive victories for congressional Republicans, who developed a coalition capable of passing legislation over Johnson's veto. The most significant new law was the Civil Rights Act, which Johnson vetoed in late March and Congress quickly passed again with the necessary majority. In its final form, the Civil Rights Act reflected the Republican consensus on the meaning and limits of civil rights. The law established birthright citizenship as the law of the land, and it provided that all U.S. citizens "have the same right" to enter into contracts and to convey and hold property and to the "full and equal benefit of all laws and proceedings for the security of person and property, as is enjoyed by white citizens."[103]

It is difficult to overestimate the novelty of the Civil Rights Act. In the antebellum era, citizenship was most often discussed as a state or local status, while national citizenship remained relatively underdeveloped both conceptually and legally. As the 1857 *Dred Scott* decision notoriously made clear, birth in the United States did not automatically entitle even freeborn people to citizenship. But the Civil War had put antebellum visions of citizenship into motion. Most famously, in the fall of 1862 Lincoln's attorney general released an opinion supporting the concept of birthright citizenship, a document that gave considerable hope to African Americans looking for evidence that the war would open a way to secure their status as citizens. The 1866 Civil Rights Act codified this new vision of birthright citizenship and established, in broad strokes, the kinds of rights to which individual citizens would be entitled.[104]

Yet the exact "civil rights" protected by the law remained in dispute. Congress did not see fit—either in the Civil Rights Act or in the Fourteenth Amendment it passed that summer—to delineate exactly what constituted "the full and equal benefit of all laws and proceedings." Historian Robert J. Kaczorowski has noted this ambiguity, stating that the Civil Rights Act left "the right to vote or hold public office" as well as "jury service, access to public schools, and the use of public transportation facilities and accommodations" in a "gray area."[105] The act made clear that state laws must avoid racially discriminatory language, but that did not mean private companies or employers could not discriminate on the basis of race or color. If African Americans encountered racial discrimination in schools, streetcars, restaurants, employment, or housing, would these be considered violations of the new law? Or was protection accorded only when the law itself discriminated, as in the postwar black codes, statutes that created different crimes and punishments for blacks than for whites?

Besides leaving the content of "civil rights" ambiguous, the Civil Rights Act also helped create a conceptual separation between what contemporaries understood to be "civil rights" and what they knew as "political rights." Republicans could generally agree on the propriety of guaranteeing blacks basic civil rights described in the law, but they were bitterly divided about the wisdom of guaranteeing racial equality in voting rights, as well as rights to hold office and to serve on juries. During the debate over the Civil Rights Act, Republicans had rejected broad language that might have implied that the right to vote was among the civil rights protected by the new law, choosing instead more specific terminology that seemed to exclude the right to vote. Indeed, many who helped pass the law over Johnson's veto believed voting rights for black men would be disastrous, and Republicans' divisions on the issue of black men's enfranchisement would have dramatic consequences in the future.[106]

Notwithstanding its absences and ambiguities, supporters and detractors alike saw the Civil Rights Act as a remarkable innovation. It so dramatically brought the federal government into the affairs of the states that many people, including some who favored it, believed it represented an unconstitutional overreaching of federal power. Supporters in Congress moved to secure the law's constitutionality through passage of the Fourteenth Amendment, while opponents insisted that it was illegitimate, not least because the states of the former Confederacy were not represented in the Congress that passed it. Black Washingtonians saw the law as momentous, and a group of black women presented flowers to each senator who voted for it, with special baskets for Charles Sumner and the bill's author, Senator Lyman Trumbull of Illinois. According to one witness, cards attached to each bouquet read, "We exercise the Civil Right to express our gratitude."[107]

Days after the law passed, African Americans celebrated the fourth anniversary of emancipation in the District of Columbia with an enormous parade organized by a coalition of church and civic organizations. This was certainly not the first time since emancipation that Washington's African Americans had publicly celebrated in the city's federal spaces, but it was a particularly meaningful one, in light of their new status as U.S. citizens and the advent of federally enforceable civil rights. The parade featured companies of black soldiers and independent black militia, brass bands, colorful flags, and delegations from each Washington ward and from the Union League, Odd Fellows, Masons, and other associations. Paraders passed sites of national significance—the Executive Mansion, the home of General Ulysses S. Grant, the headquarters of the Department of Washington, the Treasury Department, and the Capitol—at most points eliciting greetings from the federal officials they meant to honor.[108] Parade organizers had invited members of both houses of Congress to join the celebration, and the War Department furnished cannons to be fired "as the head of the procession reaches the front of the Executive Mansion."[109] Government support for the celebration, the paraders' occupation of the most significant streets of the national capital, and the array of African American associations on display all dramatized the striking and ongoing democratization of local and national political culture.[110]

The parade's significance was not lost on Democrats. Editors of the *Constitutional Union* professed to feel pity as they "witnessed the joy" with which the celebrants "swallowed down the mockery wherewith Congress has lately cheated them." The "unfortunate creatures" believed, the paper sneered, "that Congress can melt down a white man and build him up again with a black skin."[111] Expressing the conservative preoccupation with African Americans' new public assertiveness and with the idea that more prerogatives for African Americans meant fewer for whites, William Owner recorded in his diary his fear that "all the nigs" would "take possession of the avenue," making it "difficult for a white man or woman to escape being run down by them." Infuriated that the celebration had garnered approval from the highest echelons of the federal government, Owner lamented that "any white man who says boo to them will be arrested and placed under guard according to law and the 'Equal Rights bill.'"[112]

The parade culminated at Franklin Square, where the throng gathered to hear speeches by eminent men. The crowd had been polite to President Johnson as it passed the Executive Mansion, but, the *Chronicle* commented, if the president had "scanned the mottoes that were carried passed him," including banners for "Equal political rights," and "Universal suffrage," he would have known Washington's black community, en masse, did not share his views. On the dais that day, Henry Highland Garnet led off with praise for Congress, John Forney, and Lincoln. "I suppose it will no longer be considered a presumption to call you *fellow-citizens*," he told the crowd, "since the Constitution has been so amended as forever to prohibit upon American soil slavery and involuntary servitude . . . and since the 'civil rights bill' has become a law of the land." A letter from Sumner outlined the next phase of the struggle. Equality "in what are called civil rights" was only "*semi-equality*," his message declared. Without the right to vote, "the freedman . . . is only *half a man*."[113]

Several weeks after the ebullient celebration, leaders of the Lincoln Reserves, one of the militia units that had marched in the Emancipation Day celebration, met with O. O. Howard, the commissioner of the Freedmen's Bureau, to request that their organization be made part of the District's regular militia

FIGURE 3.6. "Celebration of the Abolition of Slavery in the District of Columbia by the Colored People, in Washington." In an illustration that captures the ebullience of the day, raised banners recall the importance of black associational life for demonstrating status and claiming belonging. The figures in the foreground, with their varied styles of dress, represent the class diversity of black Washington. *Harper's Weekly*, May 12, 1866, 300. Courtesy Library of Congress, LC-USZ62-33937.

and that the government sell them arms.[114] This was a dramatic request. It was one thing to muster in black soldiers in a national emergency but quite another to acknowledge that black militia would be a permanent part of local civic life. Militia participation had always been a potent sign of membership in a community of male stakeholders and, not coincidentally, had always been the exclusive domain of white men. In the antebellum years, black activists, particularly in Ohio and Massachusetts, had demanded an end to the exclusion of black men from state militia organizations. But to no avail. Supreme Court chief justice Roger Taney had made clear the connections among race, militia service, and citizenship, observing in his *Dred Scott* opinion, "Nothing could more strongly mark the entire repudiation of the African race" than black men's exclusion from state militias. Militia service was "one of the highest duties of the citizen," and "the African race" was exempt from that duty because its members were not counted among the "people." The black man "forms no part of the sovereignty of the State, and is not therefore called on to uphold and defend it," the chief justice concluded.[115] For Taney, black men's exemption from militia duty both revealed and justified their exclusion from citizenship. In light of this history of exclusion and the links between militia service and citizenship, it is no wonder that black civil war veterans in Washington sought official recognition for their militia.

The sensitivity of the issue might explain why the leaders of the Lincoln Reserves approached Commissioner O. O. Howard first. They probably thought they would receive the most sympathetic hearing from the abolitionist head of a bureau designated specifically for the protection of freedpeople. But Howard was not prepared to decide the matter himself and sought advice from Edwin M. Stanton, the secretary of war. In his letter to Stanton, Howard at first recommended giving the Lincoln Reserves permission to organize as part of the District's (heretofore exclusively white) militia. Before sending the letter, however, Howard decided against that recommendation and simply asked whether Stanton had "any objection to their organizing as an independent regiment" and whether the government could supply them with arms. Stanton's office returned an unsigned, undated note stating that the secretary saw no reason to allow such an organization and that the final decision would lie with President Johnson.[116]

Meanwhile, to the extent that black militia leaders were motivated not just by a desire for the full privileges of free manhood but also by a sense of vulnerability to white violence, events in the summer of 1866 would confirm their fears. Echoing uprisings of whites in Norfolk and Memphis that spring, in July whites rioted against African Americans in New Orleans. Closer to home, tensions seemed to grow with the federal sanction of black citizenship and civil rights. One poor white woman squatting in an old house in Washington told Julia Wilbur, "There'll be a bloody war here before long. There'll be no niggers left here, I know, I hear the men talk." Black men "wont work, have everything given them," she charged, "while white folks that belong here have to starve & freeze, but it wont be so much longer." For its own part, the *Constitutional Union* continued to ply its readers with frightening stories of black criminality and even suggested that the best strategy for dealing with assertive African Americans was a "Vigilance Committee" to "take the matter in hand, and with a stout rope and convenient tree or lamp-post rid the community of some thousands of these pests."[117]

That September, Allen M. Bland, colonel of the Lincoln Reserves, went directly to Stanton with a number of pressing questions related to the status of black militias in the capital. Informing Stanton that he and others were forming a battalion, he asked whether members of the militia could continue to wear uniforms they had worn "in the volunteer service" and whether they could expect to "parade the streets of the city without fear of interruption by the Government or City officials." Bland also made clear that the Lincoln Reserves would be directed by black officers, a departure from the army's wartime practice of appointing white officers for black troops. Reflecting his own consciousness of the importance of laws and also of the dynamic legal climate of 1866, Bland queried, "Is there any law prohibiting a colored militia regiment, officered by colored men from becoming a part of the militia organization of this District? If there is no law have you not the power to issue the necessary arms, and equipments, and will you not grant the order for arming the Lincoln Reserve Guards?"[118] Bland neither invoked the 1866 Civil Rights Act nor claimed a right to form a militia. Yet his inquiry as to whether any racially discriminatory militia laws were in effect revealed his intention to push the federal government to make good on its newfound commitment to equality before the law. Stanton demurred, affirming his earlier position that the president must authorize the formation of militias in the District. "No reason is known to this Department why new militia organizations should now be made here," he added. "All volunteer organizations, white and black, have been ordered to be mustered out of service." Therefore, Bland must "take no steps towards a militia organization" without President Johnson's approval. Separately, the office of the adjutant general (whose charge was War Department personnel matters) instructed the local army commander to summon Bland and "notify him to stop his proceedings."[119]

Johnson never approved black militia organizations in the capital, but black men nonetheless continued their efforts. Just over a year later, military officials would count three separate black militias in Washington. Amid whites' fears that the organizations were planning an uprising, Charles B. Fischer, a Union veteran and militia officer, acknowledged that about 800 black Washingtonians had joined two battalions, but he insisted that "the objects of our organizations are benevolent, not political." The capital's black militiamen merely sought "to keep up the associations engendered by our companionship in camp," he wrote, and to "relieve the necessities of the widows and orphans of our comrades who fell in the late struggle for liberty." Fischer attempted to portray the militias as apolitical social organizations, but the reality—as black militiamen and their critics alike realized—was that the social or civic existence of militia organizations was tightly linked with their political and coercive power. In this sense, then, black Washingtonians who continued to form militias even without official approval made unambiguous claims to both civil and political equality.[120]

During 1865 and 1866, African Americans had transformed the public spaces of the District of Columbia, making it clear that, despite the congressional consensus on a narrow definition of "civil rights," they would continue to claim new prerogatives in an ever-greater array of spaces. Sometimes, as in the streetcar struggle, African Americans pressured Congress, and congressional action in turn cleared space for new popular claims. Other times, as in confrontations with the police, black Washingtonians pushed up against a rigid institution but continued to insist that their claims to dignity and a place in the civic body be acknowledged.

The public activism described in this chapter represented a variety of styles of engagement. It included confident and seasoned activists such as Augusta and Truth, well-connected first-timers like Kate Brown, and people whose names are lost to history but who attended Congress, marched in parades, and generally demanded a part in the civic life of the national capital. In his third autobiography, Frederick Douglass explained his sense of the dynamic between prominent individual protesters and the multitudes of people who stood with them in spirit, if not always in body. Douglass described how "friends" in antebellum New England had "liked very well to have me take passage on the first-class cars and be hauled out and pounded by rough-handed brakesmen, to make way for them." Douglass believed "that someone must lead the way, and that if the colored man would have his rights, he must take them."[121]

In Washington, men and women like Sojourner Truth, Kate Brown, Alexander Augusta, and Allen Bland helped lead the way. But others who made more anonymous claims on streetcars, in the militia, and in the streets also did much to create and claim new rights. Indeed, it was not just an elite few who pushed for an ever-broader definition of equality. Masses of African Americans marched, drilled, paraded, stepped onto streetcars, and entered hitherto forbidden spaces, all the while rejecting slavery's deferential postures. If this seems an overly romantic portrait of what might have been simply a question of showing up, sometimes for a party, remember that the regime of slavery had been intensely concerned with exactly these same matters: with the performance of deference and the regulation of people and space in the city. The ordinary African Americans who insisted that those days were over were, in effect, insisting that emancipation would mean little without a thorough obliteration of the laws and customs that had upheld slavery.

For all the dynamism of 1865 and 1866, however, one major issue remained entirely unresolved: whether the federal government would take a stand on African American men's right to vote. Congress had purposely excluded voting rights from the 1866 Civil Rights Act, and although the Fourteenth Amendment threatened diminished representation in Congress for states that prohibited black men from voting, it made no direct provision for black men's voting rights. The House had passed a bill for black men's enfranchisement in the capital in January 1866, but the Senate had not acted. Those who hoped Congress would move toward black men's enfranchisement were encouraged by the fall 1866 midterm elections, in which northern voters delivered a ringing victory to Republicans and a repudiation of Johnson's lenient policies toward ex-Confederates. The election results indicated that Americans could expect confident Republicans to return to Congress ready to remake Reconstruction policy with little regard for Johnson's preferences, and that voting rights for black men would receive serious consideration. Yet the issue of black men's enfranchisement had the potential to divide Republicans and to outrage conservatives. Indeed, the far-reaching importance of political power and the deep doubts of so many white Americans about African American men's capacity to properly wield the vote would make black men's enfranchisement the most divisive and passionately fought issue of any in this divisive and passionate period.

A parade designed by local Republicans to welcome the Thirty-ninth Congress back to Washington in early December 1866 seemed to forecast trouble. Turnout was much lower than expected, particularly among white organizations. The event was a "melancholy and deplorable failure," wrote the editor of the *National Republican*. While the "colored troops" had "turned out strong . . . the white end of the procession was very shabby in point of numbers." Julia Wilbur was surprised too, jotting in her diary, "Chilled through. Procession all Colored! . . . Where were the white societies advertised in the Programme?"[122] Where indeed? Perhaps white groups' failure to turn out suggested simmering divisions within the party. Perhaps Republicans' projected turn toward black men's enfranchisement was already weakening local whites' support. At the same time, hostile observers like William Owner saw in the parade further evidence of incipient chaos. "A decent white man was scarcely allowed to walk on the pavements, such was the insolence of the negroes, they were shoved off into the gutters," he seethed. "How long is this to be submitted to?"[123]

❖ ❖ ❖ ❖ ❖ ❖ 4 ❖ ❖ ❖ ❖ ❖ ❖

First among Them Is the Right of Suffrage

THE VOTE AND ITS CONSEQUENCES

One of the most peculiar and important facets of the struggle over African American men's right to vote was the insistence, by its opponents, that it would bring about "social equality." During the debate about black men's enfranchisement in the capital, Washington's *National Intelligencer*, a pro-Johnson newspaper, made clear the cascading connections so many conservatives saw between racial equality in voting rights and myriad other arenas. First, black men would obtain the right to vote, the paper predicted, and then Washington's white residents would "go to the polls with good conscience, with a crowd of ignorant and wretched blacks, who will throng here from Virginia and Maryland." From there, they would

> vote for negroes who might, by the hocus-pocus of caucus, out-wit
> and out-vote whites for a nomination; would distribute votes for them;
> rally their black friends to the polls; serenade them when successful;
> assist their ceremonious induction to office; recommend white men to
> hold offices under them; sit with them in grave councils; serve with them
> on juries; stand for long hours for audience for office-seeking purposes;
> mingle in the levees and in fashionable gatherings of "that set;" send
> their children to the same schools; and finally, not to particularize to the
> fatiguing point, have and hold all the relations in business or other as-
> sociations as if they were of the same race, blood, stock, or lineage.[1]

Black men's access to the vote, the editors believed, would lead inevitably down a slippery slope toward office holding, jury service, and ever-more-intimate spaces, to the point where African American men would "have and hold" whites in the most private of places.

Why would anyone have believed, or at least argued, that voting rights for

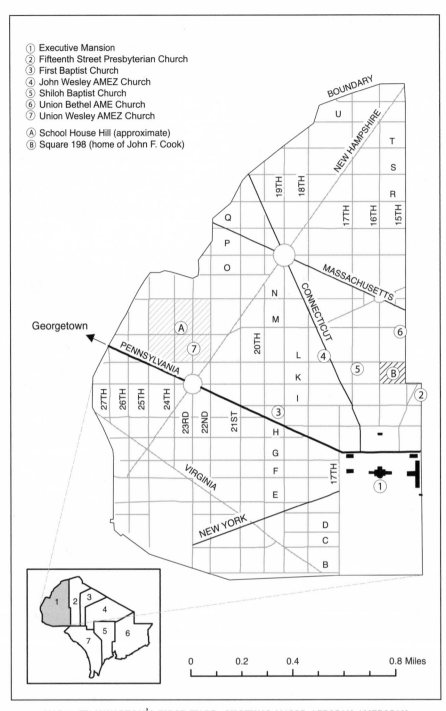

① Executive Mansion
② Fifteenth Street Presbyterian Church
③ First Baptist Church
④ John Wesley AMEZ Church
⑤ Shiloh Baptist Church
⑥ Union Bethel AME Church
⑦ Union Wesley AMEZ Church

Ⓐ School House Hill (approximate)
Ⓑ Square 198 (home of John F. Cook)

Georgetown

BOUNDARY

NEW HAMPSHIRE

MASSACHUSETTS

CONNECTICUT

PENNSYLVANIA

VIRGINIA

NEW YORK

0   0.2   0.4   0.8 Miles

MAP 3. WASHINGTON'S FIRST WARD, SHOWING MAJOR AFRICAN AMERICAN
CHURCHES AND OTHER LANDMARKS

black men would inevitably lead to racially mixed schools, associations, social events, and marriages? The logic of what contemporaries often called "social equality"—with its fantasies of proximity and equality between whites and blacks in a variety of increasingly intimate arenas—was so widespread and ultimately so powerful that it demands an explanation. Time and again, when African Americans argued that equality before the law must extend beyond the simple absence of discriminatory statutes and encompass public accommodations or public schools, their opponents insisted that they were demanding much-maligned social equality. In the debate about black men's enfranchisement, concerns were rampant that voting rights for black men would lead to racial equality in a range of other semipublic or private spaces. Some historians have argued that whites' fears about social equality reflected their anxieties about the prospect of sex, whether forced or consensual, between black men and white women. Others have written that condemnations of social equality were, in effect, rejections of the prospect that the government would intervene too heavily in private, economic relationships, acting to level class differences that almost all Americans agreed were natural and perhaps even necessary.[2]

Both perspectives help us understand what social equality meant to Americans in the mid-nineteenth century, but neither grasps the crux of the problem, which was the difficulty of determining where public life left off and private life began. It is no wonder that it was hard for contemporaries to draw this distinction; the realm of social relations and civil society had always been intimately connected with politics. Ostensibly private attributes such as wealth, respectability, or prestige had long been tied to public privileges, including the franchise. Many people continued to see the vote as a privilege that acknowledged a person's high standing in a community, whether that standing derived from his status as a taxpayer, as a property holder, or as a white man. Moreover, the culture of contemporary politics—which often involved picnics and barbeques and in which political meetings were regularly held in pubs, churches, and private meeting halls—promiscuously mingled social and associational life with public functions.[3] With no obvious delineation between the ostensibly public world of voting and political life and the private world of shared meals, social occasions, and civic organizations, it was difficult indeed for many contemporaries to imagine that black men's enfranchisement would *not* lead to upheavals in the most intimate areas of life.

As events in Washington would reveal, there was also some truth to the argument that black men, once enfranchised, would seek policies that favored an expansive vision of racial equality before the law. African Americans and radical whites did have a strong critique of the prevailing view that civil rights, narrowly conceived, were sufficient to guarantee African Americans' safety and opportunities to advance. Before the Civil War, many abolitionists had insisted not only that the franchise should be considered a right, not a privilege, but also that public schools and public accommodations should be open to African Americans on an equal footing with whites and that duties of citizenship such as service on juries and militias should be expected equally of black men and of white. Conservatives who charged that black men's enfranchisement would end in social equality no doubt foresaw that as voters, black men would support political candidates who favored expanding the realm of government-backed racial equality beyond civil rights as they were narrowly construed. And such would indeed be the case in Washington, where, after enfranchisement, African Americans and their white supporters demanded equal access to the city's restaurants and entertainment venues, to labor and professional associations, and to the whites-only public schools.

As they did so, however, they largely denied that they were seeking something called "social equality." Rather, those who supported black men's right to vote and an expansive vision of racial equality insisted that the public and private realms were strictly separate and that their demands, which they considered demands for meaningful political and civil equality, would not lead to the leveling of social distinctions. They argued that even if all men were made equal for political purposes they would remain manifestly unequal in private life. They also insisted that policies that prohibited racial discrimination in new areas, such as public schools and public accommodations, were not examples of government-enforced social equality, as opponents charged, but were in fact extensions of the principle of equality before the law. The case was clearest when it came to public schools, which owed their existence to local government and were funded by local taxes. But advocates of expansive equality before the law also insisted that streetcars, railroads, restaurants, and even labor and professional associations were essentially public institutions because they were chartered and regulated by government. Requiring such institutions to observe principles of racial equality was therefore consistent with the principle of equality before the law. It was appropriate public policy, not an untoward advance of government into private arenas.

Congress enacted universal manhood suffrage for the District of Columbia, over the veto of President Andrew Johnson, in January 1867. The congressional debate was lengthy and difficult. Early in 1866, congressional Republicans were divided on the issue, and later that year the Senate debate was diverted by a days-long discussion of voting rights for women. But when black men finally began to vote, in the spring of 1867, their voice in formal politics changed everything. Since the advent of emancipation, black Washingtonians had been arguing that freedom must entail not just the absence of slavery, but also respect for their associations and institutions and racial equality in public life. Now, African Americans could use their power as voters to demand concrete changes in municipal policy. With white voters divided between the two major parties, African Americans could wield considerable power if they voted together. Overcrowding and unemployment continued, and black laborers mobilized to insist on a fair share of employment on the public works. Members of Washington's free black elite allied themselves with freedpeople, confounding white conservatives who hoped class differences among African Americans would trump solidarities of race. Local African Americans had high hopes for the presidency of Ulysses S. Grant, who succeeded Johnson in the spring of 1869 and who seemed likely to use the chief executive's influence to further the Republican project of racial equality in public life. This was the apex of democratic possibility, the moment when it looked as if heretofore marginal visions of expansive equality before the law and universal standing and dignity might actually become a reality.

Claiming the Vote

The movement for voting rights for black men in the capital officially began with a massive rally on the grounds of the Executive Mansion on July 4, 1865. A collaborative effort between local black leaders and eminent black northerners, the gathering honored Sabbath school students and the memory of Abraham Lincoln, and it placed voting rights at the heart of the political agenda. In a speech to the assembled crowd of thousands of adults and children, Senator Henry Wilson of Massachusetts, a steadfast champion of emancipation and legal equality in the capital, noted that the mayor, Richard Wallach, was not in attendance. "I have a . . . dim idea," Wilson suggested, "that if you held the right of suffrage, Mayor Wallach and perhaps the whole city government would be here."[4] The senator urged the assembled group to petition Congress for the right to vote and promised to introduce suffrage legislation in the upcoming session. In the coming months, African Americans would mobilize a District-wide campaign for black men's enfranchisement, invoking both the Enlightenment tradition of equal individual rights and the more hierarchical view that voting was a privilege reserved for worthy individuals or groups.

Washington's African Americans were well prepared to organize for the vote, in no small measure because black churches provided a robust organizational infrastructure. Always hubs of associational life, the churches also had a long-standing tradition of cooperation across neighborhoods and denominations. Shortly after the July 4 festivities, leaders from several churches met at Second Baptist Church and created a United Franchise League. The group passed resolutions demanding "an equality of all our rights before the law, first among which is the right of suffrage." Reflecting its nondenominationalism, the organization planned to hold future meetings at Asbury Methodist and Israel AME churches. By the end of July it had fielded delegates from each of the city's wards and Georgetown and was organizing a petition to submit to Congress in the fall.[5]

Meanwhile, activists in the first ward formalized a First Ward Civil Rights Association, which sought to further develop African Americans' political voice. That the first ward emerged as the center of such organizing is not surprising. Encompassing the northwest side of town, from 15th Street to Rock Creek and south to the canal, the ward had the highest concentration of African Americans of any ward in the District. Dating from before the war, the ward was home to some of the District's most well-to-do black people, including government employees, teachers, and business owners. The ward boasted several politically and socially prominent churches, and a succession of African American private schools had been located on School House Hill, near Union Wesley AME Zion Church.[6] The first ward's black institutions and high concentration of relatively prosperous African American residents made it a particularly lively place for politics.

The First Ward Civil Rights Association developed a program for both political and economic action. While leaders worked on the voting rights petition for Congress, they also planned a boycott of businesses in their ward that did not support their political goals. Denouncing those who profited from African Americans' patronage and "yet invariably voted and threw their influence against them," the leadership encouraged the ward's African Americans to "turn their patronage to good account as political capital" by directing business toward "their friends and against their enemies." At the same time, the leaders advised members of their community "to organize and establish different kinds of business among themselves, and to stand by and help each other." Sources do not reveal the effectiveness of the boycott, but the description of the plan alone shows the ecumenism of the association's leadership. Leaders were thinking not only about racial equality in the wider community but also about black economic advancement and autonomy.[7]

By the end of November, African American leaders were assembling their monumental voting rights petition for submission to Congress. Ward by ward, committees met to adopt the memorial and obtain signatures from black residents. By early December the petition bore 2,500 signatures. The document was striking for drawing on both the Declaration of Independence and the vision of the vote as a privilege not a right. It began with the universal principle that "governments derive their just powers from the consent of the governed" and insisted that "the Colored American citizens of the District of Columbia are denied the benefits of this conceded principle." Yet the petition went on to link the right to vote with African Americans' taxpayer status, honest labor, and military service. It argued that "a large portion of the Colored citizens" were "property holders" and paid "no inconsiderable amount of taxes." They were hard-working people who obeyed the laws, and they had contributed over 3,500 enlisted men to the Union war effort.[8] The argument was not so much that freedom or even free manhood entitled black men to the vote, but rather that African Americans' virtues—as laborers, soldiers, and taxpayers—revealed them as collectively worthy of the vote.

When local municipal leaders responded with incredulity to the idea that African Americans would claim the vaunted category of "taxpayer" and otherwise insist on their collective high standing, John F. Cook Jr.—one of the most visible leaders of the voting rights movement—answered that the taxes paid by African Americans in his square of the first ward alone exceeded the amount that city council leaders claimed all black District residents paid. In a letter to the Republican *Chronicle*, Cook further argued that official tax totals, which usually included only levies on real estate, should also include taxes paid on personal property such as "carriages, vehicles of other description, licenses, &c." Cook, who owned considerable real estate himself, insisted that people who paid taxes on personal property contributed to the general well-being and should be understood as "taxpayers." Although he based much of his argument for voting rights on the taxpayer status of many of the District's black residents, Cook closed his letter by calling into question the link between economic status and the right to vote. It "might easily be shown," he suggested, "that in a government of the character of ours so large a body of men, whether property-owners or not, are entitled to every means of protection, the elective franchise being one of the greatest."[9]

The voting rights petition, as well as tabulations of the amount of property owned by black Washingtonians and evidence of their rich associational life, became powerful tools for African Americans' allies in Congress. In early January, Representatives James Wilson of Iowa and William Kelley of Pennsylvania described black Washingtonians' extensive schools, churches, and literary societies and the value of the property they held, both as individuals and as church organizations, as evidence that black Washingtonians were worthy of the right to vote. Later, when Lot Morrill, chair of the District of Columbia Committee, introduced the bill into the Senate, he alluded to the "memorials of some twenty-five hundred persons who style themselves colored citizens of the District of Columbia, citizens of the United States." The petitioners had emphasized, said Morrill, that they had served in the Union military forces, that "they are sufficiently intelligent to vote, industrious, [and] self-supporting," that they supported their own churches and common schools, and that they educated their children "without any aid from the general school fund."[10] Congressmen who supported black men's enfranchisement seemed to understand that they needed to make the case not on the grounds of abstract, universal rights, but rather in terms of the respectability and worthiness of the District's African Americans as a group.

Standing Up for This Little Community

The campaign for black men's enfranchisement in the capital provoked outrage from local newspaper editors, politicians, and other public figures, who believed the fabric of their community was on the verge of destruction. To reduce white Washingtonians' arguments against voting rights for black men to simple racism or to dismiss them as only so much political rhetoric would be to miss their significance. These commentators drew on crucial themes in American political thought. They mobilized not only a local history of frustration with Congress but also traditional arguments against suffrage expansion. And they added to that mix the newer problems of slave emancipation and the perceived threat of social equality. Conservatives thus created a powerful constellation of arguments that, although unsuccessful in the early postwar years, would later be mobilized to great effect.

To dramatize their opposition and argue for the principle of local sovereignty, the municipal governments of Washington and Georgetown decided to hold a vote on the question of black men's enfranchisement as Congress reconvened in December 1865. The capital's two most venerable local papers, the moderate *Evening Star* and the conservative *National Intelligencer*, urged an enthusiastic turnout to show Congress that local voters opposed black men's suffrage and to demonstrate support for President Johnson, who opposed congressional intervention in local election regulation, even in the District of Columbia.[11] The results of the poll gave numerical specificity to the powerful opposition to black enfranchisement among local whites. Of the 6,626 Washingtonians who voted, only 35 voted in favor of black men's enfranchisement. In Georgetown, 1 voter among 813 said yes. In both cities, turnout was large, allowing the city governments to claim that, as Americans entitled to self-government, local white residents deserved nothing less than to have their expressed wishes honored. The *Intelligencer* pointedly noted that the poll had been peaceful and added confidently that even committed Republicans had been seen voting against black suffrage.[12]

The confrontation between the local government and Congress was familiar in some ways. Local voters had often considered themselves subject to the whimsy of congressmen who lived in the District only a few months each year, paid little heed to local affairs, and were stingy in appropriating money for municipal improvements.[13] Before the war, however, city leaders had little cause to quibble with the congressional consensus on slavery and African Americans' rights. After all, Congress had been the bastion of what Don Fehrenbacher called the "slaveholders' republic," and its antebellum consensus had been to uphold slavery and the black codes in the nation's capital. Now, however, the issue was not simply congressional power per se, but also the fact that Congress threatened to subject white residents to the humiliation of sharing political power with African Americans or, at the extreme, the dreaded possibility of a government controlled by freedmen. "We are the veriest slaves on earth—at the mercy of fanatics and unscrupulous politicians," the *Constitutional Union* complained as Congress began the debate about black men's enfranchisement in the capital.[14]

Members of the local political and commercial elite were convinced that the enfranchisement of black men would destroy the very foundations of local government. There was "nothing so repugnant to this people as the conferring of the right of suffrage upon the negroes of this District," insisted Thomas E. Lloyd, chair of Washington's board of aldermen. It was horrible to imagine that "this little community, this Corporation organized only for the protection and improvement of property, should be controlled by contrabands flocking in from all quarters."[15] Lloyd was not alone in arguing that black men's enfranchisement would lead to economic catastrophe and civilizational decline. The

National Intelligencer insisted that voting rights for black men must lead to the "manifest hurt, if not destruction, of every monetary interest and all the other things pertaining to society in an age of exalted civilization and refinement."[16] And, drawing on a similar language of civilizational progress and regression, the *Evening Star* speculated that black enfranchisement would render "the national capital a negro Utopia," making Washington look like "the capital of Dahomey rather than a civilized nation."[17] Many news outlets predicted that the damage would be compounded by white laborers, who would lash out against the elevation of black men to their political stature. The *Intelligencer* forecast that white laborers around the country would "sympathize with their depressed brethren here" and vote to unseat congressmen who supported black men's enfranchisement.[18] Threatening "revolutionary redress," the newspaper noted, "If all legal forms of relief and protection fail . . . *we have a war of races in prospect.*"[19]

Perhaps most revealing of conservatives' strategies was their use of the concept of social equality. In law and in popular political culture, contemporaries often used three categories to discuss the appropriate contents and limitations of legal equality: civil, political, and social. Although the categories had existed before the war, they took on increased importance as legislators and ordinary people sought to determine how far the government would go to legislate equality. People used social equality as a gloss for inappropriate government interference in relationships that should properly be considered private matters of personal taste. Maryland senator Reverdy Johnson, for example, argued in 1864 that mandating racial integration on the capital's streetcars amounted to a social equality measure. Protection of African Americans' "life and property" was one thing, he argued, but the question of "political rights and social enjoyment" was quite another. The former was a properly legal matter, he insisted, while the latter was an issue of the natural or God-given "preference on our part for the society of those whom we deem God has created our equals."[20]

The social equality shibboleth had particular power in the case of voting rights. Democratic opponents of black men's enfranchisement repeatedly argued that voting rights for black men would lead to an inexorable slide toward other kinds of more private or intimate equality between races. The *Intelligencer* claimed that if black men in the capital were granted "that most exalted privilege of citizenship . . . equality in the holding of offices and in the social condition will follow as 'the light to the day.'" In the Senate, Garrett Davis of Kentucky insisted, "The races are either equal or unequal. . . . If they are equal, they not only have the right to vote, but they have the right to be eligible to all offices; they not only have the right to civil protection and to enjoy all civil rights, but they are entitled also to all political and all social rights."[21] With their repeated references to social rights and social equality, Democrats argued that black men's enfranchisement threatened to explode conventions of white supremacy and black deference in every realm. That prospect was particularly galling to those who believed race was a biological, natural category that determined people's basic character and influenced their private choices about whom to affiliate with. In their minds, policies that would lead to social equality were offenses against nature itself.

Not only did Democrats invoke the social realm frequently; they also sought to define it as broadly as possible. The *Intelligencer*, in its extreme opposition to black men's enfranchisement, even called "negro suffrage" in the District a "purely social question" as a way of arguing that Congress had no business legislating on it.[22] In fact, the genius and power of the discourse of social equality was that it evoked a large and amorphous realm—whether social or private or sociable—where Americans had long imagined that they had liberty to choose with whom to associate. Against the backdrop of expanding political democracy, some had sought to separate the "social" from the "political" and to insist that the social realm was one of exclusivity, choice, and taste. For example, the author of an antebellum New York society manual, reflecting on the differences between democracy in political life and exclusivity in "society," stated that political equality "did not extend to the drawing-room." She continued: "None are excluded from the highest councils of the nation, but it does not follow that all can enter into the highest ranks of society."[23] Similarly, during Reconstruction, the radical *Chronicle* used two stereotypical New York neighborhoods to dramatize the distinction between appropriate political equality and dreaded social equality. "Fifth avenue and the Five Points are politically equal," an editorial commented, "but in a social point of view they are as far removed from each other as the poles."[24]

As the *Chronicle*'s comments suggest, radical Republicans usually denied that black men's enfranchisement would lead to social equality. Indeed, almost no one openly supported social equality because the term implied the overthrow of cherished ideas about taste, choice, and social distinction. Radical Republicans instead attempted to draw a strict line between certain kinds of rights—which they called political and civil and which they supported—and social rights or equality, which they did not. Political equality was "regulated by law," while social equality was "outside the arena of legislation," the *Chronicle* argued. "Congress might as well attempt to legislate upon a man's daily habits as to pass a law regulating his social relations, or prescribing the character of the company he shall keep." Meanwhile, if political equality would inevitably lead to social equality, as conservatives charged, then why did those conservatives not invite "into their parlors" some of the "thousands of ignorant foreigners" who had equal privileges at the ballot box? That they did not, radicals claimed, revealed the social equality argument as a fallacy.[25]

To be sure, radical Republicans, and particularly African American activists, sought complete removal of all references to race or color in laws, including marriage laws, and insisted that African Americans must have equal access to schools, restaurants, and theaters and sometimes also churches and cemeteries. Yet few did so by affirming that they sought something called "social equality" or "social rights." For most black activists, it was both dangerous and unappealing to risk being misconstrued as promoting not only black men's sexual access to white women but also government-led destabilization of hierarchies of class, taste, and culture—hierarchies that many black leaders themselves believed important. Instead, they sought to place their claims—whether for equal access to streetcars and railroads, or to voting rights, public schools, or first-class accommodations—within the domain of civil or political rights and thus fit them into a broad vision of equality before the law.

Proponents of voting rights for black men eventually won the day, but over the longer term, the objections conservatives raised in the 1865 and 1866 debate over black men's enfranchisement would prove powerful. As black men began voting and became a crucial part of the Republican coalition in the city, conservatives continued to profess concern that the political change would have devastating economic consequences. At the same time, as African Americans increasingly demanded access to conventionally white arenas, including public accommodations and the white public schools, opponents continued to charge them with foolishly seeking to obliterate all distinctions of class and race. As it turned out, the discourse of social equality offered potent language for limiting Reconstruction's most racially progressive possibilities.

The Wide Sea of Universal Manhood Suffrage

In Congress, the question of voting rights for black men in the nation's capital generated a wide-ranging debate that touched on virtually all the facets of the issue. In the House debate in January 1866, Republicans divided on whether all black men should be allowed to vote, or whether qualifications should be imposed. When the Senate debated the matter, almost a year later, moderate

Republicans had come to the conclusion that black men's enfranchisement was crucial for a meaningful Reconstruction policy. Leading Republicans pitched the right to vote as a virtually universal entitlement, while opponents of black men's enfranchisement questioned why the Republicans did not favor voting rights for women as well. By the time Congress passed universal manhood suffrage for the District of Columbia over President Johnson's veto, on January 8, 1867, Americans rightly saw the move as a harbinger of Reconstruction policies to come.

During the House debate, moderate Republicans made a serious effort to limit black men's suffrage by requiring literacy, military service, or taxpayer status. Indeed, the far-reaching implications of black men's enfranchisement made the issue divisive among Republicans. As a matter of principle, only the most radical white Republicans favored unqualified or "universal" manhood suffrage. Other Republicans favored special restrictions on black men that did not apply to white men, as Abraham Lincoln had proposed for Reconstruction in Louisiana in 1865, or they supported "impartial" suffrage, which allowed for restrictions on men's voting rights, but not by race. The capital's pro-Johnson Republican newspaper, the *National Republican*, supported qualified suffrage for black men, which it said would bolster the "orderly and industrious" element of "the colored population which makes such a large portion of our numbers." Voicing widespread fears that slavery had rendered African Americans unfit for the full rights enjoyed by whites, the *Republican* argued that universal manhood suffrage would only make the masses of African Americans "'puppets' of political shows and intrigues" as they were "tossed about like a shuttlecock from one political battledore to another."[26]

During three days of intense debate in the House, however, radical Republicans (led by Pennsylvanian Thaddeus Stevens) and Democrats alike rejected proposals for qualified suffrage. In the end, these unlikely allies joined in voting for a universal franchise bill that simply removed the word "white" from all local laws "prescribing the qualifications for electors for any office." The radicals truly favored the bill; the Democrats gambled, unwisely as it turned out, that forcing a vote on unqualified manhood suffrage would divide the Republicans sufficiently to sink the bill or, at least, result in passage of a bill that revealed the Republicans' dangerous extremism.[27]

The scene at the capital was striking. African American spectators turned out in force to witness the proceedings, and when the bill passed by a large margin, the chamber echoed with the jubilant shouts of "black and white, women and men." Gratification on one side was mirrored by devastation on another.

The *Evening Star* linked the twin specters of black rights and federal power, noting facetiously that the ebullient crowd heralded the "'glorious dawn' of negro equality and negro centralization." A correspondent for the *New York Herald* graphically represented fears of social equality in his description of the scene: "Coming down from the galleries big darkies jostled loftily against the high born dames of this District and trod upon their drapery with an air of divine right. In the street cars they hobnobbed with successful Congressmen and grinned familiarly in the faces of the heretofore ruling race."[28] Even the prospect of the right to vote, this writer suggested, made black men feel they had license to violate all manner of familiar hierarchies of race, sex, and class. The implication was clear: If enfranchised, black men would demolish such hierarchies, elevating themselves as "divine" while attacking conventions of gender and respectability and demeaning American democracy itself.

Nothing changed immediately after the House passed the District of Columbia suffrage bill. The Senate had yet to take up the matter and was busy with other Reconstruction issues. The lull during the volatile winter of 1866 gave partisans the chance to take the issue to a national audience, making it a proxy in the intensifying war between Congress and the president. Radicals applauded the bill and hoped that its passage signaled a broader turn by Congress toward enfranchising black men in the ex-Confederate states. The *Chicago Tribune* observed how Congress had once again made the District of Columbia a laboratory for antislavery policy: "As with the abolition of the slave trade, and of slavery, the District of Columbia is made the test case—the entering wedge. The policy which is carried out there, will in due time be extended to the entire country."[29] Opponents hoped that was not the case. Pro-Johnson newspapers noted that northern states had repeatedly rejected referenda on black suffrage and condemned congressmen for seeking to impose on the District policies they would never pursue in their own states. The president's supporters deluged him with letters advising him to stand fast against black men's enfranchisement. It was a "monstrous" prospect, one correspondent wrote, but must be handled carefully, for it "is a great national question." Johnson likely did not need much persuading, and in late January he told a group of senators that the bill was "ill-timed, uncalled for, and calculated to do great harm."[30]

Although a Republican coalition in favor of universal manhood suffrage was developing, many white Republicans nonetheless remained ambivalent about a policy that would acknowledge that all men—regardless of race, class, or respectability—were entitled to the right to vote. A cartoon in *Harper's Weekly* visually suggested how even Republicans who supported universal manhood suffrage could not quite let go of the significance of such distinctions in public life. The cartoon showed an eminently respectable (and light-skinned) African American woman riding in a Washington streetcar next to a brutally caricatured Irish woman who seemed completely unaware of—or unable to comply with—the demand for respectable comportment on common carriers. Indeed, the fish she carried not only evoked the Catholic custom of eating fish on Fridays but also suggested an offensive odor in the confined space of the car. Through its caption, the cartoon contrasted the egalitarian space of the Washington streetcars—integrated the year before by congressional legislation and African Americans' sustained efforts—to the continuing exclusion of black men from formal politics. The caption read, "Mr. McCaffraty Voted against Negro Suffrage," presumably an allusion to the December canvass held by the Washington government. The implication, of course, was that it was absurd to allow the likes of Mr. McCaffraty to participate in politics while excluding people like the black woman's husband, who seemed far more worthy of political equality. Yet for all of its overt support of black men's voting rights, the cartoon also played to the conventional view that respectable comportment made people worthy of rights. By contrasting a respectable black woman with a disheveled Irish woman, the cartoon implicitly questioned not only whether the likes of Mr. McCaffraty deserved the right to vote, but also whether destitute freedpeople did as well.

The tumultuous politics of 1866 ultimately allowed the District of Columbia suffrage bill to succeed. The Senate took up the bill that spring but postponed discussion, in part because the bill's sponsor was ill and probably in part because supporters thought the bill more likely to pass after the fall elections. In those midterm elections, northern voters overwhelmingly voiced support for congressional Republicans and against the president, expressing approval of congressional passage of the Civil Rights Act and the Fourteenth Amendment and rejecting Johnson's lenience toward former Confederates. Meanwhile, the intransigence of white southern leaders became clear as southern state legislatures one by one refused to ratify the Fourteenth Amendment. Congressional Republicans realized they must shift course in order to secure meaningful change in the former Confederacy. Thus, when the Senate finally debated the District of Columbia franchise bill, in December 1866, it was a new day in national politics. And although congressional Republicans continued to honor principles of federalism in their policies toward the states, they had no reason to be concerned about that issue when it came to the capital.[31]

Lot Morrill, the chair of the Senate committee on the District of Columbia,

FIGURE 4.1. "Holy Horror of Mrs. McCaffraty in a Washington City Street Passenger Car. [Mr. McCaffraty Voted *against* Negro Suffrage.]" *Harper's Weekly*, February 24, 1866, 128. Courtesy Library of Congress.

reintroduced the bill with considerable fanfare in December 1866. Morrill was one of those moderate Republicans who were swayed by developments in the South that year. A former governor of Maine, Morrill had immediately joined the Senate's committee on the District of Columbia when he became a senator in 1861 and became its chair in December 1865. In the winter of 1866, Morrill had supported qualified suffrage for all men, not universal manhood suffrage. By the end of the year, however, he declared a new vision of national cohesion founded upon the equal rights of all individuals: "The bond of our national unity is not expressed by epithets 'rights of States,' 'State sovereignty,' 'community rights;' . . . but in unity of faith in human rights, unity of spirit and purpose for the development and protection of individual rights." Morrill proclaimed that "human rights" and "individual rights" guaranteed by the federal government would now replace old status hierarchies of slavery and servitude enforced through tyrannies large and small. "All attempts in this country to keep alive the old idea of orders of men, distinctions of class, noble and ignoble, superior and inferior, antagonism of races," he argued, "are so many efforts at insurrection and anarchy."[32]

Morrill's sweeping pronouncement provoked much opposition. Voicing a traditional argument against suffrage expansion, West Virginia senator Waitman T. Willey maintained that imagining all individual male citizens on equal footing was a dangerous fallacy and that literacy and property qualifications were crucial for ensuring good government.[33] Other senators emphatically brought race to the fore. Senator Garrett Davis of Kentucky, for example, argued that the elevation of African Americans to equal citizenship status with whites was an affront to the natural order of things, and he cited as evidence the "primitive" conditions of African life, the supposed failure of self-government by people of African descent in Haiti and the British West Indies, and the divinely ordained order of the "races."[34]

If arguments for the racial inferiority of people of African descent were by now predictable, Pennsylvania senator Edgar Cowan's argument for women's enfranchisement was much more novel, at least in the U.S. Senate chamber. Cowan, a very conservative Republican, took his cue from woman suffrage leaders such as Elizabeth Cady Stanton, who, along with other suffragists, saw the postwar debate about the meaning of the vote as an opportunity to press for voting rights for all women as well as for all men. At the first postwar national women's rights convention, held in New York the previous spring, woman suffragists had lamented that the second section of the Fourteenth Amendment promised to reduce the congressional representation of any state that denied its otherwise qualified "*male* inhabitants" of "the right to vote." The Constitution had never before specified that men were more entitled to the vote than women.[35] Indeed, out of frustration with Republicans' support of "universal" voting rights for men only, some leading suffragists were entertaining the idea of seeking alliance with Democrats, who vehemently opposed voting rights for black men.

Like the woman suffragists, Cowan rightly saw a contradiction in the Republicans' argument for a polity without classes. Cowan declared himself opposed to any change in voting rights laws but added, "If we are to adventure ourselves upon this wide sea of universal suffrage, I object to manhood suffrage. I do not know anything specially about manhood which dedicates it to this purpose more than exists about womanhood."[36] "Female suffrage," Cowan added, might help mitigate the baleful effects of "negro suffrage." Invoking conventional ideas about women's peaceful, moral natures, he insisted "that if there is any one influence in the country which will break down this tribal antipathy, which will make the two races one in political harmony and political action . . . it is the fact that woman and not man must interfere in order to smooth the pathway for these two races to go along harmoniously together." Cowan even cited approvingly two woman suffragists, Frances Gage and Susan B. Anthony, who had recently argued that women ought not be subjected to taxation without representation.[37]

Cowan's proposal initiated a three-day Senate debate over the logic of race and sex restrictions on voting rights, a debate woman suffrage activists watched with great interest.[38] Some senators argued that polling places themselves were no place for women, or at least not for *their* women. Reverdy Johnson of Maryland, for example, opined: "I do not think the ladies of the United States would agree to enter into a canvass and to undergo what is often the degradation of seeking to vote, particularly in the cities, getting up to the polls, crowded out and crowded in. I rather think they would feel it, instead of a privilege, a dishonor."[39] Ohioan Benjamin Wade, one of the few senators to argue extensively and sincerely for woman suffrage, insisted that no city's political culture—not even Baltimore's—was "so barbarous and rude that a lady could not go to the polls to perform a duty which the law permitted without insult and rudeness."[40] Woman suffragists had been making such arguments for some time, but in the staid Senate, Wade was in a tiny minority.

Senate conservatives who pushed for women's enfranchisement in the capital knew full well that most Republicans opposed it. Predictably, then, Morrill considered the injection of the woman suffrage question "ridiculous and absurd" and demanded a decision on the original question: black men's enfranchisement.[41] Revealing the limitations of his individualism, Morrill contended that extending suffrage rights to women "would contravene all our notions of the family; 'put asunder' husband and wife, and subvert the fundamental principles of family government, in which the husband is, by all usage and law, human and divine, the representative head." Even Wade said that regardless of the nuances of abstract principle, black men now needed the vote to protect African Americans as a group (including women and children), in a way that women as a group did not.[42]

Cowan's gambit succeeded in revealing that most Republicans' universalism was for men only. In other respects it failed. The Senate rejected his proposal and then passed the District of Columbia voting rights bill by a vote of 32 to 13, with seven members absent.[43] At this juncture, the matter of voting rights for women had none of the same political urgency as voting rights for black men in the South. Republican legislators would not be persuaded to take an unpopular stand on principle, when partisan or perhaps even national survival was at stake. Theoretically, legislators could have made the District an exemplar of universal suffrage rights for both men and women. In fact, as the next chapter will show, woman suffragists continued to push them to do just that. Yet, as the debate over Cowan's amendment revealed, most Republican legislators believed conventional gender relations were more important than theoretical consistency. Fantasies of homes torn asunder, gender roles inverted, and senators' oft-mentioned "wives and daughters" degraded in the unruly, masculine space of the hustings made it difficult for senators to take woman suffrage seriously.

President Johnson duly vetoed the District suffrage bill, offering a lengthy treatise against black men's enfranchisement. Echoing the arguments of the city's white elite, Johnson insisted that if black men were permitted to vote, the city would be deluged with new black migrants, freedpeople would be subject to coercion by "designing persons," and race war would ensue. On the authority of "the people who are daily witnesses of their mode of living," the president stated that black Washingtonians were "not yet competent to serve as electors, and thus become eligible for office." He also drew a bright line between civil and political rights. Citing the 1866 Civil Rights Act, he argued that black Americans already "possess[ed] the 'full and equal benefit of all the laws and proceedings for the security of person and property as is enjoyed by white citizens." By contrast, the ballot was "a privilege and a trust." "To give it indiscriminately to a new class, wholly unprepared by previous habits and opportunities to perform the trust which it demands, is to degrade it, and finally to destroy its power."[44]

Many Americans applauded the veto and the principles that supported it, but Republicans in Congress promptly overrode it. A broad coalition was now strong enough to defeat the president, even on the controversial matter of black men's enfranchisement. Once again, Republicans in Congress had chosen to use the capital as a laboratory for policy experimentation. When it came to the former Confederate states, the question of voting rights for black men was complicated not only by divisions on the issue itself but also by concerns about party building in the South, about punishing ex-Confederates, and about maintaining an appropriate balance between federal power and the prerogatives of the states. Because Congress's jurisdiction in the capital was "exclusive," policy toward the District was far more straightforward. Congress would move on to mandate universal manhood suffrage in newly forming western territories. Months later, black men's enfranchisement in the former Confederacy would become a reality, with passage (again over Johnson's veto) of the Reconstruction Act, which placed the former Confederate states under military rule while new state governments organized under the principle of universal manhood suffrage. The "loyal" border states of Missouri, Kentucky, Delaware, and Maryland were permitted to keep their civil governments intact, giving African Americans and white Republicans there fewer chances to build political power.[45] Neither a state nor part of the former Confederacy, the District of Columbia was not included in the federal Reconstruction Act. Yet, as in the former Confederacy, in the capital Congress overrode the sentiments of a majority of local whites by providing for the enfranchisement of African American men.

A Fair Share

Immediately after Congress passed the Act to Regulate the Elective Franchise, black Washingtonians and their white Republican allies began mobilizing for the upcoming municipal elections. Black and white Republican organizers moved from ward to ward, assembling groups and preparing them to register and vote. One newspaper correspondent noted that black Washingtonians had "made a thorough canvass of the city" and were creating a "list of all who were to be challenged as having been active rebels." Josephine Griffing, a freedmen's relief worker who was promoting freedpeople's migration out of the capital, reported that men refused to leave "till after the first of June, when they will vote." The capital's African Americans were a diverse lot, separated by education, wealth, and experiences in slavery and freedom, but they quickly united under the Republican banner.[46]

Black men's enfranchisement ushered in a period of extraordinary change. At roughly one-third of the population, African Americans entered politics as a significant bloc and, at least at first, voted together. Newly minted black voters worked with white colleagues to elect Republicans to office, and black Washingtonians coalesced across classes to demand a fair share of public works employment. At the same time, however, African American men's entry into formal politics did not mean ceding independent institutions or conforming to the agendas set forth by white political leaders. To the contrary, as a controversy over policy concerning the black public schools reveals, black Washingtonians continued to contemplate adopting independent political positions and continued to use churches as spaces of independent political debate.

Black church buildings became hubs for Republican politics immediately after enfranchisement. Churches had long served not just as houses of worship but also as centers of intellectual and cultural life as well as mutual aid and poor relief. Now black Washingtonians turned church buildings to the service of formal politics. Israel AME Church near the Capitol, Wesley Zion in southwest Washington, Third Baptist in the fourth ward, and many others played host to early meetings of local Republicans, both black and white. Pastors and church elders often attended, and when participants became rowdy, it was not uncommon for someone to remind the assembly to respect the building as a house of worship.[47]

The change since the prewar days was dramatic. Black codes had once required African Americans to obtain white people's permission to hold church services and other meetings. Now black Washingtonians invited whites into their spaces as political equals. Holding meetings in black churches moved the sociable rituals of politics into black spaces, giving greater authority to African American elders and political activists than they would have had as strangers in "white" buildings. Church buildings also linked the decidedly male culture of party politics to the broader African American community. Although newspaper accounts of Republican meetings do not mention women attending, churches were used for so many activities—including Sabbath schools, day schools, clubs, and choirs—that meetings there probably brought party activities close to nonvoters in the community.[48]

The nation watched closely as the District's black men went to the polls, first in Georgetown on February 25 and three months later in the city of Washington. The police braced for "violent demonstrations, riot, and bloodshed," and black voters began assembling before dawn to ensure that they would have access to the polling place come daylight. In the end, predictions of violence and harassment by "roughs and bullies" proved unfounded.[49] Still, there was a clear sense that black men were being put to the test. Amid arguments that most black men were not sufficiently educated or civilized, black voters had to demonstrate that they were entitled to what many still considered the *privilege* of the franchise. Their supporters were pleased at the result. After the Georgetown election, one reporter noted approvingly that black voters "approached and departed from the polls" with "dignity and decorum."[50] James A. Handy, the pastor at Union Bethel, praised Washington's black voters in similar language. "Forgetting the injustice of the past, they dealt with the present as *men*," he reported. "Thus acting, they compelled old citizens of this District . . . to say that the conduct of the black citizens in exercising the franchise, for quietness, fairness, noble-bearing, and gentlemanly conduct has no equal in the political history of this city."[51] Julia Wilbur, an abolitionist and woman suffragist, noted that the act of voting seemed to transform the newly enfranchised: "Each man after depositing his vote looked several inches taller as he walked away," she wrote in her diary. "His countenance beamed with a new light. It was to me *intensely interesting*."[52]

The act of voting meant a great deal, but the results of the election were important too. In Washington's first biracial election, the Republican coalition of African Americans and whites, many of whom were northerners by birth, succeeded in electing the city collector, register, and surveyor, as well as four of seven aldermen and thirteen of twenty-one councilmen. Considering the party had been a negligible force in local politics until then, this was a note-worthy accomplishment. All the newly elected officials were white, in part be-cause the city's charter still contained a racial restriction on office holding. The new council, however, appointed black men to several high-profile positions, and that summer the secretary of interior decided to appoint the first African American member of the Board of Trustees of Colored Schools.[53] It was clear that the conservative hold on city politics was beginning to crack and that more robust definitions of racial equality in public life were in the offing.

In a valedictory address to the city council, William W. Moore, the outgo-ing president of the Board of Common Council, took special note of the alli-ance between freedpeople and members of the city's long-standing black elite that had made the Republican success possible. Black property owners ought to have joined with the white elite to elect politicians who would "assist in protecting their home and employments from dangerous innovations," Moore argued. Yet they had cast their lot with the freedmen and, in his view, thus "proved themselves callous to those higher virtues which most exalt and en-noble manhood." Indeed, it seemed to him that the "better informed portion of the African race residing in this city" had joined with the freedpeople "for the purpose of overshadowing the white race, and wresting from them all political power."[54] Moore's comments echoed the "race war" rhetoric common among conservatives, but his central observation was apt: members of the black elite had indeed chosen to make freedpeople their political allies.

The issue that most effectively solidified that political alliance was public works employment. Finding and keeping work in the city was an acute prob-lem for all African Americans, skilled and unskilled alike. The huge migrant population suffered from serious underemployment. Nor could black skilled

FIGURE 4.2a. "The Georgetown Election—The Negro at the Ballot Box." Partisan lines are clearly drawn in this illustration. A black man votes for the Republican candidate, while a top-hatted white Republican looks on. President Andrew Johnson clings to his veto, and a Confederate veteran stands supportively beside him. *Harper's Weekly*, March 16, 1867, 172. Courtesy Library of Congress, LC-USZ62-100971.

FIGURE 4.2b. "Significant Election Scene at Washington." In this scene, black men stand in line to vote and another black man serves as an election judge. *Harper's Weekly*, June 22, 1867, 397. Courtesy Library of Congress.

laborers hope to find support from their white counterparts in unions. After the war ended, the capital's white skilled laborers organized cross-craft working-men's assemblies and lobbied employers for an eight-hour workday. Government employees—both skilled craftsmen and white-collar clerks—demanded that the federal government take the lead in instituting an eight-hour day.[55] But white workingmen's organizations did not welcome black members, nor did economic realities in the capital lend themselves to the formation of black-only or interracial unions. In more industrial and commercial southern cities like Baltimore, Richmond, and Charleston, black laborers—often with support from local Republican politicians—organized and often struck for higher wages and better hours.[56] In the capital, however, there were no major industrial worksites, such as docks or factories, where black laborers could coalesce in black-only or interracial craft unions.

Such conditions made public works employment all the more important for African Americans. As voters, black men could pressure the city government to distribute patronage to them or risk losing their political support. Fair treatment in the distribution of public work could help black day laborers, skilled workers, and contractors, all of whose private sector opportunities were undercut by white organizations that excluded them. Thus, on the eve of the 1867 election, seventh-ward resident Anthony Bowen tied political change to greater economic opportunities for black men, stating his hope "that the time would soon come when a change would occur in the municipal government, and the colored man would have an equal chance with the whites to gain a living in this city."[57]

Anthony Bowen was one among many relatively prosperous black Washingtonians who recognized that a political alliance with freedmen would redound to everyone's benefit. Born a slave in Prince George's County, Maryland, Bowen had purchased his freedom and moved to the capital as a teenager, in roughly 1826. Having learned to read and write, he secured work as a laborer in the U.S. Patent Office. He was also an AME Zion minister, a leader in Sabbath school organizations, and the founder of the nation's first African American YMCA. Like many other literate free black Washingtonians, Bowen was poised to exert considerable leadership as emancipation dawned. And, like many others, he involved himself deeply in the affairs of freedpeople, notwithstanding his own relatively secure economic circumstances. Indeed, many members of the black elite did not consider migrant freedpeople their social or educational equals, but in politics they cast their lot with the maligned "contrabands," forging an alliance based on their perceptions of shared economic interests, racial solidarity, and in some cases a commitment to racial uplift.[58]

Fortunately for those who hoped that black men could use their newfound political power to obtain public works employment in the capital, substantial infrastructure improvements were in the offing. No one could deny that the city needed help. The masses of soldiers, horses, and armaments that had passed through the capital during the war had wreaked havoc on the city's already notorious streets. Moreover, local businessmen were determined to fight an effort, led by western boosters, to move the national capital west of the Mississippi River. The greatest obstacle to improvements remained what it had always been: the municipal governments' paucity of funds. Yet times had changed. Following the heightened patriotism of the Civil War, the capital enjoyed new affection and respect, and Republicans in Congress, with their broad interests in infrastructure improvement and economic development, were sympathetic to enterprising Washingtonians' desire to improve the city.[59]

The question was how African Americans and their white Republican allies could ensure that black men were given a fair share of public works employment. Mayor Wallach had a reputation for doing business with contractors who used the city's relatively large population of Irish immigrants and people of Irish descent as their pool of unskilled laborers and who refused to hire black men. Yet Wallach evidently understood that new black voters must be cultivated, and before the 1867 election his administration made noises about distributing public work to African Americans. That spring, the city council also passed a law requiring laborers "of the Corporation" to be paid at least $2.00 per day, a nod to the white organized labor movement but a policy that hypothetically stood to benefit black laborers as well.[60]

Thus it was that black mechanics and laborers began to organize independent associations in the summer of 1867. Black activists in the first ward founded the Lincoln Radical Republican Laboring Association, which planned to build the movement throughout the city and to lobby the municipal government for a fair distribution of city employment. The association, composed of both skilled and unskilled laborers, insisted that black laborers receive one-third of the city contracts, in proportion to the black population in the city. Under the leadership of Alexander Henderson, members of the group investigated the city's public works projects "and found that colored men were not employed as a general rule." A committee visited Mayor Wallach, who informed them that responsibility lay with the ward-based commissioners of public works. The commissioners in turn blamed the mayor. The organization also publicized the fact that after the spring elections laborers who voted Republican had been subjected to reprisals from employers.[61]

By December, the black labor movement had generated enough momentum to hold a mass meeting of "colored workingmen" from across the District, with a goal of obtaining "a fair share of employment upon the public works." With help from J. Sayles Brown, a white Republican activist, black labor leaders attempted to persuade Congress to get involved.[62] At the mass meeting, they debated a petition that described in considerable detail the challenges black laborers faced in the capital. "There is still such prejudice against our color, and especially against our condition as freed people of color, that we are excluded from almost every sphere of employment except those which are burdensome, temporary, and menial in character," the document explained. White laborers would not work alongside them unless blacks occupied a subservient position. Contractors yielded to such discrimination, "although it is against their real interests and that of every citizen, as they have now to buy their labor, much of it, in a market where there is no competition, and the few control it for their own profit." Addressing stereotypes against the newly freed, the petition added, "Prejudiced and unthinking people speak of us as 'hordes of lazy contrabands' and as 'idle negroes,' while they little know our desire for honest employment and the difficulty we find in obtaining it." The petitioners requested not direct aid but, rather, "that men may be put in charge of this public work who are not unfriendly to our people, and who will give us a fair share of the employment under their direction." After considerable debate, the mass meeting adopted the petition. In the coming weeks, almost 5,000 laborers would sign on.[63]

Alexander Henderson and the black laborers' petition adopted a language of basic justice, not of civil rights, because the concept of equality before the law, as it was then interpreted, did not support a right to nondiscriminatory employment opportunities. Mainstream ideas about civil rights held that African Americans had an equal right to enter into contracts and have them honored, but that did not mean they would have an equal opportunity to be considered for employment. The decision of whom to hire remained in the hands of the employer, even if that employer was the city government or its contractors. Indeed, no one argued that a public employer like the city government must not consider race when hiring. Organized black laborers thus demanded not a *right* to be hired but rather "a *fair share* of the public work, considering their numbers and necessities."[64]

Black laborers made little headway until Sayles J. Bowen was elected mayor of Washington in June 1868, at which point the political climate changed dramatically. A native of upstate New York, Bowen had come to Washington in 1845 to take a clerkship in the Treasury Department. He was active in Republican politics from the party's earliest days, and after Lincoln's inauguration he held several local federal appointments before being made D.C. postmaster in 1863, a position he retained until becoming mayor. Bowen was close enough with Republicans in Congress to have their ear in proposing legislation, and he took credit for having authored the 1862 law establishing public schools for black children in the capital. He was active in local freedmen's relief work, served on the original board of trustees of colored schools, and led the fight to force Wallach's administration to relinquish funds owed to the black schools. When Bowen became a vocal supporter of universal manhood suffrage in the capital, friends of President Johnson tried to have him removed from the postmastership.[65]

Like many white Republicans of this era, Bowen was often accused by his enemies of being incompetent and corrupt. It is true that Bowen was politically ambitious, but he was also committed to principles of legal and political equality, as well as to economic fairness for freedpeople. Sometimes his ambition generated skepticism about his motives. For instance, when Bowen, serving as a trustee of the colored schools, hired three black teachers in the spring of 1867, Emma V. Brown, herself an African American teacher, commented to a friend, "Mr Bowen's sudden preference for colored teachers is easily accounted for. Colored men can vote now. Mr B. hopes to be mayor so say folks."[66] Bowen also cultivated connections with black voters in late 1867, when he helped found the Lincoln Cooperative Building and Deposit Association, a savings and loan organization for freedpeople that held monthly meetings in African American churches.[67] By 1868, when he challenged Wallach for the mayoralty, he was an apt representative of white radicalism in Washington. He had been in the capital long enough to avoid being considered a complete outsider, and his close ties with northern Republicans and his long-standing efforts on behalf of dignity and equality for African Americans made him a popular choice for both white and black Republican voters.

The mayoral election of 1868 was extremely closely fought, and votes were tallied amid competing victory claims by both parties. Although Bowen appeared to be the winner, Mayor Wallach refused to cede the keys to the mayor's offices, and conservatives alleged illegal proceedings by the Republican city register, Frederick A. Boswell.[68] Meanwhile, Democrats on the common council challenged the election of Carter Stewart, an African American merchant and barber, insisting that black men's enfranchisement had not negated the portion of the city charter that restricted office holding to white men.[69] Municipal business came to a standstill for several weeks while the election controversies were debated in public, in Congress, and in the District of Columbia Supreme Court. By the summer's end, authorities had rejected the most serious of the Democrats' protests, and Bowen, along with Stewart, had officially assumed office.

Still, the new mayor faced formidable obstacles to governing. That spring, local Republicans had pressed Congress to amend Washington's charter to increase the power of the city council at the expense of the mayor. They had hoped to undermine Mayor Wallach, but they ended up with a law that impeded their own goals, once a Republican was elected mayor.[70] Democrats on the city council were hostile to Bowen and, of particular importance to the black laborers' movement, refused to cooperate with Bowen's plan to end the "contract system" of distributing work and hiring laborers. Citing the shoddy work of private contractors and agreeing with black labor activists that city contractors favored white laborers over black ones, Bowen had proposed that mayoral appointees, not private contractors, supervise the city work and that laborers be hired by the day or week, rather than by the job. But Bowen's opponents on the council commanded enough votes to stymie his efforts to bring more regularity and racial equality to the processes by which city laborers were hired.[71]

Despite opposition on the council, Bowen pushed forward extensive public works projects that employed thousands of black and white laborers. During his administration, crews graded streets and the riverbank, laid miles of pavement, and constructed sidewalks and sewers.[72] The Bowen administration's projects included developing the western periphery of Swampoodle and pushing the urbanized area of the city toward the northwest. In fact, the changes were so dramatic that the *Evening Star* worried that Pennsylvania Avenue would be left "wilting." The enterprising mayor seems to have circumvented the council on some of these measures, to the dismay of opponents, who repeatedly sought explanations for who had authorized the improvements and how they would be financed.[73]

Besides attempting to improve opportunities for Washington's African American day laborers, Bowen's administration did much to transform the tone and practices of public institutions in the city. Immediately upon taking office, the mayor created an uproar by appointing two black men to the fire department. He flouted whites' resistance to having African Americans in

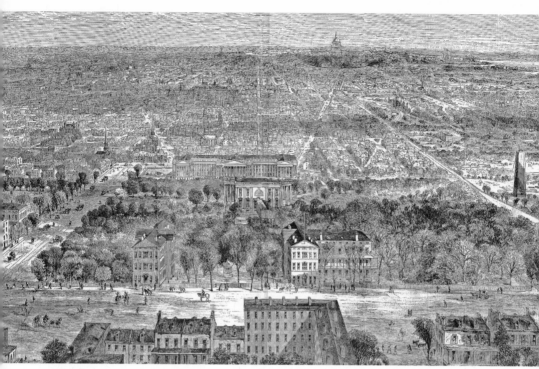

FIGURE 4.3. "Washington City, D.C." This panorama, published in the spring of 1869, shows a bustling city with the Capitol in the background. The National Mall and the unfinished Washington Monument are on the right. *Harper's Weekly*, March 13, 1869, 168–69. Courtesy *Harp Week*.

supervisory positions by naming black men as ward commissioners, whose work included supervising white laborers, and by appointing Andrew W. Tucker, a black doctor, as public health physician in one ward.[74] When the National Colored Labor Convention convened in Washington in December 1869, Bowen praised its efforts in "asserting and securing the rights of your race in the maintenance of the rights of labor."[75]

With Bowen's election, the local black labor movement that had taken shape during 1867 was absorbed into the Republican machinery. Ward-based black workingmen's associations became biracial, incorporating white skilled and unskilled laborers as well. Yet the associations continued in their original mission of lobbying the city government for work for the ward's laborers. Labor historians looking for an independent black labor movement in this era have often been disappointed to see close and continuing ties between labor leaders and the Republican Party.[76] In Washington, however, black laborers' goal of obtaining a fair share of the public employment was, of necessity, tied to politics, and it was a mark of their success that their organizations became crucial to the distribution of political patronage. Nor was black laborers' alliance with politicians a strategic mistake. To the contrary, given the dearth of industrial employment and the hostility of white laborers in the private sector, a close connection with organized Republicans was their most promising option.

Bowen's administration was not entirely satisfying to its African American constituents, however, particularly when it came to the management of Washington's black public schools. Bowen hoped to make improvement of the city's black and white schools a centerpiece of his administration.[77] In his first public message as mayor, he announced his support for congressional legislation that would place the District's black and white schools under the administration of a single school board. Yet Bowen made clear that the integration of students would not accompany the consolidation of school boards. Acknowledging that "some have advocated the mixing of white and colored children in the same schools," the mayor claimed that black and white residents alike opposed school integration and insisted that streamlining the boards would in fact benefit the black schools.[78]

Bowen's plan to remove the black schools from the authority of the Interior Department reflected a grave misunderstanding of the importance black Washingtonians placed on their schools' autonomy. The black public schools were the literal and figurative descendants of the private schools African Americans had struggled to maintain in the antebellum decades. Since the outset of the public school system, African American parents and educators had sought to maintain a voice in the schools' operations and had cultivated relationships with successive interior secretaries in order to do that. The schools had only recently begun to thrive, since it was not until 1867 that Mayor Wallach—faced with a lawsuit by the trustees and more stringent legislation from Congress— began to relinquish the public funds the city government owed to the black public schools. Many black Washingtonians feared that the three-man school board was ill-equipped to handle the expansion of the schools, and they wanted to see the black school system offer higher levels of instruction. These concerns notwithstanding, however, they were highly skeptical of Bowen's proposal, not least because it threatened to disrupt the relatively stable and fruitful relationship between the schools and the Interior Department.[79]

On February 8, 1869, when Congress passed the bill to mix the school boards but not the schools, black Washingtonians erupted in debate, holding meetings in churches throughout the city. The central question was whether to acquiesce in the new arrangement or to ask President Johnson—never a friend—for a veto. At a mass meeting in Israel Church, seventh-ward activist Anthony Bowen sided with the mayor and thought it a poor idea to ask Johnson for help. But among those who favored requesting a presidential veto were prominent locals such as John F. Cook, as well as some recent arrivals, including Sella Martin, the new pastor of 15th Street Presbyterian Church, and Duke W. Anderson, the new pastor at First Baptist. These men were not ready to trust the city government with their schools, particularly if integration of the school boards was not matched by integration of the students themselves. After a long debate, those convened at Israel Church resolved that the secretary of interior had "rendered perfect satisfaction to us as a people" and condemned the action of Congress. Citing that resolution, Johnson duly vetoed the measure, only too happy to exploit the irony of defending "the colored citizens" of the District against the incursions of congressional Republicans.[80]

The school administration controversy had two serious consequences that Bowen surely did not intend. First, his initiative alienated prominent black civic and religious leaders and seems to have exacerbated simmering racial tensions within the local Republican Party. After the president's veto, the local party convened a mass meeting where Anthony Bowen and other Mayor Bowen stalwarts proposed to request a congressional override of the veto. They viewed the Israel Church resolutions and the request for a veto as a betrayal of the mayor and Republican allies in Congress. Their opponents, who were also in attendance, downplayed the importance of loyalty to the mayor and expressed frustration with the constraints of partisan allegiances. Longtime local leader Francis Taverns argued that black Washingtonians ought to be able to support allies in Congress while still opposing the school bill, and he declared that "he had long since ceased to have any confidence in the white men of the District." Bowen's proxy at the meeting, Major William S. Morse, called Taverns's statement "dangerous" and "an invasion of his rights as a white man."[81] Morse tried to persuade the crowd that the bill would, in fact, promote racial equality in the schools, but he ended with a severe warning: "If by the exertions of colored men this bill shall fail to become a law, the weight of the wrong inflicted upon the common rights of mankind will fall upon the very men who are clamoring for an equality of rights."[82]

In addition to alienating prominent black Republicans and exacerbating racial tensions, Bowen's school gambit also—again, probably unintentionally—helped give momentum to African Americans' nascent demands for access to Washington's white public schools. Several speakers at the pivotal Israel Church meeting suggested that they would approve mixing of the school boards only if the schools themselves were mixed as well. Later, the congregation of 15th Street Presbyterian Church, under Sella Martin's leadership, passed a resolution voicing its support of "free schools and equal school rights, under a school system embracing white and colored children" and deprecating "any legislation that does not abolish *in toto* the present system, built upon distinctions of race and color." One black educator expressed the same sense that there must be complete mixing or none it all, insisting "that as long as a colored school-house stands there should be a separate board of trustees." Some black leaders insisted that only a small minority of Washington's African Americans supported mixed schools, but prointegration voices would grow increasingly forceful as the year went on.[83]

By the winter of 1869, black men's enfranchisement had wrought remarkable changes in local political culture. A radical Republican mayor was in office, black men held elected and appointed offices, and black laborers had become a political force to be reckoned with. But, as the debate about mixed schools demonstrated, fractures were also becoming evident. On the school issue, African Americans disagreed among themselves about the importance of partisan loyalty versus independent action and about school integration itself. Racial tensions between black and white Republicans had surfaced, as had moderate Republican opposition to Bowen's racial and economic policies. Such intraparty divisions would later become the basis for full-blown factionalism among Republicans. For now, however, local partisans could look forward to the inauguration of the first bona fide Republican president since Abraham Lincoln.

Caste as Caste Must Go to the Wall: The Summer of 1869

During the summer of 1869, the rising power of local Republicans, together with the inauguration of President Ulysses S. Grant that spring, combined to create a remarkable sense of possibility in black Washington. Grant signed legislation opening the way for black men's office holding and jury service, and his administration proved willing to appoint African Americans to clerical and skilled labor positions heretofore reserved for whites only. Early that summer, the city council passed its first law banning racial discrimination in theaters, restaurants, and other public accommodations. Black men insisted on admission to white-only labor and professional organizations. And by the fall, black parents were demanding an end to racial exclusivity in the capital's white public schools. Coming in a dramatic rush in the months following Grant's inauguration, all these advances reflected rising hopes that it would be possible to implement an expansive vision of racial equality in the national capital, one premised on the idea that government should take the lead in outlawing discrimination, not only in laws themselves but in other arenas as well. But the strenuous resistance black activists encountered, particularly as they sought access to labor organizations and the public schools, was a reminder of how deeply their claims challenged prevailing ideas about race and public life.

The first signal that Grant's presidency marked a new era for the capital was the president's signature on a federal law that allowed black men to hold elected office and serve on juries in the capital. As the slippery-slope rhetoric of social equality often suggested, many people considered office holding and jury service even more hallowed privileges than the vote itself. Jury service in particular was widely seen as a duty reserved for elite members of the community, men who (at least in theory) were widely respected and whose decisions would be considered fair. The proposal to admit black men to such privileges, and to allow them to help decide the fate of white men and women, struck many whites as an absurd inversion of traditional hierarchies of race and power. Congress had twice passed legislation to remove "white" from all the District's municipal laws and therefore open office holding and jury service to black men. But President Johnson had refused to sign. Grant signed the bill as soon as he took office, cementing what many people saw as the "political equality" of African Americans in the national capital.[84]

Grant's inauguration raised African Americans' hopes for fairer treatment from the police, since members of the police board and some local judges were presidential appointees. At a national convention of black men, held in Washington in January 1869, Duke W. Anderson, pastor of First Baptist Church, condemned the police for holding innocent African Americans in jail and proposed a resolution asking Grant to appoint at least two African American justices of the peace in the capital.[85] Police superintendent A. C. Richards suggested to Charles Sumner that even one black representative on the police board "would streangthen my hands as the Superintendent of the police force, by showing to the colored people that their citizenship is recognized and their rights protected in the person of a member of the Board of their own color." No black appointee to the police board was forthcoming, but that spring, Anderson and Orindatus S. B. Wall became the capital's first African American justices of the peace; and by early June, three black men had been appointed to the police force.[86]

Wall and Anderson were part of a stream of migration by northern black civic and religious leaders who found opportunities for political leadership and civic engagement in postwar Washington. Anderson was one of the most prominent black clergymen of his era. A native of Illinois, he had presided over black Baptist churches in the eastern United States and in Canada. After the war ended, he accepted an invitation to become pastor at Washington's First Baptist, moving to the capital with his wife, Eliza. His new church prospered under his leadership, by one estimate attracting some 1,000 freedpeople as members. Anderson also became involved in civic affairs, serving as a trustee of Howard University and of the Freedman's Bank, and as a commissioner of the Washington asylum.[87] O. S. B. Wall also thrived in postwar Washington. Wall's father, a North Carolina slaveholder, had sent the children he fathered with an enslaved woman to a Quaker settlement in Ohio, where he later bequeathed them property. Wall attended Oberlin College and then settled in Oberlin, marrying Amanda A. Thomas. During the war, Wall worked to recruit black soldiers for the Union army, often alongside John Mercer Langston, the famed lawyer and activist, who was married to Wall's sister. In 1865, Wall was appointed a captain in the army, becoming one of the very few black men to be commissioned as an officer. After a stint with the Freedmen's Bureau in South Carolina, Orindatus and Amanda moved to Washington, where he continued working for the Freedmen's Bureau and she worked as a teacher. People like the Walls and the Andersons began the postwar period as strangers to Washington, but many of them soon settled in, finding employment with the black public schools, Howard University, or the government.[88]

Grant and members of his cabinet proved willing to appoint African Americans to clerical positions in the federal government, something Johnson had never done. Julia Wilbur noted in her diary, "Charles Douglass & others (colored) have got appointment in Treasury." Emma V. Brown, a black public school teacher, received a clerkship in the Pension Bureau; Anthony Bowen, the civic and religious leader and longtime Patent Office employee, was finally promoted to a clerkship as well. Among the few black women to become clerks were Eleanor and Agnes Ketchum, the nieces of a prominent white lawyer and abolitionist from New York and daughters of a black Bermudan woman. The 1869 Colored National Labor Convention recognized Agnes as a leader among black women professionals who "illustrate an aptitude and ability among colored women" that must be "recognized and encouraged by colored men."[89]

At the same time that Grant's administration opened new opportunities on the federal level, the Republican advance in local affairs enabled the city council to pass measures banning racial discrimination in the city's public accommodations. On the eve of the June 1869 municipal election, the council passed legislation prohibiting discrimination in theaters and at other entertainments and exhibitions licensed by the city government. The next year, it would pass a supplemental law, extending the prohibition on discrimination to "any licensed hotel, tavern, restaurant, ordinary, sample-room, tippling-house, saloon, or eating-house" and imposing a penalty of no less than $50 on violators.

These laws attacked practices that were commonplace in the capital. White-run venues for concerts and other performances typically insisted on racially segregated seating, even when the performers themselves were African American. Members of the black elite often refused to attend under such circumstances. For example, Julia Wilbur reported that when black pianist "Blind Tom" played in Odd Fellows Hall, elite African Americans refused to go, having "too much respect for themselves" to sit in the small gallery reserved for black patrons. Months later, when Blind Tom returned to play at Anderson's First Baptist in the first ward, the "house was crowded with the elite" of Washington and Georgetown, who had "no chance to hear him when he sings for white folks, unless they sit apart in a negro gallery." Just after the public accommodations law passed, John F. Cook declared that he had never set foot in the prestigious National Theater, "for the reason of its making *the distinction* on account of color."[90]

Local laws that forbade racial discrimination in theaters, restaurants, and other places of amusement represented a significant advance from the civil rights allowed in the 1866 Civil Rights Act and from the prohibition on segregated transportation enacted by Congress for the District in 1865. The new public accommodations laws rejected the argument often made by proprietors that the common law principle of "reasonable regulation" entitled them to offer separate accommodations to black and white patrons. Rather, they drew on the municipal government's universally acknowledged power to license and regulate local businesses and, by their very existence, insisted that local government should take a leading role in wiping away the vestiges of slavery. Yet it was harder for many contemporaries to imagine integration of theaters, restaurants, and other such places than it was for them to contemplate the integration of streetcars. Interactions in theaters and restaurants seemed perilously close to being social relationships, which, many people believed, ought to be governed not by law but by taste and custom. Democrats and some Republicans as well derided the 1869 public accommodations law as a "social equality" measure that would unsettle the very foundations of local life. The Republican *Chicago Tribune* insisted that hotels and theaters "offer entertainments and amusement merely" and that the "only function the government has in relation to them is to preserve order, not to regulate the class of people who shall go to them." Meanwhile, the *Evening Star* predicted that few "colored people will avail themselves of the privileges given them by the law," since they "are acquiring a good deal of self-respect, and are not disposed to thrust themselves, socially, where they are not wanted."[91]

African Americans, however, fully intended to see that the new laws were tested and enforced. The prestigious and popular National Theater was first on the agenda. This theater had previously permitted black spectators to sit in the gallery but had excluded them from "first-class" seating. When the law passed, the theater was closed for a summer recess, but it was reported that the proprietor planned to "set apart a portion of his theatre for the exclusive use of the higher order of the colored folks," on the grounds that he would be forced out of business if he provided indiscriminate seating.[92] When a rumor circulated that African Americans would *not* seek access to the theater's first-class seating, John F. Cook indicated in a letter to the *Chronicle* that he would pull no punches. "I have no compromise or truce to make on this matter with any manager or any body else," he wrote. "I . . . shall avail myself often of the privilege that I, with others, have labored to secure for the colored people of our city."[93]

If the 1869 public accommodations law was one sign of the rise of an expansive vision of racial equality in Washington's political culture, the results of the 1869 municipal election were another. Republicans won every seat on the twenty-one-member common council, and they would now outnumber Democrats on the board of aldermen by eleven to three. Every ward sent a black delegate to the common council. Carter Stewart was elected to the aldermanic board, and Cook was voted city collector.[94] Sayles Bowen could thus look forward to working with a friendlier city council as he sought to advance his agenda. In his annual message, the mayor was explicit about how the twin programs of city improvement and employment for laborers converged. The "idle poor" were "willing and anxious to work, but are totally unable to get it," he said. The city government would put them to work "performing labor on the streets," thus reducing poverty and the crimes associated with it. That poor relief would be distributed as labor would also assuage middle-class concerns about providing charity to the undeserving.[95]

Bowen now expressed support for school integration, a marked change from his position the previous summer. "The distinction of color is no longer recognized in our charter nor at the ballot-box, in the courts of justice, the lecture-room, the hall of public amusement, the public conveyances, nor in the City

Councils," he announced. "It should be eliminated as speedily as possible from our school system." In a private letter, Bowen told Senator Sumner that he had previously opposed school integration because he believed whites would abandon the public schools if black children were let in. Popular sentiments had shifted, he reported. "We have now advanced far enough to make the trial and I think there will be few white parents found who are willing to punish their own children by keeping them out of school for fear of contamination," he wrote. Perhaps seeking to affirm his commitment to the eventual consolidation of the boards, Bowen also appointed George B. Vashon, a black educator from Pennsylvania, to the board of trustees of the white public schools.[96]

During the hopeful summer of 1869, black Washingtonians began demanding admission to associations of skilled tradesmen and other professional associations whose status as private, clublike organizations made the case for a right to access particularly difficult. First-ward activists again led the way, passing a resolution that condemned "every man and every combination of men that shall . . . endeavor to trample down the right to labor by excluding from the different branches of trades arts, &c., a large portion of honest mechanics, artists and laborers because of their color."[97] Lewis Douglass, Frederick Douglass's son, confronted the discriminatory practices of the powerful local printers' union, generating a case that garnered widespread public attention. Douglass worked at the Government Printing Office, where his supervisor, a Grant appointee named Almon M. Clapp, supported his bid to join the Columbia Typographical Union No. 101, one of the oldest labor organizations in the District. The union refused to admit Douglass and brought its case before the national printers' convention, which sustained the local's right to determine whom it allowed to join. As Douglass's struggle with the printers' union unfolded, the city council resolved to support Douglass and Clapp, while the Soldiers and Sailors Union, a white veterans' organization, symbolically crossed the color line by electing Douglass an honorary member.[98]

Yet other local labor unions also remained intransigent. Grant's naval secretary opened heretofore "white" jobs at the Navy Yard to black men. But when two black bricklayers, both of them Union veterans, applied for union cards, the president of the local bricklayers' union denied the request and the organization demanded that Navy Yard bricklayers walk off their jobs rather than work alongside black men. White Navy Yard workers' protests quickly foundered, but white labor organizations continued to exclude black men. Indeed, weeks later, the local house carpenters' union added the word "white" to its constitution, making official its refusal to admit black carpenters.[99]

That same summer, black and white physicians protested the exclusion of black doctors from the Medical Society of the District of Columbia. The controversy began when three black physicians associated with the Freedmen's Bureau and Howard University (whose medical school had opened the previous fall) applied for membership in the Medical Society, a professional association chartered by Congress in 1819. The society refused to admit the black physicians, although it had no objection to licensing them to practice medicine. Membership in the society was "merely a privilege of association and social reunion," the society contended, as it condemned "certain individuals who have settled amongst us of late" for making a "tyrannical attempt to punish [the society] for the exercise of an undoubted and legitimate right" to exclude doctors Charles B. Purvis, Andrew W. Tucker, and Alexander Augusta. The black doctors and their allies were pushing against the limits of contemporary theories of equality before the law. As the *National Intelligencer* put it, "All unions and associations of professions and trades throughout the country have hitherto determined not to admit negroes to fellowship in their organizations, leaving the colored guilds and professions to form and foster their own associations."[100] In this view, the Medical Society, like a labor union, was a private association that could make its own rules about whom to include. Black physicians had no right to become members of a private association whose existing members did not want them.

When Congress reconvened late that fall, Charles Sumner brought the matter before the Senate, using testimonials from Purvis and Augusta to demonstrate that the society's claim to be "merely" a social organization was disingenuous. In fact, Sumner showed, the society prohibited its members from consulting with nonmember physicians, a policy that stood to prevent black doctors from building their businesses and pursuing their professions.[101] The Senate adopted Sumner's recommendation that the Senate D.C. committee consider revoking the Medical Society's charter, and that winter the committee heard testimony from all parties involved. The committee report, which Sumner authored, reviewed the evidence and asserted that the Medical Society was acting "as if slavery still ruled." Introducing a bill to revoke the society's charter, the committee concluded, "A corporation which ceases to be in harmony with the spirit of the age, which insults a large body of fellow-citizens, and is a stumbling-block to harmony, cannot expect the continued sanction of Congress."[102]

The logic of the report provides important evidence of Sumner's thinking about equality and the law as he began to press for a federal civil rights law that would "supplement" the 1866 Civil Rights Act. For Sumner and others who wanted to see the federal government move beyond banning racially discriminatory laws or guaranteeing only a narrow bundle of basic civil rights, the status of associations that received government charters—often including labor and professional associations, churches, cemeteries, and even schools—was very much at issue. If those institutions were considered essentially private, as the Medical Society argued, then they could determine their membership as they saw fit. But if their publicness was emphasized, as Sumner advocated, then they were accountable to the public body that had chartered them, and a case could be made that they could be forced to honor what Sumner called "human rights." Once again, the special relationship of Congress to the District of Columbia offered Congress a chance to make a statement. Congress should revoke the society's charter, Sumner insisted, "in the name of equal rights, and for the sake of the example which will be felt throughout the country."[103]

Despite their efforts, Sumner and the black doctors proved unable either to revoke the society's charter or to win access for black doctors. The Medical Society remained intransigent, and the Senate refused to act. Black and white doctors who protested the Medical Society's policy formed their own association and took their argument before the American Medical Association, which supported the local society in its exclusionary policy. Indeed, notwithstanding ongoing lobbying by black District of Columbia doctors, many of them professors at the preeminent black medical school in the country, the local medical association remained racially exclusive until after World War II.[104]

If there was a single event during the summer of 1869 that most dramatized how black activism and political changes were helping transform local institutions, it was the trial of Minnie Gaines, an African American woman who was charged with bludgeoning her white lover to death. The case's dramatis personae represented contemporary Washington remarkably well. Gaines was a freedwoman originally from Fredericksburg, Virginia. Her lover, James Ingle, had been a watchman at the Department of Interior, one of the thousands of young men who had migrated to the capital to work for the newly expansive federal government. Gaines's lawyers, former Ohio congressman Albert G. Riddle and former Freedmen's Bureau lawyer Andrew K. Browne, were well known in Republican circles. Lawyers for both sides called some sixty witnesses, among them some of the capital's best-known physicians. For more than a week in July, witnesses discussed slavery, sex, violence, and insanity, as rapt onlookers filled the courtroom.

The facts in the case were relatively straightforward. Gaines, who worked as a servant in a boardinghouse, had become pregnant with the child of James Ingle, a boardinghouse resident. When she confronted him and demanded that he support the unborn child, he refused and threatened several times to kill her. Desperate, Gaines came to Ingle's room with a pistol and attempted to shoot him. When the pistol malfunctioned, she picked up a hammer or an axe and beat him, delivering a head wound that ultimately killed him. Gaines immediately turned herself in to police. In court, the question was whether Gaines would be convicted of premeditated murder, as the prosecutor wished, or of some lesser crime, such as murder or manslaughter, or whether she would be declared not guilty because of temporary insanity.[105]

Besides the raw sensationalism of the trial, the public took great interest in the fact that Gaines was the capital's first murder defendant to be tried before a racially mixed jury. Washington's first mixed-race grand and petit juries had been empanelled in June, and the Gaines case gave Washingtonians a chance to see how a mixed jury would decide a case that was, itself, the product of Washington's changed climate.[106] Newspaper reporters followed the jury avidly, and the jurors—six black men and six white men—seemed conscious of their place in history. The jurors publicly broke taboos of race and space, practically enacting the "slippery-slope" argument against political equality. While sequestered, they took their meals together and were quartered together at a "third-class" hotel. One Sunday, they held a private prayer meeting and, later in the afternoon, "rode out into the country with the bailiffs" on an omnibus. The men also had their picture taken at a photographer's studio. There was little more they could have done to demonstrate that racial equality in public venues like the jury box could well lead to interracial socializing and perhaps friendships. Skittish observers were no doubt thankful that jury service was a facet of citizenship still closed to women.[107]

Politically active women in the capital were fascinated by the trial and attended regularly. One of them, a black woman named Louisa Butler, visited Gaines in her jail cell every day. During the trial, A. G. Riddle, one of Gaines's lawyers and himself an advocate of voting rights for women, gave a stirring defense that emphasized Gaines's subjection, as a slave, to the sexual predation of her former master and spoke more generally of "woman's" subjection to man. When the trial was over, Josephine Griffing declared in a letter to the *Revolution*, Elizabeth Cady Stanton's New York–based weekly, that it had been of "rare interest to woman" and a testament to the need for sexual equality before the law. "I shut my eyes to the glaring injustice of excluding women from the jury," she remarked, "who were, by law, required to put themselves in the place of the prisoner" and to form their opinions based on "what *they* would do, were they in the case of this poor woman."[108] The privilege of jury service had been opened to black men, but women could expect no jury of their peers.

How would the jury decide? Julia Wilbur recorded in her journal that Duke Anderson, the pastor at the church Gaines attended, "fears the *colored* jurors will not be likely to acquit Minnie Gaines & gives plausible reasons for the same." Wilbur did not explain Anderson's reasoning, but we might speculate that Anderson worried that the black jurors would feel pressure to avoid the impression of undue leniency on an African American defendant.[109] Justice George Fisher's instructions to the jurors also reflected the political sensitivity of the jurors' mandate. After outlining the range of possible verdicts, Fisher reminded them that they could not acquit Gaines "from a feeling of sympathy in consequence of her sex, and pregnant condition, and the fact that she was once a slave," nor could they acquit "from a feeling of prejudice against slave-holders," or against "the deceased" for making death threats against a vulnerable woman. In the end, the jurors seem not to have felt constrained by a need to prove themselves tough on this black woman defendant.[110] They deliberated for just ten minutes before returning with the verdict that Gaines was not guilty by reason of insanity. Perhaps the evidence simply seemed overwhelming. "I do not see how any other verdict cd. have been given," Wilbur recorded in her diary.[111]

Following the verdict, federal officials sentenced Gaines to an unspecified amount of time in the Government Hospital for the Insane (now known as St. Elizabeth's), where she stayed in newly built facilities for the "colored insane." Louisa Butler visited her there. Hospital officials diagnosed Gaines with "mania hysterical" and reported that she was prone to "attacks" of the disease. They believed her mental condition stabilized in October, with the birth of her son, and in February they invited her father to come from Fredericksburg to retrieve her. She "appears to be well and wishes to have you take her home," a hospital supervisor wrote. Having stayed almost nine months, Gaines was released on April 16, 1870. She presumably returned to Virginia, carrying with her the infant son she had named Daniel Webster Gaines.[112]

That fall, the schools again took center stage in African Americans' broader campaign for access to public and quasi-public institutions. First, a group of black and white parents in the rapidly growing fourth ward asked the city council to furnish them with a single school for their neighborhood's black and white children. The parents argued that since their area had only about ninety children it was most efficient to build one school, not two. The white school board responded positively, requesting that the city council strike out the word "white" in the city school ordinance to permit the board to offer a mixed school. In a report to the city council, Alonzo E. Newton, a white educator from New England who had previously served as the superintendent of Washington's black public schools, approved the proposal as an initiative from parents. "Whatever opinions may exist as to the propriety of *compelling* the association of children of the two races in the same school, against their own or their parents' wishes," he wrote, "that question does not arise here." Alert to Congress's continuing interest in the District's schools, and perhaps to Senator Charles Sumner's plan to introduce legislation to desegregate the capital's schools from on high, Newton warned that if school officials "refuse to permit or encourage the removal of caste distinction in our schools *when the people themselves call for it*" their decision would likely invite Congress to "compel the wiping out of these distinctions."[113]

In late November, Sella Martin, the Presbyterian minister, pushed the issue still further by attempting to send his daughter to the most prominent white school in the city. Franklin School had opened to great fanfare the previous month and was touted as a symbol of local and national investment in public education. The building itself was designed by Adolf Cluss, Washington's most sought-after architect of public buildings, and it exemplified state-of-the-art school design. It was located at the corner 13th and K Streets, in a rapidly developing downtown neighborhood near the homes of such luminaries as Edwin M. Stanton.[114] In making Franklin School the target of his family's protest against the exclusion of black children from white schools, Martin thus literally moved the integration debate from the city's periphery—a distant fourth-ward neighborhood—into its symbolic center.

Martin had a long history of political and religious activism. He had escaped slavery in North Carolina as a young man and had become known on the abolitionist circuit and as a Baptist minister. After the war, he worked in England and continental Europe as an agent of the American Missionary Association. In the second half of 1868, he came to Washington to pastor the elite and politically active 15th Street Presbyterian Church.[115] The next year, he placed himself and his family at the heart of the burgeoning local debate about school integration when he protested his six-year-old daughter's exclusion from Franklin School. Josie Martin had obtained a "ticket" admitting her to the school from George Vashon, the one black member of the school board.[116] When she arrived at school, however, her teacher refused to admit her to class.

FIGURE 4.4. Franklin School, designed by architect Adolf Cluss. Courtesy Library of Congress, LC-USZ62-15046.

The family appealed, but the local sub-board of schools concurred with the teacher.

As public attention intensified, Martin insisted that Josie was entitled to attend Franklin School because it was closer to their home than the closest black school. The crux of his argument was that the school could not exclude Josie because the law eliminating the word "white" from the city charter, signed by Grant the previous spring, had implicitly outlawed racial discrimination in the schools. Supporters of separate schools insisted, however, that Congress had created the segregated school systems separately from the city charter and that the law striking racial distinctions from the charter did not apply to school matters. The *Evening Star* added that, since taxes were allocated to the separate school systems based on the proportion of black and white children in the District, it was only fair that white children should attend white schools and black children, black schools. The case was complicated by questions about race itself. The teacher at Franklin School professed to have initially thought Martin's daughter was white, and some people wondered what legally constituted a "colored" child.[117]

While the city waited for the corporation attorney to weigh in, Martin preached a well-attended sermon at 15th Street Presbyterian Church, in which he advanced the long-standing abolitionist argument that "in case of doubt the law shall be construed on the side of freedom." "The time has come," he demanded, "through the power of Christianity, when caste as caste must go to the wall."[118] As it turned out, the city government disagreed. Corporation counsel William A. Cook, whose job was to advise the city government on legal matters, ruled that since a school board member had given Josie a ticket, she was entitled to attend the school. But Cook refused to judge the larger questions of whether the recent law removing "white" from the city charter affected school policy, and of how to determine whether a child was "negro." He claimed that he was not obliged to address such matters because a neighborhood sub-board, not the full school board, had asked for his opinion. He also suggested that his view was of little significance, since the new Congress would likely decide the matter for itself. School board members rushed to assure students at Franklin School that Josie Martin was permitted to attend only because she was being considered "white," and that, as the superintendent of schools put it, "there will be no colored children admitted to the schools."[119]

Julia Wilbur felt the decision was "a triumph for the Colored people." Yet the effort had produced little movement by city officials, who preferred obfuscation and banal compromise to grappling directly with the fact that white schools continued to exclude black children. At the same time, the *Evening Star* and others sought to discredit Martin's protest by suggesting it was the brainchild of outsiders and did not represent the desires of local people. The black men who had been most visibly involved—Martin and Vashon, as well as George T. Downing, another newly arrived vocal advocate of mixed schools—

were in fact migrants from elsewhere. Yet plenty of local people also believed African American children should have access to the white public schools, including John F. Cook and labor activist George Hatton, as well as the fourth-ward parents who had requested an integrated school for their neighborhood.[120] Still, the issue was a divisive one among African Americans, and many black educators and other leaders did not think it wise to demand that white schools open their doors to black students.

In arguing that principles of racial equality should apply to workingmen's and professional associations, public schools, and public accommodations, black activists and their allies drew not only on principles of basic justice but also on a pragmatic assessment of the inseparability of civic associations from government. Time and again, they insisted that governments use their regulatory or police powers to demand that ostensibly private corporations or associations admit black and white people on an equal basis. This was the case when African Americans demanded access to the streetcars and Congress used its power to charter corporations in the capital to prohibit racial discrimination on common carriers. It was also the case in the municipal public accommodations laws, which merely extended the city government's existing power to regulate theaters, restaurants, and other accommodations into a new area. Black doctors' demand for admission to the Medical Society drew on the same logic; since Congress had chartered the Medical Society, it could also demand that the society not discriminate and revoke its charter if it did not comply. In each instance, black activists and their allies implicitly recognized that ostensibly private institutions were inseparable from the public world of government and policy. The common law had long treated public accommodations as a particular kind of corporation, chartered by government and beholden to the public. Nor were clubs, associations, and other kinds of corporations cordoned off in their own world, apart from government. In fact, these activists realized, such organizations were often constituted by and (they hoped) beholden to government. Moving forward, those who believed slavery's end must be accompanied by a thoroughgoing eradication of racial inequality in public life would mobilize similar arguments as they continued to press for the extension of legal equality into quasi-public institutions, and they would maintain their position that government policy must shape cultural norms, not vice versa.

Yet they would also continue to face potent opposition and charges that what they sought was dreaded social equality. Conservatives too realized that public life and private life were intimately intertwined. That is why they saw African Americans' demands for voting rights as the top of a slippery slope that would lead to racial equality in all manner of relations. That is also why they sought to define so many arenas as "social" or as places where black activism would lead to "social equality." Defining the social or private realm very broadly, conservatives cast doubt on the legitimacy of radicals' demands. For if a given area—a labor organization or a theater, for example—was truly a social space where liberty and taste should reign, then the government had no business intervening to regulate relations there.

Conservatives' reactions to black men's enfranchisement were often hyperbolic, but there is no denying that black men's votes transformed Washington. As freedmen became crucial constituents in local politics, the composition of the city government dramatically altered. Under Mayor Bowen, the municipal government lacked the financial resources to lift former slaves out of poverty through public works programs, but its attention to the needs of the African American poor were striking. Meanwhile, the new public accommodations laws expanded African Americans' access to heretofore white spaces, while Bowen's practice of appointing black men to high positions meant that black men now supervised white men and women in city affairs.

The moment of greatest possibility was contested and tragically short-lived. Washington's June 1869 municipal election itself suggested that trouble was at hand. The campaign season was defined by intraparty factionalism, and election day turned disorderly when a group of African American Republicans mobbed a black voter who was attempting to vote for the opposing "Citizens" party. Commentary on the election "riot"—both in Washington and in northern papers—forecast a nascent reaction against black men's enfranchisement. Northerners were particularly interested in the Washington canvass because the states were debating ratification of the Fifteenth Amendment, which would force them to drop racial restrictions on voting. Democratic newspapers suggested that the passions and furies of Washington's election day were the natural outcome of black men's enfranchisement. Amid an avalanche of breathless coverage, the *New York World*, perhaps the country's most powerful Democratic outlet, printed a lengthy article alleging, among other horrors, that African Americans were kidnapping white people from Washington's streets, robbing them, and dumping their bodies in the putrid canal or the Potomac River with impunity. The article was widely reprinted and discussed in commentary that made the national capital—with its large African American population, black office holders, and civil rights laws—an exemplar of pernicious "negro rule."[121]

Dissent also festered among local Republicans, as Bowen outspent his meager budget, the city government's debts grew, and day laborers went unpaid. Critics both inside and outside the administration charged that the mayor's cronies reaped fortunes at the expense of poor laborers. Democrats and many moderate Republicans had little tolerance for black political leadership, were not persuaded by the mayor's focus on employment and aggressive infrastructure improvements, and believed too much money was spent pandering to an undesirable electorate. Many who accepted basic "civil rights" as defined by the 1866 Civil Rights Act could not tolerate advances in what so many people called "social equality." Radical leaders struggled to maintain party unity, but the glue of partisan loyalty, weak to begin with, gradually dissolved.

5

Make Haste Slowly

THE LIMITS OF EQUALITY

Josephine Griffing was one of the woman suffragists whose imagination had been fired by the December 1866 Senate debate over women's voting rights in the capital. Weeks after black men voted for the first time in Washington, Griffing traveled to New York for the annual meeting of the American Equal Rights Association, the woman suffrage movement's national organization. There she urged delegates to focus their energies on the District of Columbia. Griffing, who had been an abolitionist and women's rights activist before the war, placed the drive for women's enfranchisement in the context of the recent history of slave emancipation. The question had arisen "from the great fact that at the South there were four millions of people unrepresented," she argued. "The fact of woman's being also unrepresented is now becoming slowly understood." The timing was perfect for an organized effort to demand voting rights in the capital. "It is easier now to talk and act upon [the] subject in the District of Columbia than ever before, or than it will be again," Griffing insisted.[1] That summer, Griffing and other Washington activists founded a local Universal Franchise Association to press for women's enfranchisement in the capital.

Woman suffragists like Griffing saw the debates about equality that ensued at slavery's end as an opportunity to demand equal rights for women and, in particular, the right to vote. The ascendant Republican discourse of individual rights, they recognized, opened spaces for women to claim that they, too, should be recognized as individuals. Thus, Griffing and many others in her cohort did not challenge the Republican Party's decision to make black men's enfranchisement a policy priority, nor did they see black men's enfranchisement as an insult to women. Instead, they emphasized that the logic might lead from racial equality before the law to a more genuine universalism in which women would have the same political rights as men. This orientation made it possible for white women like Griffing to form coalitions with African American women who shared similar goals. And, in fact, black and white women mobilized in Washington wards and demanded the right to vote in both 1869 and 1871.

Not all woman suffragists agreed with the universalistic approach of Griffing and her allies, however. In Washington, a cohort of white suffragists broke off from the Universal Franchise Association and inaugurated a separate movement for white women's suffrage, advocating a set of ideas to which black woman suffragists in the capital could never have subscribed. The schism in Washington mirrored a broader break in the national movement, as a group of activists led by Elizabeth Cady Stanton and Susan B. Anthony adopted new idioms of civilizational hierarchy and ethnic and racial difference and argued that white women—or sometimes educated or "intelligent" women—would exert a purifying or reforming influence on a degraded electorate. Historians have long debated how to understand the apparent conflict in leading woman suffragists' arguments for greater, yet more restrictive democracy. In ways that have rarely been recognized, however, the woman suffragists who turned to ideas about civilizational hierarchy and even racism were, in fact, quite in tune with their own times.[2]

Indeed, the schism in the woman suffrage movement reflects an even broader controversy over voting rights and representative government that animated politics, particularly in cities, in the 1860s and early 1870s. During these years, partisan alignments and political concerns were undergoing a dramatic shift. As sectional tensions waned, politicians and the public began to reflect on the impact of recent events on the structures and functions of government. Suddenly, everyone was talking about corruption. In this context, as historian Mark Summers has argued, the "corruption issue" provided a way for the relatively weak Democrats to attack the incumbent Republicans. Talk of corruption allowed Republicans disillusioned with President Grant to find common cause with their former political opponents; and it enabled everyone to attack Reconstruction and racial equality without resorting to crude racism.[3] The woman suffragists who were concerned that poor, black, and immigrant men would corrupt the electorate shared much in common with the urban reformers in cities, North and South, who increasingly charged their local electorates with dishonesty and ignorance. To be sure, such woman suffragists wanted to see a greater voice for (some) women than did most of their male counterparts. But in the main, they shared the goal of protecting government against the baleful influences of an overly democratic polity.

The post–Civil War crisis of democratic government was especially acute in cities, where members of the economic elite blamed ignorant voters for rising municipal debts and misgovernment. Public debts, which were ubiquitous, generally resulted from a demand for urban infrastructure improvements that far outpaced the ability of city governments to raise money to finance them. Yet representatives of commercial and landholding interests often laid blame for public debts with poor voters, whom they saw as the core supporters of machine politicians who drove cities into debt and kept voters in line through the distribution of patronage.[4]

The nineteenth-century urban crisis had distinct, racialized dimensions in the postemancipation South. Many southern cities entered the postwar period in need of basic infrastructure—roads, sewers, and railroad connections— long since established in northern cities and towns. With cash in short supply, southern municipal governments often assumed more debt than even the debt-ridden cities of the North had. Moreover, southern city dwellers faced not a gradually growing population but a rapid influx of migrants from surrounding areas, large numbers of whom were freedpeople and therefore considered by most whites to be degraded, racially distinct, and probably unfit for urban life. When freedmen became voters, their political power was—like that of working-class voters in northern cities—potentially dangerous to the propertied elite. Yet attached to freedpeople were particular suspicions about their capacities for thrift, independence of thought, and survival in freedom itself, derived from contemporary ideas about the impact of slavery and the meanings of race. In the urban context, freedpeople posed not just a class-based threat to elite priorities but a racial one as well.[5]

In Washington, as elsewhere in the urban South, elite Democrats and moderate Republicans responded to the intertwined problems of black men's enfranchisement and growing municipal debt with "citizen" and "taxpayer" movements that advocated retrenchment on every front. With the Republicans in power at the federal level and the growing possibility of local alliances between Democrats and disillusioned Republicans, however, southern municipal reformers avoided direct condemnations of black men's right to vote and focused instead on economic issues. They complained about municipal debts, advocated "progress," and chipped away at the newly biracial electorate by redistricting city wards, creating "at-large" rather than ward-based representation and turning city governments over to county boards or state governments. As a result, as historian Howard Rabinowitz found in his study of five southern state capitals, "although blacks continued to exercise the franchise, their votes brought them much less."[6]

This is the context in which to view the multifaceted and extended municipal reform movement in the capital, which began in the mid-1860s with a movement to consolidate the District's three municipal governments and ended with Congress's establishment of a commission government for the capital in 1874. This two-stage process of governmental reform was the capital's version of "redemption." Many of Washington's redeemers, both locally and in Congress, were Republicans. Most of them talked more about economic prosperity than about their desire to reduce African Americans' political power. Yet Washington's early redeemers were doing precisely what their counterparts did in many other southern cities: changing the structures of government to reduce the power of poor and African American voters, while advocating the rights of citizens and taxpayers.[7]

All the while, local activists and congressmen alike continued to see the District of Columbia as a laboratory for policy experimentation. The principle of federalism limited what Congress could do in the states, but it had no bearing on the capital, where Congress's jurisdiction was virtually unchallengeable. Thus, the woman suffrage movement pressed Congress to follow its experiment with black men's enfranchisement in the capital with a similar one in women's voting rights. Likewise, African American leaders, including prominent northerners who had moved to the capital after the war, worked with Senator Charles Sumner to push Congress to establish racially integrated public schools for the capital. School integration remained extremely controversial, among both black Washingtonians and Republicans in Congress. The Senate's debate, which touched on proper jurisdiction over public schools, the civilizational status of freedchildren, and the boundaries of social equality, exposed the limits of many Republicans' views on equality.[8]

Indeed, if Congress could expand equality, it could also contract it. The homegrown movement to curtail the power of District of Columbia voters targeted Congress in its bid to transform the capital's governing structures. Black men's enfranchisement had not yet passed Congress when businessmen and wealthy "old citizens" began discussing the possibility of reorganizing government in the capital so as to diminish voters' power. The bipartisan consolidation movement avoided explicitly racist attacks on the electorate and emphasized the need for good government, balanced budgets, and infrastructure improvements. But the consolidators used the unpopularity of black men's enfranchisement among local whites to their advantage as well. Consolidation advocates decried the waning influence of "taxpayers" and "intelligent" people in the current system of government, allusions to the ill effects of black men's voting rights. And newspapers sympathetic to the consolidation movement ridiculed Republican ward politics, the backbone of black politics since enfranchisement. The movement to consolidate the District's three governments did not succeed for several years. Finally, in February 1871, a Republican-controlled Congress made the District of Columbia into a federal territory governed largely by appointed officials. The creation of the territorial government was the first in a two-stage process by which District of Columbia voters were completely disfranchised.

From the late 1860s through 1871, then, public life in the national capital was characterized by multiple and often conflicting impulses. While some activists sought to put into practice the most egalitarian ideas of the era, others argued for the restriction of political power to those who were wealthy, educated, or white. A bipartisan movement sought to reduce democracy, while African American political leaders defended black men's enfranchisement. Mayor Bowen's promises of jobs for municipal workers began to ring hollow as the impoverished city proved unable to pay its employees. Irish Republicans organized in separate ward-based Republican associations, giving the lie to the party principle that differences of race and ethnicity were immaterial in public life. And, in the 1870 election, a fusionist coalition called the Independent Reform Republicans triumphed over Mayor Bowen and his Republican allies, as black voters split between the two factions. Local Republicans proved too divided to mount an effective opposition to the consolidationists, who enjoyed support in Congress and from President Grant. The last word in this chapter goes to the laborers of the capital, who walked off their jobs the day the territorial government took office. Facing a new government in which they would have few channels for representation, black laborers demanded not social equality, but decent wages and basic dignity.

Paradoxes of Woman Suffrage

Woman suffrage activists could already see in 1865 that postwar reconstruction of the South would require a national conversation about voting rights and that Congress would be at the heart of that debate. Ramping up a movement begun well before the war and placed on hold during it, Elizabeth Cady Stanton and other leading woman suffrage activists now argued for "universal suffrage" as the principle on which to reconstruct the U.S. electorate. They rejected all "class legislation" aimed at enfranchisement of any particular group, insisting instead that voting rights must not be limited by race, sex, or literacy.[9] In their postwar universalism, woman suffragists sought to exploit the tensions between Republicans' professed belief in individual rights and their conviction that the most important rights were for men only. Because congressional radicals had shown that the District of Columbia was high on their agenda for egalitarian reform, many woman suffragists saw the capital as a promising place to make their case.

Conditions were auspicious. The capital was home to an unusual concentration of elite white women intensely interested in politics. Among the local movement's leaders, some had Republican affiliations and many were professionals who came to the city in search of opportunities. Moreover, female government clerks provided the movement an unusual, and unusually strong, cohort of grassroots supporters. The exigencies of war and the expanding federal bureaucracy had pushed the government to turn to white women as waged workers in the executive departments, beginning with the Treasury Department. As historian Cindy Aron found, women clerks were often unmarried, relatively well educated, and from middle-class backgrounds. Such characteristics made them an excellent constituency for the suffrage movement. Their single status meant that they could not imagine themselves represented, politically, by their husbands and that they could easily see in their paychecks evidence of discrimination against women in federal wages. At the same time, women without children or husbands were more likely than married women to have time to commit to voluntary activities outside the home, such as attending woman suffrage meetings.[10]

From its organization in the summer of 1867, the capital's Universal Franchise Association held regular meetings in which numerous issues were addressed and debated. Echoing refrains familiar from the drive for racial equality before the law, the Universal Franchise Association organized a national petition drive asking Congress to "equalize the laws respecting women" in the District and the federal territories. Here, attention focused not only on the vote but also on "the right of woman to the guardianship of her own children, the right to her own earnings, and to hold property in her own name." The association also demanded equal wages for women federal clerks, who were paid less than men as a matter of policy. The association's supporters in Congress served as sponsors for legislation and advocates of its petition drives, while men involved in local Republican politics attended meetings and assisted in campaigns.[11]

As woman suffragists in the capital developed momentum, however, they faced internal divisions over black men's enfranchisement. The issue was a source of tension in the national movement, but it was particularly pointed in the District, where the impact of black men's enfranchisement was evident in everyday life and where it was particularly clear that black men's voting rights had opened the way for consideration of women's enfranchisement.[12] Some white women activists, including Josephine Griffing, continued in the universalistic vein established at the end of the war. They were inclined to work with black women in suffrage activities, and they did not see black men's enfranchisement as an affront to women.

Others felt differently, however. From the earliest discussions of the Fourteenth Amendment, Elizabeth Cady Stanton had worried that the vicissitudes of Republican politics and the situation in the South would push Congress to take action on black men's enfranchisement while ignoring demands for voting rights for women. Stanton began to move away from her earlier advocacy of universal suffrage. Particularly after Congress passed the Fourteenth Amendment, which included a provision punishing states that did not allow all *men* otherwise eligible to vote, Stanton and Susan B. Anthony explored alliances with Democrats and regularly argued that black men were too "degraded and oppressed" to vote.[13]

Such trends in the national movement were also evident locally. In the spring of 1868, a group broke off from the Universal Franchise Association and attempted to form a "White Woman's Intelligent Franchise Association." Their leader was Dr. Mary Walker, a physician famous for her service on Civil War battlefields and her advocacy of dress reform. Walker was precisely the kind of suffrage activist the press liked to deride, and many woman suffragists found her too radical for their tastes. Yet Walker had enough credibility in Washington to organize a meeting that garnered broad attendance. Opening the meeting, Walker announced that the new organization would "work for the franchise until every white woman who could read a ballot and write her name should have the right now extended to all male citizens."[14] Some at the meeting argued for educational, not racial, qualifications on voting rights. A strong contingent, however, favored voting rights for white women only. The meeting's secretary "warmly advocated the rights of white women," arguing that "after this freedom had been attained, it would be time enough to advocate the rights of the colored women to vote." To applause from the crowd, she added,

"White women are superior in education and equal in intellect to the colored man, and should have the same rights."[15]

The suffrage movement's divisions over voting rights for black men made things difficult for Josephine Griffing and others who did not believe that black men's voting rights diminished the cause of women. When Griffing invited Frederick Douglass to speak at a convention of the Universal Franchise Association, to be held in Washington in January 1869, Douglass firmly refused. Although he supported the cause, he said he was too busy with the more urgent struggle for black men's suffrage, which was a matter "of life and death." He considered voting rights for women less pressing, he wrote, since "woman has a thousand ways to attach herself to the governing power of the land and already exerts an honorable influence on the course of legislation." Douglass also disapproved of Stanton and Anthony's argument "that no negro shall be enfranchised while woman is not." "The conduct of these white women, whose husbands, fathers and brothers are voters, does not seem generous," he wrote.[16] Griffing was no doubt disappointed that Douglass declined, but she continued to work with Stanton and Anthony.

The animus brewing within the woman suffrage movement boiled over at the meeting that Griffing had worked to organize. That meeting has been much less studied than the subsequent convention of the American Equal Rights Association in May of that year, at which Stanton and Anthony split off and formed their own association. Yet the proceedings of the January meeting in Washington forecast that rift and etched, more clearly than ever before, how Stanton and Anthony's strong opposition to black men's voting rights, and more broadly their adoption of racial and ethnic stereotypes to discredit an array of poor men as voters, irrevocably divided the movement.[17]

All eyes were already on Washington that January, as Congress debated the Fifteenth Amendment, which would forbid states from depriving men of the vote because of race, color, or previous condition of servitude. Lobbyists for African Americans' and women's rights traveled to Washington to be part of the debate, to stage their own conferences, and to advance their demands before the nation's legislators. In fact, the Universal Franchise Association's meeting convened just as African Americans were concluding the biggest and most widely noticed black convention ever. Delegates to the National Convention of Colored Men of America had discussed establishing labor organizations in the South and had decided to inaugurate a lobbying organization in the capital, the National Executive Committee. While the delegates voiced strong support for the Fifteenth Amendment, a few made a point of arguing that vot-

FIGURE 5.1. "The National Colored Convention in Session at Washington, D.C." As this illustration makes clear, Harriet Johnson was not the only black woman who attended the convention. *Harper's Weekly*, February 6, 1869, 85. Courtesy Library of Congress, LC-USZ62-100970.

ing was a right of citizenship and that Congress must secure enfranchisement for women as well as black men. The delegates also signaled their openness to some forms of women's equality by admitting as a delegate Harriet Johnson, an educator from Pennsylvania. Among those who supported Johnson's admission was Sella Martin, who argued that the conveners were "not tied down to any conventionalities—they had no right to exclude any Delegate."[18]

Delegates from the woman suffrage convention invited members of the African American gathering to join them, and when the women's event opened, several black activists were present, including George T. Downing, the president of the new black men's Executive Committee. But tensions between the two movements surfaced immediately. Stanton opened the woman suffrage convention with a blazing critique of the Fifteenth Amendment. She argued for a new amendment that would make suffrage "the inalienable right of every citizen who is amenable to the laws of the land, who pays taxes and the penalty of crime." According to Stanton, however, it was not only taxpayer status that separated desirable voters from frightening ones. It was also their position in the hierarchy of civilization, a position that was not unrelated to their race or ethnicity. Stanton contrasted "the nobler types of American womanhood" with "the dregs of China, Germany, England, Ireland, and Africa." Invoking the threat posed by "lower orders of foreigners now crowding our shores" alongside that presented by people of African and Asian descent, she enjoined the audience to "think of Patrick and Sambo and Hans and Yung Tung, who do not know the difference between a monarchy and a republic, who can not read the Declaration of Independence or Webster's Spelling-book." It was folly, Stanton argued, for woman suffragists to "hold their own claims in abeyance until all men are crowned with citizenship." Remember, she warned, "the most ignorant men are ever the most hostile to the equality of women."[19] Stanton had moved far from the universalism she had earlier espoused. She now grouped Americans by race, ethnicity, and class, as well as by sex, and brashly argued that some groups made better voters than others.

Following on her speech, Stanton offered two resolutions that split the convention along the same lines that would permanently divide the movement months later. Her first resolution stated that black men's enfranchisement in the South would lead to "injustice and oppression toward woman," and the second argued that "a *man's* government is worse than a *white* man's government, because, in proportion as you increase the tyrants, you make the condition of the disfranchised class more hopeless and degraded." Integral to both resolutions was the assumption that black men would use their power as voters—and the elevated status that accompanied it—to oppress women. Stanton did not specify whether she thought black women or white women, or both, would be threatened by black men's enfranchisement, but her invocation of women's degradation by black male voters surely evoked whites' simmering concerns about sexual aggression by black men toward white women. Stanton's vehement condemnation of black men's enfranchisement provoked strong reactions. Catherine Stebbins, a white woman suffragist who was in attendance, commented afterward, "I never heard her speak when she had so little of what we have always deemed the true philosophy of Reforms, and when she gave less expression to the genuine democratic idea."[20]

Responding to Stanton's provocation, George Downing offered two resolutions of his own. The first rebutted the argument that black men's enfranchisement was bad for the woman suffrage movement. The ballot was "an individual right, not restricted by the color or sex of the individual," Downing proposed, and it could not be "withheld on the plea that another individual is unjustly denied the same." The second resolved, in a direct refutation of Stanton's proposals, that "no one should assume, that a person would, if given their right, abuse it." The convention elected to adopt Downing's resolutions, not Stanton's, an outcome that presaged the opposition Stanton and Anthony would face that May, when the American Equal Rights Association refused to condemn the Fifteenth Amendment.[21]

While national leaders increasingly split into two camps, local activists embarked on a new project. Mary Walker and others continued to advocate voting rights for white women only, but Josephine Griffing and other former abolitionists seized the initiative by organizing a ward-by-ward campaign to register to vote in the spring 1869 municipal elections.[22] The effort involved both black and white women, many of whom had ties to abolitionism, freedmen's relief, or African American education. One of the white women was Julia Wilbur, whose remarkable diary provides a window into how the campaign worked in the first ward.[23]

Wilbur lived an extraordinarily rich social and cultural life in Washington. A native of the Rochester, New York, area, she had never married and had devoted herself to abolitionism, women's rights, and freedmen's relief. During the war, she worked in Alexandria, Virginia, as an agent of the Rochester Ladies' Anti-Slavery Society, where she was a close associate of Harriet Jacobs, author of *Incidents in the Life of a Slave Girl*. She then moved to Washington, where she worked for the Rochester society and the Freedmen's Bureau, before getting a job as a clerk in the Patent Office. In her spare time, Wilbur attended lectures and debates in Congress, went to social events and the theater, and visited schools for freedchildren, often in the company of members of Washington's black elite. Most of Wilbur's social contact with African Americans seems to have been with members of the educated elite, but she also cherished her relationship with a couple named Charlie and Emma Newman, freedpeople she first met in Alexandria who were now making their lives in Washington.[24] She was an astute observer of racial conventions. After a dinner at her close friend Louisa Butler's house with about a dozen of Butler's friends, Wilbur commented in her diary, "I was the only 'white' woman present, although some of them were whiter than myself."[25]

Long-standing social associations among Wilbur, Butler, and several other black and white women of the first ward provide crucial context for their attempt to register to vote. Wilbur spent a great deal of time with Butler, whom she considered "an elegant woman" and "intelligent & refined."[26] The two women often exchanged social visits, particularly after Butler's husband left Washington on a trip to California with his employer, former secretary of state William H. Seward. Wilbur and Butler often called on Eliza Anderson, wife of prominent Baptist minister Duke Anderson. Another acquaintance whom Wilbur mentioned less frequently was Amanda Wall, the Oberlin-educated wife of O. S. B. Wall.[27] Wilbur was closest to Butler and Anderson. The three women often met several times each week, visiting one another's homes or attending lectures and other events.

Thus, when Wilbur, Butler, Anderson, Wall, and others undertook to register to vote in Washington's first ward, they acted within established social networks in which trust and affinity had long been cultivated. On April 22, 1869, Wilbur recorded in her diary that she had "called on Mrs. Butler and Mrs. Anderson" and at the M Street School "to get ladies to go with me to the Registration office this P.M." "After dinner," she continued, one of their male allies drew up a petition and the women signed it. Next, Wilbur, Wall, Butler, another white woman, and two white men headed to Hibernia Engine House in the first ward, where voter registration was under way. The women asked to register and presented their petition, which stated that they believed themselves "entitled to the franchise" and that they deplored their "exclusion from the highest privilege of American citizenship." That night, Wilbur transcribed the text of the entire petition in her diary. Reflecting her commitment to ward-based organizing for the vote, she added, "It is hoped that ladies in every ward will do the same, that it may be apparent the women do wish to vote. I am convinced that when a sufficient number ask for the suffrage they will get it."[28]

The 1869 campaign proved unsuccessful. Even at the apex of Republican radicalism in local affairs, city officials would not accept the women's argument that "no law compelled or authorized the Board [of Registration] to exclude" women from the voter registration rolls.[29] First, ward-based election judges rejected their claims, and later the board of registration as a whole made their defeat official. Yet the women's efforts did garner attention from newspapers in Washington and elsewhere. The *New York Tribune* offered the snide remark that if the women wanted to vote, they should "assume all the duties of citizenship," including "duty on the highways," in the jury box, and in the militia. For its part, the *New York Times* acknowledged that despite the defeat one of the election judges had been favorably disposed toward the women.[30]

Undeterred, woman suffragists continued to demand consideration from Congress. Few could forget the Senate's three-day debate about voting rights for women in the capital in December 1866 or ignore the possibility that Congress might actually be persuaded to undertake an experiment in women's enfranchisement there. Beginning in 1868, woman suffragists made every congressional debate about rechartering the District's municipal governments into an opportunity to lobby Congress and present petitions in favor of their cause.[31] In 1871, as the House of Representatives debated a wholesale reorganization of the District's governing structures, woman suffragists again argued for women's enfranchisement. At suffragists' behest, radical Republican congressman George A. Julian of Indiana proposed that the word "male" be eliminated from voter qualifications in the new District government. Julian argued that "the question of woman's rights necessarily involves the question of human rights" and that he could not "accept as a real democracy, or even a republic, a government 'half slave and half free.'" Julian's proposal was quickly defeated by a vote of 117 to 55. Yet Susan B. Anthony considered it a victory just to have had the issue debated and put to a vote. Julian's amendment had given them a national platform, she told a colleague. "No matter how many *votes* we get—we have secured *universal* discussion—and that is *gain beyond* measure."[32]

Meanwhile, woman suffragists devised another strategy for obtaining the vote in Washington and elsewhere. By 1870, movement leaders were arguing that women were, in fact, already enfranchised by the Fourteenth Amendment. According to this argument, which was often called "the New Departure," the amendment had secured their citizenship, and as citizens they were entitled to the right to vote. Victoria Woodhull, an emerging and controversial leader in the movement, brought that argument to the Capitol in the form of a petition demanding federal legislation to affirm women's presumed right to vote under the Fourteenth Amendment. With help from radical Republican congressmen Julian and Benjamin Butler, Woodhull and other woman suffragists (including Josephine Griffing) obtained a hearing before the House Judiciary Committee in January 1871.[33]

New Departure advocates faced considerable obstacles, however. The first part of their argument, that women were citizens under the Fourteenth Amendment, was essentially beyond doubt. But the second part, that citizenship entitled them to the right to vote, was highly controversial, since the prevailing interpretation of the Fourteenth Amendment was that the rights it protected did not include the right to vote. Predictably, then, the House Judiciary Committee reported adversely on Woodhull's proposed bill, arguing that the Fourteenth Amendment did not permit Congress to regulate suffrage in the states. But the committee left open the possibility of testing the constitutionality of women's disfranchisement in state courts and in the District of Columbia.[34]

Building on years of local activism, and with assurance of legal representation from Albert G. Riddle, a lawyer and former congressman, local suffragists

FIGURE 5.2. "The Judiciary Committee of the House of Representatives Receiving a Deputation of Female Suffragists, January 11th—A Lady Delegate Reading Her Argument in Favor of Woman's Voting, on the Fourteenth and Fifteenth Amendments." *Frank Leslie's Illustrated Newspaper*, February 4, 1871, 349. Courtesy Library of Congress, cph 3a05761.

thus decided to make a new test in the spring of 1871. During the first voter registration under the newly formed territorial government, a group of women, including Julia Wilbur, Amanda Wall, and Josephine Griffing, publicly signed a voting rights petition and marched to the city registrar, accompanied by no less a figure than Frederick Douglass. After a protracted discussion, members of the board of registration allowed each woman individually to ask to be registered and then duly denied each woman her request.[35] At Riddle's urging, the women attempted to vote on election day. They were again denied. Woman suffragists filed two separate lawsuits in the District's Supreme Court, one protesting being prohibited from registering and one for denial of the vote itself. Many suffragists hoped those cases would yield an important ruling on the New Departure argument.[36]

In the current climate, however, there was little chance anyone could have persuaded the court, led by Chief Justice David Cartter, to expand the suffrage to women. Cartter accepted the women's argument that the Fourteenth Amendment made women U.S. citizens. But, like the House Judiciary Committee, he rejected the implication that citizenship entitled them to the right to vote. U.S. citizenship was national, Cartter argued, while states (or the local government, in the case of the District of Columbia) were entitled to determine voter qualifications for themselves.[37] Yet Cartter went beyond ruling on the women's case to opine on the state of the franchise more generally. Consistent with the growing suspicion, locally and nationwide, of popular enfranchisement itself, Cartter held that "the legal vindication of the natural right of all citizens to vote would, at this stage of popular intelligence, involve the destruction of civil government." The judge, himself a mover in the effort to consolidate the District's three governments and thereby reduce voters' power, directed particular concern to "our large centers and cities," where the result of manhood suffrage was "political profligacy and violence verging upon anarchy" as well as "the utter neglect of all agencies to conserve the virtue, integrity, and wisdom of government, and the appropriation of all agencies calculated to demoralize and debase the integrity of the elector."[38] As his activism on behalf of consolidation implied, Cartter had grave doubts about the capacity of urban voters to properly exercise the suffrage. He thought that too many people voted already. Ironically, many woman suffragists agreed with him on that issue and had expressed very similar views about poor men as voters. They diverged only in the fact that Cartter rejected those suffragists' claim that educated women (or white women) would reduce poor men's political influence and lift electoral politics out of barbarism.

School Integration and the Limits of Racial Equality

Just as the woman suffrage movement came up against the limits of contemporary thinking about equality—both within the movement and outside it—so too did the drive for racial equality in the District's public schools. After the 1869 fight over consolidation of the white and black school boards, prominent African American leaders continued to push Congress to make the capital's heretofore white-only public schools open to all. In the spring of 1870, members of the newly formed National Executive Committee explained to the Senate that racially segregated schools had a "depressing effect" on African American children. Echoing the arguments of antebellum school reformers, they insisted that separate schools created "class" feelings and therefore "satisf[ied] prejudices having their origin in slavery and its degrading anti-republican influences." The Executive Committee emphasized the distinction between public and private schools, arguing that racial prejudice might "find refuge" in private schools but should be banished from "schools belonging in common to the public, which the government controls, which *the people's* money and not *a class* maintains." Most of the signers—men such as John F. Cook, George Downing, George Vashon, and Sella Martin—had been involved in the previous winter's contretemps over consolidating the school boards and were among those who had insisted that they would only accept mixed school boards if the students, too, could be mixed.[39]

The Executive Committee's petition was intended to support Senator Charles Sumner's efforts to bring the issue of school integration into the national debate. The Massachusetts senator was a leading congressional advocate of expansive racial equality, and he had done much to make the capital a national showcase for legislation that aspired to erase the legacies of slavery. Sumner's reciprocal relationship with leading black Washingtonians dated at least to his support for Alexander Augusta's 1864 protest against discrimination on the city's streetcars. He corresponded with black men such as Augusta and Martin, and he was particularly close with Downing, who ran an oyster house in the Capitol building and was president of the National Executive Committee. In addition to proposing and pursuing legislation for racial equality, Sumner also urged local African Americans to demand it. For instance, at an 1870 celebration of the ratification of the Fifteenth Amendment, Sumner reminded black Washingtonians that despite recent progress on voting rights black children were still excluded from white schools "on account of color." Urging them to fight the practice, Sumner emphasized that black Washingtonians were in a unique position. In working against racial proscription in the public schools, he told them, "you will not only work for yourselves, but will set an example for all the land, and most especially for the South."[40]

African Americans were far from united on the question of whether to demand access to the white public schools, however. Some worried that black students would not thrive in classrooms with white children, while others rightly perceived that black teachers would not be hired in "mixed" schools, thereby reducing employment opportunities for African American teachers. Indeed, opposition among Washington's African Americans was such that in the winter of 1871 a group visited Senator James Patterson, chair of the District of Columbia Committee and an opponent of school integration, to inform him that local African Americans did not want mixed schools.[41]

Meanwhile, most white Republicans endorsed the concept of taxpayer-supported schools, but they did not see mixed schools as a natural outcome of the battles over rights and citizenship of the Reconstruction era. In fact, when it came to race, public schools were much touchier than public accommodations. No matter that public schools were, by definition, created and funded by government and therefore in a fundamental sense public institutions. To many people, the "publicness" of public schools was mitigated by their inseparability from the private realm of parental authority and familial customs and tastes. Thus, for cultural reasons no less than legal ones, African Americans' struggle for access to white public schools proved more difficult than did the struggle for equality in less obviously "public" institutions such as streetcars, railways, hotels, and theaters. Indeed, many Republican legislators believed that legislation prohibiting racial discrimination in public schools crossed into the realm of taste and personal choice, posing the threat of government-mandated social equality.

Senator James W. Patterson was a case in point. A leader in the New Hampshire common school movement before the war, Patterson was a staunch supporter of public education for black and white children but an adamant opponent of racial integration. Patterson joined the House of Representatives in 1863 and became a senator in 1867. He served on the District of Columbia Committee in both houses, and he made schools one of his signal issues. Patterson was chair of the District of Columbia Committee in the winter of 1871, when the Senate again discussed a bill to consolidate the District's schools under one administration. While the bill was in committee, Sumner had introduced an amendment forbidding "distinction on account of race, color, or previous condition of servitude . . . in the admission of pupils" or in their education.[42] Sumner's amendment survived the committee discussion and was part of the bill that came to the Senate floor. But Patterson opened discussion by stating that he opposed Sumner's antidiscrimination measure and moving that it be removed. The New Hampshire senator believed Congress should not tell the people of the District of Columbia how to manage their schools. Rather, legislators should follow the model of "our northern states," where state legislation "simply leaves it to the board of education in each school district to determine for themselves whether they will mix the whites and blacks or have separate schools for each." Northern state governments (except Massachusetts) had, in fact, traditionally left decisions about racial integration in the hands of local school boards.[43] But the senator did not acknowledge that in postslavery communities throughout the South, where whites controlled the levers of politics, it was virtually certain that local control would result in segregated school systems at best, and at worst the complete denial of public education to black children.

Patterson's defense of segregated schooling relied on the view, widespread among Republicans, that while "race" as such may have been immaterial, black children's civilizational level was lower than that of whites. He compared black children's "level of intelligence and morality" unfavorably with white children, and he argued that segregated schools should persist until black children had improved enough that whites' "prejudices, which are transitory, will pass away, and the children of different races and different colors will mix in the schools."[44] Patterson also insisted that white parents would withdraw their children from school if Congress insisted that the white schools admit black students. He professed to "regret" whites' opposition to racial mixing in the schools. Yet he defended that opposition by explaining that the liberal vision of equality among individual "men" was consistent with the view that mankind was divided into ethnic or national groups at divergent levels of civilization. "We hear that it is the right of every man to enjoy self-government," Patterson said, "but my friend [Matthew Carpenter, a Republican who favored school integration] will hardly say that you could introduce a democracy or a republic in the Micronesian islands, among barbarians; and yet they have all the natural rights which we have." Patterson's analogy separated "natural rights," which were universal, from other rights and privileges, which should only be granted as groups were ready for them. Until black children progressed out of the barbarism of slavery, he argued, racially segregated schools were both necessary and justified. "And so I hope the day will come," he continued, "if we educate the colored and white children alike in this District—and this bill gives equal privileges—when they will be willing to mix in the schools."[45] When black children's period of collective tutelage might end, Patterson did not say.

Many senators were neither so liberal nor so sanguine about the benefits of public education itself. Democratic senator Allen Thurman of Ohio, for example, began his speech by emphasizing that the provision of public education already encroached on "individual liberty" by forcing "hundreds of thousands of parents in this country" to pay taxes for schools to which they could not, "in conscience," send their children. Thurman voiced a concern common among Catholics, who rejected the Protestant components of American public education and often sent their children to parochial schools instead. Now, Thurman complained, Congress proposed to make a bad situation even worse. A school policy that "disregard[ed] the marked differences of race that the Almighty himself has stamped upon the people" was essentially "despotism."[46] Republican policies in the South were forcing the black "minority into an antagonism with the superior and the dominant race of the country," he argued, and school integration in the capital would only increase the likelihood of primordial racial conflict, a conflict African Americans would inevitably lose.[47] Moreover,

Thurman insisted, the radicals were misguided in pushing for social equality measures such as this. "We were told that when you gave to the colored race the right of suffrage, there you intended to stop; that it was only political rights that you intended to give them; that you did not intend to enforce social equality; that you did not intend to say to the white race and the colored race, 'Intermarry with each other, mingle with each other in the private parlor or at the private dinner table.' . . . That is what you said, and yet here we have had bill after bill to do what? Not to give them political equality, for that is already given, but to enforce social equality."[48]

There was, of course, a good deal of truth to Thurman's contention. After legislating emancipation itself and an end to the black codes, radical Republicans in Congress had demanded an end to discrimination on public conveyances and then equal rights for black men to vote, be elected to office, and serve on juries. Once black men could vote and therefore influence local politics, local officials went on to pass laws barring discrimination in quasi-private places like restaurants, theaters, and hotels. Charles Sumner and Howard University doctors had even talked of forcing the Medical Society to admit black doctors. Yet whereas men like Thurman believed such developments revealed the slippery slope from political equality to enforced equality in zones where personal liberty ought to reign, those who supported school integration in the capital denied that something called social equality was on the agenda.

In fact, both camps rejected government-enforced social equality. The point of contention was the location of the boundary between social equality and other kinds of more acceptable equality. For example, Matthew Carpenter, a Republican from Wisconsin, connected school policy to political equality. "There is no more ground or reason in discriminating as to color in . . . the common schools of the District than there is in voting at the polls, and one cannot be granted and the other justified," he maintained. Dinner parties, Carpenter said, were the kind of occasions where social equality might be relevant. If a senator "chooses to give a dinner party," he argued, "he may make such discriminations as he pleases; he need not do it on the ground of color only." Deciding whom to invite to a dinner party—whether the guest list would mingle black and white or wealthy and poor—was entirely different from making school policy. School policy was a matter of government concern; whom to invite to a party was not.[49]

Like his prointegration Republican colleagues, Hiram Revels of Mississippi, the nation's first African American senator, also insisted that mixed schools did not promote social equality. Revels was born free in North Carolina and had attended college in the Midwest. An AME minister, he helped recruit black troops during the war and worked for the Freedmen's Bureau in Mississippi before entering politics. Revels argued that integrated schools in antebellum New England had demonstrated that students "may walk along together," study together, and play together, "but that is the last of it." After attending mixed schools, Revels claimed, "the white children go to their homes; the colored children go to theirs; and on the Lord's day you will see those colored children in colored churches, and the white children in white churches; and if an entertainment is given by a white family, you will see the white children there, and the colored children at entertainments given by persons of their own color."[50] Countering the argument that equality in one place would automatically lead to equality in others, Revels insisted that even where public schools were integrated, private preference still dictated who attended which churches and parties, and who entered whose homes.

The two camps also diverged in what they saw as the proper role of government. And while the precise issue concerned Congress's reach when it came to the capital, their arguments reflected broader divisions over whether government could, and should, play a role in ending the practices of racial segregation and humiliation to which so many white people turned after slavery was abolished. Revels and others who advocated school integration were adamant that the government must take action to ban racial discrimination from properly "public" places like schools and public accommodations. "Let lawmakers cease to make the difference, let school trustees and school boards cease to make the difference, and the people will soon forget it," he argued. In contrast, Democrats and conservative Republicans believed the government could not change people's deeply held beliefs. Thurman had insisted that racial "prejudices . . . are as much a part of our nature as the color of our skin or the features of our face" and that "no law in this world" could "obliterate" them. Patterson, for his part, had argued that the "race" question would adjust itself gradually, as black people uplifted themselves and whites, in response, slowly abandoned their prejudice.[51] In their view, racism would end or not as a result of personal actions and decisions; the government had little role to play in such matters. Yet radicals continued to insist, as they had in the debate over common carriers, that in the public and quasi-public places where governments could claim jurisdiction, legislators must positively affirm principles of nondiscrimination.

The 1871 Senate debate about school integration in the capital foreshadowed many of the issues that would arise in discussions of Sumner's "supplemental" civil rights bill, which would be debated intermittently from 1872 until a diminished version of it passed in 1875. Congressmen would continue to argue over whether school integration was a social equality measure and over how much any government—but particularly the federal government—could encroach on the "individual liberty" of white adults who preferred to send their children to all-white schools or of white business owners who preferred to exclude or segregate black patrons. In the nearer term, Congress opted not to pass the 1871 District of Columbia school bill at all. A major reorganization of the capital's government was at hand, and senators deemed it prudent to postpone action on the public schools until that work was completed.

Consolidation and Its Discontents

The impetus for a thorough overhaul of government in the District of Co-lumbia came from a powerful movement, energized by both Republicans and Democrats, to persuade Congress that the capital's current governments were no longer viable. The consolidation movement claimed that the three exist-ing municipal governments (Washington City, Georgetown, and the county's Levy Court) were unwieldy and inefficient, and that Washington's government was hopelessly mismanaged and debt-ridden. There was considerable truth in these claims. Yet the consolidators' preferred method for solving these prob-lems—the creation of a government run largely by presidential appointees—suggests another important facet of their critique. The consolidators' coalition of Republicans and Democrats was organized around a shared contempt for black men's newly acquired political power. Some who favored consolidation blamed black voters directly for Washington's problems. Others were more circumspect about the issue of race and emphasized efficiency and infrastruc-ture improvements instead. Yet they, too, attacked the District's black elec-torate by insisting on the rights of "taxpayers" and control by "intelligent" Washingtonians. Indeed, when viewed in the context of Reconstruction and of the biracial government the consolidators sought to dismantle, the movement's demand for a government run by presidential appointees must be understood as an effort to "redeem" the District from what its members saw as the excesses of Reconstruction.

Talk of instituting a commission government for the District of Columbia began in the fall of 1865 as a direct response to the debate over black men's en-franchisement. As Congress prepared to debate the issue and city officials ex-pressed vehement opposition, newspapers reported that property owners and politicians already had an alternative plan in mind. Should black men's enfranchisement be adopted, the city governments of Washington and Georgetown could surrender their corporation charters, thereby placing administration of the cities in the hands of a board of commissioners to be appointed by the U.S. president. As one newspaper put it, "their object" was "to quiet the agitation of the suffrage question, as well as to secure economy and greater benefits in the expenditure of money collected from them by the present system of taxation." The conversation continued even after the suffrage bill passed the House of Representatives, as the *New York Herald* reported that ward politicians proposed to vacate the charter, leaving appointments to the president and depriving the "despised African" of the vote.[52]

Similar suggestions emerged among business leaders on the infant Washington Board of Trade. The men involved in the Board of Trade, founded in the fall of 1865, represented a range of occupations and political orientations. The Board of Trade's founders self-consciously modeled the organization on similar entities in Philadelphia and Chicago. They intended it to be nonpartisan, interested strictly in the economic prosperity of the capital. Because the city's economic elite was relatively small, organizers decided to keep dues rather low ($10 per year) and to admit any man who transacted business, rather than restricting membership to those involved in large enterprises.[53] Among the founders of the Board of Trade was Alexander Robey Shepherd, a native of Washington whose father had owned slaves as well as estates in both Washington City and the county. Shepherd, a Republican, was in the plumbing and pipe fitting business and had prospered as Washington expanded.[54] Ambitious and politically savvy, Shepherd had served on the common council during the Civil War and, as the war ended, had successfully positioned himself at the forefront of the local business community.

About a month after the Board of Trade's inauguration, Shepherd proposed that the organization urge Congress to consolidate the District's three governments into one. He claimed that the measure "was a business necessity, and should not be mixed up in any degree with politics, negro suffrage or anything else." Although many on the board supported the proposal, board members ultimately decided to defer a decision. Undeterred, Shepherd raised the issue again several weeks later, this time offering more background. He argued that recent government consolidation efforts in Philadelphia, New York, and Brooklyn proved that cities worked best when contiguous municipalities were merged together. Invoking the ongoing conversation in conservative circles about vacating the city charter, he said, "This question had been suggested to him by some of the oldest citizens of the District, who felt it would be beneficial to have Congress control the whole." He claimed the proposal did not violate the Board of Trade's commitment to nonpartisanship. Shepherd was looking at the matter from a "business point of view," and "nine-tenths of the *bona fide* taxpayers and property holders of the District favored a consolidation."[55] Shepherd cleverly attempted to fuse the Board of Trade's interest in cultivating commercial development with the "oldest citizens'" outright rejection of black men's voting rights. Conservatives had always argued that black men's enfranchisement would be bad for business. Now Shepherd saw the makings of a powerful coalition if conservatives' concerns could be merged with those of the Board of Trade, which itself included many Democrats as well as wealthy Republicans. The time was still not right, however. Members of the Board of Trade once again demurred, with prominent members registering doubts about the association involving itself in politics.

The board's reluctance notwithstanding, Lot Morrill, the chair of the District of Columbia Committee, introduced legislation in the Senate the next month to consolidate the District's governments into a single government run by a presidentially appointed commission. Why Morrill proposed legislation for a commission government of the capital is not entirely clear. His proposal came in January 1866, just after the House of Representatives passed its District of Columbia suffrage bill, and it may have been, at least in part, a response to what he saw as the House's unwise course in approving universal manhood suffrage for the capital. It is also possible that the legislation was suggested to him by District of Columbia activists such as Shepherd. Historians have never discovered direct evidence that Shepherd or others on the Board of Trade wrote the legislation (and Morrill's personal papers are not available in any archive). But Shepherd's own ambitions, along with the easy access that prominent Washingtonians had to members of Congress and the similarity of Morrill's proposal to those already under discussion among the capital's economic elite, make the connection highly plausible. Morrill's gambit generated little interest in 1866, but it would become the template for Shepherd and his allies as they continued to pursue an overhaul of the District's governing structures and a diminution of voters' power.[56]

After black men began voting in 1867, conditions were increasingly favorable for a measure like Morrill's. Many white Washingtonians had never supported black men's enfranchisement, and the growing power of radical Republicans in city government illustrated the changes wrought by the new voters. The debate intensified when Washington's charter was about to expire in May 1868, just before Sayles Bowen's run for mayor. A mass meeting of "citizens" appointed a committee to propose legislation to Congress, similar to the original Morrill bill, that they "deem[ed] requisite for the good government of the District." The committee included Shepherd, D.C. Supreme Court justice David Cartter, the superintendent of the police board, and other prominent Republicans. Once again, they made little headway. The new chair of the Senate District of Columbia Committee was James Harlan, a radical Republican from Iowa. Harlan was unsympathetic to the citizens' movement, and he led senators to reject consolidation proposals in favor of rechartering the city government basically as it stood.[57]

The consolidators did not give up easily, however. The city's press increasingly supported them, making arguments about black voters' incompetence that meshed with long-standing concerns among respectable people of both parties that freedmen were not ready for voting rights and that black men's enfranchisement endangered the capital's financial well-being. Democratic and conservative newspapers remained willing to criticize black voters as such. For instance, after Sayles Bowen's election in June 1868, the *National Intelligencer* portrayed itself as an advocate for "taxpayers" and businessmen against a Republican administration that promised to use public employment as poor relief and to appoint too many dependent black men to patronage positions. Black enfranchisement and the threat of "negro rule," the *Intelligencer* insisted, were driving investors out of the capital.[58] The outlook became even worse in the wake of the 1869 canvass, when black men were elected to the council from every ward during an election that was marred by violence. The Democratic *New York World* now warned, "Let no Northern man, be he Democrat or Republican, for his life or his property set his foot in Washington with a dollar; for under the municipal rule now in force, neither is safe. Before this riot, capitalists have shunned this place. Let them do so forever more. The town is doomed and damned."[59]

Racialized fears of economic decline had been central to conservative opposition to black enfranchisement, and Shepherd and his allies exploited those fears as they lobbied for reform of the District's government. The Republican *Evening Star*—of which Shepherd was part owner—joined the conservative condemnation of local Republican rule. Although the *Evening Star* was loath to blame black voters explicitly, the newspaper frequently noticed that other papers were representing "negro rule" as a problem and alluding to Washington as the worst-governed city in the country. During the summer of 1869, the paper expressed concern that all manner of changes in the capital—from the tumultuous municipal election to the presidential transition from Johnson to Grant—were depressing the local economy. The paper worried that the Republican-dominated city council would raise taxes, thus constricting business opportunities even more. That winter, the paper turned decisively against Bowen and the ward-based Republican associations that continued to support him. It ridiculed the disorderly, raucous, and folksy qualities of popular politics, and it contrasted ward activists who supposedly said things like "shoo fly" in meetings against "citizen" reformers who sought "harmonious government."[60] Showing how visions of black voters' vulnerability translated easily into fears of political corruption, the *Evening Star* claimed that the Bowen administration, "instead of encouraging the colored people to habits of industry and thrift," made "every effort . . . to degrade and enslave them . . . by vice and politics."[61]

Those charges resonated strongly with many white Republicans' skepticism about freedpeople's worthiness of the rights and privileges white people expected and often enjoyed. Even Freedmen's Bureau agents, freedmen's relief agents, and others sympathetic to the plight of freedpeople had often expressed the view that freedpeople must show, through their personal comportment, that they were worthy of such rights. That outlook had given many Republicans and their allies impetus to uplift freedpeople by tutoring them in housekeeping, personal habits, and literacy. Yet, as debates over black men's enfranchisement had made clear, it had also instilled doubts about freedmen's political capacities. Many moderate and conservative Republicans had come to support universal manhood suffrage, but that did not mean they had ceased to fear that freedmen's lack of formal education and ostensible dependency in slavery would make them dangerous as voters.

Business leaders like Shepherd translated such doubts about the civil and political capacities of African Americans in general and freedpeople in particular into a new context. The novelty of black men's enfranchisement was fading and the congressional commitment weakening, but among Republicans the dedication to formal racial equality remained. Thus the consolidators professed not to care about black enfranchisement as such but argued, as Shepherd had in his proposal to the Board of Trade, that "taxpayers" and "intelligent citizens" favored consolidating the District's government.[62] Claims of special prerogatives for citizens and taxpayers helped consolidators argue for reducing the political power of the capital's poor black residents without offending Republicans in Congress, who rejected outright racism but were not immune to suggestions that freedmen were not ready to vote. Indeed, unlike later white supremacists, Shepherd and his cohort did not seek to racially purify the electorate. They did not mind if black men continued to serve in office, provided that the white business elite controlled the agenda. But in order to obtain such control, the consolidationist coalition energetically denigrated black voters and the men they elected to office, essentially arguing that universal manhood suffrage had proved a failure.

Leaders of the consolidation movement learned as they went along, and by the winter of 1870 they had arrived at an effective strategy for winning congressional support. Accommodating the preferences of Republicans in Congress who were still reluctant to fully disfranchise voters, as the 1866 Morrill bill had proposed, the consolidators rallied behind a bill that would render the District of Columbia a federal territory—on the model of administrative districts preparing to be admitted to the United States as states. They understood, as Shepherd put it at a meeting early that winter, that "the idea of suffrage would have to be recognized." How much suffrage remained a question to which Shepherd himself had many answers. He told a meeting of consolidationists that he supported the idea of a governor and upper legislative house appointed by the U.S. Senate, with a lower house elected by the people. Days later, however, he told a meeting of the first-ward Republicans that he advocated having all officers "from the Governor down to the Common Councilors, elected by the people." Ward Republicans evidently found him unpersuasive. After Shepherd's speech, they resolved that the consolidation movement was led by "men who have always opposed the right of suffrage to colored men" and whose object was "the oppression of the laboring men."[63]

The consolidation movement gained momentum as the Senate debated a bill that would establish the District of Columbia as a territory with elected upper and lower legislative houses. The consolidationists formed a General Committee of One Hundred to lobby Congress, and they allied themselves with the Boys in Blue, a large veterans' organization. Faced with charges that they represented only the interests of a small elite, they sought to build a popular movement by organizing ward-based associations, canvassing neighborhoods, and lobbying every member of Congress. They even planned to hold a torchlight procession celebrating ratification of the Fifteenth Amendment, a brazen attempt to prove themselves good Republicans who, in theory if not in their own community, favored black men's enfranchisement. With its provisions for elected upper and lower houses, the Senate's territorial bill gained support from some prominent white Republicans active in freedmen's affairs, the most significant of whom was O. O. Howard himself. The Senate passed its territorial consolidation bill in May 1870, but the House did not take it up, allowing another contest for Washington mayor and city council to go forward in June.[64]

All along, the consolidators faced vehement opposition, from both white and black elected officials and from an African American community that was virtually unified on the issue. In 1868, a group of city officials charged that the Morrill bill was "prepared by a few interested citizens" and did not represent the viewpoint of the majority of residents or of the local Republican Party. They objected to consolidation on grounds of both race and class. Not only would it "place our municipal affairs in the control of a few monied men and speculators, but it substantially strikes down that great privilege of the elective franchise," they insisted.[65] The popular outcry against the consolidationists should not be surprising. Indeed, it was largely because voters and their political representatives would not submit to the priorities of the business elite that Shepherd and others sought consolidation and disfranchisement in the first place. Members of the black elite opposed consolidation in stark terms. In view of historians' portrayal of that class as disconnected and antidemocratic, it is particularly noteworthy that some of the city's most prominent black men, including John F. Cook Jr., George Vashon, and Sella Martin, were on record opposing consolidation in strong terms. In the main, black Washingtonians seemed to agree with Vashon, who charged at the National Convention of Colored Men in January 1869 that the capital's consolidation movement was "a base plot, designed to defraud the eight thousand freedmen therein of the elective franchise, and cheat them of their newborn freedom."[66]

The *New Era*, a black weekly founded in the winter of 1870, became an important voice in opposition to consolidation. Several prominent Washington African Americans had begun planning the newspaper in 1869 and had urged Frederick Douglass to be its editor. Douglass, then living in Rochester, was skeptical at first. By the end of the year, however, he had agreed to serve as corresponding editor, and Sella Martin had resigned his position as pastor of 15th Street Presbyterian Church to become the paper's Washington-based editor. Martin found the job exhausting and left the city in the summer of 1870. By that time, Douglass was ready to take the reins, and in September he became the paper's major editorial voice, a position he held for about two years before passing the business to his sons, Lewis and Frederick Jr.[67]

Under Martin's editorship during the winter of 1870, the *New Era* railed against consolidation. It was the consolidators, not the voters, who sought to block "the wheels of progress," the editors insisted. The paper assailed the consolidationists for using the rhetoric of progress to obscure their real goal, which was disfranchisement. "In plain Anglo-Saxon," the editors claimed, "the old fogies are opposed to negro suffrage; and as they cannot withdraw it, they seek to diminish if not destroy, the opportunities for its exercise. Here is the whole secret of the recently inaugurated movement to take away our municipal government."[68] Another editorial sought to counter the consolidators' relentless efforts to link African Americans with poverty and outsider status. "White people flock here from all parts, too," they wrote, "Clerks, appointment clerks, —even, heads of departments—come here, and never pay one cent into the city treasury." Contrary to the claims of the consolidators, the *New Era* insisted that ex-slave voters and the officials they elected were not to blame for the District's financial problems. The problem, the paper argued, was "not the form of government, but the insufficiency of the supplies."[69]

Although the consolidation movement faced formidable opposition from black leaders and from many white Republican politicians as well, by the winter of 1870 the most obvious alternative—the administration of Mayor Sayles Bowen—was none too attractive for many Republican voters. Indeed, building a unified movement in opposition to the consolidationists proved impossible, in large part because the Republicans had become so fractured. Mayor Bowen and his allies had had a difficult year. Some Washingtonians had hoped a Republican mayor would be able to extract more generous funding from Congress, but Bowen proved unable to persuade Congress to end its miserly attitude toward the capital. Bowen vowed to balance the budget and spend only what the city could afford, but he attempted a sweeping program of improvements funded by a new bond issue and by what he hoped would be increased tax revenues resulting from an 1869 reassessment of property values. Bowen was already reviled by Democrats, and the prospect of higher taxes and larger municipal debts alienated moderate Republicans on the city council as well. A former commissioner of improvements, John H. Crane, charged the mayor with corrupt contracting, and although a high-profile investigation exonerated Bowen, the episode only highlighted the growing divisions among Republicans. Bowen also lost support from African American constituents over his inept handling of school issues, and laborers and contractors on the public works grew impatient with delayed or unpaid wages.[70]

The waning support of black laborers was probably Bowen's biggest problem outside of the juggernaut of the consolidation movement. As mayor, Bowen had done much to meet black laborers' demands for an equitable share of public works, and he had included Irish laborers in the patronage as well. The multitudes of workers in the employ of the city government, if paid regularly and decently, might have continued to support the mayor. But the city government was perpetually short of money and thus could not be relied upon for jobs, or even to pay its laborers for work already done. Ward-based workingmen's associations, which were biracial and included both common laborers and contractors, sent representatives to the mayor's office to lobby for work and press for timely and fair payment of city laborers. But Bowen often delivered unwelcome news to those representatives—that he could not guarantee them employment or that he could not pay them. The representatives, in turn, brought such tidings back to the men of their wards, many of whom relied on city employment for their livelihood. By the winter and spring of 1870, many ward-based laboring men's associations had become magnifiers of disappointment and dissent.[71]

The political trajectory of labor activist George Hatton, who first supported Bowen but then turned against him, shows how support for Bowen diminished among some African Americans who made labor issues a priority. Hatton was born in slavery in nearby Prince George's County, Maryland. His father purchased several of his children and his wife from their owner, and Hatton moved to the capital to take an apprenticeship in a Pennsylvania Avenue pharmacy. During the wartime recruitment of black soldiers, Hatton, who was about twenty years old at the time, emerged as a powerful and popular speaker and became a noncommissioned officer in the 1st USCT. Wounded in the war, he returned to the capital and worked with the Freedmen's Bureau to help his father donate land in nearby Oxon Hill, Maryland, to a school for freedpeople. Hatton also immersed himself in Republican politics. From his base in the fourth ward, he participated in the drive for black men's enfranchisement and was part of a group that petitioned Congress to remove the word "white" from the city charter. After enfranchisement, he turned to labor issues, taking a leading role in the Fourth Ward Laboring Men's Association. Hatton had significant political ambitions, and by 1869 he was strongly aligned with Mayor Bowen, arguing for Republican unity against a short-lived fusionist opposition and ceding the more radical ground on labor issues to a rival in the ward, plasterer Marcellus West.[72]

In the June 1869 election, fourth-ward voters elected Hatton to the Washington common council on the regular Republican ticket. But Hatton soon became disillusioned with Bowen, and by the next year's municipal election he had become a vocal opponent of the mayor. Hatton's reasons for the break with Bowen were myriad. A strong proponent of both autonomy for the black public schools and school integration, Hatton was frustrated with Bowen's clumsy school policies. A labor advocate, he also became disillusioned with the Bowen administration's inability or unwillingness to make good on its obligations to workingmen. Finally, he developed a personal grievance against Bowen in the summer of 1869 when he was the only African American member of a delegation of city officials who traveled to Gettysburg, Pennsylvania, for a commemoration at the historic battlefield. Hatton charged that during the trip, council members and Bowen himself abandoned him when they went out for dinner in Baltimore and then refused to make a stand for his right to eat breakfast in the restaurant of their hotel in Gettysburg. Bowen and his allies vehemently denied all the charges, no doubt insulting Hatton even further. For all these reasons, by the time the 1870 election season was at hand, Hatton was ready to become a leader in the newly formed Independent Reform Republican movement, which sought to unseat the mayor and his allies.[73]

The weakness of the local Republican operation was also clear in the formation of Irish Republican associations, which flourished in many wards during 1869 and 1870. The capital was a national hub for a short-lived flurry of Irish Republican organizing, which began during Grant's presidential campaign in 1868. The Irish Republican movement was a dissident movement among Irish Americans, who were overwhelmingly Democrats. Nationally, Irish Republicans promoted Irish defections from the Democratic Party, proclaimed support for the Fifteenth Amendment, advocated a protective tariff, and supported the Republicans' hard line against England in foreign policy. After Grant's election, the national Irish Republican movement became a mechanism through which Irish supporters sought presidential patronage. It also allowed people of Irish origin to proclaim both loyalty to the Republican Party and an ethnic identity that shaped their views on the political issues of the day.[74]

Locally, Irish Republicans organized clubs in various Washington wards and a central association to oversee matters throughout the city. With Republicans dominant in city affairs, Irish Republicans indicated that they expected that their political loyalty would be rewarded with jobs and other benefits. As one leader put it, Irish Republicans "could not deny that they were members of the bread and butter brigade, for they were all looking for their bread and butter."[75] Mayor Bowen and the mainstream Republicans seem to have agreed that a Republican-Irish alliance could be useful. Irish immigrants were the capital's second-largest group of unskilled laborers, next to African Americans, and in closely fought elections their votes could be pivotal. Evidence is limited, but it seems likely that Bowen, a savvy politician, went out of his way to oblige. Indeed, one black man who opposed Bowen in 1869 complained that "'the Radical Irish' had the work that year."[76]

It was not always easy to make the case that more united African American and Irish Republicans than divided them. In the winter of 1870, leaders of the Fourth Ward Irish Republican Club were forced to respond to rumors that Irish Republicans "by forming into an association exclusive in its character, wish to avoid coming into contact and affiliating with the colored man." Club members resolved to dispel that impression, announcing that they were "anxious that the most friendly feeling should prevail between ourselves and our colored political friends" and pledging to support "the colored Republicans throughout the city." On hand at that meeting were two black labor leaders who sought to cement the alliance. One of them, John Freeman, spoke vividly about the power of a coalition of Irish and African American voters under Republican auspices. "The success of the party depended on those who had been oppressed—the Irish and the negro," Freeman argued, "and they should not saddle any particular man on their backs; but nominate and support men who will work for the interests of the poor man." Defending the Bowen administration against attacks by both the consolidation movement and the Independent Reform Republicans, Freeman insisted that the city government "had done more in giving work to the laboring man in one ward than had heretofore been done in the entire city."[77]

Why did local Irish Republicans in Washington feel the need to organize separately from the mainstream party organizations? As black activists and white Republican regulars sought to work with the Irish Republicans, no one seemed inclined to point out that the very existence of separate Irish Republican associations undermined the Republican ideal of a party in which differences among men were vanquished by more universal interests. Republicans' case for formal equality and their broader vision of equal citizenship implied that, at least in formal politics, ethnic and class differences were irrelevant. Yet mainstream Republicans seemed to accept that their professed universalism would not banish, even within the party, people's desire to align themselves with their ethnic groups. In fact, German Republicans also organized their own associations in Washington.[78] As later events would reveal, however, white Republicans could accept both equality and difference in the party only when it came to white people; when African Americans attempted to form independent black Republican associations in 1873, white party regulars responded with screeds about race war and Haiti.

Weakened by myriad internal divisions, in 1870 the local Republican Party under Bowen's leadership faced its first formidable opponents, the Independent Reform Republicans. The Independents built a successful fusion organization that exploited the various breaches in the local Republican Party. The movement was characteristic of a moment, seen nationwide in a variety of guises, in which party alignments that had coalesced around slavery and the sectional crisis were breaking apart. Particularly after passage of the Fifteenth Amendment, which many Republicans believed was the culmination of Reconstruction policy, new issues animated politics. The Republican Party, always a somewhat tenuous coalition, began to shatter, while the weaker Democrats sought points of alliance with Republicans who were ready to assert independence from the Grant administration or the Reconstruction program. On the national scene, this impulse reached its apex in 1872, when Liberal Republicans aligned with Democrats in support of New York editor Horace Greeley as a candidate for president.

In Washington in 1870, the Independent Reform Republicans likewise sought to bring together the broad range of Washingtonians who were disillusioned with the Bowen administration. They charged Bowen and his allies with corrupt distribution of patronage and complained that Bowen had betrayed the African American laborers who had voted for him in such large numbers.[79] The party's platform decried special interests of race and class and advocated a kind of universalistic republicanism long important in Republican Party rhetoric but submerged, in the Bowen administration, by the more adversarial politics of divergent group interests. The Independents' nominee for mayor, Matthew Emery, was a native of the region, a wealthy contractor with a reputation for being a fair employer.[80] There was space in the party for labor organizations and labor leaders like George Hatton; for Democrats seeking a way into the District's heavily Republican politics; and for businessmen reformers like Shepherd, who worked for the Independents' success even as he continued to lobby for a complete overhaul of the capital's governing structures.

Faced with the onslaught of both the Independents and the consolidation movement, leading supporters of Bowen struggled to keep Washington Republicans in line but quickly found they could command little discipline. Bowenites insisted that the consolidators stood for disfranchisement and that the Independent movement was a stalking horse for the Democrats. Defending the Bowen administration's employment policies against charges that black laborers had been hired for "unessential work," Anthony Bowen argued that the municipal administration employed freedmen "in the improvement of property, and thereby made it valuable, and kept you in so doing from starvation, thus benefiting both the poor and the rich." By contrast, he argued, "reformers propose that no improvements shall be made: that Washington shall revert back to old slavery times." But it must have been difficult to believe that last claim, when men such as George Hatton—who was, like Anthony Bowen, a former slave—were prominent in the Independent party and when it surely felt like slavery to work for the city government and receive no wages. Josephine Griffing made a last-minute plea that Senator Sumner issue a letter "counselling a Union of the Loyal Men" to "save this city." Sumner evidently declined to weigh in.[81]

The masses of black voters faced a difficult choice. Bowen's administration had indeed done much to support African Americans' bid for a fairer distribution of public works, and he had advanced racial equality by appointing black men to positions of authority in city government as well. Yet he had fumbled on school issues, and, perhaps most important, his administration had too often proven unable to actually pay the many laborers it hired. Conversely, the Independents promised a new regime that would pay its employees and treat everyone fairly. The movement had support from Hatton and other respected black leaders who refused to fall into line behind the Republican Party organization. Yet the Independents were led by white men who had never done much to advocate African American equality, and the party actively sought support from Democrats, whose positions both locally and nationally were anathema to black rights and to Republican Reconstruction policy.

In the end, the Independents triumphed in a resounding victory. Emery beat Bowen in all of Washington's seven wards, and Bowen stalwarts won only five of twenty-one city seats on the city council. Emery's electoral triumph resulted from an alliance between Democrats and the many black and white Republican voters who had decided that it was time for a new municipal administration. Bowen and his allies had proven too tainted by accusations of corruption and too overpowered by the forces arrayed against them to withstand the Independents' challenge.[82]

White moderates and conservatives might have viewed Emery's election as proof that, contrary to their assumptions, black men did not vote as a mass, coalitions could shift, and incompetents could be voted out of office. Indeed, by exploiting divisions among both whites and African Americans and by taking advantage of fissures among Republicans, the Independents had succeeded in putting a businessman reformer in the mayor's office without radically transforming the structure of city government. But Shepherd and his allies were in no mood to slow down. Even as Emery assumed the mayoralty, it was clear that the existing structure of Washington City government would likely be eliminated once the House of Representatives took its turn at hammering out a municipal government reform bill.

In fact, Matthew Emery had been in office for less than a year when, on February 21, 1871, Congress finally passed legislation establishing an entirely new form of government for the District of Columbia. The nation's lawmakers made the District of Columbia into a federal territory with a legislative upper house, governor, and board of public works appointed by the president. The only remaining elective offices were the lower house of the territorial legislature (the House of Delegates) and a nonvoting representative in the U.S. House of Representatives. There would be neither voting rights for women nor integrated schools. The federal government would now be liable for special assessments, but federal property still could not be taxed directly, and Congress made no other provision to support the District financially. Leaders of the consolidation movement did not get all they had wanted, but they had good reason to celebrate. A coalition of Democrats and moderate Republicans that, as historian Alan Lessoff put it, "anticipated the emerging consensus against Radical Reconstruction" had defeated radical Republican senators' attempt to stop the bill.[83] And the new charter accomplished their basic goals of streamlining the District's governments and dramatically shrinking the power of the newly biracial electorate.

The Attenuation of Popular Politics

President Grant's appointments to the territorial government revealed the enthusiasm with which he supported the consolidation movement's goals. To promote the business agenda advocated in the consolidation movement and to reward the organizers of that campaign, the president appointed Alexander Shepherd and several other consolidation activists to the five-man Board of Public Works. The territorial charter left the board's role ill-defined, but Shepherd would make it the most powerful entity in the entire government. Grant chose as territorial governor Henry D. Cooke, brother of famed financier Jay Cooke and the manager of Washington's First National Bank.[84] Grant's appointments to the new District of Columbia government helped cement the vision of economic progress, elite rule, and popular disempowerment that Shepherd and his allies had long promoted.

Yet the consolidationists' vision of an improved and modernized city required not only investors and managers, but laborers as well, and the capital's workingmen quickly demonstrated they were not ready to accept the new government on its own terms. Consolidationists had talked vaguely about how city improvements would bring prosperity to everyone, but they had never done much to elicit support from the capital's laboring population, preferring instead to represent themselves as "citizens" and "taxpayers." Perhaps consolidation leaders believed they had little to worry about when it came to Washington's corps of unskilled laborers. Even at the height of Bowen's public works program, the population of unskilled black laborers had remained far in excess of those who could be employed. The interchangeability of those laborers, and the seemingly endless supply, helped keep wages down and probably made organized opposition seem unlikely. Thus territorial officials may well have been surprised that on the day they took office, the capital's day laborers launched a dramatic general strike, which lasted more than a week. At first, white men and black men alike walked off their jobs on public works projects. After several days, however, the strike took a more radical turn, as white men returned to work while black laborers continued the strike.

The June 1871 strike is significant not just for revealing racial factionalism among the city's laborers and the growing militancy of the strikers, but also for demonstrating how labor activism became a form of political expression when other political channels were closed off. Black men had demanded fairer distribution of public works employment from the moment they were enfranchised. Under the traditional structure of municipal government, black laborers knew that city officials must take their demands seriously or risk being voted out of office. As a result, Mayor Bowen and other city officials had made strong efforts to distribute jobs more equally and to appoint black men to patronage positions. Now, however, the consolidationists had succeeded not only in getting control of the government but also in transforming the relationship between voting rights and patronage. With far fewer offices up for election and far more power resting in the hands of appointed officials, the city's black laborers were no doubt wary of the new form of government itself. And if that were not enough, they had little reason to trust the personnel now in charge. The consolidationists had never sought support from African Americans, and African Americans—through the *New Era* and other outlets—had vehemently opposed consolidation.

Rumblings of labor unrest began the week before, but the general strike of city workers coalesced on the morning of June 1, the day the territorial government took office. Some 300 black men assembled near a worksite of the Columbia Street Railway and announced that they would "stand for their rights at $2 per day and eight hours' labor." As strikers spread out across the city and police fanned out to contain them, rumors circulated that Governor Cooke was prepared to offer $2.00 per day on all city work. When a crowd of 1,000 laborers approached city hall, however, they learned that the governor had not yet arrived at work. Laborers continued to walk off their jobs throughout the day, and in the evening, an overflowing crowd gathered at Union League Hall to discuss next steps.[85]

The leaders who assumed the dais that night were both black and white and represented both the stalwart and the Independent Republican factions in municipal politics. Henry Himber, a white supporter of Sayles Bowen from the first ward, presided; George Hatton, black Union veteran and former Bowen opponent, served as secretary.[86] Speakers representing the many facets of local Republican politics exhorted the laborers to calm and deliberate action. A committee drafted a statement to Governor Cooke promising to renounce strikes in exchange for $2.00 for an eight-hour day of work. The prevailing rate of pay by "contractors executing public work" was $1.25 to $1.50 for a ten-hour day, they stated, while laborers for the federal government and "the corporation" itself made $2.00 per day. As one Republican politician noted during the strike, the 1867 city ordinance mandating a minimum of $2.00 per day for corporation laborers had "never amounted to anything."[87] Most city work was farmed out to private contractors, who evidently were not held to the city's wage standard. The striking laborers argued that given the high cost of rent in the capital it was impossible for a man to support his family on $1.25 per day.[88] Their demand for a living wage was founded on a vision of manhood and basic dignity, and it implied that the municipal government should step in on behalf of laborers by establishing wage rates not only for its own employees but also for those working for private contractors.

The strike continued to spread, as workers at railroad and streetcar projects, bridges, a sea wall, and a saw mill all walked off their jobs. But Governor Cooke promised "mature and careful consideration" of laborers' demands and convened a meeting between contractors and labor representatives. According to the *Chronicle*, the parties struck an agreement that the current contracts would continue at $1.50 per day but future contracts would be let at $2.00. Meanwhile, a member of the District's legislature introduced legislation to establish a meaningful minimum wage, and George Hatton forecast "the beginning of a new party in this country, without respect to former party affiliations, which was a labor movement against capital."[89] Despite the contractors' conciliatory tone and Hatton's hope for translating the mass action into a labor party, however, the strike was far from over. After a weekend hiatus, laborers continued their demand of $2.00 for an eight-hour day, and the contractors flatly refused.

The strike now moved into a more radical and more intensely racialized phase. Many of the white strikers resumed work, as some 1,000 African American men and "a large crowd of white men" convened at City Hall to discuss how to proceed.[90] Members of the committee that had brokered the failed deal with the contractors—Hatton, Himber, and others—were not in evidence.[91] Amid rumors that the committee had sold out to the contractors, a new group of protest leaders assumed the dais. Freed from the institutional ties of their more staid spokesmen, they ratcheted up their language, inveighing against American "aristocrats" and vowing no compromise until their demands were met. Marcellus West, a longtime critic of the Bowen administration and a rival of Hatton's in the fourth ward, advised attendees to return to their wards and form "labor unions," from which representatives would meet in a "general convention" to demand "laborer's rights." He complained that the Board of Public Works and the governor were "swindling us," and "if they refuse to do what is right, [there will be] 'blood for blood.'" Addressing the strikers as ex-slaves, West said contractor Albert Gleason was "down on all niggers" and "worse than our old masters." Others who spoke that night seconded West's denunciations of "aristocrats" and condemned the recent reorganization of the District's government.[92] When Hatton finally put in an appearance at the meeting's end, it was too late. A new group of leaders had emerged.

The general strike reverberated beyond Washington, as laborers for a Georgetown coal hauling company demanded a 50 percent increase in their wages and black laborers at a marble quarry in Loudon County, Virginia, making just fifty or sixty cents per day heard of the Washington strike and walked off their jobs as well.[93] But the black strikers quickly found themselves isolated and under siege, as many of their white allies returned to work for $1.50 per day. Contractors had exploited racial divisions in the labor force from the outset. In particular, the much-maligned Albert Gleason employed Irish laborers at $1.50 throughout the strike and openly dared black strikers to try to recruit his loyal employees to their side.[94]

As the strike became increasingly black and increasingly untethered from established political figures, it was universally condemned in the city's white newspapers. The *Evening Star* branded the strikers as communists, likening them to the radicals who had recently overtaken Paris and organized the Paris Commune. It advised them to abandon the streets for "respectable labor associations after the fashion of the Trades Unions of the mechanics . . . [and]

to demand and enforce their rights in a dignified, self-respecting, law-abiding way." The Democratic *Patriot* called the strikers "Our Ku-Klux," implying that they were racial terrorists in the same mold as the Ku Klux Klan, whose practices had been described in dramatic hearings at the Capitol that winter. The *Chronicle*, heretofore the city's radical Republican organ, surprised many readers by condemning the strike as well.[95]

The territorial government and the police converged in an all-out effort to quell the strike. Policemen themselves no doubt had little sympathy for the black strikers in an atmosphere suffused with racial tension, and police superintendent A. C. Richards seemed willing to bring the force's entire capacity to bear in quashing the disorder.[96] Meanwhile, on the strike's sixth day, the Board of Public Works issued a formal decision that wages would remain at $1.50 per day (the number of hours was unspecified), insisting that this was the maximum the city government—and the taxpayers who ostensibly funded it— could afford to pay. Most strikers now resumed work. In the face of government intransigence, hostility from the police and white laborers, and a lack of resources to support the strike, it was impossible for them to go on. The "compromise" wage of $1.50 was at least an improvement on the $1.25 that many black men had earned before the strike began.[97]

In launching their general strike at the moment the territorial government took office, black laborers not only alerted the new administration to their demand for higher wages, but also drew attention to the attenuation of political structures that heretofore had held such mass actions at bay. Since black men's enfranchisement in 1867, the demands of unskilled laborers had been channeled through the Republican Party, the ward-based workingmen's associations, and the distribution of patronage in the form of work for underemployed freedmen in the city. With the reorganization of the District's government and the installation of a cadre of political leaders largely unaccountable to voters, those structures threatened to give way, causing laborers to take to the streets to demand redress. The ex-politicians' efforts to harness strikers' demands to traditional political channels failed. They had little to offer by way of influence, and labor radicals' condemnations of the local aristocracy no doubt rang true after the recent co-optation of the District's government by the wealthy. In subsequent years, laborers in Richmond and elsewhere would translate dissatisfaction with mainstream political parties into labor-based third party movements. In the District, however, the extended process of disfranchisement—beginning with the installation of the territorial government—meant that black and white laborers could not channel their demands into politics.[98]

It mattered a great deal that the striking laborers were largely African American, and mostly former slaves at that. In the wake of the strike, the *Evening Star* continued the demeaning harangue against supposedly dependent black laborers and ignorant black leaders that it had begun in earnest in the winter of 1870.[99] The position of the heretofore "radical" *Daily Morning Chronicle* was more noteworthy. Throughout the 1860s, the *Chronicle* had been allied with the radical Republicans and their wide-ranging demands for racial equality. But John W. Forney was no longer the editor, and in response to the strike the paper staked out a very different position. The *Chronicle* did condemn its peers for comparing the strikers to the Paris Communards and for lambasting the government's "compromise" of $1.50 per day. It also pointed out that "if a majority of the strikers had been white men and not colored this anxiety would have been less intense, and the deliberation and judicious forbearance of the Governor [would] have been a subject of eulogy instead of censure."[100] Yet the newspaper condemned the strikers for demanding too much, too soon.

As the strike ended, the *Chronicle*'s editorial page endorsed an anonymous letter headed "Make Haste Slowly," noting that its author was a "life-long friend of the oppressed."[101] Addressing the "colored population of the District of Columbia," the writer warned black residents to beware of demagogues like those who had tricked black laborers into going on strike. And he counseled patience. It was "but a few years since they were endowed with the full rights and privileges of citizenship," the writer explained. "The colored man is . . . entitled to full protection under the guarantees of law, but here *the question of equality finds a limit with all men.* All beyond, in political preferment and business success, is to be won by intellectual and moral merit and well-directed efforts" and not by attempts to "force results outside these influences."[102] Like those who used the bogey of "social equality" to delineate a broad realm of custom and taste and a concomitantly narrow zone of rights and equality, this writer asserted that equality already existed where it could be mandated by policy. By contrast, the writer maintained, "political preferment and business success" must be won by hard work and merit alone, without help from equalizing government policies (such as an effective minimum wage law). In singling out "the colored population" for a lecture on behavior, the writer also reiterated the familiar argument that African Americans suffered debilities uniquely associated with their race and ex-slave status. As the *Chronicle's* endorsement suggests, the strikers—as black men and as laborers—had sketched a vision of equality that was intolerable to most white Republicans.

This was a moment of great tension in Reconstruction politics. Eric Foner wrote that in 1869 and 1870 Congress "stood poised between retreating from Reconstruction and pressing further with its Southern policy."[103] Ku Klux Klan violence temporarily pushed Congress off the fence, and in 1870 and 1871 congressional Republicans passed Enforcement Acts designed to protect southerners from political violence. Yet Congress showed the District of Columbia its retreating side. The political terrorism of the Klan was a blatant affront to democratic principles and seemed to demand a strong response. By contrast, the consolidators, though they too sought to constrain democracy, were much more like congressmen themselves. They worked through conventional political channels, and their goals were economic prosperity and elite control of the political machinery. Although some radical Republicans in Congress had rejected the consolidators' demands for less democracy in the capital, they could not muster sufficient support from their moderate colleagues. Thus, instead of standing up for the Reconstruction experiment in biracial democracy in the capital, the Republican-controlled Congress had approved the first stage of its redemption. After 1871, Congress would more often retreat from than advance policies designed to safeguard the rights of African Americans in the South. In this sense, Congress's creation of the District's territorial government was more representative of its future direction than were the better-known Enforcement Acts.

Congress's trajectory toward retrenchment would be abundantly clear in its 1874 dismantling of the territorial government it had established just three years earlier. In the interim, Alexander Shepherd and his allies poured immense energy and capital into improving Washington's streets and other infrastructure. Their ambitious projects spurred an extraordinary real estate boom whose results, in the form of large, ornate Victorian homes, are still on display in the Dupont Circle neighborhood. And yet the territorial government's penchant for vast spending and Shepherd's autocratic style of governing quickly alienated Washingtonians of many political stripes. The campaign of wealthy conservatives to end both the territory and popular government itself was the second chapter in the larger story of how local leaders collaborated with Congress to make the District of Columbia the nation's leading example of disfranchisement.

6

To Save the Common Property and Respectability of All

THE RISE AND FALL OF THE TERRITORIAL GOVERNMENT

On July 4, 1873, the *National Republican* began a series of articles on the dramatic development of northwest Washington under the territorial government. The stories, which ran on Saturdays that summer and fall, touted the northwest side's newly paved streets, its streetcar lines, and its fashionable new masonry homes, which featured large porches, picture windows, and mansard roofs. The improvements were harbingers of "modern civilization," the newspaper informed readers, as it condemned opponents of the territorial government as "old fogeys" who refused "to walk boldly out into the sunlight of our modern improvements and make life a pleasure as well as a reality."[1] As the series began, editors touted the democratic spirit of the recent improvements. Grading and paving projects that "pass the tenements of the poor and uninfluential portion of our population bear the same impress of care and forethought . . . as those which pass the property of the millionaire," they professed.[2] Yet the business orientation of the newspaper, and of the territorial government itself, was clear in the tenor of the articles, which praised real estate agents and speculators, offered block-by-block lot prices, and even informed readers which lots were currently for sale. As the series ended, the newspaper ran an editorial summing-up of the recent triumphs of the municipal government. Under the direction of Henry Cooke and Alexander Shepherd, it boasted, "this city of Washington, which was the disgrace of the country, has blossomed into a beauty and a loveliness so that it is to-day the most attractive city in the Union. Its capital has almost doubled, the value of its real estate has been increased nearly fifty per cent, and in substantial growth we have surpassed almost every community on the continent."[3]

Such bravado notwithstanding, the *National Republican* was probably more concerned about the territorial government than it let on. In the summer and fall of 1873 the territorial government was under siege from many directions. Fiscal conservatives had long been outraged by the government's outsized spending and the high taxes and debts that spending generated. African Americans were angry that the government seemed intent on undermining the black schools and refused to listen to black leaders who continued to insist on a broad vision of equality. The territorial government's financial situation was precarious, as it had blown through two bond issues and was hard-pressed to find more money to continue financing its projects. To make matters still worse, reformist newspaper editors in New York and elsewhere had made Shepherd an exemplar of urban misrule, having successfully taken down his New York City peer, "Boss" William Marcy Tweed.

Shepherd's reign as head of the powerful Board of Public Works has sometimes been seen as the apex of Republicanism in the capital. The Shepherd government was closely associated with President Ulysses S. Grant, spent extensively on infrastructure improvements as Republicans did elsewhere in the South, and was perceived to be closely aligned with local working-class African American voters. Yet the reality was far more complicated. As the previous chapter showed, Shepherd had risen to power by allying himself with Democrats and by arguing that "citizens"—not the newly biracial electorate—must control the levers of local government. It was, therefore, no coincidence that the territorial government over which Shepherd presided was designed to minimize the power of elected officials. Voters elected representatives to the lower house of the legislature, but the most powerful components of the government were not accountable to the people at all. The excesses of spending and development under the territorial government were less the result of too much democracy, as conservatives charged, than the product of an extremely ambitious and at times corrupt appointed leadership.

Local politics in the early 1870s reflected not just the diminution of political democracy in the capital but also the subversion of other egalitarian promises of the era. African American leaders continued to press for the obliteration of racial discrimination in public life, and many in the black elite worked to support Senator Charles Sumner's proposed civil rights act, which would bring federal power to bear on quasi-private institutions that continued to exclude or discriminate based on race. Yet these activists found themselves on the defensive, as opponents of the Sumner bill invoked the specter of "social equality" to insist that churches, schools, and even streetcars and restaurants were more akin to homes than to public places. The territorial legislature passed new public accommodations laws during the territorial period, but the D.C. Supreme Court cast doubt on their legitimacy and local proprietors continued to circumvent them.

Meanwhile, mainstream Republicans used the principle of racial equality to challenge African Americans who sought to organize a black political movement. In 1873, a cohort of black leaders who were fed up with the territorial government sought to build a movement for independence from Shepherd's Republican organization. The mainstream Republicans reacted harshly, not only condemning the Equal Rights League's apostasy but also raising the familiar threat of "race war," should black people seek to organize on their own. Republicans had accepted independent Irish and German Republican associations, apparently understanding that ethnic groups might have their own bases of solidarity and separate interests. When African Americans sought to organize on the basis of race, however, they were treated as a threat to democracy itself. The territorial period was one of great dynamism as far as public and private enterprise was considered, but it was largely one of retrenchment in racial politics.

When a Republican-controlled Congress terminated all elected offices in the capital in the spring of 1874, it cemented the second of two stages of the capital's "redemption." The disfranchisement of the capital was part of a broader elite reaction against urban and black voters, in both the North and the South. Yet nowhere else did contemporary suffrage reform go so far. Congress's exclusive jurisdiction and the perception that the capital city was a unique case helped justify this extraordinary move. But the District's large black population also had a great deal to do with it. Conservatives had long insisted that universal manhood suffrage would wreak havoc on the city, unnaturally elevating black men to positions of power, provoking violence among white laborers, and leading to instability and economic decline. Many Republicans had also harbored doubts about black men's enfranchisement, worrying that slavery had rendered freedpeople unready for the prerogatives of citizenship and unable to exercise the judgment required of voters. Many among the capital's economic elite therefore associated the excesses of the Shepherd regime with black voters, asserting that the territorial government survived by manipulating the black vote and suggesting that the government's economic crisis was the inevitable outcome of universal manhood suffrage. In a moment of national economic instability and waning support for the democratic and egalitarian impulses of Reconstruction, a reconfigured cohort of local reformers found considerable support in Congress. And Congress, with its singular authority over the District of Columbia, not only ousted Shepherd but also brought the Reconstruction experiment in manhood suffrage to a close.

"Citizens" and the Scourge of Black Voters

The territorial government was immediately unpopular among elite conservatives, who opposed the enormous and expensive improvement plans proposed by Alexander Shepherd and the Board of Public Works. Democrats scowled as President Grant appointed only Republicans to the new government, a policy that did not seem to recognize the bipartisan nature of the consolidation movement. Grant named too many African Americans to the government for Democrats' tastes, appointing three black men (including Frederick Douglass) to the upper house of the territorial legislature and John Mercer Langston, a professor of law at Howard University, as legal counsel to the territorial Board of Public Health. Then, the territory's first election yielded a two-thirds Republican majority in the House of Delegates, a reminder to Democrats that they were on the weak side of the partisan divide and would likely remain so as long as whites divided their votes between the two parties. The election of Norton P. Chipman as the District's nonvoting representative to Congress particularly rankled. Chipman had led the controversial war crimes prosecution of Confederate prison guard Henry Wirtz, and conservatives considered the Iowa lawyer a rank carpetbagger. Democrats had good reason to feel that a new Republican ring had merely replaced the old.[4]

The outrage of wealthy Democrats and other fiscal conservatives only increased as territorial officials announced their extraordinarily ambitious plans for improving the capital. Early on, Alexander Shepherd placed himself in charge of letting contracts for the Board of Public Works, a position so powerful that conservatives began to suspect he had engineered it ever since the days of the consolidation movement.[5] Weeks after assuming office, the Board of Public Works released a "comprehensive plan" for improvements in the capital. The proposal called for extensive grading and paving, new sewer projects, and other structural changes, including eliminating the fetid canal that ran through the middle of downtown. The board proposed to place first priority on Washington's center—Pennsylvania Avenue and the National Mall—and then move northwest to the Connecticut Avenue corridor. The estimated cost was $6,578,397, of which one-third would be paid by special assessments on property abutting the improvements and two-thirds would be funded through a bond issue. The board pledged state-of-the-art construction and an effort coordinated with the army engineers, who were responsible for overseeing federal properties in the capital.[6]

From Shepherd's perspective, the proposal made sense despite its astounding cost. The territorial government had assumed power at a moment of unprecedented appetite for improvements in Washington. In the wake of the war, many commentators believed the capital's hodgepodge of unpaved streets, wide avenues, poor housing, and dust and mud were a sorry representation of a newly strengthened nation emerging from the trials of a great war. The movement to remove the capital to the West had been defeated, and the consolidators had persuaded Congress that new energy and enthusiasm could transform the city from a southern town closely associated with slavery into an apt symbol for a reunited nation. Not least, the highest territorial officials served at the pleasure of the president, and they had good reason to think Grant would be a loyal ally.[7]

But wealthy conservatives were not willing to stand by as Shepherd raised property taxes and plunged the territory deeply into debt. That summer, they sought an injunction against the $4 million bond issue proposed in the comprehensive plan. With legal assistance from Walter S. Cox, the former fugitive slave commissioner (and future District of Columbia Supreme Court justice), they argued that Shepherd and the Board of Public Works had failed to clarify their plans and that the proposed bond issue exceeded the legal limit of municipal debt. Justice Andrew Wylie, the most conservative member of the District's Supreme Court, granted the injunction, which forced a halt—during valuable summer workdays—to the government's first major wave of improvements.[8]

Shepherd had no intention of bowing to such pressure. The territorial government obtained a temporary loan from the House of Delegates and announced that it would seek popular approval for the loan through a plebiscite in November. With that, the warring parties took their quarrel to voters in the capital's twenty-two election districts. Representatives of the territorial government held mass meetings to explain the purposes of the loan. They emphasized that extensive improvements would result not only in rising land values but also in work opportunities for unskilled laborers. Proponents of the improvements promised, as Mayor Bowen had done before them, that although the costs might seem painful in the short run, everyone would benefit as infrastructure development raised land values and generated outside investment in the city. Among the public spokesmen for the loan was O. O. Howard, who had deep ties both to the territorial government and to local African Americans, many of whom associated him with the Freedmen's Bureau's work on behalf of freedpeople.[9]

The conservatives, for their part, constituted themselves as the Citizens Association of the District of Columbia and started a newspaper, the *Citizen*. They sought to broaden their appeal beyond the relatively small cadre that had initiated the injunction, arguing that the territorial government's proposed increases in property taxes and the public debt would harm not only the economic elite but also small real estate owners and even renters. The Citizens Association found some allies among black activists, including labor leader and former city councilman George Hatton, who gave speeches insisting that landlords would pass the cost of their increased property taxes on to the poor people who rented from them.[10]

Yet the Citizens Association's economic concerns had a racialized twist, for its leaders saw freedmen voters as the root of the problem. Mobilizing themes long present in both Democratic and Republican rhetoric, they argued that supposedly passive, ignorant black voters posed a threat to the city's political and economic well-being. Without overtly lamenting black men's enfranchisement itself, the Citizens Association and its allies drew on long-standing and ubiquitous doubts about black men's fitness for the privilege of voting. The Citizens were so convinced that the territorial government would recruit African Americans from the surrounding countryside to vote illegally in the plebiscite that they offered a $50 reward to anyone who provided information leading to convictions for illegal registration or voting. In one characteristic editorial, the Citizens likened Shepherd's relationship to the territorial legislature to that of a slave driver and a slave. "Never did a slave, smarting under the lash of a slave-driver, obey more supinely than the dirt-eating flunkeys who compose a majority of the Legislature have obeyed the commands of the Board of Public Works."[11] The analogy may have been designed to appeal to freedmen voters who remembered the horrors of enslavement, but it also reinforced the perception that slaves were dangerously passive and uncivilized, an outlook often used to discredit freedmen's claims to political equality and full citizenship.

The Citizens Association's fight against the territorial government represented a rupture within the District's economic elite over the desirable pace and extent of improvements. Members of the business and commercial elite had temporarily united in support of the consolidation movement, but they now split over how political and economic power should be used. Conservatives wanted the government to move more slowly and avoid accruing enormous debt. By contrast, allies of the territorial government saw themselves as progressives who would jolt the capital into urban modernity. In his detailed study of the two groups, historian Alan Lessoff found that members of the Citizens Association were far more likely than allies of Shepherd to have been born in the District. Leaders of both sides were wealthy, but members of the Citizens Executive Committee were particularly so. Occupational differences between the groups were not enormous, but leaders of the Citizens Association were more often merchants or lawyers, while territorial allies were more likely to be engineers or architects.[12]

Two bankers, George W. Riggs and William Wilson Corcoran, were among the most prominent members of the Citizens Association movement and perfectly fit the typologies laid out by Lessoff. Georgetown-born Corcoran was a Democratic financier and Confederate sympathizer who had fled to Europe during the war. On his return, he quickly regained an esteemed place in local social and political life. A devoted art collector, Corcoran opened his gallery to great fanfare in February 1871, as the District government reorganization was in process. Riggs also came from a prominent Maryland and Georgetown family and was also a Democrat. Unlike Corcoran, Riggs had remained in Washington during the war, and afterward he was prominent in the Board of Trade and the consolidation movement. Riggs was quick to turn against Shepherd, however, when he understood the speed and ambition with which Shepherd planned to prosecute his program.[13] Not all the leading members of the Citizens Association were locals and Democrats, however. The movement also attracted Republicans like Albert G. Riddle, the lawyer and former Ohio congressman who had helped defend Minnie Gaines and who supported the woman suffrage movement. Riddle and others like him were, by 1871, disillusioned with President Grant, the Reconstruction agenda, and the perceived excesses of popular politics, and they were ready to ally with Democrats in hope of shifting the balance of power.[14]

It is striking, but not surprising, that conservatives chose to identify themselves as a movement of "citizens." Prior to Reconstruction, citizenship was usually considered a local or state status, not a national one. "Citizens" were typically considered to be the local men charged—by traditions of republicanism and patriarchy—with stewardship over the entire community. This unabashedly inegalitarian vision of citizenship placed great importance on hierarchies of race, sex, and wealth. In this view, "citizen" was almost the same as "taxpayer," and citizens were entitled to a greater say in community affairs than those without substantial resources. During Reconstruction, conservatives purposefully invoked this increasingly antiquated usage of the term "citizen" against African Americans' claims that they, too, were citizens, and against the ideas expressed in the 1866 Civil Rights Act and the Fourteenth Amendment that a citizen was any American-born or naturalized individual and that all citizens were equally entitled to an array of basic rights. Thus when the debate about black enfranchisement in the District began, conservatives claimed that "citizens" opposed black enfranchisement, and in 1869 a "Citizens' Ticket" sought to oust Bowen by uniting moderate Republicans with Democrats in an argument for fiscal restraint and the promotion of commerce. New York City's "citizens" movement is perhaps best known to historians, but in many southern cities besides Washington—in places like Charleston, Memphis, and New Orleans—business elites also constituted themselves as "citizens" as they attempted to oust Republican governments.[15] In the postemancipation context, those who mobilized as citizens and taxpayers insisted on the relevance of the older vision of hierarchical citizenship against the new one associated with racial equality and individual rights.

Leading "citizens" who attempted to undermine the likes of Shepherd, New York's "Boss" Tweed, and other powerful urban politicians often found themselves stymied by a numerically more powerful opposition. The District of Columbia Citizens Association was no exception. Despite their considerable efforts and financial resources, the Citizens failed to persuade voters to oppose the loan. On November 21, District voters approved it by a vote of 12,748 to 1,202. The low turnout and lopsided result suggested that Democrats had opted to stay home rather than participate in a poll they would likely lose.[16] Yet the Citizens were determined to fight on, outside the realm of electoral politics. In fact, voters' overwhelming support for the loan only solidified their perception that the territorial government was dishonestly allied with abject voters who were helpless in the face of coercion by contractors and politicians. In a memorial to Congress signed by 1,000 property owners, they demanded an inquiry into the territory's business practices and into the loan vote itself. Contractors allied with the government had coerced their employees to vote for the loan, they charged, and voters had been imported from surrounding Maryland. The District of Columbia Committee of the House of Representatives began an investigation that February.[17]

House investigators proceeded as if African Americans had voted as a unit for the loan, and as if they had done so largely because they had been coerced and pressured by conniving politicos. For instance, investigators and many of the witnesses proved remarkably adept at converting black voters' political strategies—their efforts to form associations, deliberate about politics, and protect themselves against fraud—into signs of dependency and malleability. Black voters had been marching to the polls in groups since enfranchisement in 1867. The practice helped protect illiterate voters, who were susceptible to being deceived into voting for candidates they did not support. As J. W. Green, a black minister and opponent of the loan, explained in his congressional testimony, freedmen voters "depend upon others more than the white voters generally, because they are uneducated."[18]

Yet congressional investigators saw the appearance at the polls of "squads" of black laborers as evidence that outsiders were exerting unfair influence on them. For example, they charged that Joseph Voorhees, a white timekeeper on a project improving Seventh Street Road north of Boundary Street, had inappropriately influenced working-class black voters who lived near Fort Slocum, in northern Washington County. Voorhees explained that the night before the election the Fort Slocum Republican Club had decided to "march in a body to the polls and vote," and to vote for their district's black candidate for the House of Delegates, O. S. B. Wall. Each member of the club, they resolved, "would receive a ticket only from the president, the reason being that they should not be imposed upon."[19] On arriving at the polls, Voorhees testified, supporters of the white candidate made a "grand rush" toward the Fort Slocum group, proffering tickets with which to vote for their candidate. As president of the club, Voorhees had "asked every member . . . whom he wanted to vote for, and I was very careful that they should vote for any man they wanted. . . . I distributed the tickets along just as they asked for them, and I showed them the window to which they should go to deposit their ballots." Under questioning, Voorhees acknowledged that he had also tried to sway voters' opinions "by talking to them and explaining things."[20] Investigators seemed skeptical of Voorhees and other witnesses who testified that "squads" of black men and Republican club leaders were not signs of corruption or coercion in the political process. Discussion and persuasion were fundamental to democracy. Yet, because of widespread doubts about black laborers' ability to perform the deliberative work required of voters, men like Voorhees made the investigators uneasy. The perception that African American voters were passive and corruptible permeated the investigation, as investigators repeatedly impugned black voters' rationality and emphasized their susceptibility to demagogues.

The dangerous flip side of vulnerable voters was corrupt politicians seeking to exploit them. Under questioning from investigators, some witnesses contended that antiloan contractors had threatened to fire employees who voted for the loan. Others claimed that loan advocates had promised paid labor in exchange for votes or had refused to make antiloan ballots available. There was no doubt some truth to such charges. The Shepherd government was not above offering financial incentives in exchange for support at the polls, and testimony confirmed that the government had paid all the District's major newspapers—including the Democratic *Patriot*—to publish "advertising" designed to encourage favorable coverage. Yet the testimony unearthed no compelling evidence that the government had purposely ramped up construction projects before the loan vote or brought in black voters from surrounding states to support the loan, as critics alleged. Shepherd's opponents charged that contractors and others coerced black voters to support the loan, but plenty of others insisted that nothing outside the bounds of conventional politics had occurred.[21]

The reality was that the relationship between African Americans and the territorial government was complicated. There was, in fact, something of an alliance between black voters and the government, but it was not necessarily founded on coercion and vote buying. The government recognized the importance of black voters by employing black laborers on public works projects and appointing black men to about one-third of the menial jobs at its disposal. Territorial leaders also appointed black men to more prestigious positions: John F. Cook was city registrar; John T. Johnson, an educator and barber, was the treasurer; and the commissioner of the Washington asylum was longtime AME church leader John A. Simms.[22] Black laborers who looked at the appointment and employment practices of territorial leaders would have had reason to believe they would benefit from the public works employment generated by the prospective improvements. Indeed, the members of the Citizens Association were correct in their conviction that the masses of Washington voters had class interests that were quite different from theirs.

At the same time, however, black support for the loan bill was neither as unified nor as potent as the Citizens Association and many congressional investigators suggested. A number of black leaders publicly opposed the loan, including Hatton, former councilman Frank Gaines, and minister J. W. Green. That fall, editors of the *New National Era* continued their skepticism of Shepherd, insisting that the consolidation movement's preeminent goal had been to reduce the power of the black vote. The paper objected to white Republican leaders who marginalized prospective black candidates just because they were black, condemned the racial conservatism of many of the territorial government's appointees, and criticized contractors who tried to coerce black voters to support proterritory candidates.[23] The Citizens' portrayal of African Americans as herdlike followers of Shepherd and the contractors was ill-founded.

Moreover, although the Citizens blamed black voters for the passage of the loan vote, black voters could not have been solely responsible. African Americans made up 33 percent of the population and 38 percent of registered voters in 1871. Even if every single black voter had supported the loan, the measure would not have passed without the help of whites who either voted in favor or abstained. In fact, the Board of Public Works had done a great deal to win whites' support, distributing contracts to Democrats as well as Republicans and to Irish contractors as well as black ones.[24] Thus, plenty of white people had good reason to join with African Americans in support of the loan.

In the end, Shepherd and his peers escaped the 1872 congressional investigation almost unscathed, both because of the dearth of concrete evidence against them and because powerful political alliances worked in their favor. Chair of the investigating committee was Connecticut Republican Henry H. Starkweather, a friend and ally of both Cooke and Shepherd. With Starkweather at the helm and Grant as president, the committee's majority concluded that the territorial government was "entitled to the favorable judgment of Congress, and [was] . . . to be commended for the zeal, energy, and wisdom with which they have started the District upon a new career of improvement and prosperity."[25] Outraged critics immediately cried foul, and two Democratic committee members published a scathing minority report. But Shepherd's peculations were not yet offensive enough to attract universal condemnation, and the broader reaction against Reconstruction and black rights was not yet far enough along. The conservatives would have to wait, but it would not be long before conditions would favor a dismantling of the last remaining vestiges of elective government in the capital.

Against Caste

While conservatives were developing their case against the territorial government, members of the capital's black elite continued to advance an expansive interpretation of racial equality before the law. When Senator Charles Sumner's supplemental civil rights bill came to the Senate floor in the winter of 1872, black Washingtonians lobbied in its support. Meanwhile, public accommodations laws passed by the city councils were going unenforced, and local

African Americans continued their efforts to secure racial equality in restaurants, bars, and other accommodations. Historians have often regarded such efforts, in Washington and elsewhere, as evidence that the black elite sought outside recognition of its own elevated class status and was disconnected from the masses of African Americans, who struggled for basic survival. Yet these black activists believed they were fighting racial caste, not class, and that their efforts to secure equal treatment in public accommodations would help open the way for upward class mobility for all African Americans. The times proved less than auspicious for such goals, however. In Congress and in the capital alike, opponents of laws requiring nondiscrimination in restaurants, bars, and hotels insisted that these were essentially private, almost domestic spaces, where proprietors' authority ought not be constrained by government. That a weakened version of the Sumner bill passed in 1875 did little to mitigate the overall trend. The U.S. Supreme Court would overturn the law just eight years later, arguing, in part, that Congress had no business intervening in "what may be called the *social rights* of men and races in the community."[26]

Charles Sumner's federal civil rights bill aimed to place a federal ban on racial discrimination in a variety of arenas not clearly covered by the 1866 Civil Rights Act. After passage of the 1866 law, African Americans had tested whether federally enforceable civil rights included access to public accommodations such as streetcars, bars, and restaurants. Results had been mixed. Some judges interpreted the act expansively; others maintained that it applied only to the specific—and largely economic—relations the act described; and many held that separate but supposedly equal accommodations complied with the act's mandate. Rather than rely on federal statutes, in the late 1860s and early 1870s some Republican state governments in both the South and the North passed their own public accommodations laws. Yet racial discrimination continued, and black activists realized that local and state courts could not be relied upon to uphold the new laws. Thus, as historian Elsie M. Lewis wrote in a study of black leadership in the postwar years, "Negroes became committed very early to a policy of federal control and extension of federal power."[27]

This is where Sumner's proposal came in. Sumner's bill promised to address racial discrimination and exclusion in public schools, public accommodations, and, in the words of his initial proposal, "church organizations, cemetery associations, and benevolent institutions incorporated by national or State authority."[28] Sumner himself often justified the measure by invoking the broad vision of natural rights expressed in the Declaration of Independence. Yet the bill had a legal and constitutional logic that went beyond the abstract ideal of universal equality. In the fight over the District of Columbia Medical Society, Sumner had argued that because Congress chartered the society and had the power to regulate it, it could also demand that the society not practice racial discrimination. The logical extension of this argument was that the Fourteenth Amendment, which prohibited states from discriminating, therefore also prohibited states from chartering corporations and associations that discriminated. This case for federal power to prohibit not only discriminatory state laws but also discriminatory action by corporations and associations held out hope of securing for African Americans the broad range of rights and privileges they had long demanded.[29]

Members of the District of Columbia's black elite, many of whom saw themselves as stewards for African Americans' interests everywhere, saw the supplemental civil rights act both as necessary for securing racial equality and as a test of the Republican Party's commitment to its African American constituents. Students and faculty at Howard University held mass meetings and passed supportive resolutions. At racially mixed meetings at First Congregational Church, nationally renowned black leaders, including Frederick Douglass and John Mercer Langston, testified to their humiliating experiences with racial discrimination in public accommodations. At one such meeting, John F. Cook explained that he and his wife had been "thrust" from a ladies' car into a smoking car when changing trains in Baltimore en route to Philadelphia. Perhaps more bitingly, he mentioned having been forced to ride in the smoking section on the Lady of the Lake, the steamer that linked Washington with Norfolk and happened to be owned by the territorial governor, Henry Cooke.[30]

At the same time, many black leaders argued that the failure of a Republican Congress to pass the bill would suggest a broad disregard for the views of loyal black constituents. Nationally, Grant and his allies faced a formidable challenge from the Liberal Republican movement, which was organizing for the 1872 elections. The Liberal Republicans planned to meet in Cincinnati in early May to devise their platform, and Sumner himself had expressed his support. With the Liberal Republican challenge in mind, some black leaders indicated that passage of the Sumner bill would shore up black support for Grant and the regular Republicans. Southern black leaders attending a Washington civil rights meeting warned that failure to pass the bill would "have the effect of creating an apathy among the colored voters detrimental to the Republican Party."[31]

Supporters of the Sumner bill faced a daunting battle, however. Sumner's influence in the Senate was at a low ebb. He had alienated the president and his supporters in Congress by opposing Grant's bid to annex San Domingo, and he had widened the breach by indicating that he would support a reform candidate for president in 1872. Sumner had been unable to get his civil rights bill out of committee in 1870 and 1871, but he forced the issue in 1872 by making the bill a rider on an "amnesty bill" aimed at restoring the political rights of ex-Confederates. Since Congress was determined to resolve the amnesty question, Sumner's move brought his measure before the full Senate.[32]

Yet many Senate Republicans, as well as Democrats, opposed the civil rights bill in principle. The discourse of "social equality" had come to define the debate over the limits of equality, and advocates of an expansive definition of equality before the law were now almost entirely on the defensive. Some opponents couched their objections to the bill in constitutional terms, arguing that the Thirteenth and Fourteenth Amendments did not so augment Congress's powers as to permit federal authority over corporations and associations in the states. More striking, however, was how the bill's opponents invoked the shibboleth of "social equality" and reframed the bill as a "social rights act." Putting aside the nuances of constitutionalism, moderate Republicans and Democrats alike stressed that the law would interfere with individuals' presumed right to choose with whom they dined in restaurants, attended theater, and shared other quasi-public spaces. Such arguments stirred deeply felt convictions about the meanings of biological race, personal taste, and economic liberty. For instance, the *Chicago Tribune*, formerly a radical Republican organ now turned Liberal Republican, called the bill a "Compulsory Social Equality Measure." Characteristically eliding the political with the social and the public with the private, the editors refused to concede "that because the negro has, by virtue of his birthright as an American, the privilege of sharing the ballot-box with us, he may also demand to share the butter-plate with us."[33]

Black leaders went to great lengths to combat such arguments. After Senator Lot Morrill argued that the question of equal access to public accommodations did not belong in Congress because it concerned "rights of a strictly domiciliary nature," George T. Downing submitted a letter to the editor of the *Chronicle* that Charles Sumner later read to the Senate. "A man's private domicile is his own castle," Downing argued. "But the public inn, the public or common school, the public place of amusement, as well as common carriers, asking the special protection of law, created through its action on the plea and for the benefit of the public good, have no such exclusive right as the citizen may rightfully claim within his home." It was ridiculous, Downing said, to imagine "that the colored people . . . are designing to break into social circles against the wish of those who compose them." Morrill himself had argued that "equality before the law" was a constitutional right, Downing pointed out. The Sumner bill simply represented a codification of that reasoning.[34] Downing's case was cogent, but the entire colloquy demonstrated that supporters of an expansive vision of equality before the law had made little headway in persuading opponents that even public schools and common carriers were decidedly public institutions.

The Sumner bill was fated to three more years of inaction before it finally passed, in a much-weakened form, in early 1875. In the spring of 1872, Senate Republicans, hoping to stem the Liberal Republican movement's momentum by passing the amnesty bill, removed the Sumner rider's provisions concerning schools, churches, and cemeteries. That change made the rider palatable to Democrats and thus enabled the Senate to pass the amnesty bill with the civil rights rider attached. The House did not act, however. Sumner's death in the spring of 1874 gave Congress new momentum to secure a measure that recognized the controversial senator's lifelong quest for an expansive vision of equality before the law. In the spring of 1875, Congress passed the watered-down version of the Sumner bill, making racial discrimination in "inns, public conveyances . . . and other places of public amusement" and in the selection of juries a federal crime. Overall, however, congressional Republicans' lack of commitment to the bill, and particularly to the school integration clause, fed African Americans' growing frustrations with the party and fostered continuing discussions about the possibility of defection.[35]

During the 1872 discussion of the Sumner bill, the institutions and spaces of the national capital again became the focus of pointed debate over the meaning of equality. Mary Clemmer Ames, one of the few prominent women journalists of the era, described Washington as a place where African Americans enjoyed equality a little too much. In her widely read column in the *New York Independent*, Ames acknowledged that the Sumner bill might do some good elsewhere. But she complained that black women spectators in the Senate galleries during a recent Sumner speech on civil rights had refused to make way for "white ladies of position and fashion." She was aghast that on Washington streetcars "the most unctuous contraband from its slums can plunge herself beside you or possess your seat." And she lashed out at what she saw as the airs of Washington's black elite, describing the capital as a place "wherein African people have already become rich and prosperous, where they rejoice in caste and 'sets' among themselves . . . where they elbow you or supplant you on the public thoroughfare with all the assured rights of free citizenship."[36] As Ames

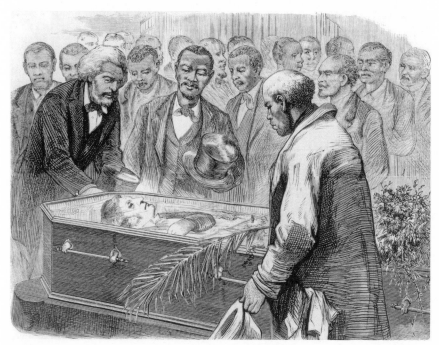

FIGURE 6.1. "The Late Senator Sumner—Ceremonies in the Capitol—Colored People of Washington, Headed by Frederick Douglass, Viewing the Remains." In a commemorative issue with Sumner on its cover, *Frank Leslie's* recognized the senator's special commitment to racial equality and his rapport with leading black men in the nation's capital. *Frank Leslie's Illustrated Newspaper*, March 28, 1874, 45. Courtesy Library of Congress.

cataloged the various public and quasi-public places where African Americans had refused to resume old conventions of racial deference, she placed particular emphasis on affronts to white women like herself. In Washington, she suggested, African American men's and women's claims to equality impinged directly on white women's ability to preserve the bubble of respectability that was meant to surround them in public.

The *New National Era* quickly published a defiant response to Ames, which rejected the distinctions of gender, race, and class on which her column had relied. Writing as "Faith Lichen," a columnist asserted that all people had the same "natural rights." "The public seats of Washington belong to those who come in time to occupy them, let this be understood, and we shall have no more growling championship of lazy or indifferent 'white ladies of position and fashion,' or implied tolerance of slightly bronzed ladies, educated and refined, to the exclusion of 'unctuous contrabands.'" Those "contrabands," Faith Lichen insisted, were as entitled to ride on the streetcars as anyone else. She called on Ames to stop "pricking . . . colored people whenever opportunity offers" and called her attacks "intensively mean, unendurable," and "futile." In any event, she asserted, integration in Washington's public places was a fait accompli: "Meet them at public places you will, unless you stay at home; and have them take *their* seats in the *street cars* of the city of Washington, you must."[37]

Years of popular and legislative struggle had, in fact, created a capital city where elite African Americans enjoyed access to an expansive range of public spaces and where they were not expected to perform traditional rituals of racial deference. Yet, even for the black elite, Washington was far from a bastion of racial equality. Racial exclusion and segregation persisted in the city's schools, as well as in its finer restaurants, hotels, and theaters. A Pennsylvania Avenue saloon refused to serve a U.S. district attorney and two deputy marshals because one of the deputies was black. Labor leader Marcellus West was denied service in a bar and took the proprietor to court.[38] Far from assuming that their patronage would be accepted at any establishment or that they had all the rights to which white people were entitled, black Washingtonians knew that vestiges of slavery remained ubiquitous in public life. Indeed, in June 1872, the territorial legislature passed a new public accommodations law specifying that businesses could neither explicitly discriminate on the basis of race nor use more informal techniques designed to discourage black patronage, such as not posting prices and then insisting that black customers pay more than whites. Anyone found in violation of the law, which applied to restaurants, bars, and "ice-cream saloons or soda fountains," would be fined $100 and forfeit his or her operating license.[39]

After the law passed, African Americans launched a series of test cases to ensure its enforcement. In police court hearings, a judge duly convicted violators and held them accountable with fines and license forfeitures. Proprietors then appealed to the District's Supreme Court, and late in 1872 Justice Arthur MacArthur handed down a decision that essentially vitiated the law. MacArthur asserted that "the proprietor of a hotel or restaurant was the proper judge of who should have either refreshments or lodgings in his house, and no one could dispute his authority on that matter."[40] The judge thus rejected the argument, advanced by Sumner and local activists, that licensed public accommodations were institutions of a different stature from conventional private property. Indeed, his use of the term "house" to describe restaurants and inns signaled his conviction that public accommodations were akin to private homes and that the law was essentially a "social equality" measure. The District of Columbia court's ruling anticipated the U.S. Supreme Court's 1883 decision in the *Civil*

Rights Cases, which struck down the Sumner Civil Rights Act of 1875, in part by emphasizing the rights of proprietors of public accommodations. Indeed, both decisions continued the decades-long erosion of common law tradition, as courts increasingly regarded proprietors of public accommodations as private entrepreneurs whose rights trumped the privileges of the public. And, as courts elevated the rights of one category of individuals, they undermined those of another.

Some historians have argued that black leaders who focused on public accommodations were unfortunately distracted from more important issues such as land reform and labor rights. And they have asserted that their efforts to gain access to such relatively luxurious accommodations as first-class train cars and dress circle seating in theaters was about seeking outside recognition of their own high status in relation to the masses of African Americans.[41] There can be no doubt that many of the black leaders who focused attention on public accommodations—many of them college educated, refined, and well off—felt intensely the slight of being refused admission to facilities solely on account of their color or "race." Besides their personal feelings, however, elite black activists had more egalitarian motivations for demanding an end to discrimination in places where most African Americans could never afford to go in the first place. The argument was about the persistence of caste. The exclusion of "colored gentlemen" and "ladies" from "first class" or "ladies'" accommodations, they believed, was different from exclusions based on other attributes, such as comportment or dress. Proponents were not claiming that disheveled or ill-behaved people had a "right" to attend the theater, even if they could pay for a ticket. What they were arguing was that race in particular (or "color" or "previous condition") could not be used to justify exclusion or segregation. This perspective helps explain why it was so important for activists to argue that they were not seeking to level so-called social distinctions. They were not fighting against class, but rather against caste.[42]

But there was a deeper principle here, too, one embedded in the liberal ideals of individualism and upward mobility. The denial to elite African Americans of access to first-class accommodations or integrated seating arguably epitomized racial oppression better than did the exploitation of black laborers. For even if African Americans could escape the drudgery of labor and a hand-to-mouth existence, the racial "caste" system meant they could never command the same respect as their white counterparts. A focus on the upper reaches of racial discrimination did not necessarily imply inattention to the plight of the black poor. To the contrary, many of the African American leaders who worked for passage of the Sumner bill were also involved in efforts to achieve better wages and working conditions for African American laborers. They saw the fight against caste as a struggle to ensure opportunities for all African Americans. To be sure, this was a liberal vision premised on the ideas of upward mobility and racial progress, but it was not a narrow vision of special prerogatives for the black elite.[43]

African Americans and the "New Washington"

Once exonerated by the 1872 congressional investigation, territorial officials moved forward with dramatic improvements to the capital's infrastructure, funded by bond issues and built by local laboring men, both black and white. Their accomplishments were remarkable. During the territorial period, laborers and contractors for the government laid more than 150 miles of road, 120 miles of sewers, 30 miles of water mains, and 39 miles of gas lines. They built 208 miles of sidewalks and planted over 60,000 trees. The territorial government oversaw the elimination of the putrid canal running through the city's center, the creation of a new railroad station just off the National Mall, and the extension of street railroads to open suburban development. It also collaborated with the army engineers to beautify parks and other green spaces. Commentators in the capital and elsewhere began to hail the "New Washington," a national capital people could be proud of, a city that might even serve as a model of municipal government.[44]

The territorial government was not nearly so accomplished when it came to matters of race and equality. Officials did appoint black men to government positions and distribute labor to the capital's black working class, but their mode of doing business ensured prosperity for their wealthy allies and dispossession for the poor. Meanwhile, proterritory newspapers, particularly the *National Republican*, trafficked in racialized ridicule of black politicians who opposed the government, mobilizing long-standing ideas about African Americans' political incompetence that, ironically, conservatives were using against the territory itself. Black political leaders continued to insist that the territorial government neglected African Americans in its appointments, and in 1872 many black voters defected to a "Bolter" faction, which sought to challenge Republican regulars running for the House of Delegates. Tensions between African Americans and the territorial government would boil over during 1873, when territorial officials appointed an African American opponent of school integration as president of the Board of Trustees of Colored Schools. A cadre of black political leaders pushed African Americans to abandon the local Republican machine, bringing forth a barrage of criticism from white Republicans that revealed the complexities and shortcomings of the Republican vision of racial equality.

The territorial government's vast improvements and the general prosperity of the years before the economic crash of 1873 produced an extraordinary market in land speculation and building. The Board of Public Works hired private contractors to level hills, grade streets, and eliminate nuisances. Investors in real estate—sometimes themselves contractors or territorial officials—then traded on the prospective value of the land abutting the newly improved streets. The *National Republican* reported in the summer of 1873 that firms devoted entirely to real estate suddenly ranked "among the most prominent and important of our business firms, having offices which rival in elegance of furniture and completeness of arrangement the best counting or banking houses in the city." The agencies, the paper added, "are operated by some of the most respected and influential of our citizens." Hallet Kilbourn and James Latta, real estate brokers who had been prominent in the consolidation movement, had offices at 15th and G Streets, just north of the portion of 15th Street known as the "Wall Street of Washington," for its eminent banking establishments (including Jay Cooke's bank) and the U.S. Treasury Department.[45]

Builders, realtors, and speculators had good reason for optimism. With the continuing expansion of the federal government, congressmen and employees of the executive departments more often brought their families to the capital and established permanent residences. Elite social and cultural life flourished as never before. In fact, it was the dynamism of Washington in this period and the baroque manners and petty rivalries of the city's socially conscious elite that inspired Mark Twain and Dudley Warner's 1873 parody, *The Gilded Age*. Social and political connections among the capital's improver elite—politicians, contractors, bankers, and real estate agents—facilitated the speedy and profound transformation of the District during the territorial period. Those networks also opened doors to insider dealings and out-and-out corruption. For a time, however, the territorial government and its allies seem to have felt invincible. As real estate prices rose, they enjoyed the support of the Grant administration and business-minded Republicans in Congress, who were themselves often investors in city property.[46]

Members of the white business and political elite were not the only ones to benefit from booming land prices in the increasingly fashionable West End. African American real estate owners in the newly graded areas of the first ward—

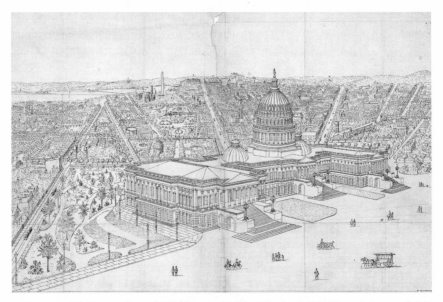

FIGURE 6.2. Bird's-eye view of Washington City, by George A. Morrison. In a remarkably detailed 1872 drawing, the Capitol dome is depicted between Pennsylvania Avenue on the left and New Jersey Avenue on the right, drawing viewers' attention to the city's northwest quadrant, where the territorial government and private contractors were energetically making improvements. Courtesy Library of Congress.

west of Connecticut Avenue along streets like L, M, and N—held tenaciously to their land despite efforts to buy them out. On M Street near New Hampshire Avenue, for example, the going rate of 35 cents per square foot attracted speculators, but black owners were not selling.[47] Black investors also improved their land when they could. On prestigious K Street, property values lowered precipitously when one crossed Connecticut Avenue going west. There, two black men built "small, six room bricks" that presented a stark contrast to the "small frame tenements of the most temporary character" that surrounded them. The homes were modest compared with the mansions built by magnates and politicians, but their permanence made an impression.[48] That some African Americans became wealthy, even under the increasingly straitened political circumstances, is confirmed by economic historian Loren Schweninger, who found that Washington was at the heart of a trend toward growing affluence among African Americans. Between 1870 and 1890, Schweninger showed, the proportion of African Americans in the District who owned their own homes increased from 10 percent to 15 percent. Although the great majority of African Americans continued to rent, the growing rate of homeownership suggested that African Americans did have opportunities for economic advancement in the nation's capital.[49]

By other measures, however, the period was not nearly so auspicious. The city's real estate developers and their clients valued cultural homogeneity and social exclusivity, and those values shaped the development of residential Washington. It was barbaric, many members of the nineteenth-century bourgeoisie believed, for people of different classes and races to live alongside one another. As one columnist for the *Atlantic Monthly* exclaimed of Washington, "Never, surely, were greater incongruities tolerated in any civilized community!" "In other places," she added, "people of wealth and taste like to get as close together as possible, so as to form solid streets, or at least squares, of respectability and order. But in Washington their instinct seems to be, choosing the Presidential mansion for a centre, to back farther and farther away from it and from each other." She complained that, as a result, "the great houses of millionnaires or of high government officials will, more likely than not, have a tumbledown tenement, a mean grocery, or a negro-shanty not a block off, and not seldom they are next-door neighbors."[50] Such mingling, it was believed, suppressed land values and reflected the city's primitive stage of development.

The bourgeois vision of residential exclusivity encompassed both class and race. Yet the pro-Shepherd *National Republican* singled out black property owners for special disdain in its laudatory coverage of the city's housing boom. It maligned the "frail tenements" of "a laboring class of people, mostly colored," that—amid the increasing lavishness of the rapidly developing area west of 14th Street and just north of P Street (immediately northwest of what is now Logan Circle)—"rather impede than enhance the value of real estate."[51] On another occasion, the paper sneered at "several dilapidated old frames, mostly owned by colored people," that stood between two new mansions on K Street. Notwithstanding efforts "by several of our more prominent real estate firms to purchase this property for gentlemen of wealth," it reported, "the owners, suspicious through ignorance, have interpreted the frequent applications for purchase into a scheme to get the advantage of it." The owners hardly seemed ignorant, however. They were demanding $5.00 per square foot for the land, roughly the price brought by real estate in the so-called Wall Street area of downtown 15th Street.[52]

Under the territorial government, the displacement of poor residents, particularly African Americans, proceeded not as explicit public policy but as a by-product of public and private cooperation in development. Some of Washing-

FIGURE 6.3. With a well-dressed white woman in the foreground and a substantial masonry building on the left side, this drawing, "Negro Shanties," visually emphasizes the race and class diversity of some Washington neighborhoods. Washington's real estate developers and cultural critics hoped to eliminate this sort of heterogeneity. *Harper's New Monthly Magazine*, March 1881, 544. Courtesy The Newberry Library, Call Number A5.391.

ton's poorest residents had always rented houses built in alleys behind the city's main streets. Drawing on census data, historian James Borchert found that between 1860 and 1880 the population of those alleys increased and also became increasingly African American, as whites found housing elsewhere. At the same time, real estate owners who had formerly lived adjacent to their alley properties increasingly lived in different neighborhoods.[53] The real estate agents and speculators who pressured black property owners to sell their land contributed to the intensifying racial and class segregation of the city and in particular to the growing concentration of poor African Americans in the city's alleys. By the dawn of the twentieth century, northwest Washington, once home to large concentrations of African Americans and important black institutions, had become predominantly white.

Despite Shepherd's successes in promoting economic development, however, his business practices became the subject of increasing scrutiny, as allegations of corruption in both the territorial and the federal governments roiled the city and the nation. The entire Washington milieu seemed scandalous, not just because of "Boss" Shepherd and the large population of freedpeople who supposedly supported his every move, but also because it was home to the federal government. Many Americans, disdainful of office holders and suspicious of federal power, had long doubted the morals of the capital city and its inhabitants. Although Washington benefited from a brief postwar period of nationalism and admiration for federal power, the capital city soon came to represent the undesirable excesses of Republican-led Reconstruction policies. The District of Columbia was, after all, the center of the entire edifice of Reconstruction. During and immediately after the war, it had become a center of black migration, education, and political power and a laboratory for congressional experimentation with equalizing legislation. It was home to Congress, the newly enlarged executive departments with their thousands of clerks, and the scandal-ridden Freedman's Bank. All these characteristics led many Americans to view the city as an exemplar of all that was untrustworthy and misguided about the Republican Ascendancy.

The territorial government itself also contributed mightily to the capital's reputation as the epicenter of unscrupulous politics. The local outcry against Shepherd broadened as time went on. In areas undergoing extensive improvements, small property owners were inconvenienced or bankrupted by the unpredictable, careless, and expensive work of the Board of Public Works and its contractors. Those not lucky enough to own land in the West End felt that their neighborhoods were being left to languish, their property values and investments stagnating. There were lawsuits, charges of favoritism, and bitter complaints of increased assessments and grading projects that left homes above street level or with entrances blocked.[54]

At the same time, the territorial government's finances began to collapse. Having spent the funds from the original $4 million bond issue, the government was out of money by the spring of 1873 and hard-pressed to collect taxes. A second bond issue had sold poorly, and District officials scrambled to invent what seemed ever more outlandish ways of trading on the prospects of development. Laborers, policemen, public school teachers, and other civil servants went unpaid, despite a congressional appropriation of $3.5 million to cover the costs of improvements on federal property.[55] Prominent New York newspapers—energized by their success in ousting "Boss" Tweed, by animus toward President Grant, and by the spirit of retrenchment against Reconstruction—subjected Shepherd to increasing scrutiny and contempt. And the territorial government's clear cronyism and undisguised willingness to reward loyalty with jobs only intensified charges of bossism and comparisons with Tweed.[56]

Shepherd's supporters fought back by touting the government's extraordinary modernization of the capital and the concomitant rise in real estate values. *Lippincott's Magazine* even went so far as to call Washington "in most respects the best-governed city of its size in the United States."[57] By late 1873, however, few people were persuaded. To the extent that the improvements had come at the hands of a debt-ridden administration linked with a highly suspect electorate, the Shepherd administration was extremely vulnerable, particularly as Republican fortunes plummeted. Throughout the country, elite Americans increasingly saw uneducated and unpropertied urban voters as the source of urban problems in general and of corrupt "boss" rule in particular. The reaction against ostensibly ignorant and dangerous urban voters had begun before the Civil War, but it reached new heights in the early 1870s. Arguments for elite rule in cities drew on familiar themes: that propertyless voters had no investment in municipal prosperity; that poor voters would use the levers of government to redistribute wealth; and that working-class voters would incite class conflict and undermine business prosperity. All those objections, long part of northern debates about universal manhood suffrage in the cities, possessed new power as critics assessed the Reconstruction experiment with black men's voting rights in the postemancipation South.

Meanwhile, territorial officials' indifference toward matters of racial equality and their opposition to school integration pushed a politically vocal subset of African Americans into outright revolt. During the summer and fall of

1873, black leaders throughout the country discussed abandoning the Republican Party in the upcoming elections out of frustration with its lack of responsiveness to their concerns. In Washington, the movement began as a response to a series of school-related controversies and boiled over into a critique of the high-handed policies of the territorial government. By the end of the summer, African American leaders were considering fielding black candidates to run insurgent campaigns against the Republican candidates chosen by the Shepherd-controlled Republican Central Committee. The movement eventually collapsed, but not before it had created a vociferous debate over the propriety of continuing to recognize race in public life.

The 1873 school controversies revealed both the continuing importance of school integration in local political life and a factional dispute between African Americans who opposed the territorial government and those allied with it. First, Congress gave the territorial government control of the District's black public schools. Black school leaders had long valued their schools' relationship with the Department of Interior and the schools' resulting protection from the vicissitudes of local politics. Now not only was their relationship with the Interior Department severed but the territorial government appointed Henry L. Johnson, a well-known African American opponent of school integration, as chair of the school board.[58] Second, Thomas W. Chase, an African American member of the popularly elected House of Delegates, proposed that a public normal school under discussion in the legislature be open to black students as well as white ones. Chase's proposal passed the House of Delegates, but a black member of the appointed upper house, John H. Brooks, opposed it, resulting in the initiative's failure. Finally, the newly constituted school board fired the charismatic and prominent principal of the city's African American preparatory high school, Richard T. Greener, a Harvard graduate and an editor of the *New National Era*, which in April 1873 was rechristened the *New National Era and Citizen*.[59]

During July and August, African Americans convened in mass meetings, and debates about school matters merged into questions of how to loosen the territorial government's iron grip on local politics. High school students mobilized to protest Greener's firing. The mother of an elementary school student stood up at a public meeting to complain that her daughter could not attend school because the black school was too far away and the two local white schools would not admit her.[60] The *New National Era and Citizen* also intensified its criticism of the territorial government. Under the direction of Richard Greener and Frederick Douglass's sons, Lewis and Frederick Jr., the newspaper charged that Brooks and Johnson were toadies of the Shepherd administration and complained that the school trustees were "responsible to no one," not even to the governor.[61]

As school issues receded in favor of a broader discussion of African Americans' fate in the territorial government, it became clear that many black leaders were angry at how territorial officials chose black appointees. The editors of the *New National Era and Citizen* charged that black appointees were selected from "the small set of hungry office-seekers who gain by fawning and sycophancy their private ear." Such men, they argued, did not represent "the great heart of the negroes of this district." Charles Purvis, a doctor at Freedman's Hospital, provocatively alleged that Governor Cooke appointed men he knew to be good servants, a demeaning comment that drew countercharges of elitism from black territorial appointees.[62] In some ways, the debate over who could faithfully represent Washington's diverse and divided African Americans in the halls of power resembled the 1862 controversy over the delegation to Abraham Lincoln. At that time, as in 1873, many African Americans had rejected the process by which representatives were chosen and charged that white leaders were listening to people who did not in fact represent black opinion. The mayoral structure of government, during the period of universal manhood suffrage, was certainly not a perfect democracy. But it had offered a popularly legitimate mechanism for choosing representatives. (African Americans, at least, had thought so.) Confirming the severity of the problem, Governor Cooke refused protestors' request that he remove Johnson, the chair of the black school board. He told a delegation of black men that he would consider their wishes but added, "I must be frank with you. I do not think that you are a unit upon this, as also [on] many other subjects before."[63]

Unable to vote leaders out of office and unsuccessful in lobbying Cooke, activists began holding secret meetings to organize formal opposition to the territorial government in the upcoming elections. The *National Republican* first reported on a movement to create a "black man's party with a view of running a man for Congress purely on the ground of color."[64] The *New National Era and Citizen* remained mum on the subject, but at the end of August the *National Republican* managed to get a reporter inside one of the meetings, and the paper went public with an extensive report that the summer's school agitators were organizing an African American "Equal Rights League" with the intention of nominating their own candidates in the October municipal elections.[65]

That some black leaders dared to directly challenge the territorial government made powerful, proterritory Republicans apoplectic, and they used every means at their disposal to undermine the nascent movement. The pro-Shepherd *National Republican* was particularly dogged. The newspaper discounted black leaders' complaints against the government and insisted that they were motivated only by frustration at not having been appointed to office themselves. Above all, it ridiculed those who dared to organize against the territorial government. Even those who had once been respectable, the paper argued, were now corrupted by politics and the potential rewards of office holding. The paper insisted that "intelligent" African Americans did not support the movement and that its leaders were charlatans.[66]

Opponents of independent black political organizing also hammered away at a conundrum brought into existence by the ratification, during the Republican ascendancy, of the principle of racial equality before the law. Those opponents demanded "consistency" on matters of race, challenging the summer's agitators to explain how they could demand the end of racial distinctions in places like public schools while at the same time arguing for the importance of electing black men to office. African American legislator John H. Brooks was one of the earliest to express that viewpoint. Amid criticism for defeating the bill for an integrated normal school, Brooks had condemned those who argued that, as a black elected official, he had an obligation to support school desegregation. In a speech in his home district, Brooks wondered whether "colored men" would now "take the position of forcing any one of their number who may be elected or appointed to office to act in their interest solely upon the ground of color." Portraying his position as the true fulfillment of ideals of racial equality, Brooks suggested that "if it was just for colored men to legislate upon the basis of color, it was equally right for white men; and if the whites were forced into that position, colored men must be forced to the wall."[67] Brooks's point that a strict racial division in Washington politics would be bad for African Americans was certainly valid. It was ironic, however, that he made the argument against "color" as a basis for politics while defending racially segregated schools.

Correspondents to the *National Republican* took up Brooks's argument against any recognition of race or color in local affairs. They were particularly harsh on school integration advocates William J. Costin and John T. Johnson and his son Jerome, whom correspondents criticized for refusing to serve black clientele in their barbering businesses. One pseudonymous writer claimed he favored the "abolition of the separate school system" but demanded that "men who maintain color distinctions in barbershops and newspapers, and insist on making a representative responsible only to persons of his color" must step aside. "We must rise above mere considerations of race," the writer insisted.[68] Radical Republicans had long argued that race was an arbitrary category not appropriate in politics and the law. Now pro-Shepherd Republicans turned that argument back on black activists, charging them with mobilizing race in a manner that was divisive and backward looking.

In fact, black activists themselves had debated the importance and propriety of independent black political organizations ever since the principle of racial equality had begun making inroads in American political culture. Delegates to the 1869 National Convention of Colored Men in Washington, for instance, had clashed over whether to continue building an African American "equal rights league." Some, including Henry McNeal Turner, the former pastor of Israel Church who was now based in Georgia, argued that "some systematic organization should be perfected, that would bind the colored people together in one common cause." But others, including physician Charles Purvis, had insisted that "there should be no colored leagues but simply leagues of American citizens, irrespective of color."[69] In the first half of the 1870s, there were still those, like lawyer John Mercer Langston, who argued for the eradication of racial distinctions in every aspect of American life, a position that (not coincidentally) fit with the Grantist argument that the Reconstruction constitutional amendments were sufficient guarantors of racial equality. But others, including Frederick Douglass, voiced a more complicated view. At a December 1873 convention organized to lobby for passage of Sumner's civil rights bill, Douglass acknowledged that the measure was, as critics charged, "special legislation." That is, by specifying that there must be no discrimination on account of race, the bill singled out race as a category of difference that demanded particular attention. Opponents had objected that such measures granted special privileges to African Americans. Yet Douglass argued that positive legislation against racial discrimination remained necessary. "We have for at least four generations been made the subjects of special legislation—this against our will, as it was against our interest. Now the last hour for special legislation has struck. . . . Give us our rights, and the noontide of the Republic is reached."[70] Until the legacies of slavery were expunged from public life, Douglass suggested, it would be appropriate to recognize race in policy and law.

Most white Republicans were not nearly so nuanced. The *National Republican* provocatively called the emerging Equal Rights League a "Black Man's Party" and intimated that a "race war" was at hand. The newspaper claimed that the party's organizers were "supporters and advocates of every measure calculated to stir up bitterness and strife between the two races" and argued that independent black political organizing threatened the very idea of republican government. Making "color a distinctive issue in the coming campaign" by running African American candidates to appeal to African American voters was "unrepublican and contrary to the spirit and genius of republican institutions." Such a policy threatened to render the District of Columbia "a sort of Hayti, where black men alone shall rule and hold office."[71] To be sure, there were purely partisan reasons why stalwart Republicans did not want to see African Americans form an independent organization that threatened the authority of the Republican Central Committee. But their invocations of Haiti, race war, and the violation of republican ideals suggest that the problem transcended mere politics and stood for something much more threatening.

African Americans began to point out that mainstream Republicans did not panic when Irish and German immigrants and their descendants organized their own political associations. A correspondent to the *New National Era and Citizen* reminded readers that Americans of European origin lobbied for their own ethnic interests without inciting charges of disloyalty: "Whilst there are Irish and German organizations in this city and country, working exclusively for the preeminence of their respective nationalities, and at the same time are enjoying all the rights that belong to Americans, newspapers should not demur against colored men, whose privileges are so circumscribed, for organizing to obtain by lawful means what justly belongs to them as citizens."[72] Irish and German Republican associations in the District had raised virtually no outcry. Why, African Americans asked repeatedly, was there such an uproar when African Americans sought to organize independently?

Black Americans were in fact being judged differently from ethnic whites. To be sure, "white" was a variegated category. Yet many contemporaries also believed a gaping chasm separated those who were sometimes called "Caucasians" from racial others. In the law and in popular political culture, white people had long been considered a separate and privileged class, as the history of the word "white" in federal and state statutes granting privileges and delineating the responsibilities of citizenship demonstrated. And, in fact, during discussions of the Sumner civil rights bill, many white commentators made clear that they saw African Americans as racial others, not as assimilable immigrants like the Irish or the Germans. The *Chicago Tribune* made a typical distinction in the winter of 1872, when it claimed that the Sumner bill would force patrons of theaters and other establishments "to ignore and suppress all prejudices . . . against promiscuous association with negroes, Indians, Chinamen, or other persons of uncongenial complexion."[73] Such allusions were common enough, as opponents of expansive racial equality found new justification for their position by grouping African Americans with others whom they saw as definitively not white.

Black Washingtonians were not the only African Americans who thought about asserting their independence from the Republican Party in the summer and fall of 1873. Black northerners were frustrated by racial discrimination in the distribution of federal patronage, and a group of leaders gathered in Chillicothe, Ohio, to discuss abandoning the party. In Virginia, African Americans upset that state Republicans had fielded an all-white ticket headed by an ex-Confederate also talked of forming a separate organization.[74] In Washington, Equal Rights League organizers hoped to influence the process by which Republican candidates for the territorial House of Delegates were chosen. At least according to the hostile *National Republican*, the league's plan was to put up candidates who supported its agenda and then "pack" the nominating meetings to get its candidates onto the Republican ticket over the candidates chosen by the Republican Central Committee.[75]

When leaders of the Equal Rights League spoke for themselves, they were alternately defensive and defiant. After the *New York Times* ran two articles on the movement—with the second one headlined "The Colored 'Know-Nothings'"—Richard Greener sought to explain the situation to a national audience. African Americans in the District were "a unit for the Republican Party," he wrote, but they were dismayed at the territorial government's "indifference" to their concerns. The government had appointed to the school board "men notoriously the most incompetent, conceited, and dogmatic," he claimed. And although he personally favored integrated schools, the first priority was to have qualified administrators for the separate black schools.[76] Soon after, a letter signed "Equal Rights for All," published in the *New National Era and Citizen*, defended African Americans' "perfect right" to form black-only organizations. The writer, who was probably Greener, asserted that it was manly for African Americans to escape their subservient relationship to the Republican Party and rebuffed charges that black defectors were misguided or dupes. "It is the old cry, to attribute the negro's demand for civil rights to the suggestion of the Democrats or the negro's disregard of what Abraham Lincoln and the Republican party have done for him," he wrote. "We are not frightened by these taunts, nor intimidated by insinuation. We owe it to ourselves to be men, honest, earnest, citizens, to demand all of our rights as citizens, and to be prepared to render everything that may be due from citizens. This is our platform."[77]

It was difficult to stake out an independent position in local politics, however, when African Americans were a majority of registered voters in just three of the capital's twenty-two election districts and when the territory's Republican Central Committee was dedicated to keeping black voters aligned with the mainstream of the party. As the election season began, the Central Committee, probably responding to the threat posed by the nascent Equal Rights League movement, attempted to exert new control over the process of selecting Republican nominees. Many voters bridled at the new rules and charged that the Shepherd "ring" had designed them in hope of forcing black voters into line. In the contentious twenty-first district, for example, longtime black residents Michael Shiner and his son, Isaac, insisted that African Americans must protect their political autonomy. "The white men seek to use them on election day as if they were dumb sheep," the son insisted. His father, a former slave and longtime Navy Yard employee, argued for "the rights of the black men to identify themselves with any party which would act most honest by them."[78]

School-related issues continued to figure prominently in the debate. In several districts, voters demanded to know Republican candidates' positions on "mixed" schools in general, and on the controversial normal school bill in particular. In the eighth district, much of the jockeying among Republicans concerned the fact that the incumbent, Thomas W. Chase, had authored the provision for an integrated normal school.[79] No doubt hoping to quell African Americans' discontent with recent management of the black schools, the *National Republican* published a lengthy story touting the increasing capacity of the "colored schools," the high pay of the teachers, and the black preparatory high school.[80] Yet many black activists were unmoved. When the territorial government sent a team of white men to investigate management of the black schools, the *New National Era and Citizen* complained, "We would have preferred a mixed committee," for the prevailing feeling among the "white people in this community" was that "anything in the way of schools is good enough for 'niggers.'"[81] One correspondent explained that black students' continuing exclusion from the white schools, in itself, demonstrated the need for a "colored man's party." If a "colored citizen" living near Franklin School tried to send his child there, wrote "Sphinx," he would be informed "that this is a white children's party." Continuing insults made the race-blind universalism demanded by white Republicans seem naive. "If we are to be constantly reminded of the fact . . . that we are a distinct party, stamped by the complexion of our skin," "Sphinx" argued, "it is time that we should accept the situation in politics, where our power can alone be felt."[82]

The fall's debate about the merits of independent black political organizing was soon interrupted by economic and political changes of seismic proportions. First, Governor Cooke resigned, finally acting on the advice of his brother, Jay, who had been urging him to separate himself and his family's fortunes from the increasingly maligned territorial government. Grant quickly appointed Shepherd governor, feeding critics' suspicions that the District government was a vast machine for distributing presidential patronage.[83] Then, just days after the governor's resignation, Jay Cooke's banking empire failed, and banks across the country quickly followed suit. A nationwide financial panic ensued, as the New York Stock Exchange and affiliated banks temporarily closed and panicked investors found banks unable to remit their savings.[84] The crash had immediate and dire ramifications in the District of Columbia. As governor, Henry Cooke had invested considerable public funds in his brother's now bankrupt projects. The territorial government, on weak financial footing for more than a year, now appeared to be collapsing.[85]

The economic crash was a blow to the already subsiding movement to field independent black candidates. Even before the cataclysm, talk of the movement seemed to quiet as the Republican Central Committee tried to corral opposition and control the selection of nominees. Then, on the day Cooke's firm failed, men representing the District of Columbia Equal Rights League convened at the offices of the *New National Era and Citizen* and marched to Alexander Shepherd's home, where they serenaded him and then congratulated him on being appointed territorial governor. Inside Shepherd's home, John T. Johnson, who was the treasurer of the territorial government (and also an advocate of mixed schools), offered the loyalty of "those here present . . . not as black men, nor as a black man's party, but as men in the full sense of the term." Johnson clearly sought to distance the Equal Rights League from anyone who would advocate independent black political organizations and to embrace the race-blind Republicanism touted by the Shepherd government and its allies in the press. Shepherd, characteristically, did not acknowledge the group's "equal rights" agenda but, instead, discussed the difficulties of governing and his hope for financial support from Congress.[86]

The serenaders' link to the *New National Era and Citizen* bespoke a larger shift in the paper's position. Soon after the "Equal Rights for All" letter, the Shepherd serenade, and the banking crisis, the newspaper ran an editorial condemning efforts to run independent candidates and supporting Shepherd, Grant, and the regular Republican nominees for the House of Delegates. The same issue announced that Richard Greener was no longer employed in the editorial department in "consequence of the assumption of other duties."[87] After the election, the newspaper would return to a somewhat more critical stance, attacking those who argued that local African Americans were "non-producers" and therefore not entitled to a voice in the administration of their schools and offering encouragement to those "seeking for equality before the law, and equality in the enjoyment of public rights."[88] It was likely no coincidence that the paper's editorial voice sounded a great deal like Frederick Douglass, who remained adamant that African Americans must support the Republican Party even as he continued to advocate for an expansive vision of racial equality. Perhaps the senior Douglass had reasserted control of the paper in the fall of 1873, as Greener's editorials diverged too much from his pro-Republican stance and the economic crisis increased the likelihood of a Democratic onslaught in the fall elections.[89]

Despite the work of Douglass, Sella Martin, and other African Americans who remained committed to the complete package of Shepherd, Grant, and the Republican Party, black Washingtonians remained politically divided. Jockeying for Republican nominations in the districts continued until the eve of the election. Revealing the continuing impact of the fall's movement for black political independence, in four districts independent black candidates ran against nominees approved by the Republican Central Committee. Their bids were largely unsuccessful, however. The only place where an insurgent African American candidate won election was in the first district, where Republican regular Frederick Douglass Jr. was defeated.[90] The Republican Central Committee, with its high-profile black allies, proved able to largely neutralize the local movement for black independence from the Shepherd machine.

It is difficult to imagine, however, that the election results felt like a genuine victory to men like Douglass and Martin. Turnout had been low, suggesting popular disengagement. Five of the twenty-two official Republican candidates were African American, but only one of them was elected. Three black incumbents lost bids for reelection, including Thomas Chase, author of the normal school integration bill. His district had a small majority of African American voters, but he was defeated by a coalition of African Americans disillusioned with the Shepherd machine and whites who opposed his position on the normal school. The new House of Delegates would have only two black representatives; previously it had had five.[91] The *Evening Star* proclaimed that weak turnout and uncontested elections in some districts were proof that the territorial government represented "the progressive spirit of the age."[92] After all, who would want to run against history? But perhaps the better explanation was that, particularly in the face of economic crisis, few people cared to compete over representation in the virtually powerless House of Delegates, a bit player in a government that many Washingtonians—particularly Democrats and African Americans—had never seen as legitimate in the first place.

African Americans' divisions over whether to support Shepherd and his government had more to do with divergent views on the importance of loyalty to the Republicans than it did with divisions of class or prewar status. After Shepherd was removed from office, Sella Martin assured him that "the better classes of the colored people fully appreciate you."[93] Yet Martin certainly exaggerated, since it was Harvard graduate Richard Greener and other members of the political elite who had led the charge against the territorial government the preceding summer. Early on, Shepherd may have purchased the goodwill of many African American constituents through the distribution of appointments and employment on public works projects. But the government gradually lost what black support it did enjoy, primarily because it was increasingly unable to pay employees and because it refused to satisfy the more progressive leaders of black Washington. By the summer and fall of 1873, many black Washingtonians were searching for alternatives to the Shepherd regime. As the Republican Central Committee attempted to reassert control over that fall's election, however, it benefited enormously from the argument that, as Douglass famously put it, "the Republican party is the ship and all else is the sea."[94] Black defections from the Republican Party in the capital would not have unseated the powerful appointees who ran territorial government. But in places where politics were more democratic, leaving the Republican Party might open the way for a dangerous Democratic ascendancy. For African Americans, the vicissitudes of two-party politics could be a source of great frustration and disillusionment.

Race and Suffrage Reform

The territorial government never regained momentum after the failure of Jay Cooke's banking empire. President Grant continued publicly to support Shepherd and the territorial government, but reformist newspapers persisted in their investigations into the government's business practices, looking for evidence that would discredit both Shepherd and the U.S. president. That winter, the *New York Tribune* and the *Sun* found what they were looking for and published damning letters that revealed collusion among contractors, District officials, and Henry Starkweather, the 1872 congressional committee chair. Memorialists, many of them members of the original group of injunctionists from 1871, then presented Congress with a petition charging corruption and maladministration and demanding another investigation.[95]

Congress's joint, bipartisan investigating committee of 1874 exposed the stunning amounts of money the territorial government had spent and ultimately found significant breaches of the public trust. Members of the Board of Public Works claimed they had not surpassed the broad authority given them by the territorial charter, but Shepherd himself acknowledged that the board had spent close to $19 million, exceeding by roughly $12 million the budget that had been touted in the "comprehensive plan." Shepherd stated in his own defense that he had believed Congress would absorb much of the debt his government had accumulated. The congressional committee was not sympathetic. There had been no oversight of the District's auditor, accounts were in disarray, and it was impossible to determine how money had flowed in and out of the treasury. The committee insisted that the board did not work closely enough with the territorial legislature. "Good faith," it pronounced, "required that so great burden[s] as have been imposed should, in some manner, have received in advance legislative sanction."[96] Above all, the congressional committee could not square the welcome improvement of the District's public services and real estate values with the public debt that had made these changes possible. "While your committee join in the general expression of gratification at beholding the improved condition of the national capital," it wrote, "they cannot but condemn the methods by which this sudden and rapid transition was secured."[97]

The committee also distributed blame beyond Shepherd to the residual features of democracy in the capital. Investigators faulted the legislative assembly for passing acts "simply devised for the purpose of raising money with which to pay previously-incurred obligations, and continue the improvements."[98] The committee also complained that the government had plunged the municipal corporation too deeply into debt without sufficient consent from "the people." District voters had approved the $4 million loan by a landslide, but they were not *the people* the committee had in mind. In fact, the committee indicted the voters, who had "in the most emphatic way possible, indorsed and approved the action of the legislative assembly and the board of public works in the expenditure of a large sum of money."[99] In blaming voters for endorsing the loan and elected delegates for rubber-stamping the proposals of the Board of Public Works, the committee accepted the vision of public affairs that "citizens" and "taxpayers" had been advocating for the previous five years. Irresponsible voters and their elected representatives, the committee alleged, had failed to stop Shepherd's dangerous spending binge. It was now for Congress to design a new government whose policies would be more satisfactory to "the people," as conservatives defined them.

Congress acted quickly. Two days after the investigating committee issued its report, Congress abolished the territory through legislation creating a three-man commission to govern the capital. The idea of a commission government had long been dear to conservatives, who had been seeking a form of government entirely free from popular control ever since black men's suffrage had come up for debate in Congress. The commission form implied immaturity or infirmity in government. The capital had been governed by three commissioners at its outset; elsewhere, too, state and county governments had sometimes established temporary commissions while more permanent, representative governments were devised. In fact, during the economic crisis of the 1870s, other cities would turn to commissions or other forms of government that combined legislative and executive functions as interim solutions while debts and defaults were addressed. Congress's creation of a commission government for the District, and its 1878 decision to make that form permanent, conveyed its lack of faith in the capacity of residents to govern themselves.[100]

Members of the territorial House of Delegates, the capital's last vestige of local self-government, protested vehemently, petitioning Congress and protesting to newspaper editors. Speaking as "citizens" of the District, they argued that a commission would give too much power to "officials not of their choice and not responsible to them." They warned Congress that a "denial of suffrage . . . would be most impolitic," since it would send a message that Congress believed "the new voting population of the District are unfit to be entrusted with the suffrage here or any where else."[101] But there was nothing they could do to reverse Congress's course. Arguments for universal manhood suffrage and citizens' sovereignty now seemed feeble when counterpoised with economic depression, vast municipal debt, the sinking fortunes of Grant, and a climate of retrenchment against Reconstruction policies and the democratic visions they often represented.

Having made no headway through conventional political channels, members of the House of Delegates pulled a prank that many people immediately saw as confirmation that local voters' representatives were unfit to govern. Upon concluding what was destined to be the last meeting of elected local officials in the District for close to a century, local legislators apparently looted their chamber. According to breathless accounts in the *Evening Star*, delegates appeared at the legislative hall with forged papers stating that they were authorized to remove desks and other furnishings from the building and carry them home. Guards stood by as the now-obsolete politicians confiscated desks, clocks, soap, mirrors, a feather duster, and other small objects.[102] Publicity mounted, and the delegates proffered explanations, claiming they had borrowed the furniture or removed it for repairs—or that the whole escapade had been a joke. Shepherd and other officials ordered the objects returned, and the next day the *Evening Star* acknowledged that its early coverage had exaggerated the extent of the looting and reported that almost everything had been returned.[103]

If some onlookers saw the incident as further evidence of corruption in government, others probably found it hilarious. After all, many believed it was the likes of improver Alexander Shepherd and conservative George Riggs who were the thieves, the men who had stolen legitimate government away and rendered democracy in the District a farce. If a three-year orgy of building and speculation by the capital's wealthiest residents ended with the creation of a government still more favorable to the wealthy, why should not the duly elected representatives of the people help themselves to a small morsel as the regime collapsed? By the time the delegates seized public property in the council chambers, the stunt probably seemed a fitting and low-stakes protest against developments ultimately beyond their control.

To opponents of the legislature and of representative government, however, the prank only confirmed broader doubts about black voters and the officials, both white and black, they tended to elect. In almost every report, the *Evening Star* provided some version of a list of "desks, chairs, clocks, water coolers, mirrors, ink-stands, wash-stands, towels, combs, brushes, soap, and even the second-hand toothbrushes." Lists of luxurious or mundane items charged to—or stolen from—public coffers were typical of the assault on Reconstruction-era Republican governments and on the idea of political equality among men. Republicans were not alone in using public money for personal profit in this era, but biracial governments run by Republicans were uniquely vulnerable to charges of profligacy and corruption that drew strength from widespread assumptions about the incapacity of black men to responsibly use their newfound political power.[104] A long tradition of caricature dating back to the antebellum image of the black "dandy" or "Jim Crow" character had identified black people with unrestrained and inappropriate consumer appetites, and since emancipation northern and southern elites alike had worried that freedpeople would be profligate spenders. The Reconstruction discourse that linked public debt with black men's enfranchisement drew on such visions of black profligacy, even when—as was the case in the District of Columbia's House of Delegates—most of the government officials in question were white. One popular 1873 pamphleteer, for example, commented on the "mock grandeur" of the territorial government and stated that "for expense, for cheap pomp and circumstance, our territorial government, so-called, could beat Hayti." Liberal Republican journalist Donn Piatt wrote of the District legislature, "As a morbid excrescence on the body politic it has no equal except that of the South Carolina amalgamation," clearly a racialized reference to the ongoing corruption controversy in the black-majority South Carolina legislature.[105]

Commentators continued to make racialized allusions to black voters' childishness and barbarism as they grappled with how to explain the termination of representative government in the capital of a nation supposedly dedicated to popular sovereignty. In the fall of 1874, the *Evening Star* impugned local suffrage by calling it "a childish toy, with which the voters play at electing officers who have no real powers." The *Nation* later used a similar civilizational language to condemn black men's enfranchisement in Washington and throughout the South, complaining that the "ballot had been exalted into a kind of talisman or fetish, the mere possession of which elevated a man instantly, morally and intellectually." Invoking Africa and the primitive magic of the fetish, the magazine condemned black voters by linking them with cultural backwardness and implying they were unable to exercise the reason required to take part in political life.[106]

Indeed, commentary in the reformist Republican press explicitly blamed black voters for the governmental crisis in the capital. The *Nation* charged that Shepherd's Board of Public Works had controlled all branches of government "through the ignorant negro voters, its employees." The magazine marveled that "six thousand ignorant negro laborers, called in from the surrounding country by the Board of Public Works to the eight hours and loaferdom of city life, living in cabins and barracks, and knowing no one but the contractors who employ them could effectually saddle a debt upon the Chief-Justice's property." Voting rights intended to "safeguard" property against the state were rendered "utterly worthless" by black men's enfranchisement, it continued.[107] *Harper's Weekly*, no longer a staunch proponent of Reconstruction-era democratic reform, similarly blamed black men's enfranchisement for placing city government in "the hands of white persons imbittered by long minority, and resentful for their ostracization in former years." "Property-holders" had become "discouraged" and "rougher whites . . . [had become] turbulent." Meanwhile, "the negroes armed themselves to execute their new privileges," and "the course of improvements was suspended." Fortunately for the city, a "conservative Northern element" had come to the rescue, "in order to save the common property and respectability of all."[108]

The *Nation* later reflected directly on the difference between political reform in New York and in the District of Columbia. Discussing the situation in the capital, it blamed corruption on "newly-emancipated and very ignorant freedmen" who, on arriving there, "were at once converted into municipal voters who, though hardly knowing what municipal government was, were charged with the power of appropriating the property of the residents in the form of taxation." The magazine registered qualms about a government entirely shorn of voters, but it suggested that the extreme situation in Washington (that is, the preponderance of freedmen in the electorate) merited extreme political reform. By comparison, proposals to "temper" universal suffrage in New York were "milder and more carefully-designed."[109] The *Nation* suggested that New York reformers could look to Washington and feel vindicated for their tolerance of a modicum of democracy and happy to live in a center of migration for the *European* poor. These accounts did not make recourse to essentialist arguments about racial character or destiny, but they emphasized at every turn that the problem in Washington was "negroes," "ignorant negro voters," and "ignorant freedmen," a population considered racially and experientially distinct from the urban masses of the North.

As many people recognized, the total elimination of self-government in the nation's capital was a remarkable move, particularly for a Congress still controlled by Republicans, the party supposedly committed to democratizing southern politics. Elsewhere as well, elite Americans were interested in diminishing the power of undesirable voters, but nowhere else were they as successful. In 1875, the governor of New York, Democrat Samuel Tilden, appointed a commission to investigate reorganizing the New York City government. The "Tilden Commission," a body of New York City intellectual and business elites, recommended a new municipal government dominated by appointed commissions and by a powerful "board of finance," whose members would be elected by men who held at least $500 worth of property or paid at least $250 a year in rent. Historian Sven Beckert calculated that the measure would have disfranchised close to 70 percent of the city's voters. The commission's efforts were ultimately stymied, however, by a coalition of farmers and urban laborers who believed the problems of which the urban elite complained "were not significant enough to justify a step entirely out of the bounds of the political-constitutional framework of the United States."[110] Congress and the capital's economic elite did not mind transcending those bounds, and once the contested presidential election of 1876 had been resolved, they made permanent the commission form of government. For close to a century, appointed officials would govern the District of Columbia, absent any formal mechanism for taking residents' views into consideration.

As the New York City example indicates, Washington was certainly not the only place where elite reformers blamed voters for keeping a corrupt urban boss in power. As municipal debts grew during the 1870s, northern suffrage reformers campaigned against poor, urban voters, particularly Irish immigrants, whom they considered too ignorant and dependent to safely exercise political power. Some contemporaries emphasized the parallels between enfranchised former slaves in the South and Irish voters in northern cities, as did an 1876 Thomas Nast cartoon showing a caricature of a black man and an Irish man sitting on a scale balancing "South" against "North," "black" against "Irish." Recent historians have drawn on such comparisons to argue that northern suffrage reformers lumped freedmen and Irish voters together as members of a dangerous laboring class and that they cared little about the supposed "race" of the troublesome voters in question. Members of the northern Republican elite, Heather Richardson has argued, believed they were living through a crisis in "political economy" and feared, first and foremost, the threat of "disaffected workers."[111]

Yet to argue that disfranchisement in Washington was really about class, not race, would be to miss the important ways that racialized visions of political and economic competence shaped how reformers diagnosed and sought to cure the political problems that bothered them. To be sure, the era's leading Republicans and liberal reformers often eschewed the language of race and racism. Yet as we have seen, Washington's municipal reformers—both Shepherd's consolidation movement and the Citizens Association—nonetheless mobilized other powerful ideas about inequality to attack popular government. Drawing on long-standing traditions, they insisted that the true local citizens were the wealthy and that economic status should be the foundation of political power. Further, by representing themselves as citizens, they contrasted themselves with freedpeople, whom they designated the most marginal members of the local community and the least entitled to govern.

Municipal reformers used arguments that exploited the particular problems African Americans faced as they sought to claim full citizenship in the community. Even Freedmen's Bureau agents and their allies had believed freedpeople must prove themselves worthy of their new rights. Municipal reformers charged—implicitly if not explicitly—that they had not done so. They asserted that black voters were ignorant and easily led, ridiculed African Americans' political meetings, and ignored or maligned black leaders who disagreed with them. Their campaign against African Americans as voters and politicians, begun in earnest in 1869, laid the groundwork for the actual disfranchisement of 1874. We cannot know whether Congress would have ended self-government in the District if its laboring population had been largely of European descent, but there can be no doubt that it was easier to justify denying self-government to masses of black Washingtonians than it would have been if the voters in question had been of European or even Catholic origin. Even when their votes had little power, as in the capital during the territorial period, black voters still seemed threatening, not just as laborers but also as people of African descent whose experiences with enslavement ostensibly hampered their morals and left them unprepared for the responsibilities of citizenship.

Notably, however, even as Washington's municipal reformers sought to discredit freedmen as voters and freedpeople as local citizens, they did not challenge the prevailing interpretation of racial equality before the law. In fact, the institutionalization of that principle may have been one of the signal accomplishments of the period. The growing acceptance of formal racial equality meant that it was no longer tolerable in some circles to appeal directly to racial prejudice, and it circumscribed the possibilities for overt, race-based discrimination in some arenas. As the curtain closed on representative government in the capital, there was no talk of returning to black codes or other explicitly discriminatory legal proceedings. Yet the limited impact of these accomplishments must also be recognized. By the mid-1870s, notwithstanding the passage of the Sumner Civil Rights Act, the most commonly accepted interpretation of the principle of racial equality before the law offered no protection against discrimination in public schools, on common carriers, or in other public accommodations; it did not guarantee African Americans the right to vote or hold office; and it certainly did not protect them against discrimination by employers or landlords. Moreover, when allies of the territorial government used the rhetoric of race-blind Republicanism to bludgeon the nascent Equal Rights League, they revealed how the Republicans' principle of formal racial equality —when abstracted from real and persistent race-based inequities—could be used to further the interests of the white elite. The Republican repudiation of racial distinctions in public life had begun as an attempt to create a more racially egalitarian society in the wake of slavery. But those committed to understanding racial equality narrowly had always been hard-pressed to fathom the intransigence of racism and the complexity of the challenge posed by emancipation.

In the summer of 1873, Charles Sumner, frustrated with the lack of progress on school integration, had described the capital's history as the vanguard of "all the great reforms born of the war": "Emancipation, the colored suffrage, the right of colored persons to testify, and the right to ride in the street cars—all these began here," he emphasized.[112] Less than a year later the capital was at the forefront of another kind of change, born in large part from the reaction against precisely the principles Sumner and his allies had long espoused. By creating a commission government for the District, Congress placed the capital at the cusp of antidemocratic municipal reform. The permanent commission government established in 1878 had not a single elected official, but it did commit the federal government to paying 50 percent of the District government's expenses. The local business elite, never enamored of popular self-government, had no quarrel with trading voting rights for a guarantee that Congress would substantially share in the burden of paying for municipal upkeep and improvements. Some Republicans in Congress tried to fight the tide, as did white Alabama carpetbagger George E. Spencer, who in 1877 argued that the permanent commission set a precedent that "threatened" "the franchise of the poor man throughout the United States, whatever his race, his color, his nationality, or his creed," and even forecast "the abolishment of an elective government altogether." But Spencer's brief for democracy was ill-suited to the era. It would be almost a century before elected government returned to Washington.[113]

Epilogue

In the weeks before Congress reconvened in the fall of 1874, District of Columbia radical Republicans still held out a modicum of hope that Congress would not make the commission government permanent. At the very least, they wanted to draw attention to their view that the decision was a momentous one. Andrew K. Browne, the white lawyer who had worked for the Freedmen's Bureau and helped defend Minnie Gaines and who had also served in the territorial House of Delegates, was clear on this point. If Congress wiped out self-government in the District, he told a reporter for the *National Republican*, it would be a declaration of retreat from the egalitarian goals of the Reconstruction era. "Following on the great progress of the last ten years," he argued, disfranchisement in the capital "would strike the whole world with astonishment, and would be a denial of the right of self-government that this people cannot afford to make."[1]

Such arguments proved to be in vain, however. In the upcoming session, Congress would opt to continue the temporary commission it had established the previous spring, and in 1878 it would make the commission form of government permanent. The end of local self-government was not just symbolic of the federal government's waning commitment to Reconstruction; it was also highly significant for residents of the capital. Voting rights and ward-based municipal government, however disorderly and sometimes inefficient, had given impoverished Washingtonians a means for shaping the city government's priorities. Even in the territorial period, voters and their representatives continued to demand a measure of accountability from city officials. Once the commission government was created, only elite Washingtonians, organized in private "Citizens Committees," had access to the federal appointees who controlled the purse strings in their city. As one turn-of-the-century political scientist reflected, the government was "a benevolent despotism" and "in practice . . . a representative aristocracy."[2]

In the late nineteenth century, as northern urban reformers continued their debate about how cities should be governed, the anomalous form of government in the nation's capital remained an example of considerable interest. Under Washington's old, "mediaeval" government, the *Nation* explained in 1884, the suffrage had been "at least as bad as can be found in any Northern city, but different, because it was principally made up, since the war, of ignorant negroes." Under the commission form, the "city government was a despotism," and that was generally an improvement.[3] Was the District's government "fundamentally opposed to the spirit of American institutions," wondered a writer in *Century Magazine*. The "citizens" of Washington might feel that way, he concluded, but their voices should carry little weight, since the federal District was designed only as a "creature and protégé" of the federal government.[4] No one in the capital had a *right* to vote, these outlets argued, and in some situations it was best to deny people the privilege.

It is not surprising that amid the national conversation about the benefits of nonelected government Alexander Shepherd returned to Washington in 1887 and was feted as a hero. Following the territorial government's demise, he had moved with his family to northern Mexico, where he had taken charge of a silver mine. On his first trip back to the capital, local business leaders honored him as a leader of great wisdom and foresight, celebrating him with fireworks and an hour-long parade along Pennsylvania Avenue. Shepherd's reputation only improved in coming years, as elite white Americans continued to question the wisdom of urban democracy and began to prize expert management above all other qualities of municipal governance. In 1909, city fathers erected a statue in Shepherd's likeness at the entrance to the municipal building and sang his praises as the founder of modern Washington.[5]

Yet some commentators found the contradictions of the late nineteenth-century capital unacceptable. Writing in the *Chautauquan*, a self-designated journal of radical reform, Margaret Noble Lee argued that, although the commission government promoted financial security, Americans should reject its abrogation of republican principles. "Self-government would . . . make the colored race a formidable if not preponderating power in national capital affairs," she acknowledged, but "home-rule in local affairs is a vital principle in our government." Another analyst lamented to an audience of municipal reformers in 1895 that the capital's commission government promoted real estate development while ignoring the needs of laborers and schoolchildren. White Washingtonians were loath to lobby for home rule, he said, because they feared Congress would withdraw its 50 percent appropriation. "The dread of 'nigger rule,'" he added, "is another bugbear that frightens many a good citizen either into active opposition or passive resistance to the restoration of suffrage." He concluded with a caution: "I offer you Washington as an example of a municipality where the people thereof are denied all voice and participation in their government. Do you wish to follow it?"[6]

By the 1890s, it was clear that northern reformers would seek a variety of means to limit the power of urban working-class voters but that no movement for mass disfranchisement was in the offing. By contrast, southern reformers were on their way to the almost total disfranchisement of black voters (and some poor whites), urban and rural, in the service of an explicitly white supremacist vision of governance. To them, Washington was an exemplar because of its significantly black electorate and because a Republican Congress had ended voting rights there. In an 1890 book "respectfully dedicated . . . to the businessmen of the North," Hilary Herbert, an Alabama Democrat and outspoken segregationist, recalled that during Reconstruction the "noon-day sun" had shone on the "abuse" of suffrage by black voters in the capital, pushing Congress to disfranchise the entire population rather than allow the mismanagement to continue.[7] Historian William Archibald Dunning—whose racist outlook defined the historiography of Reconstruction for generations—took special note of the "extravagance, corruption, and intolerable oppression" of the Shepherd administration, whose key supporters were President Grant and "the negro voters." It "did not fail to impress reflecting minds," Dunning added, that "the popular form of government which was so unceremoniously set aside in 1874 had been originally established as in some measure a standing national exhibition of the blessings of negro suffrage." The "promptness and thoroughness with which the Republican Congress suppressed" the exhibition, Dunning suggested, was evidence that Republicans in Congress had never really supported black enfranchisement and had only imposed it on the South to punish white southerners for secession.[8] His account was historically inaccurate, since the territorial government itself represented the first step toward rejecting black men's enfranchisement. But his overall outlook confirmed the predictions of radical Republicans such as Andrew K. Browne that disfranchisement in the capital would be a dangerous precedent for the rest of the country.

Despite the loss of the vote, the national capital, with its illustrious black educational institutions and federal employment for members of the black elite, remained a bastion of black protest. In a crucial 1883 decision known as the *Civil Rights Cases*, the U.S. Supreme Court declared that equal access to public accommodations was not among the "fundamental rights which appertain to the essence of citizenship." Signaling its acceptance of a constricted vision of racial equality before the law, the Court distinguished between the acceptable "civil rights" outlined by the 1866 Civil Rights Act and the unacceptable government incursions into private life mandated by the 1875 Sumner Civil Rights Act. Any arenas not explicitly mentioned in the 1866 law, the Court argued, concerned "what may be called the *social rights* of men and races in the community." These areas were properly adjudicated by local law and custom.⁹ In invalidating the 1875 Civil Rights Act, the Court rejected arguments that associations chartered by government were essentially public and ratified instead the capacious definition of social equality long used to stymie expansive interpretations of equality before the law.

When the decision was announced, many of Washington's most politically engaged black men assembled to discuss and condemn it. Most had begun their political lives in much more promising days, making upstart claims and demanding that slavery's end be accompanied by wide-ranging racial equality. Among them were Union veteran Charles B. Fischer, who had defended the capital's black militias in the pages of the *New York Times*; Alexander Augusta, the army surgeon and Howard University Medical School professor who had demanded a right to ride the city's streetcars and sought to join the Medical Society; and labor leader Marcellus West, the plasterer who had galvanized striking workers in 1871 by likening contractors to slave owners and aristocrats. The featured speaker was Frederick Douglass, who had settled in the capital and was the District of Columbia's recorder of deeds. In his address, Douglass addressed the uses and misuses of the language of social equality. "Social equality and civil equality rest upon an entirely different basis, and well enough the American people know it," he said. When a black man working as a servant occupied a room or a carriage with whites, no one imagined he thought he was his employers' "social" equal. The entire social equality argument was "a studied purpose to degrade and stamp out the liberties of a race," he declared. "It is the old spirit of slavery, and nothing else." In a lengthy dissent in the *Civil Rights Cases*, Justice John Marshall Harlan agreed. "Government has nothing to do with social, as distinguished from technically legal, rights of individuals," he wrote, but "the rights which congress, by the act of 1875, endeavored to secure and protect are legal, not social, rights." In fact, he argued, they were guaranteed by the Thirteenth and the Fourteenth Amendments.¹⁰

Yet these arguments—that social equality was a chimera and that the Court's majority had construed legitimate legal rights too narrowly—made little headway in the late nineteenth century or, for that matter, in much of the twentieth.

In fact, the discourse of social equality became central to the justification for segregation. "Perhaps nothing perplexes the outside observer more than the popular term and the popular theory of 'no social equality,'" wrote the Swedish sociologist Gunnar Myrdal in 1944. Myrdal had been "made to feel from the start" of his research on the "American dilemma" of race that social equality had "concrete implications and a central importance for the Negro problem in America." Yet he observed that its meaning was always "kept vague and elusive, and the theory loose and ambiguous." "One moment [the theory] will be stretched to cover and justify every form of social segregation and discrimination, and, in addition, all the inequalities in justice, politics and breadwinning. The next moment it will be narrowed to express only the denial of close personal intimacies and intermarriage," Myrdal wrote. "The very lack of precision allows the notion of 'no social equality' to rationalize the rather illogical and wavering system of color caste in America."[11] That powerful notion, which Myrdal found so central to the architecture of twentieth-century segregation, had its foundation in the Civil War–era debate about racial equality. And, from the beginning, opponents of expansive racial equality had invoked social equality with the same opportunistic inconsistency.

The men and women who made Washington a center of egalitarian aspirations during Reconstruction would have been gratified to know that a few measures they had demanded—though largely unenforced during their own lifetimes—would be dramatically revived much later. In the late 1940s, black activists in Washington, many of them affiliated with Howard University, challenged segregation in restaurants by using the forgotten public accommodations laws of the Reconstruction years. Those local laws, passed during Bowen's and Shepherd's regimes, had been ignored for decades, but they had never been repealed or overridden. In a case that resulted from activists' pressure, the U.S. Supreme Court found in 1953 that the laws were still in effect and that racial discrimination in the capital's restaurants and other accommodations was already illegal, a decision that provided momentum to a burgeoning twentieth-century movement struggling to make real the expansive vision of civil rights demanded by its predecessors in the nineteenth century.[12]

In the wake of emancipation, the capital of the United States was an example for all the land: a hub of African American activism, a crucial laboratory for federal policy, and a bridge between the North and the South. Black residents of the capital demanded respect for their familial relations and civic associations and the privileges accorded to full members of the community. Well before government policies formally granted them rights, they made upstart claims in places like streetcars, public schools, and the Capitol building itself. Kate Brown insisted on riding the ladies' car home from Alexandria, Virginia; Josie Martin attended Franklin School; and hundreds of African Americans whose names are now unknown attended debates in the Capitol and marched in the streets, insisting that freedom must also mean full citizenship. Black Washingtonians were a diverse group, composed of recently arrived former slaves as well as long-standing residents. But members of the black elite saw their future as intimately linked to that of the freedpeople and forged political alliances with them rather than holding themselves aloof.

As Congress struggled to create a Reconstruction policy for the states of the former Confederacy, it played an extraordinary role in Washington, where the Constitution gave it exclusive jurisdiction. With radical Republicanism ascendant, Congress passed emancipation, forbade racial discrimination in laws and on common carriers, enfranchised black men, and provided for black men's office holding and jury service. But it was not only the policies themselves that were significant. Often spurred by the activism of local residents, Congress's debates about equality and its limits in the District of Columbia illuminated a remarkable range of contemporary ideas about the areas in which government ought, and ought not, attempt to level inequities. It was Congress's willingness to undertake experiments with racial equality in the capital that made woman suffragists hope for similar innovations in women's rights there. Yet hopes for truly universal voting rights soon foundered. Black men's enfranchisement seemed to Republican congressmen both more urgent and less disruptive to what they saw as proper domestic relations.

The dynamics of local activism and congressional power helped place the capital at the vanguard of racially egalitarian policy and practice, but they also allowed white business leaders and conservatives to bend the governing structures of the District toward their own interests. The two-stage "redemption" of the capital from radical Reconstruction was similar in timing and tenor to other early examples of redemption, particularly in the Upper South. Indeed, the District of Columbia was distinctly southern in its large population of freedpeople, its fractious Republican politics, its brief period of radical Republicanism, and its dramatic disfranchisement. And yet, I have argued, because the capital's redemption ultimately happened at the hands of a Republican Congress and because Alexander Shepherd was so frequently compared with "Boss" Tweed of New York, it is also useful to see its story in the context of contemporaneous urban reform movements in the North. Northern urban reformers of the 1870s and 1880s, sometimes known as the "best men," saw Washington as an example of what New York was not. New York and the North had troublesome voters in the Irish and in other working-class immigrants, but when they looked at Washington, they saw difference, not sameness, and specifically they saw a significantly black electorate toward which far more dramatic disfranchisement measures could be justified. Thus the capital not only sits geographically on what is often considered the border between the North and the South; politically and historically, too, it is an intriguing link between the two regions, and its history invites further questions about race, class, and urban reform in both.

During Reconstruction, relatively new visions of equal individual rights swirled together with other, more long-standing ideas about groups, status, and privileges in the community. Amid an ongoing expansion of individualism and rights whose beginnings antedated the Civil War, African Americans and their allies used emancipation as an opportunity to frame claims to racial equality and entitlement to individual rights. But they also insisted on privileges and prerogatives in the community, and they also made claims on behalf of groups: families, church organizations, labor and political associations, and "the race" as a whole. Thus when freedpeople sought help reunifying families or insisted that existing relationships between men and women be considered marriages, Freedmen's Bureau agents converted such demands for recognition of status into claims to rights that the state could, at least in theory, secure through policy. When African Americans demanded equal access to streetcars, they went out of their way to show themselves worthy of the privilege of riding—whether as soldiers or as respectable ladies and gentlemen. Congress formally turned such claims into a right to ride by forbidding common carriers from discriminating based on race. Yet even after the law had affirmed African Americans' positive right to ride the cars, status and respectability continued to be important, as black men and women presented themselves as decorous riders and opponents insisted that black ridership degraded the city's public conveyances.

In the crucial case of the vote, demands for rights remained intertwined with convictions that only those with elevated status should vote. Black activists such as John F. Cook Jr. used both idioms, arguing that black men should be allowed the privilege of voting since so many were hard workers, soldiers, and taxpayers *and* that the vote should be a right enjoyed by all men in a diverse society. Woman suffragists knew all too well that many people believed voting was more akin to a privilege reserved for people of a certain standing in a community (that is, men) than a right to which all adult members were entitled. Yet some woman suffragists themselves argued for the privileges of some groups over others as they insisted that white women voters would exert a reforming influence on the electorate. Urban reformers likewise carried forward the long-standing view that only wealthy members of the community were true citizens. The privilege of participating in self-government must be earned, they argued, and only people like themselves deserved it.

The continuing link between status and rights made it particularly difficult for African Americans to claim equality. Many white Americans believed race as such made people of African descent unworthy or incapable of citizenship. In addition, however, many of those whites who were most interested in advancing freedpeople's fortunes—Republicans, Freedmen's Bureau agents, and educators—believed freedpeople must secure their rights through proper behavior. Such attitudes toward freedpeople's comportment reflected something more than simply class-based condescension, for freedpeople were widely considered uniquely damaged by slavery and, perhaps, disadvantaged by race itself. Judged as failures before they were given a chance, freedpeople could never have overcome most whites' presumption that they were unworthy of membership in the civic body. Many black Washingtonians adopted conventions of respectability to demonstrate that they deserved the rights and privileges they were claiming. Collectively, however, they faced brutal ridicule and degradation in public, a kind of demeaning discourse designed not only to humiliate, but also, crucially, to discredit their political aspirations.

In this context, it is not difficult to understand both the appeal of equality before the law and its limitations. Here, at least, was the prospect of ignoring the group affiliations that branded people as superior or inferior based on race, class, and perhaps even sex, and of imagining (at least for legal purposes) a deracinated individual equal to all others. Here too was the possibility that institutions such as legislatures and courts would require and then enforce such equal treatment. The principle of equality before the law also suggested that equalizing mandates would be balanced against principles of liberty and free choice. In other words, it promised to carve out two separate arenas: one where government could act to promote equality and the other where private taste and perhaps inequality would reign.

Yet, as we have seen, the placement of the crucial demarcation between these two zones posed fundamental problems. Many Democrats were reluctant to grant any concession to racial equality before the law, as the black codes passed by southern state legislatures in 1865 and 1866 indicate. But Republicans also disagreed vehemently among themselves. Many believed equality before the law meant narrowly conceived civil rights and had no bearing on the right to vote. Black activists and radical Republicans, by contrast, contended that legal equality should encompass not only the vote but also corporations and other associations that were regulated by the law and by the state. Their reasoning had a strong basis in fact, for public policy extended well beyond formal legislation; states and local governments regulated and even created a myriad of ostensibly private institutions. But the radicals' view lost out to the much more pervasive one, that equality before the law should be defined narrowly, so that only states and their laws could be prohibited from racial discrimination.

The principle of equality that made the most headway in public life during Reconstruction thus provided no remedy for discrimination or exploitation by ostensibly private parties. In an era when organized white laborers could not persuade states or the federal government to establish minimum wage or maximum hours laws for private employers, it was virtually inconceivable that private employers could be prohibited from racial discrimination in hiring or pay scales. Nor did people seem inclined to argue that citizens' fundamental rights to property and contract barred private parties from discriminating when selling land and other property. People could contest such inequities with claims to fairness or justice, but the concept of equality before the law did not encompass arenas like private housing and employment that in the twentieth century were made the domain of civil rights. The prerogatives of private parties, expressed in visions of personal taste, liberty of contract, and the prohibition on social equality, were simply too strong.

The question of postemancipation racial equality did not have a simple yes or no answer. Rather, it produced a complicated debate about who should have which rights and privileges, and in which places. That discussion engaged people in the streets and in churches, at the polling places and in legislative chambers. It touched domains of law and civil society, and it reached into the most intimate areas of people's lives. The era's struggles over where equality should be promoted and where inequality should be accepted, over how democracy should work, and over whether wealth, whiteness, or manhood should be the sources of special privileges, resonate in our own time. The parallels are instructive, if not always encouraging.

Notes

PFP	Post Family Papers, University of Rochester, Rochester, N.Y.
RACC	Records of the United States Army Continental Commands, 1821–1920, RG 393, NARA
RBRFAL	Records of the Bureau of Refugees, Freedmen, and Abandoned Lands, RG 105, NARA
RDCSC	Records of the District of Columbia Supreme Court, RG 21, NARA
RSEH	Records of St. Elizabeth's Hospital, RG 418, NARA
RSIS	Records of the Office of the Secretary of the Interior Relating to the Suppression of the African Slave Trade and Negro Colonization, 1854–72, M160, reel 8, NARA
RUSHR	Records of the U.S. House of Representatives, RG 233, NARA
RUSS	Records of the U.S. Senate, RG 46, NARA
RUSSC	Records of the U.S. Supreme Court, RG 267, NARA
USMPCDC	U.S. Manuscript Population Census for Washington, D.C.
WC	*Washington Chronicle*
WES	*Washington Evening Star*
WNI	*Washington National Intelligencer*
WNR	*Washington National Republican*
WOD	William Owner Diary, Manuscript Division, LC

Introduction

1. Editorial, *WNR*, Nov. 19, 1874; Sumner, *Charles Sumner: His Complete Works, 18:21*.

2. *CR*, 43rd Cong., 2nd sess., 1874, 103.

3. Ibid., 126.

4. This book owes a great debt to Washington historians whose work helped me understand the contours of local history and offered openings for additional exploration. Constance McLaughlin Green was the pioneer of Washington history in the twentieth century, writing a fine two-volume history of the capital, followed by a separate volume on race relations. The only published volume dedicated to Reconstruction politics was James Whyte's 1958 *Uncivil War*, which ably reflects the early stages of Reconstruction revisionism. Thomas Reed Johnson's excellent unpublished dissertation helped me immensely, as did more quantitatively driven studies of black Washington. I also benefited from a somewhat separate literature on corruption and urban development, and from Howard Gillette's *Between Justice and Beauty*, which links racial conflict and urban planning over the capital's entire history. Constance McLaughlin Green, *Washington*; Constance McLaughlin Green, *Secret City*; Whyte, *Uncivil War*; Thomas Reed Johnson, "City on the Hill"; Johnston, *Surviving Freedom*; Borchert, *Alley Life in Washington*; Horton and Horton, "Race, Occupation, and Literacy"; Horton, "Development of Federal Social Policy"; Melvin Roscoe Williams, "Blacks in Washington"; Clark-Lewis, *First Freed*; Lessoff, *Nation and Its City*; Maury, *Alexander "Boss" Shepherd*; Howard Gillette, *Between Justice and Beauty*.

5. Barkley Brown, "Negotiating and Transforming the Public Sphere"; Dailey, *Before Jim Crow*; Edwards, *Gendered Strife and Confusion*; Laurent Dubois, *Colony of Citizens*; Scott, *Degrees of Freedom*; Saville, *Work of Reconstruction*; Saville, "Rites and Power"; Cooper, Holt, and Scott, *Beyond Slavery*.

6. Eric Foner, *Reconstruction*; Eric Foner, *Nothing but Freedom*. The literature on Reconstruction has tended to focus heavily on land, labor, and freedom in a rural context. See also Berlin et al., *Slaves No More*; Schwalm, *Hard Fight for We*; Reidy, *From Slavery to Agrarian Capitalism*; Rodrigue, *Reconstruction in the Cane Fields*; Fields, *Slavery and Freedom on the Middle Ground*; Saville, *Work of Reconstruction*; Bercaw, *Gendered Freedoms*; Frankel, *Freedom's Women*; and Hahn, *Nation under Our Feet*.

7. Sumner, "Equality before the Law," in Sumner, *Charles Sumner: His Complete Works*, 3:56–64; Laurent Dubois, *Colony of Citizens*; Berlin, *Many Thousands Gone*; Frey, *Water from the Rock*; Wiecek, *Sources of Antislavery Constitutionalism*; Nelson, *Fourteenth Amendment*, 13–39; Isenberg, *Sex and Citizenship*; Kousser, "Supremacy of Equal Rights"; Finkelman, "Prelude to the Fourteenth Amendment"; Nieman, "Language of Liberation," 67–72; Frank and Munro, "Original Understanding of 'Equal Protection,'" 136–38; Levy and Philips, "The *Roberts* Case"; Ruchames, "Jim Crow Railroads."

8. I have found the following works particularly useful: Kousser, "Supremacy of Equal Rights"; Finkelman, "Prelude to the Fourteenth Amendment"; Maltz, "Fourteenth Amendment Concepts"; Sandoval-Strausz, "Travelers, Strangers, and Jim Crow"; Welke, "When All the Women Were White"; and Keyssar, *Right to Vote*. A thoughtful assessment of the field, which urges more interaction between conventional social history and legal history, is Vorenberg, "Reconstruction as a Constitutional Crisis." For a rhetorician's approach, see Wilson, *Reconstruction Desegregation Debate*.

9. Novak, "Legal Transformation of Citizenship"; Novak, "American Law of Association"; Edwards, *People and Their Peace*; Vorenberg, "Citizenship and the Thirteenth Amendment"; Sandoval-Strausz, "Travelers, Strangers, and Jim Crow"; Kerber, *No Constitutional Right*. Historians' earlier conversations about the persistence and importance of republicanism in nineteenth-century America also addressed ideals of community and hierarchical status and proposed an alternative tradition to liberalism. See, for example, McCurry, *Masters of Small Worlds*; Barkley Brown, "Negotiating and Transforming the Public Sphere"; Kloppenberg, "Premature Requiem"; and Ethington, *Public City*.

10. Novak, "Legal Transformation of Citizenship"; Vorenberg, "Citizenship and the Thirteenth Amendment"; Kettner, *Development of American Citizenship*; Kerber, *No Constitutional Right*; Isenberg, *Sex and Citizenship*.

11. See, for example, Litwack, *North of Slavery*, 64–102; and Finkelman, "Prelude to the Fourteenth Amendment."

12. Stanley, *From Bondage to Contract*; Novak, *People's Welfare*; Edwards, *People and Their Peace*; Richardson, *Death of Reconstruction*; Wiecek, *Sources of Antislavery Constitutionalism*; Goluboff, *Lost Promise of Civil Rights*; Kaczorowski, "To Begin the Nation Anew"; Cooper, Holt, and Scott, "Introduction," in *Beyond Slavery*; Nieman, *To Set the Law in Motion*.

13. Historians once tended to portray the Reconstruction black elite as detached from freedpeople, but more recent interpretations have emphasized both the malleability of class relations and solidarities across classes. Lapsansky, "Friends, Wives, and Strivings"; Barkley Brown, "Negotiating and Transforming the Public Sphere"; Schweninger, *Black Property Owners*, 143–232; Schweninger, "Black Economic Reconstruction"; Scott, *Degrees of Freedom*; Holt, *Black over White*; Powell, "Centralization and Its Discontents." Social historians have long recognized the importance of cities for the development of African American life after slavery. See, for example, Blassingame, *Black New Orleans*; Blassingame, "Before the Ghetto"; Perdue, *Negro in Savannah*; Wright, *Life*

behind a Veil; Rachleff, *Black Labor in the South*; Jenkins, *Seizing the New Day*; Lewis, *In their Own Interests*; Hunter, *To 'Joy My Freedom*; and Rabinowitz, *Race Relations*. For an emphasis on urban politics, see Fitzgerald, *Urban Emancipation*.

14. Johannsen, *Lincoln-Douglas Debates*, 52–53. See also Eric Foner, *Free Soil, Free Labor, Free Men*, 285–98; and Frederickson, *Big Enough*, 63–84, 117–26.

15. For social equality as an existing legal category, see, for example, Hyman and Wiecek, *Equal Justice under Law*, 396–98. Others have suggested that the category was mainly used by white supremacists attempting to stop the advance of racial egalitarianism. See Myrdal, *American Dilemma*, 586–92; Scott, "Public Rights"; Painter, "Social Equality"; Primus, *American Language of Rights*, esp. 153–73; Wilson, *Reconstruction Desegregation Debate*, 112–16; Rosen, *Terror in the Heart of Freedom*, esp. 138–59; and Dailey, *Before Jim Crow*, 85–93.

16. As Ann Stoler has observed, "Racial discourses work through sedimented and familiar cultural representations of difference as they simultaneously tap into and feed the emergence of new ones." "Racial Histories and Their Regimes of Truth," 190. The literature on post–Civil War southern cities, including Washington, tends to split between "Reconstruction" studies of African Americans and race relations and "city building" studies about governance and technology that treat the "New South" but slight Reconstruction. Historian Howard Rabinowitz sought to bridge the two fields, but subsequent historians have rarely followed suit. Rabinowitz, *Race Relations*; Rabinowitz, "Continuity and Change"; Rabinowitz, "Reconstruction to Redemption"; Rabinowitz, "Segregation and Reconstruction." For black community studies, see note 13 above. The contrasting literature on southern urban development includes Russell, *Atlanta*; Platt, *City Building in the New South*; and Carl Vernon Harris, *Political Power in Birmingham*. More suggestive about the conjunction of Reconstruction, race, and political reform are Berkeley, *Like a Plague of Locusts*; Fitzgerald, *Urban Emancipation*; and Wrenn, *Crisis and Commission Government in Memphis*.

17. *Views of the Minority*, 44th Cong., 2nd sess., 1877, S. Rept. 572, p. 13. For southern and northern reform and disfranchisement, see Kousser, *Shaping of Southern Politics*; Perman, *Struggle for Mastery*; Keyssar, *Right to Vote*; McGerr, *Decline of Popular Politics*; and Sproat, *Best Men*.

Chapter 1

1. "The President's Interview with a Committee," *San Francisco Pacific Appeal*, Sept. 20, 1862. For more on this meeting, see Kate Masur, "African American Delegation."

2. "The President's Interview with a Committee," *San Francisco Pacific Appeal*, Sept. 20, 1862.

3. Leech, *Reveille in Washington*; Furgurson, *Freedom Rising*; Cooling, *Symbol, Sword, and Shield*.

4. Dickens, *American Notes*, 129; Constance McLaughlin Green, *Washington*, 1:9–23; Bryan, *History of the National Capital*, 1:338–86.

5. Howard Gillette Jr., "Introduction"; Goldfield, "Antebellum Washington in Context"; Constance McLaughlin Green, *Washington*, 1:191–99; McArdle, "Development of the Business Sector," 560–65.

6. Walt Whitman to Nathaniel Bloom and John Bray, Mar. 19, 1863, in Louis P. Masur, *Real War Will Never Get into the Books*, 264.

7. Whitman, *Complete Prose Works*, 416–17; Busey, *Personal Reminiscences*, 87–89.

8. U.S. Constitution, art. I, sec. 8; Constance McLaughlin Green, *Washington*, 1:88–89, 162–63, 173–74; Bryan, *History*, 1:466–74.

9. Goldfield, "Antebellum Washington in Context," 19; Goldfield, "Pursuing the American Dream"; Einhorn, *Property Rules*; Constance McLaughlin Green, *Washington*, 1:203–4; Tindall, *Standard History*, 241, 243, 366.

10. Brown, *Free Negroes in the District of Columbia*; Arnebeck, *Through a Fiery Trial*; Provine, "Economic Position of the Free Blacks"; Constance McLaughlin Green, *Secret City*, 15–16, 27–28; Kapsch, "Building Liberty's Capital"; Allen, "Capitol Construction"; Allen, *History of Slave Laborers*.

11. Harrold, *Subversives*, 6, 11; Deyle, *Carry Me Back*, 246–53. See also Clephane, "Local Aspect of Slavery."

12. Fehrenbacher, *Slaveholding Republic*, 49–88; Deyle, *Carry Me Back*, 195–203; Constance McLaughlin Green, *Washington*, 1:143, 178–79; Harrold, *Subversives*, 94–145; Gudmestad, *Troublesome Commerce*, 35–40, 186–88.

13. Constance McLaughlin Green, *Secret City*, 25, 32; Clephane, "Local Aspect of Slavery," 230–31; Corrigan, "Ties That Bind," 87; Constance McLaughlin Green, *Washington*, 1:99.

14. Goodwin, "History of Schools," 200; Constance McLaughlin Green, *Secret City*, 27, 35–38; Constance McLaughlin Green, *Washington*, 1:143, 181; Corrigan, "Ties That Bind," 79, 85; Harrold, *Subversives*, 148–49; Rives, "Old Families and Houses," 58; Clephane, "Local Aspect of Slavery," 237; Johnston, *Surviving Freedom*, 89–90. For the Upper South more generally, see Berlin, *Slaves without Masters*, 344–63.

15. Quoted in Corrigan, "Ties That Bind," 85; and Levey, "Segregation in Education," 67–68. On Irish immigrants, see also Teute, "Wild, Desolate Place," 53; and McAleer, "Green Streets of Washington."

16. Goodwin, "History of Schools," esp. 195–222. Goodwin's detailed report has been extraordinarily useful for historians. See also Robinson, "Some Aspects of the Free Negro Population"; Cromwell, "First Negro Churches"; and Melvin Roscoe Williams, "Blueprint for Change," 366–70.

17. Goodwin, "History of Schools," 200–203; Grimshaw, *Official History of Freemasonry*, 148–49; Eric Foner, *Freedom's Lawmakers*, 49–50; Gatewood, *Aristocrats of Color*, 40.

18. Johnston, *Surviving Freedom*, 85; Corrigan, "Ties That Bind."

19. *Anglo-African*, Nov. 30, 1861, Jan. 23, 1864; Severson, *History of Felix Lodge*, 9, 10; Grimshaw, *Official History of Freemasonry*, 136–37; Busey, *Personal Reminiscences*, 22.

20. Novak, "American Law of Association."

21. *National Anti-Slavery Standard*, May 31, 1862.

22. *Anglo-African*, Dec. 12, 1863; Kasson, "Iowa Woman in Washington, D.C.," 85; Johnston, *Surviving Freedom*, 163; Whitman, *Specimen Days & Collect*, 48; "Washington as a Camp," *Atlantic Monthly*, July 1861, 107–10; Bulkley, "The War Hospitals"; Leech, *Reveille in Washington*, 167; Constance McLaughlin Green, *Washington*, 1:244–47.

23. Curry, *Blueprint for Modern America*; Bogue, *Congressman's Civil War*; James M. McPherson, *Struggle for Equality*; James M. McPherson, *Negro's Civil War*, 249–50.

24. Sayles Bowen to Emily Howland, May 31, 1862, EHP. *National Anti-Slavery Standard*, Jan. 11, 1862, May 31, 1862; Billings, "Social and Economic Conditions in Washington," 198; Conlin, "Smithsonian Abolition Lecture Controversy"; Daniel W. Pfaff, "Forney, John W.," *American National Biography Online*, Feb. 2000.

25. Alfred G. Harris, "Enforcement of the Fugitive Slave Laws," 2–16, 43; Guelzo, *Lincoln's*

Emancipation Proclamation, 92–99; Johnston, *Surviving Freedom*, 119–20; Kousser, "Supremacy of Equal Rights." See also McKay, *Henry Wilson*, 176–79.

26. "Persecution of Negroes in the Capitol—Astounding Revelations," *Frank Leslie's Illustrated Newspaper*, Dec. 28, 1861; *Daily Citizen and News* (Lowell, Mass.), Dec. 9, 1861; *Daily Cleveland Herald*, Dec. 10, 1861; *Liberator*, Dec. 13, 1861.

27. *WNI*, Apr. 12, 1862; *CG*, 37th Cong., 2nd sess., 1862, 1353–56; *National Anti-Slavery Standard*, May 31, 1862; *WNR*, Feb. 14, 1862; Berlin et al., *Destruction of Slavery*, 366; Fields, *Slavery and Freedom on the Middle Ground*, 111–13.

28. *CG*, 37th Cong., 2nd sess., 1862, 1496. See also ibid., 1300, 1338–39, 1478, 1500, 1523; *WNI*, Apr. 4, 1862, Apr. 3, 1862; Alfred Garrett Harris, "Slavery and Emancipation," 263; Kurtz, "Emancipation in the Federal City"; and Curry, *Blueprint for Modern America*, 36–43.

29. Kate Masur, "African American Delegation"; Boyd, "Negro Colonization," 144; Seraille, "Afro-American Emigration," 199; Vorenberg, "Abraham Lincoln," 35–36.

30. "Act for the Release of Certain Persons Held to Service or Labor," 377.

31. Levey, "Segregation in Education," 159–80.

32. "An Act Providing for the Education of Colored Children in the Cities of Washington and Georgetown, District of Columbia, and for Other Purposes," *U.S. Statutes at Large*, 12:407; "An Act Relating to Schools for the Education of Colored Children in the Cities of Washington and Georgetown, in the District of Columbia," ibid., 537–38; *WNR*, May 21, 1862, May 22, 1862; *WNI*, Apr. 19, 1862; Henry Barnard, *Special Report*, 49–50; Goodwin, "History of Schools," 252–53, 264–66; Levey, "Segregation in Education," 149–52.

33. "An Act Providing for the Education of Colored Children in the Cities of Washington and Georgetown, District of Columbia, and for Other Purposes," *U.S. Statutes at Large*, 12:407; "An Act Supplementary to the 'Act for the Release of Certain Persons Held to Service or Labor in the District of Columbia,' approved April Sixteen, Eighteen Hundred and Sixty-two," ibid., 539; *CG*, 37th Cong., 2nd sess., 1862, 2020.

34. *WNI*, June 18, 1863; *Constitutional Union*, June 16, 1863; Cromwell, "First Negro Churches"; *Washington Post*, Sept. 24, 1888; Higginbotham, *From Strength to Strength*, 25–31. See also Howard, *Autobiography*, 166–67; and Keckley, *Behind the Scenes*, 111.

35. *Anglo-African*, Nov. 30, 1861.

36. Johnston, *Surviving Freedom*, 106. For population numbers, see U.S. Bureau of the Census, *Historical Statistics of the United States*, 26; and Kate Masur, "Reconstructing the Nation's Capital," Appendix, Tables 1, 2, 3.

37. *Anglo-African*, Aug. 1, 1863; *WNR*, May 23, 1862; Bryan, *History of the National Capital*, 2:520.

38. *Washington Post*, June 25, 1902; Bryan, *History of the National Capital*, 2:520.

39. *National Anti-Slavery Standard*, Apr. 19, 1862, 3; Editorial, *WNR*, May 23, 1862, May 24, 1862; *WNI*, June 2, 1862. See also Pearson, *James S. Wadsworth*, 134–41; Alfred G. Harris, "Enforcement of the Fugitive Slave Laws," 9–11; Guelzo, *Lincoln's Emancipation Proclamation*, 99–100; and Leech, *Reveille in Washington*, 245–47.

40. *WNR*, Apr. 7, 1862, Apr. 9, 1862, May 23, 1862, June 10, 1863; *WNI*, June 12, 1863; *Constitutional Union*, June 11, 1863.

41. *Christian Recorder*, July 19, 1862. See also *WNR*, May 22, 1862, May 23, 1862; and *Anglo-African*, Oct. 24, 1863.

42. Editorial, *WNR*, May 24, 1862; *National Anti-Slavery Standard*, May 31, 1862.

43. Application for writ, Apr. 20, 1863, Petition of Andrew Hall, Habeas Corpus Case Files, 1863–1933 (unnumbered), RDCSC; General Term Minutes, vol. 1, 9, 11–12, ibid.; *WES*, May 12, 1863.

44. *Anglo-African*, Aug. 1, 1863; Bryan, *History of the National Capital*, 2:518–20; Noell and Downing, *Court-House*, 48–49, 94–95; Job Barnard, "Early Days of the Supreme Court," 8–11. Lincoln's appointees were David K. Cartter, Abraham B. Olin, George P. Fisher, and Andrew Wylie.

45. *WES*, May 22, 1863, May 23, 1863; *WNR*, May 13, 1863; *WNI*, May 24, 1863, May 25, 1863.

46. *WES*, May 23, 1863, May 26, 1863; *WNR*, June 4, 1863; "*In Re* Andrew Hall," in Mackey, *District of Columbia Reports*, 10–35; Noell and Downing, *Court-House*, 72. See also Proctor, *Washington*, 228–29; and Leech, *Reveille in Washington*, 252. For Hall's lawyer, John Dean, see *WNR*, May 22, 1862, June 4, 1863; *Anglo-African*, Oct. 24, 1863; and Pearson, *James S. Wadsworth*, 139.

47. Constance McLaughlin Green, *Secret City*, 99; Constance McLaughlin Green, *Washington*, 1:278–79, 324–25; Johnston, *Surviving Freedom*, 191–93; Jacqueline M. Moore, *Leading the Race*.

48. Payne, *Welcome to the Ransomed*; Cromwell, "First Negro Churches," 69.

49. *Christian Recorder*, Nov. 1, 1862, Oct. 4, 1862.

50. *Christian Recorder*, Oct. 4, 1862; [John Simms], "Notes on Union Relief Association," Metropolitan AME Church Papers, box 2, folder 33, MSRC; *Christian Recorder*, Dec. 27, 1862. On other Protestant and Catholic associations, see ibid., Mar. 28, 1863, Nov. 8, 1862, Oct. 25, 1862; and *Anglo-African*, Nov. 30, 1861.

51. "Societies in Washington, DC, for the Benefit of the Contraband," *Christian Recorder*, Nov. 1, 1862; *Second Annual Report of the Freedmen and Soldiers' Relief Association*; Ripley et al., *United States, 1859–1865*, 248–52. See also Quarles, *Negro in the Civil War*, 128–29; and Melvin Roscoe Williams, "Blueprint for Change," 367–68. Keckly's name is typically spelled "Keckley," but Jennifer Fleischner has noted that Keckly herself never used the second "e" when she wrote her name. See Fleischner, *Mrs. Lincoln and Mrs. Keckly*, 7.

52. For the quotation, *Christian Recorder*, Aug. 29, 1863. See also *Christian Recorder*, Jan. 10, 1863; *Anglo-African*, Nov. 14, 1863, May 28, 1864, July 2, 1864.

53. This account of black women's philanthropic work in Civil War Washington supports arguments advanced by other historians that black women began such work well before the Jim Crow era. Concurring arguments include Berkeley, "Colored Ladies Also Contributed"; Shaw, "Black Club Women"; Martha S. Jones, *All Bound Up Together*, esp. 133; and Coleman, "Architects of a Vision." For contrasting claims, see Gilmore, *Gender and Jim Crow*, chap. 6; and Jacqueline M. Moore, *Leading the Race*.

54. *Christian Recorder*, Nov. 22, 1862. See also ibid., Nov. 8, 1862, Jan. 3, 1863, Jan. 10, 1863. For church and Sabbath school organizing across District of Columbia neighborhoods and denominations, see *Christian Recorder*, July 19, 1862; *WNR*, Apr. 9, 1862, Apr. 28, 1862; and Cromwell, "First Negro Churches," 69.

55. *Anglo-African*, Jan. 16, 1864.

56. *Christian Recorder*, Nov. 1, 1862, 173; Shirley Dare (pseud.), "The Freedmen of the Capital," *New York World*, Feb. 25, 1865, and Griffing to Mott, Apr. 22, 1870, both in JGP.

57. *Christian Recorder*, Aug. 30, 1862, Oct. 25, 1862, Jan. 3, 1863, Apr. 4, 1863, July 1, 1863, Sept. 5, 1863; William H. Jones, "John Brown in Washington," ibid., June 13, 1863; Henry McNeal Turner, "Our Washington Correspondent," ibid., Nov. 1, 1862.

58. *Christian Recorder*, Mar. 21, 1863, Oct. 25, 1862. For similar concerns about limited resources, see Emma Brown to Emily Howland, Nov. 19, 1862, EHP; *Christian Recorder*, June 18, 1864; and *Baltimore Sun*, Oct. 16, 1862.

59. *WES*, Aug. 5, 1862; John E. Washington, *They Knew Lincoln*, 108; Testimony of William Slade, File 1, AFIC. The organization may have been modeled after—or co-founded with—an identically named organization founded in Philadelphia in 1860. For the Philadelphia organization, see Hugh Davis, "Pennsylvania State Equal Rights League," 614.

60. Testimony of William Slade, file 1, AFIC. The association may have been responsible for the publication of information about African American organizations and property ownership in the *WNR*, Apr. 15, 1862.

61. Hahn, *Nation under Our Feet*, 322, 318; "The Expedition to Chriqui," *Douglass's Monthly*, Nov. 1862, 751; "Pomeroy's Colonization Scheme Abandoned," *San Francisco Pacific Appeal*, Sept. 27, 1862; J. D. Johnson to [Abraham Lincoln], Mar. 3, 1863, and J. D. Johnson to J. P. Usher, Apr. 10, 1863, RSIS.

62. *WNR*, Apr. 10, 1862, Apr. 23, 1862, Apr. 20, 1862; *Christian Recorder*, May 17, 1862, July 19, 1862; Berlin et al., *Wartime Genesis of Free Labor*, 263–66.

63. "Colored Men Petitioning to Be Colonized," *Douglass's Monthly*, May 1862, 642.

64. "Important Meeting of the Colored People of Boston," *Liberator*, Aug. 1, 1862.

65. The large literature on the American Colonization Society and Liberia includes Burin, *Slavery and the Peculiar Solution*; and Miller, *Search for a Black Nationality*, esp. 47–49, 82–90.

66. *WES*, Aug. 5, 1862; "The People of Washington and J. D. Johnson," *San Francisco Pacific Appeal*, Sept. 13, 1862; Carter A. Stewart et al. to J. D. Johnson, ibid.; William McClain to James Hall, July 30, 1862, vol. 46, 410, Outgoing Correspondence, Letterbooks, 1839–1912, Domestic Letters, American Colonization Society Papers, LC, Reel 203; William McLain to John Orcutt, Aug. 4, 1862, 426, ibid.

67. William McClain to James Hall, July 30, 1862, vol. 46, 410, Outgoing Correspondence, Letterbooks, 1839–1912, Domestic Letters, American Colonization Society Papers, LC, Reel 203; "The People of Washington and J. D. Johnson," *San Francisco Pacific Appeal*, Sept. 13, 1862.

68. Lincoln, *Collected Works*, 371, 372, 375.

69. Edward M. Thomas to Abraham Lincoln, Aug. 16, 1862, Abraham Lincoln Papers, LC. For northern reactions, see James M. McPherson, *Negro's Civil War*, 91–97; and Blight, *Frederick Douglass's Civil War*, 140–42.

70. *WNI*, Aug. 29, 1862; *Christian Recorder*, Aug. 30, 1862; *Baltimore Sun*, Aug. 23, 1862.

71. *Anglo-African*, Jan. 3, 1863, Jan. 10, 1863.

72. *WNI*, Sept. 15, 1862; *Liberator*, Sept. 19, 1862; Kate Masur, "African American Delegation." For the diplomatic conflicts that stymied the Chiriquí colonization plan, see Scheips, "Lincoln and the Chiriquí Colonization Project," 437, 441–45.

73. *Liberator*, Nov. 7, 1862; *WNI*, Nov. 5, 1862; *San Francisco Pacific Appeal*, Dec. 13, 1862.

74. "Our Free Colored People," *Douglass's Monthly*, Feb. 1863, 798; *WNI*, Dec. 9, 1862; *Anglo-African*, Jan. 17, 1863. For other efforts by African Americans to shape public perceptions, see *Baltimore Sun*, Nov. 5, 1862, Aug. 22, 1862, Aug. 23, 1862.

75. Carter A. Stewart et al. to John D. Johnson, *San Francisco Pacific Appeal*, Sept. 13, 1862.

76. "The Expedition to Chriqui," *Douglass's Monthly*, Nov. 1862, 751.

77. Henry McNeal Turner, "Washington Correspondence," *Christian Recorder*, Aug. 30, 1862, 137.

78. Letter of Cerebus, *Christian Recorder*, Aug. 30, 1862.

79. *Christian Recorder*, Sept. 6, 1862.

80. Ibid., Dec. 6, 1862.

81. Ashon, *Official Opinions of the Attorneys General*, 382–413.

82. For the subdued initial response to emancipation, see *WNR*, Apr. 9, 1862, Apr. 28, 1862; [Unnamed] to Christian Fleetwood, Apr. 12, 1862, Christian Fleetwood Papers, LC; *New York Independent*, Apr. 17, 1862, Apr. 24, 1862; *Liberator*, May 2, 1862; *National Anti-Slavery Standard*, Apr. 19, 1862, 3; and Quarles, *Negro in the Civil War*, 141–42.

83. Turner, "Reminiscences of the Proclamation," 6; Coffin, *Drum-Beat of the Nation*, 458–59.

84. *WNR*, Sept. 19, 1862, May 24, 1862; Goodwin, "History of Schools," 203.

85. Henry McNeal Turner, "Washington Correspondence," *Christian Recorder*, Jan. 3, 1863; Emma Brown to Emily Howland, Sept. 23, 1862, EHP; Goodwin, "History of Schools," 273, 296.

86. *Christian Recorder*, Jan. 24, 1863.

87. Cullen, "I's a Man Now"; Furstenberg, "Beyond Freedom and Slavery"; Pocock, "Machiavelli, Harrington, and English Political Ideologies." Turner became chaplain of the 1st USCT and, after the war, settled in Georgia where he was active in the AME church and in politics. Angell, *Bishop Henry McNeal Turner*; Redkey, "Henry McNeal Turner"; Dittmer, "Education of Henry McNeal Turner."

88. *WNR*, May 18, 1863; *Christian Recorder*, June 13, 1863; Stoddard, *Inside the White House*, 172, 173–74. See also *WES*, June 6, 1863; and *WC*, Oct. 9, 1865. The regiment's history is discussed in Gibbs, *Black, Copper, and Bright*.

89. *WES*, May 18, 1863.

90. *WNR*, May 20, 1863. Augusta was born in Norfolk, Virginia, and was educated in Canada. For his biography and publicity about his commission, see *Anglo-African*, Apr. 18, 1863, Apr. 25, 1863, May 2, 1863; and Ripley et al., *United States, 1859–1865*, 205–6, 211n8.

91. *WES*, May 19, 1863.

92. *WNR*, May 5, 1863. See also ibid., May 2, 1863; *WES*, May 4, 1863, May 5, 1863; and "Enthusiastic War Meeting in Washington," *Liberator*, June 12, 1863. On Asbury Chapel's history as a hub of African American educational, cultural, and philanthropic efforts, see Sluby, *Asbury*, 5–37.

93. *WES*, May 18, 1863, May 28, 1863, May 29, 1863, June 1, 1863.

94. Ibid., May 23, 1863, June 2, 1863, June 3, 1863; *WNR*, May 23, 1863.

95. *WES*, June 2, 1863, June 3, 1863; *WNR*, June 2, 1863, June 3, 1863; *Anglo-African*, June 20, 1863.

96. *Constitutional Union*, June 8, 1863. Thomas Florence, a former congressman from Ohio, edited the paper.

97. *Christian Recorder*, Jan. 10, 1863; *Anglo-African*, May 2, 1863; Tindall, *Standard History*, 387–88; King, *100 Years of Capital Traction*, 3–4; Lessoff, *Nation and Its City*, 29; Brooks, *Washington, D.C., in Lincoln's Time*, 191; Warner, "Political and Social Conditions," 205. Black soldiers in other cities also protested racial discrimination on streetcars. *Anglo-African*, Sept. 19, 1863; Fischer, "Pioneer Protest," 220–22; Philip S. Foner, "Battle to End Discrimination," Part I, 269–70.

98. *WES*, June 10, 1863; *Christian Recorder*, June 20, 1863.

99. Lois Bryan Adams, "Letter from Washington," Feb. 18, 1865, in Adams, *Letter from Washington*, 235.

100. *Anglo-African*, Oct. 19, 1861.

101. *Constitutional Union*, June 8, 1863, June 12, 1863, June 16, 1863 (emphasis added). See also ibid., June 20, 1863.

102. *Christian Recorder*, June 20, 1863, 102.

103. *Constitutional Union*, June 12, 1863. See also ibid., June 10, 1863; *WES*, June 12, 1863; and *WNR*, June 12, 1863.

104. *Christian Recorder*, June 13, 1863, June 27, 1863; *WNR*, June 9, 1863; *WES*, June 10, 1863; "Case of William G. Raymond," T-87 1/2 1863, Letters Received, Colored Troops Division, RG 94 [B-402]; *Anglo-African*, Nov. 28, 1863; Whitman, *Complete Prose Works*, 420; John P. Sherburne to Capt. H. B. Todd, June 6, 1863, Letters Sent, vol. 99, ser. 642, District of Washington, RACC, pt. 2; *Christian Recorder*, June 20, 1863, 101, 102.

105. *Constitutional Union*, June 22, 1863.

106. James J. Ferree to Gen. Martindale, July 20, 1863, Letters Received, ser. 646, Department of Washington, RACC, pt. 2.

107. *Christian Recorder*, July 11, 1863. For similar allusions to manhood in the rhetoric of the (women's) Contraband Relief Association, see *Liberator*, Sept. 25, 1863.

108. *Christian Recorder*, June 27, 1863.

109. *Anglo-African*, Aug. 1, 1863; *Christian Recorder*, July 11, 1863, July 4, 1863.

110. "Eureka" (letter), *Christian Recorder*, July 4, 1863.

111. *Anglo-African*, Oct. 31, 1863; *Christian Recorder*, Oct. 3, 1863. The Odd Fellows did not feel completely secure, and organizers requested protection from civil and military authorities.

112. *WNI*, Feb. 13, 1865; *Boston Congregationalist*, Feb. 24, 1865; Garnet, *Memorial Discourse*.

113. Garnet, *Memorial Discourse*, 65. For descriptions of the crowd, see *Boston Daily Advertiser*, Feb. 13, 1865; and Lois Bryan Adams, "Letter from Washington," Feb. 20, 1865, in Adams, *Letter from Washington*, 233. See also Furgurson, *Freedom Rising*, 350–51. For earlier black spectators in the Capitol, see Chapter 3.

114. J. M. McKim, "Forty Thousand Freed Slaves in Washington," Oct. 30, 1864, Samuel J. May Antislavery Collection, Cornell University, Ithaca, N.Y.

Chapter 2

1. My account of the case of Hannah Price is based on documents enclosed in A. K. Browne to S. N. Clark, Dec. 18, 1867, Unregistered Letters Received, reel 12, DCBRFALM. For Kimball, see Goodwin, "History of Schools," 280.

2. Fredrickson, *Black Image in the White Mind*, 101–29. See also James M. McPherson, *Struggle for Equality*, 134–53. My analysis of civilizational uplift beginning in the home draws on Mehta, *Liberalism and Empire*; Holt, "Empire over the Mind"; Holt, "Essence of the Contract"; and Franke, "Becoming a Citizen." By contrast, much recent scholarship has treated the Freedmen's Bureau as an avatar of race-blind contractarianism. See, for example, Schmidt, "A Full-Fledged Government of Men"; Harrison, "Welfare and Employment Policies"; Richardson, *Death of Reconstruction*, 13–14, 20; and Stanley, *From Bondage to Contract*, 35–39, 122–30. For an emphasis on gender and reform, however, see Schwalm, *Hard Fight for We*, 236–42; Farmer, "Because They Are Women"; and Farmer-Kaiser, "Are They Not in Some Sorts Vagrants?" For the argument that Ku Klux Klan members and other nightriders sexually assaulted freedwomen and attacked freedpeople's domestic institutions in part to demonstrate symbolically that freedpeople were unworthy of respect or rights, see Rosen, *Terror in the Heart of Freedom*, chap. 5. For the apex of civilizational discourse in a later period, see Bederman, *Manliness and Civilization*.

3. A. K. Browne to C. H. Howard, Oct. 10, 1868, AMQN.

4. The rich and dynamic literature on the education of freedchildren often remains isolated from other aspects of the period's history. Important works on the history of freedmen's education include Jacqueline Jones, *Soldiers of Light and Love*; Morris, *Reading, 'Riting, and Reconstruction*;

Butchart, *Northern Schools, Southern Blacks, and Reconstruction*; Gutman, "Schools for Freedom"; Anderson, *Education of Blacks in the South*, 4–32; and Heather Andrea Williams, *Self-Taught*. For histories that tie educational efforts into a broader history of reform, see James M. McPherson, *Struggle for Equality*, 154–77; and Bentley, *History of the Freedmen's Bureau*, 171–78.

5. *Constitutional Union*, June 16, 1863, Mar. 10, 1866.

6. Kate Masur, "Rare Phenomenon of Philological Vegetation."

7. Spurgin to Clark, Aug. 31, 1865, AMQN. See also J. V. W. Vandenburgh to Wm. F. Spurgin, Nov. 2, 1865, Unregistered Letters Received, reel 12, DCBRFALM; Clark to Richard Wallach, Feb. 9, 1866, Letters Sent, vol. 1, reel 1, DCBRFAL; JWSD, Dec. 1, 1865; Letter of Frances D. Gage, *National Anti-Slavery Standard*, Jan. 27, 1866; and *Annual Report of the Secretary of War, Nov. 14, 1866*, 729.

8. Josephine Griffing to James Harlan, July 13, 1865; Richard Wallach to B. B. French, July 24, 1865; French to Harlan, July 25, 1865; Wallach to Harlan, Oct. 26, 1865; all in box 5, Patents and Misc.

9. John Eaton to O. O. Howard, Sept. 22, 1865, Letters Sent, vol. 1, reel 1, DCBRFALM. See also *CG*, 39th Cong., 2nd sess., 1867, 1242. For similar tensions between city governments and bureau officials in other cities, see Elna C. Green, *This Business of Relief*, 88–89 (Richmond); and Savitt, "Politics in Medicine" (Georgia cities).

10. For the Judge Wylie case, see John Eaton to C. H. Howard, Sept. 22, 1865, Letters Sent, vol. 1., reel 1, DCBRFALM; Wylie to Col. Taggart, Aug. 15, 1865, Unregistered Letters Received, DCBRFAL [A-9854]; B. B. French to James Harlan, with letter from Wylie, Aug. 16, 1865; and other correspondence in box 4, Patents and Misc. Sources cited with alphanumeric identification numbers were consulted at the Freedmen and Southern Society Project, University of Maryland, College Park, Md.

11. Josephine Griffing to Edwin Stanton, n.d., "Griffing, Josephine," Consolidated Correspondence File, Central Records, Records of the Office of the Quartermaster General, RG 92, NARA; Howard, *Autobiography*, 417–18; Bryan, *History of the National Capital*, 2:587–88.

12. For the special assessment system in Washington, see Bryan, *History of the National Capital*, 2:509–10. See also Einhorn, *Property Rules*; Yearley, *Money Machines*; Blackmar, *Manhattan for Rent*, esp. 149–82; Novak, *People's Welfare*; Keyssar, *Right to Vote*, 30–32; and Frisch, "Community Elite," 286–87.

13. Resolutions of Mar. 1, 1866, enclosed in T. A. Lazenby to O. O. Howard, Mar. 12, 1866, L-49 1866, Letters Received, Records of the Commissioner's Office, RBRFAL [A-9754]. The police were historically the public health arm of the local government. For the cholera threat that spring, see Rosenberg, *Cholera Years*, 175–76, 204–6.

14. George Alfred Townsend, "New Washington," *Harper's New Monthly Magazine*, February 1875, 308; O. B. Frothingham, "Washington as It Should Be," *Atlantic Monthly*, June 1884, 843; Zina Fay Peirce, "The Externals of Washington," *Atlantic Monthly*, Dec. 1873, 707. See also Press, "South of the Avenue."

15. Wm. Bartlett to C. H. Howard, Jan. 28, 1867, #1224, Letters Received, DCBRFAL [A-9822]; J. G. Hall to S. N. Clark, Jan. 20, 1866, Reports from Visiting Agents, reel 14, DCBRFALM; John K. Kimball to W. W. Rogers, May 7, 1867, MRMC.

16. A. C. Richards to the Board of Police, Mar. 6, 1866, enclosed in T. A. Lazenby to Major Genl. O. O. Howard, Mar. 12, 1866, L-49 1866, Letters Received, Records of the Commissioner's Office, RBRFAL [A-9754]. The report was frequently cited as evidence of freedpeople's decrepitude and

debauchery, and historians have used it without commenting on its contemporary context or political purpose. See, for example, Truth, *Narrative of Sojourner Truth*, 188–91; *Constitutional Union*, Mar. 22, 1866; William W. Moore, *Contraband Suffrage*; Alfers, *Law and Order in the Capital City*, 33; and Constance McLaughlin Green, *Washington*, 1:302.

17. A. C. Richards to the Board of Police, Mar. 6, 1866, enclosed in T. A. Lazenby to Major Genl. O. O. Howard, Mar. 12, 1866, L-49 1866, Letters Received, Records of the Commissioner's Office, RBRFAL.

18. *CG*, 39th Cong., 1st sess., 1866, 1507–8.

19. Ibid., 1508; "A Resolution for the Temporary Relief of Destitute People in the District of Columbia," *U.S. Statutes at Large*, 14:353. For evidence that congressmen drew on their own observations when making policy for the District of Columbia, see for example *CG*, 39th Cong., 2nd sess., 1867, 1242 (Benjamin Wade); *CG*, 39th Cong., 1st sess., 1866, 1507 (Lot Morrill); and ibid., 1508 (Willard Saulsbury). For race in the 1865 discussion of the Freedmen's Bureau bill, see Belz, "Freedmen's Bureau Act of 1865."

20. Wm. F. Spurgin to C. H. Howard, Mar. 22, 1866, #1239, Letters Received, DCBRFAL [A-9754]; Wm. F. Spurgin to W. W. Rogers, Apr. 27, 1866, #1329, DCBRFAL; *Constitutional Union*, Apr. 11, 1866.

21. For the quotation, see Wm. F. Spurgin to W. W. Rogers, Apr. 16, 1866, Unregistered Letters Received, DCBRFAL [A-9888]. See also Spurgin to Howard, Mar. 22, 1866, and C. H. Howard to O. O. Howard, Oct. 1, 1867, Letters Sent, vol. 3, reel 1, DCBRFALM. For subsequent summers, see J. V. W. Vandenburgh to W. W. Rogers, July 20, 1867, and J. V. W. Vandenburgh to D. G. Swaim, Sept. 29, 1868, AMQN. For a detailed treatment of the whitewashing campaign, see Harrison, "Welfare and Employment Policies," 81–82.

22. *Report of the Board of Metropolitan Police for the Year 1868*, 874. For the transition from bureau to police, see J. W. Vandenburgh to W. W. Rogers, July 20, 1867, and J. W. Vandenburgh to D. G. Swaim, Sept. 29, 1868, AMQN.

23. The first large-scale effort to reform housing and attack "blighted" poor neighborhoods began in the 1890s, a period of intensive urban planning. Howard Gillette, *Between Justice and Beauty*, 109–23. Freedpeople's institutions and neighborhoods concentrated on the outskirts of other cities as well. Rabinowitz, *Race Relations*, 99–101.

24. Ross, "Freed Soil, Freed Labor, Freed Men."

25. W. F. Spurgin to Clark, Aug. 4, 1865, AMQN; S. N. Clark to S. J. Bowen, Jan. 8, 1866, Letters Sent, vol. 1, reel 1, DCBRFALM; *Annual Report of the Secretary of War, Nov. 14, 1866*, 728–31. The bureau's home visits and outdoor relief drew on practices established by antebellum Christian reformers. Smith Rosenberg, *Religion and the Rise of the American City*, 80–94, 248–55.

26. Colman, *Reminiscences*, 63; JWLD, Dec. 19, 1867; John L. Roberts to J. S. Fullerton, Jan. 26, 1866, C-38 1866, Records of the Commissioner's Office, RBRFAL [A-9711]. See also Louisa J. Roberts to O. O. Howard, June 30, 1865, Unregistered Letters Received, reel 12, DCBRFALM. Conflicts between paid bureau officials (usually military men) and volunteers have been detailed in, for example, Rose, *Rehearsal for Reconstruction*; Faulkner, *Women's Radical Reconstruction*, 17–26, 83–99; and Harrison, "Welfare and Employment Policies," 89–92. My point here is that all agents, regardless of background, in some measure shared convictions about freedpeople's need for civilization and domestic reform.

27. John K. Kimball to W. W. Rogers, May 7, 1867, MRMC.

28. R. M. Bigelow and W. F. Harris to S. N. Clark, Jan. 20, 1866, Reports from Visiting Agents, reel 14, DCBRFALM.

29. *Christian Recorder*, Aug. 8, 1863; Rufus L. Perry to Directors of African Civilization Society, *National Freedman*, Feb. 15, 1866, 49; Sojourner Truth to Rowland Johnson, Nov. 17, 1864, in Truth, *Narrative of Sojourner Truth*, 177. See also Emma Brown to Emily Howland, Dec. 10, 1861, EHP. For a pathbreaking discussion of respectability and reform among African Americans, see Higginbotham, *Righteous Discontent*, 14–15 and chap. 7.

30. "Memorial of S. J. Bowen and the National Freedmen's Relief Association," Jan. 8, 1868, 40A-H5.1, RUSS; Letter from H.C., July 23, [1864], *Extracts from Letters of Teachers and Superintendents*, 18. For recognition that women faced particular problems, see also W. F. Spurgin to Clark, Aug. 4, 1865, AMQN. For free labor ideology and constructions of "dependence," see, for example, Eric Foner, *Free Soil, Free Labor, Free Men*, esp. 11–39; Stanley, *From Bondage to Contract*, 1–59; and Edwards, "Problem of Dependency."

31. *Report of the Operations of the Bureau of Refugees*. See also Alvord, *Fifth Semi-Annual Report*, 16–17.

32. Goodwin, "History of Schools," 243; A. E. Newton to James M. McKim, *National Freedman*, Nov. 15, 1865, 329. See also Goodwin, "History of Schools," 241–43. On the demand that welfare institutions be economically self-sufficient, see Rothman, *Discovery of the Asylum*, esp. 93–94, 103–4.

33. J. E. Griffing, "Report of Industrial School No. 2," *Sixth Annual Report of the Executive Board of the Friends' Association*; Catharine A. F. Stebbins, "Josephine Sophie Griffing," in *HWS*, 2:28. See also Letter from H.C., June 24, [1864], *Extracts from Letters of Teachers and Superintendents*, 18.

34. *Summary Report of the District of Columbia*, 378–79. See also Catharine S. B. Spear, Memorial for Appropriation to Establish a House for Dependent and Friendless Children to Be Designated a House of Refuge for the District of Columbia, Dec. 22, 1864, 38A-H4, RUSS; *Report of the Board of Metropolitan Police for the Year 1868*, 878.

35. *Anglo-African*, Dec. 23, 1863, Dec. 19, 1863, Feb. 13, 1864; *Letter of Daniel Breed*; and Alvord, *Fifth Semi-Annual Report*, 15. See also Dabney, *History of Schools for Negroes*, 23–73.

36. For the quotation, see A. E. Newton to Rev. B. Schneider, *National Freedman*, Dec. 15, 1865, 367; and *WNI*, Dec. 16, 1865. See also Dabney, *History of Schools for Negroes*, 82–89.

37. See, for example, *WNI*, Dec. 30, 1865, Jan. 6, 1866, Feb. 3, 1866; *WC*, Nov. 3, 1866; Alvord, *Fourth Semi-Annual Report*, 7; and Goodwin, "History of Schools," 233.

38. Goodwin, "History of Schools," 224. See also A. E. Newton to Charles Sumner, Mar. 9, 1867, reel 38, frame 304, CSP; Henry Barnard, *Special Report*, 66.

39. Alvord, *Fourth Semi-Annual Report*, 9. See also S. A. H. to Editor, *National Anti-Slavery Standard*, Apr. 18, 1868. For northern whites' curiosity about whether freedpeople could learn math and other kinds of abstract thinking, see Morris, *Reading, 'Riting, and Reconstruction*, 10–12, 31.

40. Alvord, *Eighth Semi-Annual Report*, 82–83.

41. Ibid.

42. Alvord, *Fourth Semi-Annual Report*, 85–86.

43. O. O. Howard to James Miller McKim, Dec. 20, 1866, Samuel J. May Manuscript Collection, box 15, Cornell University, Ithaca, N.Y. See also O. O. Howard, "Education of the Colored Man," mss., O. O. Howard Papers, box 53-2, MSRC.

44. Alvord, *Fifth Semi-Annual Report*, 14.

45. *Report of the Operations of the Bureau of Refugees*.

46. Robert Harrison found that about 11,000 freedpeople left the District of Columbia under the bureau's auspices. Harrison, "Welfare and Employment Policies," 95.

47. John Roberts to J. S. Fullerton, Jan. 26, 1866, Letters Received, Records of the Commissioner's Office, RBRFAL [A-9711]; *Report of the Operations of the Bureau of Refugees*; JWSD, Mar. 16, 1866, Apr. 2, 1866; P. Glennan to Sojourner Truth, Mar. 25, 1867, and Griffing to Truth, Mar. 26, 1867, PFP; A. E. Newton to J. M. McKim, *National Freedman*, Nov. 15, 1865, 329; J. G. Hall to S. N. Clark, Jan. 20, 1866, Reports from Visiting Agents, reel 14, DCBRFALM; Sayles Bowen, "Memorial of the National Freedmen's Relief Association," 1868, 40A-H5.1, RUSS. See also Cohen, *At Freedom's Edge*; Penningroth, *Claims of Kinfolk*, 170–76; Litwack, *Been in the Storm So Long*, 292–306; and Harrison, "Welfare and Employment Policies," 104–5.

48. See, for example, J. S. Griffing to Brig. Gen'l C. H. Howard, Aug. 4, 1866, #2001, Letters Received, DCBRFAL [A-9780]; John L. Roberts to C. H. Howard, [late] Oct. 1866, AMQN; J. J. Coale to S. N. Clark, Jan. 24, 1866, Reports from Visiting Agents, DCBRFAL [A-9909]; Unsigned to C. H. Howard, Oct. 30, 1866, vol. 7, 111–12, Letters Sent, DCBRFAL [A-9925].

49. Shirley Dare (pseud.), "The Freedmen of the Capital," *New York World*, Feb. 25, 1865, and Josephine Griffing to Lucretia Mott, Apr. 22, 1870, JGP.

50. C. H. Howard to O. O. Howard, Dec. 28, 1868, Miscellaneous Reports and Lists, reel 21, DCBRFALM; Everly, "Freedmen's Bureau in the National Capital," 124. In the fall of 1866, an inspector reported that a total of 945 people (from 255 families) were living in the three barracks. The next year, the barracks accommodated 1,060 people, from 277 families. E. H. Ludington to the Inspector General of the Army, Nov. 14, 1866, L-22 1866, Letters Received, Records of the Office of the Inspector General, RG 159, NARA [J-47]; Charles H. Howard to O. O. Howard, Oct. 1, 1867, Letters Sent, vol. 2, #758a, reel 1, DCBRFALM. Government housing at Freedman's Hospital, which was administered somewhat differently, continued into the 1880s. Holt et al., *Special Mission*, 13–14, 17–24.

51. A cumulative report for 1866 indicated that about 60 percent of the residents were female and 75 percent were either adult women or children under fourteen. The three barracks housed about seventeen women for every ten men. Out of the 945 residents counted in the barracks, 430 were children, and of those children, 48 were over fourteen years old. Men and boys were about 40 percent of the population in the barracks. A special census in 1867 indicated that men and boys were about 45 percent of the total black population in the capital. E. H. Ludington to the Inspector General of the Army, Nov. 14, 1866, L-22 1866, Letters Received, Records of the Office of the Inspector General, RG 159, NARA [J-47]; Henry Barnard, *Special Report*, 28.

52. N. C. Clark to W. W. Rogers, Nov. 10, 1866, #130, Letters Received, DCBRFAL [A-9792]; Wm. Bartlett to C. H. Howard, Jan. 28, 1867, #1224, ibid. [A-9822].

53. J. W. Vandenburgh to W. W. Rogers, July 20, 1867, J. W. Vandenburgh to D. G. Swaim, Sept. 29, 1868, and John L. Roberts to C. H. Howard, [late] Oct. 1866, AMQN; E. H. Ludington to the Inspector General of the Army, Nov. 14, 1866, L-22 1866, Letters Received, Records of the Office of the Inspector General, RG 159, NARA [J-47].

54. For oysters, see N. C. Clark to W. W. Rogers, Nov. 10, 1866, #130, Letters Received, DCBRFAL [A-9792]. For women's occupations, see tabular reports in Monthly Reports of Bureau Tenants, reels 20, 21, DCBRFAL. For rags and paper, see S. N. Clark to Wm. W. Rogers, Oct. 6, 1866, Letters Sent, vol. 53, 23–24, Asst. Inspector General, RBRFAL [A-9931].

55. For eviction policy, see S. N. Clark to Roberts, Feb. 20, 1866, Letters Sent, vol. 1, #417, reel 1,

DCBRFALM. For rents, see E. H. Ludington to the Inspector General of the Army, Nov. 14, 1866, L-22 1866, Letters Received, Records of the Office of the Inspector General, RG 159, NARA [J-47]; *Second Annual Report of the New England Freedmen's Aid Society*, 35–36.

56. S. N. Clark to C. H. Howard, May 28, 1866, #1534, Letters Received, DCBRFAL [A-9762]; N. C. Clark to W. W. Rogers, Nov. 10, 1866, #130, DCBRFAL [A-9792].

57. N. C. Clark to W. W. Rogers, Nov. 10, 1866, #130, DCBRFAL [A-9792].

58. John L. Roberts to C. H. Howard, [late] Oct. 1866, AMQN. For similar practices at Wisewell Barracks, see Alvord, *Sixth Semi-Annual Report*, 9; and Goodwin, "History of Schools," 241–42.

59. John L. Roberts to C. H. Howard, [late] Oct. 1866, AMQN.

60. Charles H. Howard to Oliver O. Howard, Oct. 1, 1867, Letters Sent, vol. 3, #758a, reel 1, DCBRFALM.

61. N. C. Clark to W. W. Rogers, Nov. 10, 1866, #130, Letters Received, DCBRFAL [A-9762]; S. N. Clark to C. H. Howard, May 28, 1866, #1534, ibid.; S. N. Clark to W. F. Spurgin, Sept. 25, 1865, Letters Sent, vol. 1, #157, reel 1, DCBRFALM.

62. S. N. Clark to Wm. W. Rogers, Oct. 6, 1866, Letters Sent, vol. 53, 23–24, Asst. Inspector General, DCBRFAL [A-9931]; William Rogers to John Roberts, Nov. 2, 1866, Letters Sent, vol. 2, #492, reel 1, DCBRFALM.

63. S. N. Clark to Captain W. F. Spurgin, Sept. 25, 1865, Letters Sent, vol. 1, #157, reel 1, DCBR-FALM; S. N. Clark to Roberts, Feb. 20, 1866, Letters Sent, vol. 1, #417, reel 1, DCBRFALM; E. H. Ludington to the Inspector General of the Army, Nov. 14, 1866, L-22 1866, Letters Received, Records of the Office of the Inspector General, RG 159, NARA [J-47]; *Second Annual Report of the New England Freedmen's Aid Society*, 35–36.

64. S. N. Clark to W. F. Spurgin, Sept. 25, 1865, Letters Sent, vol. 1, #157, reel 1, DCBRFALM. See also C. H. Howard to Hon. Martin Welker, June 8, 1866, Letters Sent, vol. 2, reel 1, DCBR-FALM. As Ariela Dubler has argued, widows and other unmarried women have been "regulated by marriage's normative framework even as they have inhabited terrain outside of its formal boundaries." Dubler, "In the Shadow of Marriage," 1646.

65. W. F. Spurgin to S. N. Clark, Sept. 30, 1865, W. F. Spurgin to S. N. Clark, Nov. 1, 1865, W. F. Spurgin to C. H. Howard, Mar. 1, 1866, and A. K. Browne to C. H. Howard, Oct. 10, 1868, AMQN. On marriage as a solution to women's poverty, see Dubler, "In the Shadow of Marriage." Studies of freedpeople's actual views on coupling and marriage include Schwalm, *Hard Fight for We*, 243–46; and Frankel, *Freedom's Women*.

66. C. H. Howard to Hon. Martin Welker, June 8, 1866, Letters Sent, vol. 2, reel 1, DCBRFALM.

67. Ibid. (Emphasis added.)

68. "An Act Legalizing Marriages and for Other Purposes in the District of Columbia," *U.S. Statutes at Large*, 14:236. The law continued, "And when the parties shall have ceased to cohabit before the passage of this act, in consequence of the death of the woman, or from any other cause, all the children of the woman recognized by the man to be his shall be deemed legitimate." Unlike the marriage laws passed as part of discriminatory black codes during 1865 and 1866, the federal marriage law for the District of Columbia also made it easy for people not currently living with their spouse to claim to be married, granting "legitimacy" even to those children whose fathers (or mothers) were not present. For more stringent marriage laws and their enforcement in the states, see Frankel, *Freedom's Women*, 82–84; Franke, "Becoming a Citizen," 282–90; and Edwards, "The Marriage Covenant." For evidence that Congress was at that point genuinely trying to accommodate the

particular circumstances of newly freed black men and women, see also McClintock, "Impact of the Civil War on Nineteenth-Century Marriages."

69. Clark to W. F. Spurgin, Sept. 25, 1865, Letters Sent, vol. 1, #157, reel 1, DCBRFALM; S. N. Clark to Roberts, Feb. 20, 1866, Letters Sent, vol. 1, #417, reel 1, DCBRFALM.

70. E. H. Ludington to the Inspector General of the Army, Nov. 14, 1866, L-22 1866, Letters Received, Records of the Office of the Inspector General, RG 159, NARA [J-47]; Tabular reports contained in Monthly Reports of Bureau Tenants, reels 20, 21, DCBRFALM.

71. John L. Roberts to C. H. Howard, [late] Oct. 1866, AMQN.

72. John K. Kimball to W. W. Rogers, May 7, 1867, MRMC. See also John Kimball to W. W. Rogers, Mar. 27, 1867, MRMC.

73. John K. Kimball to W. W. Rogers, May 7, 1867, MRMC.

74. See, for example, Scott, "Battle over the Child"; Edwards, *Gendered Strife and Confusion*, 48–54; Frankel, *Freedom's Women*, 135–45; Schwalm, *Hard Fight for We*, 249–54; and Zipf, *Labor of Innocents*, 40–105.

75. S. N. Clark to Judge Bond, July 26, 1865, vol. 1, Letters Sent, reel 1, DCBRFALM. For apprenticeship in Maryland and its slow demise, see Fields, *Slavery and Freedom on the Middle Ground*, 139–42, 148–49, 151–56; and Fuke, *Imperfect Equality*, 69–83. For the 1866 Civil Rights Act allowing the bureau to intervene in apprenticeships in Georgia, see Rapport, "Freedmen's Bureau as a Legal Agent," 38.

76. *American Freedmen's Inquiry Commission Report*. See also Zipf, *Labor of Innocents*, 74–83; and Franke, "Becoming a Citizen," 300–304.

77. Statement of Eliza Low, Oct. 10, 1867, Letters Received, reel 9, DCBRFAL. Generally, see Letters Sent, vol. 1, reel 1, DCBRFAL. Most of the claimants were mothers and other female kin, but some were fathers or other men. See, for example, Clark to James W. Rand, July 28, 1865, and Eaton to Richard Robinson, Aug. 21, 1865, both in Letters Sent, vol. 1, reel 1, DCBRFALM.

78. For an alternative interpretation, that freedpeople who insisted they had means sufficient to support their apprenticed offspring were "attack[ing] the very foundation of nineteenth-century citizenship ideals," see Zipf, *Labor of Innocents*, 94, 84–105.

79. S. N. Clark to Mr. John Onfit, July 24, 1865, Letters Sent, vol. 1, reel 1, DCBRFALM (emphasis added). See also Clark to Thomas Belt, Aug. 1, 1865, Letters Sent, vol. 1, reel 1, DCBRFALM; and Hahn et al., *Land and Labor, 1865*, 515. Around the same time, O. O. Howard issued an order stating that for freedpeople "the parent will have the right to the child" unless consent was given for an apprenticeship. Quoted in Fuke, *Imperfect Equality*, 97. On freedpeople using the bureau to assert new rights, see also Rapport, "Freedmen's Bureau as a Legal Agent," 50–53; and Nieman, "Language of Liberation," 75–78.

80. For the ideology of common school reform and for regional differences between the North and the South in the development of public education, see Kaestle, *Pillars of the Republic*, 75–103, 182–217.

81. Henry Barnard, *Special Report*, 49, 52–54; Levey, "Segregation in Education," 161–79; *Twenty-second Annual Report of the Board of Trustees of the Public Schools*. See also *WES*, July 5, 1864; and Beauchamp, "Schools for All," 145.

82. *Twentieth Annual Report of the Board of Trustees of the Public Schools*, 58. See also *WES*, July 5, 1864; Beauchamp, "Schools for All," 145.

83. *Letter of Daniel Breed*; Letter of Alfred Jones et al. to the Board of Trustees of Colored Schools and reply, *WC*, Oct. 13, 1865; Case 1968, Law Case Files, 1863–1934, RDCSC; Levey, "Seg-

regation in Education," 197–98; Constance McLaughlin Green, *Secret City*, 85; Whyte, *Uncivil War*, 64–65.

84. Report of the Committee on Public Schools, Nov. 25, 1867, 40th Cong., accompanying papers file, "District of Columbia," RUSHR. On the rationale for the census, see Goodwin, "History of Schools," 269. On population numbers, see Henry Barnard, *Special Report*, 57–63.

85. Alvord, *Third Semi-Annual Report*, 6; Alvord, *Fourth Semi-Annual Report*, 7, 9; *Report of the Secretary of War, Part I, Nov. 1867*, 660–61. See also Alvord, *Seventh Semi-Annual Report*, 9–10; and Dabney, *History of Schools for Negroes*, 115–16.

86. For estimates, see Goodwin, "History of Schools," 222 (1,000); Testimony of William Slade, File 1, AFIC (1,400); and J. C. Wright, "Historical Sketch," Dunbar *Liber Anni*, Class of 1924, Papers of the District of Columbia Public Schools, Sumner School Museum, Washington, D.C. (1,200).

87. Goodwin, "History of Schools," 272–74.

88. Ibid., 272–74, 276.

89. Carter H. Stewart et al. to Secretary of the Interior, Apr. 18, 1866, box 3, Patents and Misc. See also Daniel Breed to Secretary Harlan with concurrence by Sayles Bowen, Jan. 11, 1866, ibid. For a list of board members, see Preston, "Development of Negro Education," 600.

90. Petition of Albert Bolden et al., Mar. 18, 1868, 40A-H5.1, RUSS.

91. On the appointment of Alfred Jones, see Letter and Oath of Alfred Jones, July 11, 1867, box 3, Patents and Misc. For the appointment of William Syphax as the second African American trustee, see Letter and Oath of William Syphax, July 8, 1868, ibid.

92. M. A. Cary to Secretary of Interior, June 24, 1870, box 3, Patents and Misc. The letter was written by Mary Ann Shadd Cary.

93. Letter of Harriet Jacobs, Mar. 1, 1864, in Sterling, *We Are Your Sisters*, 248; Wilson quoted in DeBoer, "Role of Afro-Americans," 307.

94. On the new teachers, see Emma Brown to Emily Howland, Jan. 2, 1866, EHP. On Kimball's preferences, see Emma Brown to Emily Howland, Mar. 23, 1867, EHP. For discrimination against black teachers, see also Emily Howland to Hannah, Nov. 6, 1866, EHP.

95. For N.T., see Emma Brown to Emily Howland, Feb. 3, 1867, EHP. For another derisive reference to N.T., see Emma Brown to Emily Howland, May 19, 1867, EHP.

96. Trustees quoted in Goodwin, "History of Schools," 257. G. F. T. Cook to Wm. Syphax, Nov. 8, 1869, Records of the Superintendent of Education for the District of Columbia, RBRFAL [C-364]. For 1867, see Alvord, *Fourth Semi-Annual Report*, 8.

97. On the high school and other opportunities for advanced education in the capital, see Dabney, *History of Schools for Negroes*, 62–63, 135–37; and Alvord, *Eighth Semi-Annual Report*, 15–16.

98. For the quotation, see Goodwin, "History of Schools," 247. On the founding of Howard, see *Report of the Secretary of War, Part I, Nov. 1867*, 662; Alvord, *Sixth Semi-Annual Report*, 60; Alvord, *Eighth Semi-Annual Report*, 16, 75–76; Goodwin, "History of Schools," 245–52; and Alldredge, *Centennial History of First Congregational*, 15–18.

99. Alvord, *Eighth Semi-Annual Report*, 76.

100. Alvord, *Sixth Semi-Annual Report*, 12.

101. *Report of the Board of Trustees of Colored Schools of Washington and Georgetown*, 10. For the number of children in school in 1866 and 1867, see *Annual Report of the Secretary of War, Nov. 14, 1866*, 729; and *Report of the Secretary of War, Part I, Nov. 1867*, 660.

102. Alvord, *Seventh Semi-Annual Report*, 10. See also Alvord, *Fourth Semi-Annual Report*, 79–80; and S. A. H. to Editor, *National Anti-Slavery Standard*, Apr. 18, 1868.

103. *Sarah C. Roberts v. City of Boston*, 59 Mass. 198; Levy and Philips, "The *Roberts* Case."

104. Alvord, *Second Semi-Annual Report*, 13.

Chapter 3

1. Committee on the District of Columbia, *Report*, 12.

2. Ibid.

3. Ibid.

4. Ibid.

5. Ibid., 13.

6. JWLD, Mar. 16, 1868; *WC*, Feb. 10, 1868.

7. French, *Witness to the Young Republic*, 613.

8. The basic parameters of Kate Brown's case are cited in Maltz, "Separate but Equal," 565; Lofgren, *Plessy Case*, 124–25; and Welke, "When All the Women Were White," 281.

9. In a much-cited line, Eric Foner, *Reconstruction*, 122–23, noted "the 'politicization' of everyday life that followed the demise of slavery." By way of explanation, he continued that "day-to-day encounters between the races became infused with the tension inevitable when a social order, with its established power relations and commonly understood rules of conduct, has been swept away and a new one has not yet come into being." Approaches that emphasize the "public sphere" include Ryan, *Civic Wars*; and Barkley Brown, "Negotiating and Transforming the Public Sphere."

10. On the law of common carriers and regulation of passengers, see Sandoval-Strausz, "Travelers, Strangers, and Jim Crow"; Singer, "No Right to Exclude"; and Welke, "When All the Women Were White."

11. Garnet, *Memorial Discourse*, 65; *Liberator*, Jan. 6, 1865, 1. See also D. B. Nichols to George Whipple, May 31, 1862, in DeBoer, "Role of Afro-Americans," 299; and *CG*, 37th Cong., 2nd sess., 1862, 1339.

12. Letter of "Dixon," *Daily Advertiser*, Dec. 10, 1864 (also published in *Liberator*, Jan. 6, 1865, 1); *Christian Recorder*, May 31, 1862, July 19, 1862; *Anglo-African*, Jan. 23, 1864; Adams, "Letter from Washington," Apr. 8, 1864, in Adams, *Letter from Washington*, 106–7; Charles Douglass quoted in Vorenberg, *Final Freedom*, 207. For the general trajectory, see also *Liberator*, Jan. 6, 1865, 1; and *Zion's Herald and Wesleyan Journal*, Mar. 9, 1864, 39.

13. Letter of "Dixon," *Daily Advertiser*, Dec. 10, 1864.

14. *National Anti-Slavery Standard*, Jan. 27, 1866, 3; WOD, Jan. 19, 1866. See also Bowers, *Tragic Era*, 99–100.

15. JWLD, Apr. 4, 1866; Ritchie, *Press Gallery*, 146.

16. Welke, "When All the Women Were White."

17. *CG*, 37th Cong., 2nd sess., 1862, 1339.

18. Jacqueline Jones, *Labor of Love, Labor of Sorrow*, 68–70; Hunter, *To 'Joy My Freedom*, 4–5.

19. *Anglo-African*, Jan. 23, 1864.

20. *Frank Leslie's Illustrated Newspaper*, Feb. 1, 1868, 312; Adams, "Letter from Washington," Apr. 8, 1864, in Adams, *Letter from Washington*, 107; WOD, Dec. 5, 1865.

21. JWLD, Jan. 22, 1869.

22. *CG*, 39th Cong., 1st sess., 1866, 1508 (Saulsbury).

23. *Frank Leslie's Illustrated Newspaper*, Feb. 1, 1868, 312.

24. The image from *Frank Leslie's Illustrated Newspaper* would be modified and reprinted in sub-

sequent years, and it became an icon in the intensifying discourse of black men's political incompetence. *United States Senate Catalogue of Graphic Art*, 83, 87, 89.

25. Adams, "Letter from Washington," Apr. 8, 1864, in Adams, *Letter from Washington*, 107.

26. *Report of the Secretary of the Senate*, 1861, 15, 32, 48; *Report of the Secretary of the Senate*, 1862, 13, 24, 32, 55, 70.

27. Erving Goffman's analysis of different "regions" in work environments suggests that although black employees of the Senate may have been deferential to whites in their "front" region interactions with visitors, they may have enjoyed a less deferential relationship "backstage" with George Brown. Goffman, *Presentation of Self in Everyday Life*, 106–40.

28. Committee on the District of Columbia, *Report*, 24.

29. JWLD, June 27, 1868. In 1874, the Supreme Court sustained the D.C. court's finding that Kate Brown was entitled to $1500 in damages from the railroad company. See Kate Masur, "Personal and Political in Kate Brown's Washington," *Journal of American History*, forthcoming March 2013.

30. CG, 38th Cong., 1st sess., 1864, 817–18; Ripley et al., *United States*, *1859–1865*, 308–10.

31. JWSD, Apr. 19, 1865, Apr. 18, 1865. See also Colman, *Reminiscences*, 70; and Quarles, *Negro in the Civil War*, 342–43.

32. *Anglo-African*, July 23, 1864; MacGregor, *Emergence of a Black Catholic Community*, 3–5, 36–39; Quarles, *Negro in the Civil War*, 253–54.

33. *Celebration by the Colored People's Educational Monument Association*, 3; WES, July 5, 1865; WC, July 6, 1865; *Anglo-African*, July 8, 1865, July 22, 1865; Adams, "Letter from Washington," July 14, 1865, in Adams, *Letter from Washington*, 275–76.

34. *Celebration by the Colored People's Educational Monument Association*, 10–11.

35. Ibid., 7.

36. The principle of "reasonable regulation" is clearly explained in Welke, "When All the Women Were White," 273–74. Antebellum northern courts' approval of accommodations segregated by sex and class—and their ambiguity on racial discrimination—are discussed in Singer, "No Right to Exclude." See also Maltz, "Separate but Equal," 554–55. For African Americans' antebellum demands for access to railroads and streetcars, see also Leslie M. Harris, *In the Shadow of Slavery*, 270–71; and Ruchames, "Jim Crow Railroads."

37. Sandoval-Strausz, "Travelers, Strangers, and Jim Crow."

38. In Washington in the spring of 1865, a ticket cost seven cents when purchased from the conductor and less than six cents if bought in advance as part of a book. At the federal government's daily laborers' wage of $2.00, the 12 cents required for a round-trip commute was about 6 percent of a day's wages. WC, Mar. 29, 1865. On senators riding, see JWLD, Apr. 16, 1869. For accessibility of streetcars for laborers, see also Drago, *Black Politicians and Reconstruction in Georgia*, 98–100; and Philip S. Foner, "Battle to End Discrimination" (Parts 1 and 2), 268, 356–57, 361.

39. *Anglo-African*, Nov. 7, 1863, Nov. 28, 1863. On additional cars being provided, see ibid., Dec. 12, 1863. See also Truth, *Narrative of Sojourner Truth*, 184.

40. *Anglo-African*, Feb. 13, 1864. For more coverage, see ibid., Feb. 20, 1864. For Augusta's protest as a "crisis," see Brooks, *Washington, D.C., in Lincoln's Time*, 193.

41. "An Act to Extend the Charter of the Alexandria and Washington Railroad Company, and for Other Purposes," *U.S. Statutes at Large*, 12:805. See also Pierce, *Memoir and Letters of Charles Sumner*, 179. Aspects of this legislative history are described in Maltz, "Separate but Equal." For background on early streetcar routes and fares, see King, *100 Years of Capital Traction*, 3–8.

42. CG, 38th Cong., 1st sess., 1864, 553 (emphasis added).

43. Ibid., 553–54.

44. Ibid., 816–17. See also *Report of the Committee on the District of Columbia*. The principle that racial separation conformed with the common law and with principles of equality would emerge in federal court decisions during Reconstruction. Riegel, "Persistent Career of Jim Crow."

45. *CG*, 38th Cong., 1st sess., 1864, 1141. An early biographer credited Sumner with having ended discrimination by reporting an offending company to the police and threatening to repeal its charter if it did not comply with the law. Pierce, *Memoir and Letters of Charles Sumner*, 181. The erasure of black activism is striking.

46. *CG*, 38th Cong., 1st sess., 1864, 1159. For similar arguments by other senators, see also ibid., 1141, 1157–58 (Saulsbury), 1159 (Carlile), 1161 (Davis).

47. *CG*, 38th Cong., 1st sess., 1864, 1156. In this, Johnson echoed the arguments of antebellum abolitionists that segregation based on color was arbitrary, while selling tickets with varying prices was not a problem. See Ruchames, "Jim Crow Railroads."

48. *CG*, 38th Cong., 1st sess., 1864, 1156.

49. Ibid., 1157. For a similar claim, see also ibid., 1131 (Saulsbury).

50. Sandoval-Strausz, "Travelers, Strangers, and Jim Crow," 73–74.

51. W. J. Pond to W. L. Garrison, *Liberator*, Jan. 20, 1865, 12; JWSD, Feb. 25, 1865; Colman, *Reminiscences*, 51. Colman also noted that Elizabeth Keckly, Mary Todd Lincoln's seamstress, was "never permitted to go into the house as a caller." Ibid., 51.

52. *WC*, Mar. 2, 1865, cited in Bryan, *History of the National Capital*, 2:535.

53. Douglass, *Life and Times*, 371–72.

54. *CG*, 38th Cong., 1st sess., 1864, 817.

55. Ibid., 1158.

56. Ibid., 1141, 1158.

57. Ibid., 1159.

58. Ibid., 1185, 3060–61, 3079, 3326, 3378, 3401; "Act to Incorporate the Metropolitan Railroad Company," *U.S. Statutes at Large*, 13:328–29. The bill passed by a vote of 19 to 17. Among the moderate or conservative senators who voted in favor were Morrill, Henry Anthony (R.I.), William Fessenden (Maine), James Grimes (Iowa), and Timothy Howe (Wis.). This assessment relies on the spectrum of Republicanism developed in Benedict, *Compromise of Principle*. For opposition to slavery as a unifying force among Republicans, see Vorenberg, *Final Freedom*, 90–94.

59. Franklin Johnson, *Development of State Legislation*, 54, 124.

60. "An Act to Amend an Act Entitled 'An Act to Incorporate the Metropolitan Railroad Company in the District of Columbia,'" *U.S. Statutes at Large*, 13:573. See also Pierce, *Memoir and Letters of Charles Sumner*, 180–81.

61. *WC*, Mar. 11, 1865.

62. John Eaton Jr., in *Summary Report of the District of Columbia*, 380. See also *WC*, July 10, 1865; and R. B. Bortecon to "Colonel," Aug. 21, 1865, Unregistered Letters Received, DCBRFAL [A-9859].

63. Post to Titus, Mar. 28, 1865, and Daniels to Post, Jan. 2, 1866, both in PFP; Truth to Rowland Johnson, Nov. 1, 1864, in Truth, *Narrative of Sojourner Truth*, 177; Lamb, *Howard University Medical Department*, 13; Susie Bruce to Emily Howland, Oct. 26, 1864, and Anna M. Powell to Dear Friends, Jan. 11, 1866, both in EHP. See also Mabee, "Sojourner Truth Fights Dependence"; Faulkner, *Women's Radical Reconstruction*, 78, 123–24; and Painter, *Sojourner Truth*, 209–16.

64. Truth, *Narrative of Sojourner Truth*, 184. One of the streetcar protests described in the narra-

tive, discussed below, is corroborated by a host of other sources. The others are difficult to verify, but they accord with Truth's larger perspective on rights and her outsized public persona.

65. Ibid., 186.

66. Ibid., 186–87; *National Anti-Slavery Standard*, Oct. 14, 1865, 3. See also S. Truth to Amy Post, Oct. 1, 1865, PFP; and Laura Haviland to Editor, *National Freedman*, Dec. 15, 1865, 361. For Haviland in Washington, see Haviland, *Woman's Life-Work*, 456–65.

67. Truth, *Narrative of Sojourner Truth*, 187; *WC*, Sept. 23, 1865; *WNR*, Sept. 22, 1865; Case 3012, Criminal Case Files, 1863–1934, RDCSC; Criminal Docket Book, vol. 3, 187, RDCSC. See also Haviland to Editor, *National Freedman*; and Mabee, *Sojourner Truth*, 133–35.

68. W.P.P. to Friend Garrison, *Liberator*, Sept. 29, 1865, 156.

69. Adams, "Letter from Washington," Aug. 25, 1865, in Adams, *Letter from Washington*, 297.

70. *WC*, Dec. 25, 1865.

71. Cohen, "Safety and Danger"; Hood, "Changing Perceptions"; Scobey, *Empire City*, 146–47.

72. Reid, *Radical View*, 99.

73. *WC*, Mar. 24, 1865; *WNR*, Mar. 9, 1865.

74. *Constitutional Union*, July 5, 1866. For similarly politicized commentary on African Americans' odors, see ibid., Apr. 19, 1866 (on an Emancipation Day parade).

75. *Constitutional Union*, May 1, 1867.

76. Bortecon to "Colonel," Aug. 21, 1865, Unregistered Letters Received, DCBRFAL; and other accounts referenced herein. See also *WC*, Feb. 13, 1868; and Committee on the District of Columbia, *Report*, 22.

77. Ruchames, "Jim Crow Railroads"; Omori, "Race-Neutral Individualism"; Minter, "Failure of Freedom," 997; Maltz, "Separate but Equal," 554–55. Taking the gender asymmetry of these ideas to a logical extreme, officials in Reconstruction Louisville, Kentucky, briefly permitted black women to ride the streetcars while excluding black men. *Christian Recorder*, Nov. 19, 1870; Norris, "An Early Instance of Nonviolence," 491.

78. Black men's ability to claim respectability or other forms of elevated status has been far less examined than black women's. See Coleman, "Black Women and Segregated Public Transportation"; Minter, "Failure of Freedom"; Welke, "When All the Women Were White"; Welke, *Recasting American Liberty*, Part 3; Gilmore, *Gender and Jim Crow*; and Higginbotham, *Righteous Discontent*. For an exception, see Mack, "Law, Society, Identity," 393–98.

79. Other historians have argued that respectable black women who demanded access to common carriers in this era aspired to distance themselves from the black masses and to have their own relatively high status acknowledged. See Welke, "When All the Women Were White," esp. 285–88; and Mack, "Law, Society, Identity," 389–92.

80. Taylor, *Negro in the Reconstruction of Virginia*, 52; Fischer, "Pioneer Protest"; Hine, "1867 Charleston Streetcar Sit-Ins," 110–14; Norris, "An Early Instance of Nonviolence"; Drago, *Black Politicians and Reconstruction in Georgia*, 98–100; Fitzgerald, *Urban Emancipation*, 93, 123, 152.

81. Alfers, *Law and Order in the Capital City*, 37. For policing challenges after the war, see *Report of the Board of Metropolitan Police for the Year 1865*, 843–44; and *Report of the Board of Metropolitan Police for the Year 1866*, 597–600. See also Alfers, *Law and Order in the Capital City*, 27–28, 35–36; Sylvester, *District of Columbia Police*; and Young and Feeney, *Metropolitan Police Department*, 58. For policemen's recollections of disorder and difficult working conditions in this period, see "Rival to Boom Towns," *Washington Post*, Sept. 7, 1902; and "Heroes of the Force," *Washington Post*, May 31, 1897.

82. Sylvester, *District of Columbia Police*, 52; Bryan, *History of the National Capital*, 2:558n4.

83. R. W. Kerr, *History of the Government Printing Office*, 32; Schwartz, "H Street: A Neighborhood's Story"; Kennedy, *Population of the United States in 1860*; Walker, *Statistics of the Population of the United States, . . . the Ninth Census*.

84. *WC*, Mar. 27, 1865, July 17, 1865; *WES*, July 12, 1865. See also Sylvester, *District of Columbia Police*, 54.

85. *WNR*, Sept. 12, 1865, Sept. 13, 1865; *WC*, Sept. 25, 1865; Chas H. Tompkins to Jas. H. Taylor, Sept. 26, 1865, T-37, Letters Received, ser. 5382, Department and Defenses of Washington, RACC, pt. 1 [C-4106].

86. Editorial, *WNR*, Sept. 13, 1865.

87. John Eaton to A. C. Richards, Sept. 26, 1865, Letters Sent, vol. 1, reel 1, DCBRFALM.

88. Tompkins to Taylor, Sept. 26, 1865, and endorsements, Letters Received, ser. 5382, Department and Defenses of Washington, RACC, pt. 1 [C-4106].

89. "Rival to Boom Towns," *Washington Post*, Sept. 7, 1902.

90. Cox, "Defenses of Washington," 137; Holt et al., *Special Mission*, 8.

91. Harriet Prescott Spofford, "The Streets of Washington," *Harper's New Monthly Magazine*, Aug. 1868, 414. African Americans rarely occupied stalls inside markets in southern cities. Rabinowitz, *Race Relations*, 78–79.

92. R. B. Bortecon to "Colonel," Aug. 21, 1865, Unregistered Letters Received, DCBRFAL [A-9859].

93. W. F. Spurgin to W. W. Rogers, July 7, 1866, Letters Received, DCBRFAL [A-9769].

94. Ibid. For the neighborhood around Seventh and O Streets, Northwest, as a persistent problem, see C. H. Howard to R. Wallach (endorsement), July 10, 1866, on ibid.; and *Constitutional Union*, July 6, 1866.

95. J. Sayles Brown to C. H. Howard, July 2, 1866, #1726, Letters Received, DCBRFAL [A-9767]; Browne and Smithers to C. H. Howard, Oct. 21, 1866, AMQN; *Anglo-African*, May 2, 1863. For police violence or indifference toward blacks in Washington, see also Emma Brown to Emily Howland, Sept. 23, 1862, EHP; Catharine A. F. Stebbins, "Josephine Sophie Griffing," in *HWS*, 2:32; and Thomas Reed Johnson, "City on the Hill," 95. For parallels in other southern cities, see Rousey, *Policing the Southern City*, esp. 115; Rabinowitz, *Race Relations*, 35–36; and Rabinowitz, "Conflict between Blacks and the Police."

96. Obituary, *Washington Post*, Feb. 27, 1892; *WNR*, Nov. 21, 1873; *WC*, Nov. 12, 1867, Nov. 25, 1867, July 17, 1869. See also Westwood, "Getting Justice for the Freedman."

97. A. K. Browne to Chas. H. Howard, Oct. 10, 1868, AMQN.

98. Committee on the District of Columbia, *Report*, 13. Similarly, two black women had "dared to raise their voice against" the "brutality" of a streetcar conductor; see *Anglo-African*, Feb. 13, 1864. Such women, as Laura Edwards has suggested, "defend[ed] their respectability through publicity." Edwards, *Gendered Strife and Confusion*, 207. See also Kelley, "Congested Terrain."

99. Affidavits of Shederick Crump, Richard Clements, Mary Elizabeth Crump, Robert H. Dyson, and Charles Simon, sworn before a Bureau Agent, Sept. 5, 1865, Unregistered Letters Received, DCBRFAL [A-9875].

100. Petition of Colored Citizens of the District of Columbia, 39A-H4, RUSS.

101. The narrative of the conflict between the president and Congress in the winter of 1866 has been recounted many times. Excellent examples include Eric Foner, *Reconstruction*, 228–51; McKitrick, *Andrew Johnson*, 274–325; and Benedict, *Compromise of Principle*, 134–87.

102. JWLD, Feb. 22, 1866, Mar. 1, 1866; *WC*, Feb. 16, 1866; Editorial, ibid., Feb. 20, 1866; Editorial, ibid., Feb. 26, 1866. See also *Constitutional Union*, Mar. 21, 1866.

103. "An Act to Protect All Persons in the United States in Their Civil Rights, and Furnish the Means of Their Vindication," *U.S. Statutes at Large*, 14:27.

104. Kettner, *Development of American Citizenship*, 248–333; Novak, "Legal Transformation of Citizenship"; Vorenberg, "Citizenship and the Thirteenth Amendment."

105. Kaczorowski, "Revolutionary Constitutionalism," 926. See also Maltz, "Civil Rights Act," 620–22. Peggy Pascoe has revealed the postwar lack of consensus about whether the 1866 law invalidated state antimiscegenation laws. See Pascoe, *What Comes Naturally*, 17–74. For divergent interpretations of whether legislators sought to create federal jurisdiction over contracts between private parties or only to forbid discriminatory "state action," see Sullivan, "Historical Reconstruction, Reconstruction History"; Stanley, *From Bondage to Contract*, 55–56; Eric Foner, *Reconstruction*, 245; and Maltz, *Civil Rights, the Constitution, and Congress*, 70–78.

106. For an account of the debate, see Flack, *Adoption of the Fourteenth Amendment*, 20–35.

107. JWLD, Apr. 9, 1866. For William Owner's very different account, see WOD, Apr. 10, 1866.

108. *WNR*, Apr. 20, 1866; *WC*, Apr. 20, 1866. See also "The Negro Celebration in Washington," *Harper's Weekly*, May 12, 1866, 300 (with illustration).

109. *WNR*, Apr. 11, 1866; Petition of J. L. Hickman, Apr. 13, 1866, 39A-H4, RUSS; Asst. Adj. General to Captain, 4th US Army, Apr. 18, 1866, ser. 5375, Letters Sent, vol. 23 (439), Department of Washington, RACC, pt. 1 [C-4776]; Petition of Senators to General Dent, with endorsements, Apr. 10, 1866, Letters Received, WD 150, Ordnance Department, RG 156, NARA [YY-1].

110. Editorial, *WNR*, Apr. 19, 1866; JWLD, Apr. 19, 1866.

111. *Constitutional Union*, Apr. 19, 1866, Apr. 16, 1866.

112. WOD, Apr. 17, 1866, Apr. 13, 1866.

113. *WC*, Apr. 20, 1866; Sumner, *Charles Sumner: His Complete Works*, 14:41–42. See also Howard, *Autobiography*, 320–27.

114. O. O. Howard to Edwin Stanton, May 14, 1866, Letters Received, Records of the Commissioner's Office, RBRFAL [A-9716].

115. *Dred Scott v. John F. A. Sandford*, 60 U.S. 393 (1857); Osher, "Soldier Citizens," 371, 373–76; Litwack, *North of Slavery*, 31–33, 60. See also Mahon, *History of the Militia*, 83–85; Todd, "Militia and Volunteers of the District of Columbia"; Pocock, "Machiavelli, Harrington, and English Political Ideologies"; Kerber, *No Constitutional Right*, 236–48; and McCurry, *Masters of Small Worlds*, 265–70.

116. O. O. Howard to Edwin Stanton, May 14, 1866, Letters Received, Records of the Commissioner's Office, RBRFAL [A-9716]. For early militia laws that gave the U.S. president ultimate oversight over the District of Columbia militia, see Callan, *Military Laws of the United States*, 149–68.

117. JWLD, Apr. 28, 1866; Editorial, *Constitutional Union*, July 30, 1866; Rable, *But There Was No Peace*, 31, 33–42; Taylor, *Negro in the Reconstruction of Virginia*, 23. For black militias elsewhere in 1865 and 1866, see Saville, *Work of Reconstruction*, 144–50; Hahn, *Nation under Our Feet*, 174–75; and Fuke, "Blacks, Whites, and Guns," 330–32.

118. Allen M. Bland to Edwin M. Stanton, Sept. 6, 1866, Letters Received, ser. 5382, Department and Defenses of Washington, RACC, pt. 1. For the debate about black officers, see, for example, Osher, "Soldier Citizens," 427–33, 439–40.

119. Memorandum Stating Opinion of the Secretary of War, Sept. 11, 1866, and E. D. Townsend

to General Canby, Sept. 11, 1866, both filed with Bland to Stanton, Sept. 6, 1866, Letters Received, ser. 5382, Department and Defenses of Washington, RACC, pt. 1.

120. Joseph Roberts to Col. J. H. Taylor, Oct. 30, 1867, with endorsements from William Emory, E. D. Townsend, and U. S. Grant, Letters Received, Andrew Johnson Papers, LC; letter of Charles B. Fischer, *WC*, Nov. 9, 1867. See also Masur, "Reconstructing the Nation's Capital," 141–48.

121. Douglass, *Life and Times*, 371–72.

122. *WC*, Dec. 4, 1866; Editorial, *WNR*, Dec. 4, 1866; JWSD, Dec. 3, 1866. See also *WES*, Dec. 3, 1866.

123. WOD, Dec. 3, 1866. For a similar interpretation, see Bowers, *Tragic Era*, 148.

Chapter 4

1. Editorial, *WNI*, Dec. 20, 1865.

2. The first group includes Rabinowitz, *Race Relations*, 186–87; Rosen, *Terror in the Heart of Freedom*; Rosen, "Rhetoric of Miscegenation and the Reconstruction of Race"; Hodes, *White Women, Black Men*, 166–70, 174; and Dailey, *Before Jim Crow*, 85–93. The second group includes Richardson, *Death of Reconstruction*, 122–49; and Dale, "Social Equality Does Not Exist among Themselves." For an exploration of social equality's overlapping race and class connotations, see Painter, "Social Equality."

3. Keyssar, *Right to Vote*, 30–31, 46–65; Novak, "Legal Transformation of Citizenship"; Blackmar, *Manhattan for Rent*, 152–58; Griffith and Adrian, *History of American City Government: The Formation of Traditions*, 114–15.

4. *Celebration by the Colored People's Educational Monument Association*, 31–32. See also Editorial, *WES*, July 6, 1865.

5. *WC*, July 21, 1865; *New Haven Daily Palladium*, July 28, 1865; Sluby, *Asbury*, 41. Aspects of black Washingtonians' campaign for voting rights are also treated in Constance McLaughlin Green, *Washington*, 1:296–301; Thomas Reed Johnson, "City on the Hill," 42–50; and Harrison, "Experimental Station for Lawmaking," 35–36.

6. *Anglo-African*, Aug. 13, 1863; Preston, "Development of Negro Education," 194; Schweninger, *Black Property Owners*, 203.

7. *WC*, Nov. 23, 1865.

8. Petition of Colored Citizens of the District of Columbia, Dec. 11, 1865, 39A-H4, RUSS. See also *WES*, Dec. 12, 1865. For District black leaders claiming the vote based on taxpayer status, see also Benjamin Pond to Wm. George Hawkins, July 19, 1865, *National Freedman*, Aug. 15, 1865, 222.

9. John F. Cook to Editor, *WC*, Dec. 19, 1865. Cook had $5,000 in real estate and $200 in personal property in 1860. USMPCDC, 1860, 332.

10. *CG*, 39th Cong., 1st sess., 1866, 175, 181; ibid., 2nd sess., 1866, 39.

11. Editorial, *WES*, Dec. 18, 1865. The newly rejuvenated local Democratic Party had requested the poll, and the city council had pledged in November to hold such a poll should Congress take up the matter. *WES*, Oct. 10, 1865; *WNI*, Nov. 15, 1865; *New Haven Daily Palladium*, Nov. 22, 1865.

12. Henry Addison to L. F. S. Foster, Jan. 12, 1866, 39A-H4, RUSS; Richard Wallach to L. F. S. Foster, Jan. 6, 1866, in *CG*, 39th Cong., 2nd sess., 1866, 38–39. For an analysis of the turnout, see *WNI*, Dec. 22, 1865. In the radical Republican *WC*, Sayles Bowen, the city postmaster and an outspoken antislavery activist, had urged those who favored African American suffrage to boycott the poll. Letter of S. J. Bowen, *WC*, Dec. 18, 1865.

13. Howard Gillette, *Between Justice and Beauty*, 14–17, 21–26.

14. *Constitutional Union*, Nov. 23, 1865. See also Editorial, *WNI*, Jan. 4, 1866.

15. *WNI*, Dec. 15, 1865.

16. Editorial, ibid., Jan. 19, 1866.

17. Editorial, *WES*, Jan. 19, 1866. For civilizational language, see also Editorial, *WNI*, Dec. 20, 1865; and Editorial, *WES*, Dec. 8, 1865.

18. Editorial, *WNI*, Jan. 20, 1866.

19. Ibid., Jan. 4, 1866. For predications of white laborers' opposition to black men's enfranchisement, see also ibid., Dec. 15, 1865; Editorial, *WES*, Dec. 8, 1865; Editorial, ibid., Dec. 18, 1865; and *Journal of the Sixty-third Council*, 813–16. For "race war," see also *WNI*, Nov. 15, 1865.

20. *CG*, 38th Cong., 1st sess., 1864, 1156–57.

21. Editorial, *WNI*, Jan. 19, 1866; *CG*, 39th Cong., 2nd sess., 1866, 80–81. For a close analysis of similar ideas expressed at the 1868 Arkansas constitutional convention, see Rosen, *Terror in the Heart of Freedom*, 150–58.

22. Editorial, *WNI*, Jan. 11, 1866.

23. Quoted in Beckert, *Monied Metropolis*, 45.

24. Editorial, *WC*, Mar. 2, 1865. See also Editorial, ibid., Oct. 18, 1865; Editorial, ibid., Jan. 22, 1866.

25. Editorial, ibid., Jan. 22, 1866. For more on Republicans drawing the line on social quality, see Editorial, ibid., Oct. 18, 1865; *CG*, 38th Cong., 1st sess., 1864, 1160; Sella Martin to Editor, *WES*, Dec. 8, 1869; and Chapter 6.

26. Editorial, *WNR*, Apr. 26, 1866; Editorial, ibid., Jan. 19, 1866. O. O. Howard, the Freedmen's Bureau commissioner, in 1866 also supported "at least" an educational qualification for "the negroes." Howard, *Autobiography*, 317. For divisions among congressional Republicans and their varying concerns, see Belz, "Origins of Negro Suffrage," esp. 119–21; Benedict, *Compromise of Principle*; Cox and Cox, *Politics, Principle, and Prejudice*; and Eric Foner, *Reconstruction*, 228–80.

27. *Daily Advertiser*, Jan. 20, 1866; *Vermont Watchman and State Journal*, Jan. 26, 1866. For history and analysis of the House bill, see Maltz, *Civil Rights, the Constitution, and Congress*, 43–48; Harrison, "Experimental Station for Lawmaking," 40–41; and Wang, *Trial of Democracy*, 23, 317n95.

28. *National Anti-Slavery Standard*, Jan. 27, 1866, 3; Editorial, *WES*, Jan. 19, 1866; *New York Herald*, Jan. 19, 1866. For African Americans' ongoing lobbying for the vote, see *WNR*, Jan. 18, 1866; *New York Herald*, Jan. 19, 1866; and Petition of Citizens of Washington City, D.C., Members of the First Baptist Church, Jan. 17, 1866, 39A-J3, RUSHR [E-48].

29. Editorial, *Chicago Tribune*, Jan. 20, 1866. On the symbolic importance of congressional policy for the capital, see also Editorial, *Chicago Tribune*, Jan. 22, 1866; *Daily Advertiser*, Jan. 15, 1866; and *WC*, Jan. 24, 1866.

30. Russell Houston to Johnson, Feb. 2, 1866, in Johnson, *Papers of Andrew Johnson*, 10:14–17; *New York Herald*, Jan. 29, 1866. See also Editorial, *WNI*, Jan. 25, 1866; *New York Sun*, Jan. 22, 1866; *New York Herald*, Jan. 22, 1866; and *WNI*, Jan. 23, 1866. For additional correspondence from Johnson supporters, see Johnson, *Papers of Andrew Johnson*, 10:608–9, 626, 636. For northerners' rejection of voting rights for black men in 1865 and 1866, see Wang, *Trial of Democracy*, 22–23, 28–39, 40–41; Belz, "Origins of Negro Suffrage," 124–25; and Fishel, "Northern Prejudice and Negro Suffrage," 11–15.

31. Eric Foner, *Reconstruction*, 267–69; Maltz, *Civil Rights, the Constitution, and Congress*, 122–27; Abbott, *Republican Party in the South*, 73–74; McKitrick, *Andrew Johnson*, 449–55; Benedict, "Pre-

serving the Constitution." For postponement of the D.C. bill, see Wang, *Trial of Democracy*, 317; and Harrison, "Experimental Station for Lawmaking," 42–43.

32. *CG*, 39th Cong., 2nd sess., 1866, 41, 38; Talbot, "Lot M. Morrill." For Morrill's earlier support of taxpayer and literacy qualifications, see *CG*, 38th Cong., 1st sess., 1864, 2239; and Harrison, "Experimental Station for Lawmaking," 41–42. Benedict identified him as a powerful senator and a consistent centrist. Benedict, *Compromise of Principle*, 32.

33. *CG*, 39th Cong., 2nd sess., 1866, 41, 43, 45.

34. Ibid., 79. Morrill and others declared that suffrage legislation for the capital could serve as a model for the states. *CG*, 39th Cong., 2nd sess., 1866, 43 (Pomeroy); Sumner, *Charles Sumner: His Complete Works*, 24:229–30.

35. U.S. Constitution, amend. 14, sec. 2 (emphasis added); *Proceedings of the Eleventh National Woman's Rights Convention*. See also Ellen Carol DuBois, *Feminism and Suffrage*, 60–61.

36. *CG*, 39th Cong., 2nd sess., 1866, 47. Cowan had also tried this gambit in the 1864 debate about black men's enfranchisement in the District. *CG*, 38th Cong., 1st sess., 1864, 2140. He had also used women's diminished rights within the "marriage contract" to challenge arguments for a universal right to contract made by senators during the debate over the 1866 Civil Rights Act. Stanley, *From Bondage to Contract*, 57–58.

37. *CG*, 39th Cong., 2nd sess., 1866, 59.

38. Resolutions of the Equal Rights Convention in Rochester, N.Y., Dec. 12, 1866, in Stanton and Anthony, *Against an Aristocracy of Sex*, 7–8. For additional notice of the debate by woman suffragists, see ibid., 8–10, 11n3, 12; and *HWS*, 3:25. The proceedings are published in ibid., 2:103–51.

39. *CG*, 39th Cong., 2nd sess., 1866, 64.

40. Ibid., 64–65.

41. Ibid., 60.

42. Ibid., 40, 62–63. The broader issue of how the subordination of women has often revealed the limits of liberal individualism is treated in Pateman, *Sexual Contract*; and Stanley, *From Bondage to Contract*.

43. Wang, *Trial of Democracy*, 31.

44. District of Columbia Franchise Law Veto Message, Jan. 5, 1867, in Johnson, *Papers of Andrew Johnson*, 11:577–88.

45. Fields, *Slavery and Freedom on the Middle Ground*, 131–66; Wright, *Life behind a Veil*, 15–40; Curry, *Radicalism, Racism, and Party Realignment*; Eric Foner, *Reconstruction*, 421–23.

46. *Milwaukee Daily Sentinel*, Feb. 11, 1867; Josephine S. Griffing to Sojourner Truth, Apr. 14, 1867, in Truth, *Narrative of Sojourner Truth*, 275; *WC*, Feb. 28, 1867, Mar. 1, 1867, Mar. 6, 1867, Mar. 8, 1867, Apr. 11, 1867. See also Thomas Reed Johnson, "City on the Hill," 52–57; and Melvin Roscoe Williams, "Blueprint for Change," 380–82. Previous historians have often argued that members of the black elite were uninterested in political alliances with freedpeople. Constance McLaughlin Green, *Secret City*, 97–99; Johnston, *Surviving Freedom*, 192–93.

47. *WC*, Mar. 6, 1867, Apr. 8, 1867, Dec. 9, 1867; *WES*, Jan. 15, 1869, Jan. 22, 1869. See also Higginbotham, *From Strength to Strength*, 28, 31–32. On the significance of churches for black mobilization, political and otherwise, see also Hunter, *To 'Joy My Freedom*, 69–70; Barkley Brown, "Negotiating and Transforming the Public Sphere"; Eric Foner, *Reconstruction*, 92–95; Drago, *Black Politicians and Reconstruction in Georgia*, 201; and Higginbotham, *Righteous Discontent*, esp. 7–13.

48. For evidence of black women's political engagement and the sense that the vote belonged not only to men but to the whole community, see Barkley Brown, "Negotiating and Transforming the

Public Sphere"; Barkley Brown, "To Catch the Vision of Freedom"; Hahn, *Nation under Our Feet*, 185; and Saville, *Work of Reconstruction*, 169–70.

49. *Report of the Board of Metropolitan Police for the Year 1867*, 506; "The Washington Election," *Harper's Weekly*, June 22, 1867, 397. See also Thomas Reed Johnson, "City on the Hill," 53–56.

50. *Daily Cleveland Herald*, Feb. 28, 1867, quoting *WC*. See also "The Georgetown Election," *Harper's Weekly*, Mar. 16, 1867, 162.

51. Letter of James A. Handy, *Christian Recorder*, June 15, 1867.

52. JWSD, June 3, 1867.

53. Whyte, *Uncivil War*, 63; Bryan, *History of the National Capital*, 2:559–60; Thomas Reed Johnson, "City on the Hill," 57–60; Grimshaw, *Official History of Freemasonry*, 149.

54. Speech of W. W. Moore, *Journal of the Sixty-fourth Council*, 716, 718.

55. *Constitutional Union*, Sept. 18, 1865, Oct. 28, 1865, Nov. 2, 1865, and more generally fall 1865 and spring 1866 coverage. See also *WC*, July 18, 1867, Oct. 22, 1867, Nov. 6, 1867; Seibold, *Historical Sketch*, 25; Tracy, *History of the Typographical Union*, 231; J. Sayles Brown to Hon. T. D. Elliot [Eliot], Dec. 27, 1867, Letters Received by Thomas D. Eliot, Washington Hdqrs., RBRFAL [A-25]; and Montgomery, *Beyond Equality*.

56. Wesley, *Negro Labor*, 145, 173–77; Hine, "Black Organized Labor in Reconstruction Charleston"; Fuke, *Imperfect Equality*, 131–35; Rachleff, *Black Labor in the South*, 38, 42–45; Arnesen, *Waterfront Workers of New Orleans*, 3–60; Rabinowitz, *Race Relations*, 73–74.

57. *WC*, Mar. 1, 1867.

58. Moran, "Anthony Bowen"; McMillan, "Anthony Bowen."

59. Lessoff, *Nation and Its City*, 7–13; Keller, *Affairs of State*, 98–101; Cowdrey, *City for the Nation*, 24–25; Olynthus B. Clark, "Bid of the West for the National Capital"; Constance McLaughlin Green, *Washington*, 1:328–33.

60. *New Hampshire Statesman*, Jan. 25, 1867; *Milwaukee Daily Sentinel*, Feb. 11, 1867; S. J. Bowen to Charles Sumner, Mar. 26, 1867, reel 38, frames 517–18, CSP; J. Sayles Brown to Hon. T. D. Elliot [Eliot], Dec. 27, 1867, Letters Received by Thomas D. Eliot, Washington Hdqrs., RBRFAL [A-25]; *Laws of the Corporation of the City of Washington*, 20. The minimum wage law seems to have exempted private parties who contracted with the city.

61. *WC*, July 16, 1867, July 27, 1867, Dec. 10, 1867. According to the 1870 manuscript census, Henderson was a Virginia-born mulatto preacher who lived in the first ward with his wife, two sons, and a servant. The couple had no real estate or personal property of any value, but Henderson could read and write. USMPCDC, 1870.

62. *WC*, Dec. 10, 1867. For Brown, see ibid., Apr. 10, 1867; and General Term Minutes, June 8, 1867, vol. 1, 198–99, RDCSC.

63. Petition of Daniel Burrows and 4,871 other colored laborers of the city of Washington, D.C., HR40A-H4.1, RUSHR (also printed in *WC*, Jan. 2, 1868); *WC*, Dec. 10, 1867, Jan. 2, 1868, Jan. 3, 1868.

64. J. Sayles Brown to Hon. T. D. Elliot [Eliot], Dec. 27, 1867, Letters Received by Thomas D. Eliot, Washington Hdqrs., RBRFAL [A-25] (emphasis added). Similarly, in an address to the African American National Labor Convention in 1869, John Mercer Langston spoke in terms of fairness and access, not in terms of rights. "We ask," he said, "that trades be opened to our children . . . that for every day's labor given we be paid full and fair remuneration . . . that we may work in the printing office, whether private or governmental, in the factory, the foundry, the workshop." *Proceedings of the Colored National Labor Convention*, 18. Risa Goluboff has detailed the struggles in the 1930s

and 1940s over the extent to which the dynamic concept of civil rights included labor-related rights. Goluboff, *Lost Promise of Civil Rights*.

65. Josephine S. Griffing to Charles Sumner, Feb. 12, 1867, reel 38, frames 17–18, CSP; Sayles J. Bowen to Charles Sumner, Mar. 26, 1867, reel 38, frames 517–18, CSP; Sayles Bowen to Emily Howland, May 31, 1862, EHP; [Mary Bowen] to Emily Howland, Feb. 2, 1866, EHP; William H. Tenney to Andrew Johnson, Feb. 3, 1866, in Johnson, *Papers of Andrew Johnson*, 10:24–25; John N. Cochran to Andrew Johnson, approximately Oct. 15, 1866, in ibid., 11:352–53; Editorial, *WC*, Jan. 9, 1866; ibid., Mar. 13, 1866. See also Tindall, "Sketch of Mayor Sayles J. Bowen"; Madison Davis, *History of the Washington City Post-Office*, 54–56; Thomas Reed Johnson, "City on the Hill," 66–68; and Whyte, *Uncivil War*, 71.

66. Emma Brown to Emily Howland, Mar. 23, 1867, EHP.

67. On the Lincoln Cooperative Building and Deposit Association, see *WC*, Dec. 7, 1867, Dec. 21, 1867, Jan. 24, 1868; and *New National Era*, Dec. 15, 1870.

68. *Memorial of Soldiers in Service of the United States*; and see general coverage in local papers. See also Tindall, "Sketch of Mayor Sayles J. Bowen," 30; Thomas Reed Johnson, "City on the Hill," 70–77; Bryan, *History of the National Capital*, 2:557–68; Whyte, *Uncivil War*, 59–84; Harrison, "Race, Radicalism, and Reconstruction"; and Melvin Roscoe Williams, "Blueprint for Change," 379–82.

69. *Journal of the Sixty-sixth Council*, 1:240–42.

70. *WC*, July 17, 1867. For the congressional debate about the measure, see *CG*, 40th Cong., 2nd sess., 1868, 2260–67. See also Whyte, *Uncivil War*, 65; Thomas Reed Johnson, "City on the Hill," 73; and Bryan, *History of the National Capital*, 2:562–63.

71. Bowen, *Message of the Mayor* (1868), 8–9; *Journal of the Sixty-sixth Council*, 1:322, 323; Bowen, *Message of the Mayor* (1869), 28. See also Constance McLaughlin Green, *Secret City*, 91–92; and Thomas Reed Johnson, "City on the Hill," 76–77.

72. Bowen, *Message of the Mayor* (1869), 4; Thomas Reed Johnson, "City on the Hill," 78–79; Constance McLaughlin Green, *Washington*, 318; Glassie, "Victorian Homes," 334; Tindall, "Sketch of Mayor Sayles J. Bowen," 28–29.

73. Editorial, *WES*, Feb. 9, 1869; M. Defrees to James Harlan, July 1, 1868, 40A-E4, RUSS.

74. *WNI*, July 16, 1868; *Journal of the Sixty-sixth Council*, 2:821–22. See also *WC*, July 30, 1869.

75. *Proceedings of the Colored National Labor Convention*, 7.

76. Spero and Harris, *Black Worker*, 33; Wesley, *Negro Labor*, 187–88.

77. Goodwin, "History of Schools," 254–55; Dabney, *History of Schools for Negroes*, 117; Levey, "Segregation in Education," 218–19.

78. Bowen, *Message of the Mayor* (1868), 4–5.

79. Petition of Albert Bolden et al., Mar. 18, 1868, 40A-H5.1, RUSS; Four Petitions of Colored Citizens of Washington and Georgetown, Apr. 7, 1869, Sen. 41A-H5.2, RUSS; Petition from a Committee Appointed by Citizens . . . after a Series of Mass Meetings, Dec. 7, 1870, 41A-H5.2, RUSS. See also Chapter 2.

80. *WES*, Feb. 10, 1869; *Presidential Message Vetoing Act Transferring Duties of Trustees of Colored Schools*. See also *WC*, Feb. 15, 1869; *WES*, Feb. 15, 1869; and *CG*, 40th Cong., 3rd sess., 1869, 978. For passage of the bill, see *Journal of the Senate of the United States of America, 1789–1873*, 40th Cong., 3rd sess., 1869, 220. See also Goodwin, "History of Schools," 260–61; Cromwell, "First Negro Churches," 70; and Levey, "Segregation in Education," 227–33.

81. *WES*, Feb. 16, 1869; *Liberator*, May 8, 1863, 75.

82. *WES*, Feb. 16, 1869. See also *WC*, Feb. 16, 1869.

83. *WES*, Feb. 15, 1869; Thomas Martin to Editor, ibid., Feb. 18, 1869; ibid., Feb. 22, 1869. See also ibid., Feb. 16, 1869; and Four Petitions of Colored Citizens of Washington and Georgetown, Apr. 7, 1869, Sen. 41A-H5.2, RUSS.

84. "An Act for the Further Security of Equal Rights in the District of Columbia," *U.S. Statutes at Large*, 16:3; Edward McPherson, *Political History of the United States*, 351–52, 395. For popular support of the measure, see *WNR*, Feb. 10, 1868, clipping in 40A-E4, RUSS; Petition of Fourth Ward Republican Club, July 16, 1867, 40A-H5.1, RUSS; and *CG*, 39th Cong., 1st sess., 1866, 312. On the significance of jury service during Reconstruction, see *WNI*, Dec. 5, 1865; Forman, "Juries and Race," 910–20; Maltz, "Civil Rights Act," 623–26; and Rabinowitz, *Race Relations*, 38–41.

85. *WES*, Jan. 15, 1869, Jan. 12, 1869. Black leaders also complained that the police board distributed liquor licenses in a discriminatory way. *WES*, June 7, 1869.

86. *WC*, Apr. 23, 1869; A. C. Richards to Charles Sumner, Mar. 26, 1869, reel 45, frame 687, CSP; *New York World*, May 22, 1869; *WES*, May 21, 1869, July 10, 1869.

87. George W. Williams, *History of the Negro Race in America*, 476–503; Cromwell, "First Negro Churches," 78.

88. Fletcher, *History of Oberlin College*, 871; Biggleston, *They Stopped in Oberlin*, 207–8; DeBoer, "Role of Afro-Americans," 464, 470–71, 747n168; Berlin et al., *Black Military Experience*, 9, 93. The civic activities of Amanda Wall and Eliza Anderson are discussed in Chapter 5.

89. *Proceedings of the Colored National Labor Convention*, 22; JWSD, Apr. 21, 1869, Aug. 3, 1869; Emma Brown to Emily Howland, July 3, 1869, EHP; McMillan, "Anthony Bowen," 159. See also *New York World*, May 22, 1869; and *Philadelphia Enquirer*, July 7, 1869, quoted in *Weekly Georgia Telegraph*, July 16, 1869.

90. Letter of John F. Cook, *WC*, June 9, 1869; JWLD, Mar. 12, 1868, Dec. 14, 1868. See also ibid., Nov. 30, 1867; *New York World*, Jan. 9, 1869; and Meersman and Boyer, "National Theatre in Washington," 236–37. For the laws, see *Laws of the Corporation of the City of Washington, Passed by the Sixty-sixth Council*, 22; and Indritz, "Post Civil War Ordinances," 187–89.

91. Editorial, *Chicago Tribune*, June 15, 1869; Editorial, *WES*, June 7, 1869. See also *New York World*, June 5, 1869, June 14, 1869, Dec. 1, 1869; *Washington Express*, July 20, 1869; and Indritz, "Post Civil War Ordinances," 187–89. For governments' power to charter and regulate corporations, see Novak, "American Law of Association," 180–82.

92. *Daily Advertiser*, June 8, 1869; *Newark (Ohio) Advocate*, June 11, 1869; *New York Herald*, quoted in *Charleston (S.C.) Courier*, June 8, 1869. See also *New York World*, June 5, 1869.

93. Letter of John F. Cook, *WC*, June 9, 1869 (also printed in *Newark (Ohio) Advocate*, June 18, 1869). Although leading black Washingtonians did not press for a law affirming the right to marry across racial lines, the capital became known as a place where interracial couples could marry. The District's early antimiscegenation statute, adopted as part of the Maryland legal code when the District was founded, was never explicitly repealed. It seems to have been quietly nullified, however, perhaps by the establishment of legal equality in 1862. By the 1870s, interracial couples from Virginia, forbidden from marrying in their state, sometimes traveled to the District to marry. Dailey, *Before Jim Crow*, 92; Pascoe, *What Comes Naturally*, 48.

94. *WES*, June 8, 1869; Whyte, *Uncivil War*, 68–73.

95. Bowen, *Message of the Mayor* (1869), 8. For the contemporary use of public works employment as poor relief, see also Klebaner, "Poor Relief and Public Works"; and Gutman, "Failure of the Movement by the Unemployed."

96. Bowen, *Message of the Mayor* (1869), 14–15; S. J. Bowen to Charles Sumner, July 23, 1869, reel 47, frame 540, CSP; *Express*, July 20, 1869.

97. *WES*, May 20, 1869. For adoption in the fourth ward, see ibid., May 21, 1869.

98. *Journal of the Sixty-seventh Council*, 46; *WNI*, June 21, 1869; *WC*, July 16, 1869; Thomas Reed Johnson, "City on the Hill," 159–62; Tracy, *History of the Typographical Union*, 239–40, 246–48; Wesley, *Negro Labor*, 167–68; Spero and Harris, *Black Worker*, 20–21; R. W. Kerr, *History of the Government Printing Office*, 34.

99. *WES*, June 4, 1869, June 19, 1869, July 9, 1869; *New York World*, June 5, 1869, June 7, 1869, June 11, 1867; *New York Herald*, July 10, 1869; *Detroit Tribune*, quoted in *WC*, July 19, 1869. See also Wesley, *Negro Labor*, 166–67. For employment in the Navy Yard as a political concern in the fifth and sixth wards, see *WC*, Apr. 28, 1869, July 14, 1869, Dec. 2, 1869.

100. "An Appeal to Congress," 41A-H5.2, RUSS; *WNI*, June 18, 1869.

101. A. W. Tucker to Charles Sumner, Jan. 15, 1870, and A. T. Augusta to Charles Sumner, Jan. 16, 1870, both in 41A-H5.2, RUSS. For other accounts, see *New York World*, June 17, 1869; Lamb, *History of the Medical Society*, 100–105; Busey, *Personal Reminiscences*, 245–93; Cobb, *First Negro Medical Society*, 6–39; and Lamb, *Howard University Medical Department*, 21, 23.

102. Sumner, *Charles Sumner: His Complete Works*, 17:186–88; *Report to Accompany Bill S. 511*, 7.

103. *Report to Accompany Bill S. 511*, 6, 7.

104. *New York World*, Dec. 10, 1869, Dec. 17, 1869; "An Appeal to Congress," 41A-H5.2, RUSS; Sumner, *Charles Sumner: His Complete Works*, 17:186–88.

105. *WC*, Mar. 6, 1869, July 15, 1869, July 16, 1869, July 20, 1869, July 21, 1869; *WES*, July 11, 1869–July 21, 1869. For original reports of the crime, see *WES*, Mar. 5, 1869; and *WC*, Mar. 6, 1869.

106. *New York World*, June 22, 1869, June 23, 1869, July 21, 1869; *WES*, July 13, 1869; for the jury, see July 12, 1869, Case 6908, Criminal Case Files, 1863–1934, RDCSC.

107. *WES*, July 14, 1869, July 15, 1869, July 19, 1869; *Chicago Tribune*, July 17, 1869. See also *WC*, July 17, 1869; and *Express*, July 16, 1869, July 17, 1869.

108. J.S.G., "Lessons in the Court-Room," *Revolution*, Aug. 12, 1869, 83; JWSD, July 16, 1869, July 19, 1869, July 21, 1869; *WES*, July 13, 1869, July 15, 1869.

109. JWSD, July 16, 1869.

110. Instructions to the Jury, Case 6908, Criminal Case Files, 1863–1934, RDCSC. See also Indictment, in the same file.

111. *WC*, July 21, 1869; JWSD, July 21, 1869. See also Editorial, *WC*, July 21, 1869; and "Lessons in the Court-Room," *Revolution*, Aug. 12, 1869, 83.

112. *WC*, July 22, 1869; *WES*, Nov. 27, 1869; JWLD, Aug. 14, 1869; Case 2681, Register of Cases, 108, RSEH; [Deputy] to Anthony Gaines, Feb. 2, 1870, and [Deputy] to Hon. George P. Fisher, Mar. 31, 1870, vol. 1869–70, 13, 28, Letters Sent Relating to Women Patients, ibid.

113. *Journal of the Sixty-seventh Council*, 463–70, quotations at 466, 469. See also Levey, "Segregation in Education," 234–37.

114. Beauchamp, "Schools for All," 145–50.

115. Blackett, *Beating against the Barriers*, 185–285; DeBoer, "Role of Afro-Americans," 337–48.

116. Newspaper coverage did not mention the daughter's name, but the 1870 census lists her as Josie, age seven. USMPCDC, 1870.

117. *WNI and Express*, Nov. 25, 1869, Nov. 26, 1869; *WC*, Nov. 26, 1869, Dec. 1, 1869; *WES*, Nov. 25, 1869, Nov. 26, 1869; Editorial, ibid., Nov. 27, 1869. See, generally, the coverage in ibid. through Dec. 8, 1869.

118. *WES*, Nov. 29, 1869.

119. Letter of William A. Cook, *WES*, Nov. 30, 1869, Dec. 1, 1869.

120. JWSD, Nov. 30, 1869; *WES*, Nov. 25, 1869; Editorial, ibid., Dec. 1, 1869; *WES*, Dec. 8, 1869.

121. *New York World*, June 9, 1869. For "negro rule," see also ibid., June 10, 1869; *Weekly Georgia Telegraph*, June 18, 1869; and *Washington Express*, June 7, 1869. For the *WES*'s rebuttal, see Editorials, *WES*, June 11, 1869, and June 14, 1869. For condemnatory coverage of the election, see also *New York Herald*, June 8, 1869, June 9, 1869, June 10, 1869; *San Francisco Daily Evening Bulletin*, June 15, 1869; *Weekly Georgia Telegraph*, June 11, 1869; and *Newark (Ohio) Advocate*, June 11, 1869.

Chapter 5

1. *HWS*, 2:221. On Griffing's work in freedmen's relief, see Melder, "Angel of Mercy"; Faulkner, *Women's Radical Reconstruction*; and Kate Masur, "Reconstructing the Nation's Capital," 51–52, 61–64.

2. Ellen Carol DuBois, *Feminism and Suffrage*, 79–104, 162–202; Andrea Moore Kerr, *Lucy Stone*, 119–42; Douglass, *Frederick Douglass on Women's Rights*, 26–37; Terborg-Penn, *African American Women in the Struggle for the Vote*, 24–35; Newman, *White Women's Rights*, 59–66; Aptheker, *Woman's Legacy*, esp. 44–50. For the recent debate, see DuBois and Smith, *Elizabeth Cady Stanton*. For a similar argument to mine, see Keyssar, *Right to Vote*, 190–93, 197–200.

3. Summers, *Era of Good Stealings*, x–xi; Eric Foner, *Reconstruction*, 415.

4. Keller, *Affairs of State*, 115–21, 230–31; Monkkonen, "Politics of Municipal Indebtedness"; Frisch, "Community Elite"; Yearley, *Money Machines*, 3–35; Glaab and Brown, *History of Urban America*, 172–73. For recent cultural orientations, see Beckert, *Monied Metropolis*; Ryan, *Civic Wars*; and Ethington, *Public City*.

5. Rabinowitz, "Continuity and Change"; Holt, "Empire over the Mind."

6. Rabinowitz, "Reconstruction to Redemption," 189. See also Rabinowitz, *Race Relations*, 266–77. Early in his long career, Ernest Griffith noted perceptively that before 1880 "the desire to insure the localities against negro rule had in certain instances also been influential in strengthening the state at the expense of the locality." Griffith, *Modern Development of City Government*, 98. For "taxpayer" movements and municipal reform in Charleston, Nashville, Atlanta, New Orleans, Mobile, and Memphis, see Kornell, "Reconstruction in Nashville," 277–87; Drago, *Black Politicians and Reconstruction in Georgia*, 81; Russell, *Atlanta*, 176–82; Ryan, *Civic Wars*, 280; Richardson, *Death of Reconstruction*, 93–98; Fitzgerald, *Urban Emancipation*, 147–62, 199–206; Wrenn, *Crisis and Commission Government in Memphis*, 24–27; Berkeley, *Like a Plague of Locusts*, 228–40; and Summers, *Era of Good Stealings*, 158. On whites finding ways to circumvent prohibitions on racial discrimination, see also William Gillette, *Retreat from Reconstruction*, 38–42; and Eric Foner, *Reconstruction*, 421–22. Some of my initial analysis was inspired by Michael O'Malley's brilliant and provocative analysis of the economic and racial connotations of "carpetbagger." O'Malley, "Specie and Species."

7. Historians have typically portrayed the consolidation movement as a drive for municipal modernization while paying little attention to its postemancipation context. See Constance McLaughlin Green, *Washington*, 1:332–38; Lessoff, *Nation and Its City*; Howard Gillette, *Between Justice and Beauty*, 59–60; and Thomas Reed Johnson, "City on the Hill," 81–82, 186–87, 190–97. Yet the goals and rhetoric of the consolidationist coalition bear striking resemblance to other contemporaneous movements in what Eric Foner called the "first redemption." Foner, *Reconstruction*, 421–22.

8. New Orleans has long been recognized as the only southern city where a meaningful move-

ment for school integration developed during Reconstruction. Elsewhere in the South, it was an achievement for African American activists to obtain publicly funded schools for black children at all. Rabinowitz, "Half a Loaf"; Fischer, *Segregation Struggle in Louisiana*, 110–32; Kousser, "Before *Plessy*, before *Brown*." For the North, see Douglas, *Jim Crow*, 61–122.

9. A good statement of that position is Stanton, "Universal Suffrage," July 29, 1865, in Stanton and Anthony, *In the School of Antislavery*, 550–51. For Stanton's universalism, see also her article dated Jan. 14, 1869, in Stanton and Anthony, *Against an Aristocracy of Sex*, 201–3. For tensions in the universal suffrage movement, see also Ellen Carol DuBois, *Feminism and Suffrage*, esp. 71–74; and "Outgrowing the Compact of the Fathers," in DuBois, *Woman Suffrage and Women's Rights*.

10. Aron, *Ladies and Gentlemen of the Civil Service*, 40–61. See also Norgren, *Belva Lockwood*, 18–19, 36–39; Moldow, *Women Doctors in Gilded-Age Washington*, 10–15; and *HWS*, 3:812–13.

11. "To the Friends of Equal Rights," in Willcox, *Suffrage a Right*; *WC*, July 13, 1867, July 19, 1867, July 20, 1867; Letter of Julia A. Holmes, ibid., Aug. 27, 1867; Report of the Corresponding Secretary, June 15, 1868, in Holmes, *Report on the Condition of the Cause*, 11–12; *HWS*, 3:809; petitions from states, including Delaware, Massachusetts, Indiana, Kansas, Connecticut, and Ohio, in 40A-H5, RUSS. On pay issues, see *HWS*, 2:420, 3:811–12, 3:814; Holmes, *Report on the Condition of the Cause*, 5; and Editorial Correspondence by Elizabeth Cady Stanton, Jan. 22, 1869, in Stanton and Anthony, *Against an Aristocracy of Sex*, 206, 210n13. See also Norgren, *Belva Lockwood*, 36–39.

12. For the split in the national movement, see *HWS*, 2:92–101, 229–68; and note 2 above.

13. *HWS*, 2:214.

14. *WES*, June 6, 1868. See also *WC*, June 5, 1868, June 6, 1868; Holmes, *Report on the Condition of the Cause*, 5–6; *WES*, Jan. 29, 1869; and Willcox, *Suffrage a Right*. Recent biographical treatments of Walker do not mention this facet of her activism. Walker, *Mary Edwards Walker*; Leonard, *Yankee Women*, 105–57.

15. *WES*, June 6, 1868.

16. Frederick Douglass to Josephine Griffing, Sept. 27, 1868, JGP.

17. See Painter, "Voices of Suffrage," 51; and Andrea Moore Kerr, *Lucy Stone*, 135, 269n75.

18. Foner and Walker, *Proceedings of the Black National and State Conventions*, 354; *WES*, Jan. 15, 1866, Jan. 16, 1869. For Johnson's occupation, see Martha S. Jones, *All Bound Up Together*, 146.

19. *HWS*, 2:350, 353–54.

20. Letter of Catherine A. F. Stebbins, *Woman's Advocate*, Mar. 1869, 172. Stanton's resolutions were not published in *HWS*.

21. Letter of Catherine A. F. Stebbins, *Woman's Advocate*, Mar. 1869, 173. See also *WES*, Jan. 21, 1869; Editorial Correspondence by Stanton, Jan. 22, 1869, in *HWS*, 2:345–48; JWLD, Jan. 13, 1869, Jan. 14, 1869; *WES*, Jan. 19, 1869.

22. *WES*, Jan. 29, 1869.

23. For women attempting to register in the third and seventh wards, see *WES*, Feb. 3, 1869, Apr. 27, 1869, May 17, 1869; *WC*, Apr. 23, 1869, Apr. 27, 1869; and JWLD, Apr. 26, 1869.

24. See, for example, JWLD, Nov. 27, 1867, and Dec. 25, 1868. Griffing and her milieu are also discussed in Faulkner, *Women's Radical Reconstruction*.

25. JWLD, Mar. 11, 1869, Aug. 18, 1869.

26. JWLD, Dec. 4, 1867.

27. For Eliza Anderson, see Obituary, *Washington Post*, Sept. 27, 1898; and George W. Williams,

History of the Negro Race in America, 497. For Amanda Wall, see DeBoer, "Role of Afro-Americans," 747n168.

28. JWLD, Apr. 22, 1869. Eliza Anderson signed the petition but chose not to appear before the registrars.

29. *WES*, Apr. 27, 1869.

30. *New York Tribune* quoted in *WNI*, Apr. 24, 1869; *New York Times*, June 2, 1869. See also *WNI*, Apr. 26, 1869.

31. For 1868, see Virginia L. Minor to Elizabeth Cady Stanton, May 4, 1868, in Stanton and Anthony, *Against an Aristocracy of Sex*, 133, 135n4; "Meeting of the American Equal Rights Association in New York," May 14, 1868, ibid., 136–37; and *HWS*, 2:312, 3:810. For 1869, see woman suffrage petitions in Senate papers of the 40th Congress, 40A-H5, RUSS.

32. For Julian, see *HWS*, 2:482. For Anthony, see Susan B. Anthony to Isabella Beecher Hooker, Jan. 21, 1871, in Stanton and Anthony, *Against an Aristocracy of Sex*, 407, 408n4. For lobbying Congress in 1870, see *HWS*, 2:411–18; Diary of Susan B. Anthony, entries of Jan. 18–23, 1870, in Stanton and Anthony, *Against an Aristocracy of Sex*, 295–97; *Revolution*, Jan. 27, 1870, Feb. 17, 1870; and Briggs, *Olivia Letters*, 158–60. See also Susan B. Anthony to Isabella Beecher Hooker, in Stanton and Anthony, *Against an Aristocracy of Sex*, 292; and Susan B. Anthony to Elizabeth T. Schenck et al., Jan. 14, 1870, in ibid., 293–94.

33. Resolutions of the Washington Convention, Jan. 13, 1871, in Stanton and Anthony, *Against an Aristocracy of Sex*, 405; *WES*, Jan. 11, 1871; "The Washington Convention," *Revolution*, Jan. 19, 1871. For arguments before the committee, see *HWS*, 2:443–61.

34. *HWS*, 2:456–57; *Report of the Committee on the Judiciary*. (Butler dissented.) See also Holzman, *Stormy Ben Butler*, 200–201.

35. *WC*, Apr. 15, 1871; *Revolution*, Apr. 20, 1871; Norgren, *Belva Lockwood*, 59; Rhodes, *Mary Ann Shad Cary*, 195. For Douglass's support for woman suffrage in 1870 and 1871, see Douglass, *Life and Writings*, 231–33, 235–39; and "The Washington Convention," *Revolution*, Jan. 19, 1871.

36. *WC*, Apr. 19, 1871, Apr. 20, 1871; *Revolution*, Apr. 20, 1871, Apr. 27, 1871, May 4, 1871, May 11, 1871, May 25, 1871; *HWS*, 2:587–99. See also Norgren, *Belva Lockwood*, 60–61; "Taking the Law into Our Own Hands," in Ellen Carol DuBois, *Woman Suffrage and Women's Rights*, 126; Stanton and Anthony, *Against an Aristocracy of Sex*, 526n4.

37. Sara S. [sic] *Spencer v. the Board of Registration, Sarah E. Webster v. the Superintendents of Election*, 1 Macarthy 8467, 8468 (D.C. Supreme Court) 169 (1873). Proceedings of the case and the appeal to the U.S. Supreme Court are Case 8467, Law Case Files, RDCSC; and *Spencer v. Martin*, Case 6207, Appellate Case Files, RUSSC. Cartter's ruling foreshadowed the U.S. Supreme Court's 1874 decision in *Minor v. Happersett*. For a compelling analysis of why the U.S. Supreme Court took the Minor case rather than Spencer's, see Norgren, *Belva Lockwood*, 63–66.

38. *Spencer v. Board of Registration*.

39. *Petition of National Executive Committee of Colored People*, 130. For local African Americans' support for school integration, see also Four Petitions of Colored Citizens of Washington and Georgetown, Apr. 7, 1869, Sen. 41A-H5.2, RUSS; *WES*, Feb. 11, 1871, Feb. 17, 1871; and Chapter 4.

40. Sumner, *Charles Sumner: His Complete Works*, 18:21. See also Kelly, "Congressional Controversy." Sumner's dogged pursuit of an expansive vision of racial equality before the law in the capital and his special relationship with black leaders there has been curiously neglected. For limited attention to the matter, see Munro, "Original Understanding." For almost none, see Donald, *Charles Sumner*.

41. *WES*, Feb. 17, 1871. For local black opposition to mixed schools, see also *WC*, Mar. 10, 1870 (at a second ward Republican meeting, a black attendee said that he thought each color should have its own school; others disagreed vehemently). For opposition to school integration among northern black activists, see Hugh Davis, "Pennsylvania State Equal Rights League," 619–20; Fishel, "Repercussions of Reconstruction," 340–41; Douglas, *Jim Crow*, 45–50; and Moss, "Tarring and Feathering of Thomas Paul Smith."

42. *CG*, 41st Cong., 3rd sess., 1871, 1054; Eaton, *Eulogy on Hon. James Willis Patterson*; Patterson, *James W. Patterson*.

43. *CG*, 41st Cong., 3rd sess., 1871, 1056; Finkelman, "Prelude to the Fourteenth Amendment."

44. *CG*, 41st Cong., 3rd sess., 1871, 1054.

45. Ibid., 1057. For similar arguments used by British liberals such as John Stuart Mill to justify colonial rule in India and elsewhere, see Mehta, *Liberalism and Empire*, esp. 77–114.

46. *CG*, 41st Cong., 3rd sess., 1871, 1057.

47. Ibid., 1058.

48. Ibid., 1057.

49. Ibid., 1056.

50. Ibid., 1060; Eric Foner, *Freedom's Lawmakers*, 180–81.

51. *CG*, 41st Cong., 3rd sess., 1871, 1060 (Revels); ibid., 1057 (Thurman). For integrationists' view that the state must lead the destruction of racial prejudice, see also Letter of D. A. Straker, *New National Era and Citizen*, Feb. 5, 1874; Letter of F. M. Jackson, *Christian Recorder*, Apr. 20, 1872; and Kousser, "Supremacy of Equal Rights," 977.

52. *New Haven Daily Palladium*, Nov. 22, 1865 (also printed verbatim in *Liberator*, Dec. 15, 1865); *New York Herald*, Jan. 21, 1866. See also *Daily Cleveland Herald*, Dec. 22. 1865; and *Daily Citizen and News*, Dec. 10, 1866.

53. *Constitutional Union*, Oct. 18, 1865, Nov. 11, 1865; *WES*, Oct. 25, 1865, Nov. 23, 1865. For Elvans, see Bryan, *History of the National Capital*, 2:570–71.

54. Tindall, "Sketch of Alexander Robey Shepherd," 49–51; Lessoff, *Nation and Its City*, 48–49; Constance McLaughlin Green, *Washington*, 1:289.

55. *WES*, Nov. 23, 1865; *WNI*, Dec. 7, 1865. See also Editorial, *WES*, Dec. 11, 1865.

56. Editorial, *WNI*, Jan. 26, 1866; *Bill in Addition to the Several Acts for Establishing the Temporary and Permanent Seat of the Government*, Senate bill 97, 39th Cong., 1st sess.; *CG*, 39th Cong., 1st sess., 1866, 3191–93. See also Constance McLaughlin Green, *Washington*, 1:333; and Bryan, *History of the National Capital*, 2:550–51.

57. *Petition of the Citizens of the District of Columbia*; Petition of J. C. Lewis et al., Jan. 31, 1868, 40A-H5.1, RUSS; Petition of A. G. Hall et al., Mar. 13, 1868, 40A-H5.1, RUSS; Resolution of Washington Board of Common Council, Feb. 18, 1868, 40A-H5.1, RUSS; *CG*, 40th Cong., 2nd sess., 1868, 2260–67. The new charter, with the existing city council structure intact, passed May 28, 1868. See "An Act to Extend the Charter of Washington City, Also to Regulate the Selection of Officers, and for Other Purposes," *U.S. Statutes at Large*, 15:61–62.

58. *WNI*, July 16, 1868; Editorial, ibid., June 18, 1868. See also ibid., Feb. 14, 1868.

59. Ibid., Feb. 14, 1868; *New York World*, June 8, 1869. See also ibid., June 9, 1969. In fact, arrests in Washington declined steadily after the war, including in 1869 and 1870. The police board first noted a marked decline in crime in 1868 and attributed it to "a gradual settling down into a condition of peace." Between 1866 and 1870, African Americans were arrested at a higher rate than whites, but the total number of arrests of African Americans declined each year, along with the overall number

of arrests. *Report of the Board of Metropolitan Police for the Year 1866*, 604, 606; *Report of the Board of Metropolitan Police for the Year 1867*, 512, 514; *Report of the Board of Metropolitan Police for the Year 1868*, 880, 881, 883; *Report of the Board of Metropolitan Police for the Year 1869*, 1130–32; *Report of the Board of Metropolitan Police for the Year 1870*, 928, 930.

60. *WES*, Mar. 25, 1870, Feb. 3, 1870. See also ibid., May 14, 1870, for Bowen supporters portrayed as "boys as well as 'children of larger growth.'" On the changing editorial position of the *WES*, see also Howard Gillette, *Between Justice and Beauty*, 56–57; and Whyte, *Uncivil War*, 83–84.

61. Quoted in Howard Gillette, *Between Justice and Beauty*, 58 (spring 1870). See also Whyte, *Uncivil War*, 91.

62. David M. Kelsey to Hannibal Hamlin, Jan. 24, 1870, 41A-H5.2, RUSS.

63. *WC*, Jan. 13, 1870, Jan. 18, 1870; David M. Kelsey to Hannibal Hamlin, Jan. 24, 1870, 41A-H5.2, RUSS; Petition of William A. McCoy for Revision and Codification of Laws of the District of Columbia, Feb. 14, 1870, 41A-H5.2, RUSS.

64. *WC*, Mar. 19, 1970, Apr. 2, 1870; *WES*, Feb. 3, 1870. For the bill's trajectory in Congress, see Harrison, "From Biracial Democracy to Direct Rule," 246–49. See also Lessoff, *Nation and Its City*, 53; Bryan, *History of the National Capital*, 2:574–75; and Tindall, "Sketch of Alexander Robey Shepherd," 53–54.

65. Petition of A. G. Hall et al., Mar. 13, 1868, 40A-H5.1, RUSS. See also Petition of J. C. Lewis et al., 40A-H5.1, RUSS; Resolution of Washington Board of Common Council, Feb. 18, 1868, 40A-H5.1, RUSS; and Resolutions of the Board of Aldermen and Common Council, Feb. 3, 1870, 41A-H5.2, RUSS.

66. *WES*, Jan. 15, 1869.

67. *WES*, Feb. 17, 1870; Kate Masur, "New National Era," 441–42; Douglass, *Life and Writings of Frederick Douglass*, 225; McFeely, *Frederick Douglass*, 271.

68. *New Era*, Jan. 27, 1870. See also Tindall, "Sketch of Mayor Sayles J. Bowen," 41–42.

69. Editorial, *New Era*, Feb. 10, 1870.

70. *Journal of the Sixty-sixth Council*, 1:20–21; *Journal of the Sixty-seventh Council*, 1:80–81, 179–81; *WES*, Feb. 2, 1869; Sec. of the Senate to Hannibal Hamlin, July 12, 1870, 41A-E5, RUSS. Property was reassessed for tax purposes every five years. For Bowen's difficulties with Crane and other challenges, see *Journal of the Sixty-seventh Council*, 1:374; Whyte, *Uncivil War*, 80, 509–13, 687, 731–47, 772–73; Thomas Reed Johnson, "City on the Hill," 83, 86; and Constance McLaughlin Green, *Washington*, 1:327.

71. *WES*, Jan. 19, 1869, Feb. 17, 1870; *Journal of the Sixty-seventh Council*, 1:599. On Bowen explicitly seeking "the Irish vote" and German support, see *WNI*, June 1, 1868.

72. *WES*, Feb. 6, 1869, May 20, 1869, June 2, 1869; George W. Hatton to Mr. Kimball, Sept. 8, 1866, Unregistered Letters Received, Records of the Superintendent of Education for the District of Columbia, RBRFAL [A-10205]. Hatton's father was one of the few black slaveowners to seek compensation for his human property—in this case his remaining enslaved children—after Congress passed the D.C. Emancipation Act. *WNI*, May 21, 1862. On Hatton's early life, see also Terry, "Brief Moment in the Sun," 71.

73. On Hatton's opposition to Bowen, see *WC*, Jan. 14, 1870, Jan. 20, 1870. For Hatton on school integration, see *WC*, Jan. 18, 1870; and *WES*, Feb. 11, 1871. For the Gettysburg incident, see *WES*, July 13, 1869, July 15, 1869, July 21, 1869; and *Express*, July 12, 1869, July 13, 1869. See also Whyte, *Uncivil War*, 79–80; and Thomas Reed Johnson, "The City on the Hill," 67.

74. For the movement, see *New York Times*, Aug. 19, 1868; and *Chicago Tribune*, July 27, 1868,

Aug. 9, 1868. For the national meeting in Washington, see *Chicago Tribune*, Apr. 7, 1869. For the meeting with Grant, see *WNI*, Mar. 13, 1869. See also Gleeson, *Irish in the South*, 180; and Gibson, *Attitudes of the New York Irish*, 219–22, 233–34.

75. *WES*, Feb. 17, 1870. See also *WNI*, Sept. 25, 1868; and *WES*, Feb. 6, 1869, Apr. 16, 1869.

76. *WES*, May 5, 1869.

77. *WES*, Feb. 17, 1870. For similar rhetoric about the alliance between black and Irish Republicans, see ibid., May 14, 1869. For Irish Republican clubs in other wards in 1870, see *WES*, Feb. 11, 1870, Feb. 17, 1870.

78. For German Republican clubs, see *WC*, Apr. 8, 1867, Apr. 10, 1867. For the German Soldiers' and Sailors' Union, see *WES*, Jan. 21, 1869.

79. *WES*, Feb. 5, 1870, Feb. 19, 1870, May 7, 1870; *WC*, Jan. 28, 1870.

80. *WES*, Apr. 13, 1870. On Emery, see Henry and Spofford, *Eminent and Representative Men*, 114. See also Whyte, *Uncivil War*, 84–85.

81. Bowen quoted in Howard Gillette, *Between Justice and Beauty*, 58; and Josephine Griffing to Charles Sumner, May 26, 1870, reel 50, frame 600, CSP. Republican factionalism such as this was common in the Reconstruction South. See, for example, Powell, "Politics of Livelihood"; and Fitzgerald, *Urban Emancipation*.

82. Thomas Reed Johnson, "City on the Hill," 87–91; Lessoff, *Nation and Its City*, 43; Melvin Roscoe Williams, "Blueprint for Change," 384–92.

83. Lessoff, *Nation and Its City*, 54; Harrison, "From Biracial Democracy to Direct Rule," 246–49; Maury, *Alexander "Boss" Shepherd*, 4; Constance McLaughlin Green, *Washington*, 1:335–37.

84. Constance McLaughlin Green, *Washington*, 1:340; Maury, *Alexander "Boss" Shepherd*, 13; Lessoff, *Nation and Its City*, 50; Whyte, *Uncivil War*, 92; Osthaus, *Freedmen, Philanthropy, and Fraud*, 140–41.

85. *WES*, June 1, 1871.

86. Ibid., June 2, 1871.

87. Ibid., June 3, 1871.

88. Ibid., June 2, 1871; *WC*, June 3, 1871.

89. *WC*, June 5, 1871. The *WES* reported that the contractors had agreed to $2.00 per day, but the *WC*'s version seems more probable.

90. *WES*, June 5, 1871; *WC*, June 6, 1871.

91. *WC*, June 6, 1871; *WES*, June 6, 1871.

92. *WES*, June 6, 1871; *WC*, June 6, 1871. West later denied that he had advocated "blood for blood," though he maintained his stance on class antagonism. Card from Marcellus West, *WC*, June 8, 1871.

93. *WES*, June 7, 1871, June 8, 1871, June 6, 1871; *WC*, June 8, 1871.

94. *WES*, June 1, 1871, June 6, 1871; *WC*, June 7, 1871.

95. *WES*, June 6, 1871; *Washington Patriot*, June 7, 1871, June 8, 1871; *WC*, June 3, 1871. For similar strategies of protest by unskilled laborers elsewhere, see Montgomery, *Beyond Equality*, 144–45.

96. *WES*, June 6, 1871; *WC*, June 3, 1871, June 5, 1871, June 8, 1871, June 9, 1871.

97. H. D. Cooke to J. V. W. Vandenburg, *WES*, June 7, 1871, June 9, 1871.

98. Rachleff, *Black Labor in the South*, 82–108.

99. *WES*, June 9, 1871. The weekly *New National Era* noted that the strike was largely orderly and, in a separate story, complained of daily papers attempting "to cast odium upon colored people here." *New National Era*, June 8, 1871.

100. Editorial, *WC*, June 8, 1871.

101. Ibid.

102. "Make Haste Slowly," *WC*, June 8, 1871 (emphasis added). See also Editorial, *WC*, June 6, 1871.

103. Eric Foner, *Reconstruction*, 454.

Chapter 6

1. *WNR*, Aug. 9, 1873, July 4, 1873.

2. *WNR*, July 4, 1873.

3. Editorial, *WNR*, Sept. 15, 1873.

4. Constance McLaughlin Green, *Washington*, 1:340–45; Bryan, *History of the National Capital*, 2:592, 598–99; Whyte, *Uncivil War*, 106–9; Maury, *Alexander "Boss" Shepherd*, 7, 18.

5. Historians have never found direct evidence to that effect, but Shepherd's political acumen and extraordinary success makes the theory seem plausible. Coombs, *Address*, 2–3; *WC*, Jan. 13, 1870; Constance McLaughlin Green, *Washington*, 1:336.

6. Lessoff, *Nation and Its City*, 55–56, 84; Beauchamp, "Schools for All," 127; Constance McLaughlin Green, *Washington*, 1:346–47; Gutheim, *Worthy of the Nation*, 81–87; Maury, *Alexander "Boss" Shepherd*, 9, 32; Cowdrey, *City for the Nation*, 25–26; Bryan, *History of the National Capital*, 2:596–97; Tindall, "Sketch of Alexander Robey Shepherd," 57–58; Howe, "Board of Public Works."

7. Constance McLaughlin Green, *Washington*, 1:339; Gutheim, *Worthy of the Nation*, 81–90; Olynthus B. Clark, "Bid of the West for the National Capital."

8. Bryan, *History of the National Capital*, 2:603–5; Maury, *Alexander "Boss" Shepherd*, 9; Constance McLaughlin Green, *Washington*, 1:347; Whyte, *Uncivil War*, 114–17.

9. Chipman, *Speech of Hon. Norton P. Chipman*, 4–5. The 1871 territorial charter divided the District of Columbia into twenty-two election districts; in Washington, the new districts replaced the city's seven wards.

10. *Washington Citizen*, Oct. 6, 1871; *Washington Patriot*, Nov. 22, 1871; *New National Era*, Aug. 10, 1871; Whyte, *Uncivil War*, 120–21; Maury, *Alexander "Boss" Shepherd*, 10.

11. *Washington Citizen*, Oct. 9, 1871.

12. Lessoff, *Nation and Its City*, 57–60. See also Constance McLaughlin Green, *Washington*, 1:349–50; Maury, *Alexander "Boss" Shepherd*, 39; and Whyte, *Uncivil War*, 120–21.

13. Goldstein, "Washington and the Networks of W. W. Corcoran"; Henry and Spofford, *Eminent and Representative Men of Virginia and the District of Columbia*, 85–86; Lessoff, *Nation and Its City*, 52–53, 59; Proctor, *Washington*, 298–300; Levey, "Segregation in Education," 157.

14. *New National Era*, Aug. 10, 1871; Lessoff, *Nation and Its City*, 60–62; Whyte, *Uncivil War*, 122–23.

15. On New York's conservative "citizens" movement, which began after the 1863 draft riots, see Beckert, *Monied Metropolis*, 183–86; and Scobey, *Empire City*, 194. For "taxpayer" and "citizen" rhetoric in the South, see Beckert, *Monied Metropolis*, 227–28; Ryan, *Civic Wars*, 280; Richardson, *Death of Reconstruction*, 93, 95–97; Wrenn, *Crisis and Commission Government in Memphis*, 25; and Summers, *Railroads, Reconstruction*, 204–9, 280–85.

16. Lessoff, *Nation and Its City*, 56; Maury, *Alexander "Boss" Shepherd*, 17.

17. *Report of the Committee for the District of Columbia*, 1–2; Whyte, *Uncivil War*, 129; Summers,

Era of Good Stealings, 140. Contemporary supporters of the board cast doubt on the validity of the 1,000 signatories. Maury, *Alexander "Boss" Shepherd*, 39; Bryan, *History of the National Capital*, 2:605. For members of the urban elite pursuing their goals through courts, investigations, and tax evasion in other cities, see Ryan, *Civic Wars*, 277–80.

18. *Report of the Committee for the District of Columbia*, 373.

19. Ibid., 466–67.

20. Ibid., 467. See also ibid., 462 (testimony of R. D. Ruffin) and 475 (testimony of O. S. B. Wall). The territorial government had decided to hold an election for seats on the House of Delegates along with the loan vote.

21. Ibid., v.

22. Certificates of Appointment, box 89-1, Simms Family Papers, MSRC; Constance McLaughlin Green, *Washington*, 1:341; Bryan, *History of the National Capital*, 2:592; Whyte, *Uncivil War*, 112. See also Thomas Reed Johnson, "City on the Hill," 195–97.

23. For quotation, see Editorial, *New National Era*, Nov. 2, 1871. See also Editorial, *New National Era*, Oct. 26, 1871; and Editorial, ibid., Nov. 30, 1871. Whyte, *Uncivil War*, 150; Thomas Reed Johnson, "City on the Hill," 207–9.

24. *Report of the Committee for the District of Columbia*, 292, 442; *Washington Citizen*, Oct. 8, 1871; Maury, *Alexander "Boss" Shepherd*, 40; Whyte, *Uncivil War*, 150; Thomas Reed Johnson, "City on the Hill," 209–10.

25. *Report of the Committee for the District of Columbia*, xiii. See also Maury, *Alexander "Boss" Shepherd*, 40; and Whyte, *Uncivil War*, 130–41.

26. *Civil Rights Cases*, 109 U.S. 3 (1883) (emphasis added).

27. Lewis, "Political Mind of the Negro," 196; Kaczorowski, "Revolutionary Constitutionalism," 935–36; Flack, *Adoption of the Fourteenth Amendment*, 46–54; Franklin Johnson, *Development of State Legislation*; Riegel, "Persistent Career"; Lofgren, *Plessy Case*, 18–20; Keller, *Affairs of State*, 219; Eric Foner, *Reconstruction*, 369–71; James M. McPherson, "Abolitionists and the Civil Rights Act of 1875," 496–97; William Gillette, *Retreat from Reconstruction*, 193–96; McFeely, *Frederick Douglass*, 277–78.

28. Quoted in Avins, "Civil Rights Act of 1875," 876.

29. For a detailed account of the congressional debate, see ibid.

30. E. S. Atkinson et al. to Charles Sumner, May 6, 1872, reel 57, frame 188, CSP; Alldredge, *Centennial History of First Congregational*, 21–33; *WC*, Jan. 6, 1872, Jan. 18, 1872. See also ibid., Apr. 25, 1872, May 10, 1872.

31. *WC*, Jan. 6, 1872. See also Letter of D.A.S., *New National Era*, Feb. 8, 1872, Feb. 22, 1872, May 16, 1872; and *WC*, May 10, 1872. See also Lewis, "Political Mind of the Negro," esp. 196–97.

32. Kelly, "Congressional Controversy," 547–51; Avins, "Civil Rights Act of 1875"; William Gillette, *Retreat from Reconstruction*, 60–66, 197–210; Burg, "Amnesty, Civil Rights, and the Meaning of Liberal Republicanism."

33. *Chicago Tribune*, Jan. 24, 1872. See also "Color and Law," *Harper's Weekly*, Jan. 10, 1874, 27; *WNR*, Dec. 15, 1873; *WC*, May 10, 1872; Editorial, *Chicago Tribune*, Jan. 24, 1872; Editorial, ibid., Feb. 7, 1872; Avins, "Civil Rights Act of 1875"; and William Gillette, *Retreat from Reconstruction*, 190–94.

34. *CG*, 42nd Cong., 2nd sess., 1872, Appendix, 4; G.T.D. to Editor, *WC*, Jan. 31, 1872 (also printed in *New National Era*, Feb. 8, 1872). See also *Christian Recorder*, Apr. 20, 1872; *New National*

Era, May 2, 1872, May 16, 1872; *WC*, May 10, 1872; and Letter of George T. Downing to *WC*, in *New National Era*, May 30, 1872. Republican moderate Lyman Trubull also called the bill a "social rights" measure. Kelly, "Congressional Controversy," 548.

35. "An Act to Protect All Citizens in Their Civil and Legal Rights," *U.S. Statutes at Large*, 18:335–37; Kelly, "Congressional Controversy," 550–51; Avins, "Civil Rights Act of 1875," 894; Eric Foner, *Reconstruction*, 504–5, 532–33, 555–56.

36. M.C.A., "A Woman's Letter From Washington," *Independent*, Jan. 25, 1872.

37. Faith Lichen, "That Woman's Letter from Washington," *New National Era*, Feb. 22, 1872.

38. *WES*, Feb. 20, 1871, Aug. 9, 1871; *WC*, Aug. 10, 1871.

39. *WC*, May 10, 1872, June 12, 1872. See also Indritz, "Post Civil War Ordinances," 182–83; and Thomas Reed Johnson, "City on the Hill," 221.

40. *WC*, Dec. 7, 1872. See also Thomas Reed Johnson, "City on the Hill," 220–22.

41. For example, Fishel, "Repercussions of Reconstruction," 336–38; Welke, "When All the Women Were White," 285–88; Mack, "Law, Society, Identity," 389–92; Richardson, *Death of Reconstruction*, 133–34; and Omori, "Race-Neutral Individualism."

42. David A. Straker commented, "Our civil rights should be uniform and universal. . . . Separate schools are relics of the caste of Hindooism. Our white people the Brahmin, the negro the Sudra." *WNR*, July 9, 1873. For the fight against caste, see also *New National Era*, May 9, 1872; Letter of C. T. Garland, ibid., June 25, 1874; Letter of "LeB," *National Anti-Slavery Standard*, Dec. 4, 1869; and Sumner, *Charles Sumner: His Complete Works*, 17:34–52.

43. A twentieth-century parallel is the NAACP's postwar decision to deemphasize labor issues and focus on school segregation, as described in Goluboff, *Lost Promise of Civil Rights*.

44. *Report of the Joint Select Committee on the District of Columbia*, xv–xvi; Maury, *Alexander "Boss" Shepherd*, 51n27; Glassie, "Victorian Homes," 336–40.

45. *WNR*, July 19, 1873, Sept. 13, 1873. For the real estate market from the 1870s to the turn of the century, see Borchert, *Alley Life in Washington*, 28–35.

46. Jacob, *Capital Elites*, 66–100; Jacob, "Like Moths to a Candle"; Glassie, "Victorian Homes," 342–48; Constance McLaughlin Green, *Washington*, 1:437–38.

47. *WNR*, Aug. 9, 1873.

48. Ibid., Aug. 2, 1873, Aug. 9, 1873.

49. Schweninger, *Black Property Owners*, 180, 203–4.

50. Zina Fay Peirce, "The Externals of Washington," *Atlantic Monthly*, Dec. 1873, 703. See also Scobey, *Empire City*, 166–70.

51. *WNR*, Aug. 30, 1873.

52. Ibid., Aug. 2, 1873, Sept. 13, 1873. See also ibid., Sept. 15, 1873; and George Alfred Townsend, "New Washington," *Harper's New Monthly Magazine*, Feb. 1875, 309, 316.

53. Borchert, *Alley Life in Washington*, 23–28, 42; Johnston, *Surviving Freedom*, 7–12.

54. "Olivia" to A. R. Shepherd, Apr. 29, 1873, and "Olivia" to A. R. Shepherd, Oct. 24, 1873, both in Shepherd Papers, box 4, LC. See also Whyte, *Uncivil War*, 143–48; Constance McLaughlin Green, *Washington*, 1:352; Maury, *Alexander "Boss" Shepherd*, 24, 29, 34–35; and Glassie, "Victorian Homes," 336–40.

55. *New National Era and Citizen*, May 29, 1873; Lessoff, *Nation and Its City*, 73; Maury, *Alexander "Boss" Shepherd*, 42–43, 48; Constance McLaughlin Green, *Washington*, 1:357.

56. Adams, *Our Little Monarchy*; Crane, *More about the Washington Tammany*; Zina Fay Peirce,

"The Externals of Washington," *Atlantic Monthly*, Dec. 1873, 711; Lessoff, *Nation and Its City*, 75; Summers, *Era of Good Stealings*, 145–46.

57. "New Washington," *Lippincott's Magazine* 11 (1873): 306. See also Constance McLaughlin Green, *Washington*, 1:354–55.

58. *CG*, 42nd Cong., 3rd sess., 1873, 85, 851–52, 868, 870, 1040, 1421, 2153; *Journal of the Senate of the United States of America, 1789–1873*, Mar. 3, 1873, 561; *WNR*, Mar. 15, 1873, Mar. 17, 1873, Apr. 1, 1873, Apr. 3, 1873. The measure that placed the black schools under the territorial government's control reflected radical Republicans' ongoing diminution in Congress. In the House, the District's representative, Norton Chipman, had proposed a bill to increase the number of trustees, a goal long sought by many black residents. Representative Robert Roosevelt, a critic of the Shepherd administration, had, in turn, proposed to place the black schools under the territorial government. Roosevelt's measure lost, but the Senate's Committee on the District of Columbia soon proposed a similar measure, which eventually passed the entire Congress. Charles Sumner's marginalization in the Senate undoubtedly helped make this change possible.

59. Few preparatory high schools for black students existed anywhere, and Washington's attracted black teachers of considerable renown. In 1871, the school was located in the regal new Sumner School building (designed by architect Adolf Cluss). The principal was Mary Jane Patterson, the first black woman to graduate from Oberlin College. During the 1872–73 school year, the high school's staff included Philadelphia-born Charlotte Forten, daughter of a prominent black abolitionist, and army surgeon and civil rights activist Alexander T. Augusta, who taught anatomy, physiology, and hygiene. *Report of the Board of Trustees of Colored Schools of Washington and Georgetown*; *New National Era and Citizen*, July 23, 1873; Sterling, *We Are Your Sisters*, 285; Augusta to Board of Trustees, *New National Era and Citizen*, Sept. 11, 1873, Feb. 26, 1874. For Greener's later life, see Blakley, "Richard T. Greener."

60. *WNR*, June 28, 1873, Aug. 7, 1873.

61. *New National Era and Citizen*, June 19, 1873.

62. Editorial, *New National Era and Citizen*, July 10, 1873; *WNR*, July 9, 1873.

63. *WNR*, July 17, 1873.

64. Ibid., July 19, 1873. See also Letter of "Coming Again," ibid., July 25, 1873; and Whyte, *Uncivil War*, 165–66.

65. *WNR*, Aug. 25, 1873. See also ibid., Aug. 26, 1873.

66. *WNR*, July 10, 1873, July 19, 1873; Letter of "Coming Again," ibid., July 25, 1873; ibid., Aug. 25, 1873.

67. *WNR*, July 11, 1873. See also *New National Era and Citizen*, May 29, 1873; *New National Era and Citizen*, July 17, 1873. For the dilemma, see also Belz, "Freedmen's Bureau Act of 1865."

68. Letter of "Coming Again," *WNR*, July 25, 1873. See also Letter of "A Looking-on in Venice," ibid., July 22, 1873. As Michael Fitzgerald showed in *Urban Emancipation*, tensions between race-blind universalism and African Americans' race-based organizing also surfaced among Republicans in Mobile, Alabama.

69. Foner and Walker, *Proceedings of the Black National and State Conventions*, 366, 368. See also Hugh Davis, "Pennsylvania State Equal Rights League," esp. 617–21, 630–31.

70. Editorial, *New National Era and Citizen*, Dec. 18, 1873. For Langston, see *WC*, Jan. 6, 1872.

71. Editorial, *WNR*, Aug. 25, 1873; *WNR* quoted in *New National Era and Citizen*, Sept. 11, 1873. See also *WNR*, Sept. 2, 1873.

72. Letter of "Sphinx," *New National Era and Citizen*, Oct. 2, 1873. See also ibid., Dec. 18, 1873.

73. *Chicago Tribune*, Jan. 24, 1872. See also ibid., Feb. 23, 1870, from the *New York Herald*; sources quoted in Richardson, *Death of Reconstruction*, 134; Keyssar, *Right to Vote*, 137. See also Jung, *Coolies and Cane*, 136–45; Keller, *Affairs of State*, 153–58; Eric Foner, *Reconstruction*, 462–64; and Pascoe, *What Comes Naturally*, 77–108.

74. On Chillicothe, see *Chicago Tribune*, Aug. 23, 1873, Aug. 24, 1873, Sept. 6, 1873, Sept. 9, 1873; and Gerber, *Black Ohio and the Color Line*, 219–23. On Virginia, see *Chicago Tribune*, Aug. 29, 1873; and *New National Era and Citizen*, Sept. 11, 1873. See also *WNR*, Sept. 4, 1873; Editorial, ibid., Sept. 5, 1873; and Richardson, *Death of Reconstruction*, 109–10, 130.

75. *WNR*, Aug. 25, 1873; Letter of "One Who Knows," ibid., Aug. 29, 1873.

76. Letter of Richard T. Greener, *New York Times*, Aug. 30, 1873, Aug. 26, 1873, Aug. 28, 1873.

77. Letter of "Equal Rights for All," *New National Era and Citizen*, Sept. 11, 1873.

78. *WNR*, Sept. 12, 1873. See also *WC*, Sept. 12, 1873; and *WES*, Sept. 6, 1873, Sept. 9, 1873, Sept. 11, 1873, Sept. 16, 1873. For Michael Shiner, see *WES*, Feb. 9, 1870; and USMPCDC, 1860.

79. *WES*, Sept. 6, 1873, Sept. 2, 1873, Sept. 11, 1873, Sept. 27, 1873, Oct. 1, 1873.

80. *WNR*, Sept. 15, 1873.

81. *New National Era and Citizen*, Oct. 2, 1873.

82. Letter of "Sphinx," *New National Era and Citizen*, Oct. 2, 1873. See also Editorial, ibid., Nov. 13, 1873.

83. Editorial, *WNR*, Sept. 15, 1873; Oberholtzer, *Jay Cooke*, 417; Whyte, *Uncivil War*, 168–69.

84. Oberholtzer, *Jay Cooke*, 422–23; Eric Foner, *Reconstruction*, 512–24; Beckert, *Monied Metropolis*, 207–10; Rabinowitz, "Continuity and Change," 102.

85. *Historical Sketches of the Charities and Reformatory Institutions*, 156–59. See also Oberholtzer, *Jay Cooke*, 416–17; Whyte, *Uncivil War*, 170–72; and Maury, *Alexander "Boss" Shepherd*, 22–24.

86. *WES*, Sept. 18, 1873.

87. Editorial, *New National Era and Citizen*, Oct. 9, 1873.

88. Editorial, ibid., Nov. 13, 1873.

89. Ibid.; *Chicago Tribune*, Oct. 10, 1873; Gerber, *Black Ohio and the Color Line*, 222; William Gillette, *Retreat from Reconstruction*, 186–87.

90. *WES*, Oct. 15, 1873.

91. Ibid., Sept. 6, 1873, Sept. 16, 1873, Sept. 18, 1873, Oct. 1, 1873.

92. Ibid., Oct. 15, 1873.

93. J. Sella Martin to Alexander Shepherd, July 22, 1874, Alexander Shepherd Papers, box 4, LC. Another black supporter lamented that on canvassing "the colored people," he could "find but few who had sence enough to appreciate your work here." Isaiah Mitchell to Alexander Shepherd, June 29, 1874, ibid.

94. Quoted in James M. McPherson, "Grant or Greeley?" 50.

95. Whyte, *Uncivil War*, 176–77; Maury, *Alexander "Boss" Shepherd*, 46–48.

96. *Report of the Joint Select Committee on the District of Columbia*, vii. See also Harrison, "From Biracial Democracy to Direct Rule," 249–50; Lessoff, *Nation and Its City*, 77–83; Summers, *Era of Good Stealings*, 143–44; and Maury, *Alexander "Boss" Shepherd*, 47.

97. *Report of the Joint Select Committee on the District of Columbia*, viii.

98. Ibid., xii.

99. Ibid., viii.

100. Lessoff, *Nation and Its City*, 83; Teaford, *Unheralded Triumph*, 75–77; Griffith, *History of American City Government: The Conspicuous Failure*, 13–22, 38–41, 57–59; Griffith and Adrian, *His-*

tory of American City Government: The Formation of Traditions, 161; Wrenn, *Crisis and Commission Government in Memphis*, 29.

101. *WES*, June 23, 1874.

102. Ibid.

103. Editorial, ibid., June 24, 1874; *WNR*, June 24, 1874.

104. Editorial, *WES*, June 23, 1874. See also Adams, *Our Little Monarchy*, 16; and Joint Investigating Committee Report (South Carolina), cited in Wade Hampton, "What Negro Supremacy Means," *Forum* (June 1888), esp. 390–92.

105. Adams, *Our Little Monarchy*, 18; Piatt quoted in Whyte, *Uncivil War*, 213. For concerns that freedpeople's supposed lack of self-restraint would make them profligate spenders, see *American Freedmen's Inquiry Commission Report*, 67; *Extracts from Letters of Teachers and Superintendents*, 4; Holt, "Essence of the Contract"; and Hartman, *Scenes of Subjection*, chap. 5.

106. Editorial, *WES*, Sept. 9, 1874; "The Crime against Suffrage in Washington," *Nation*, June 27, 1878, 415. For the dual image of black political power as dangerously "Africanized" and also burlesque, see also Holt, *Black over White*, 95–98.

107. "How Shall We Govern the National Capital?" *Nation*, June 11, 1874, 375.

108. George Alfred Townsend, "New Washington," *Harper's New Monthly Magazine*, Feb. 1875, 314. See also "New Washington," *Lippincott's Magazine* 11 (1873): 306.

109. "The Crime against Suffrage in Washington," *Nation*, June 27, 1878, 415.

110. Beckert, *Monied Metropolis*, 218–24; quotation on p. 224. See also Quigley, *Second Founding*; Quigley, "Proud Name of 'Citizen'"; Summers, *Era of Good Stealings*, 148; and McGerr, *Decline of Popular Politics*, 49–50.

111. Richardson, *Death of Reconstruction*, 93–95, 114. For a like-minded interpretation of the District, see Harrison, "From Biracial Democracy to Direct Rule," 258. For another analysis of the relationship between economic and racial issues in the South, see Summers, *Railroads, Reconstruction*, 289–91. For historians' use of the cartoon, see Summers, *Era of Good Stealings*, 148–49; and Scobey, *Empire City*, 253–54. On northern suffrage reform, see also Yearley, *Money Machines*, 21–24; McGerr, *Decline of Popular Politics*; Sproat, *Best Men*; and Keyssar, *Right to Vote*, 141–46. For a contrasting perspective that emphasizes race but treats African Americans, New York Catholics, and Chinese immigrants under a single rubric, see Ryan, *Civic Wars*, 268–69, 302–3.

112. *WNR*, July 30, 1873.

113. *Views of the Minority*, 44th Cong., 2nd sess., 1877, S. Rept. 572, 24–25. For the congressional debate, see Kate Masur, "Reconstructing the Nation's Capital," 384–87; and Harrison, "From Biracial Democracy to Direct Rule," 253–56. On the restoration of home rule, see Howard Gillette, *Between Justice and Beauty*, 179, 190.

Epilogue

1. Letter of A. K. Browne, *WNR*, Nov. 21, 1874.

2. C. Meriwether, "Washington City Government," *Political Science Quarterly* 12, no. 3 (Sept. 1897): 419. For citizens' associations, see Cox, *Public Improvements*; and Lessoff, *Nation and Its City*, 204–8.

3. "A Study in City Government," *Nation*, Apr. 17, 1884, 335. See also Goldwyn Smith, "The Capital of the United States," *Macmillan's Magazine* 54 (July 1886): 169.

4. "The New Washington," *Century Magazine*, Mar. 1884, 648.

5. Lessoff, *Nation and Its City*, 98–99; Constance McLaughlin Green, *Washington*, 2:83; Cox, *Unveiling of a Statue*.

6. Margaret Noble Lee, "City Government of Washington, D.C." (Part 2), *Chautauquan*, Nov. 1895, 168, 169; Siddons, "Municipal Condition of Washington," 370, 373. For other expressions of reservations about denial of self-government in the capital, see "The New Washington," *Century Magazine*, Mar. 1884, 643; "A Study in City Government," *Nation*, Apr. 17, 1884; and Thomas Meehan, "Washington: Its Material Progress and the Cause," *Philadelphia Public Ledger*, Sept. 15, 1891.

7. Herbert et al., *Why the Solid South?*, 23–24. Similarly, see Page, *Negro*, 135–36.

8. Dunning, *Reconstruction*, 244–46.

9. *Civil Rights Cases*, 109 U.S. 3 (1883) (emphasis added).

10. *Proceedings of the Civil Rights Mass-Meeting*, 13; Harlan dissent in *Civil Rights Cases*, 109 U.S. 3 (1883).

11. Myrdal, *American Dilemma*, ix, 586.

12. Indritz, "Post Civil War Ordinances"; Beverly W. Jones, "Before Montgomery and Greensboro"; McCluskey, "Setting the Standard."

Works Cited

Primary Sources

Archival and Manuscript Collections

Bryn Mawr, Pa.
    Haverford College
        Julia Wilbur Papers
Cambridge, Mass.
    Harvard University
        Charles Sumner Papers (Chadwyck-Healey, 1988)
College Park, Md., and Washington, D.C.
    National Archives and Records Administration
        Records of the District of Columbia Supreme Court (RG 21)
        Records of the United States Senate (RG 46)
        Records of the Office of the Secretary of the Interior (1826–1981) (RG 48)
        Records of the Office of the Quartermaster General (1774–1985) (RG 92)
        Records of the Bureau of Refugees, Freedmen, and Abandoned Lands (RG 105)
        Records of the United States House of Representatives (RG 233)
        Records of the United States Supreme Court (RG 267)
        Records of the United States Army Continental Commands, 1821–1920 (RG 393)
        Records of St. Elizabeth's Hospital (RG 418)
        Records of the Office of the Secretary of the Interior Relating to the Suppression of the African Slave Trade and Negro Colonization, 1854–1872, National Archives Microfilm Publication M160
College Park, Md.
    University of Maryland
        Freedmen and Southern Society Project Archive
Ithaca, N.Y.
    Cornell University
        Emily Howland Papers and Additional Papers
        Samuel J. May Antislavery Collection
        Samuel J. May Manuscript Collection
New York, N.Y.
    Columbia University
        Josephine Griffing Collection

Rochester, N.Y.
    University of Rochester
        Frederick Douglass Papers
        Post Family Papers
Swarthmore, Pa.
    Swarthmore College
        Emily Howland Papers
Washington, D.C.
    Howard University, Moorland Spingarn Research Center
        O. O. Howard Papers
        Metropolitan AME Church Papers
        Simms Family Papers
Washington, D.C.
    Library of Congress
        American Colonization Society Papers
        Christian Fleetwood Papers
        Andrew Johnson Papers
        Abraham Lincoln Papers
        William Owner Diary
        Alexander Shepherd Papers
Washington, D.C.
    Sumner School Museum
        Papers of the District of Columbia Public Schools

Periodicals

NEWSPAPERS

Anglo-African (New York)
Baltimore Sun
Boston Daily Advertiser
Charleston (S.C.) Courier
Chicago Tribune
Christian Recorder (Philadelphia)
Constitutional Union (Washington)
Daily Citizen and News (Lowell, Mass.)
Daily Cleveland Herald
Frank Leslie's Illustrated Newspaper (New York)
Liberator (Boston)
Milwaukee Daily Sentinel
National Anti-Slavery Standard (New York)
National Freedman (New York)
Newark (Ohio) Advocate

New Era, New National Era (Washington, D.C.)
New Hampshire Statesman (Concord)
New Haven Daily Palladium (Montpelier)
New York Herald
New York Times
New York Sun
New York World
Revolution (New York)
San Francisco Daily Evening Bulletin
San Francisco Pacific Appeal
Vermont Watchman and State Journal
Washington Chronicle
Washington Citizen
Washington Evening Star
Washington Express

Washington *National Intelligencer*
Washington *National Republican*
Washington *Patriot*

Washington Post
Weekly Georgia Telegraph (Macon)

MAGAZINES

Atlantic Monthly
Century Magazine
Chautauquan
Douglass's Monthly
Harper's New Monthly Magazine
Harper's Weekly

Lippincott's Magazine
Macmillan's Magazine
Nation
Overland Monthly
Woman's Advocate

UNITED STATES GOVERNMENT DOCUMENTS

Alvord, J. W. *Third Semi-Annual Report on Schools for Freedmen, Jan. 1, 1867*. Washington, D.C.: Government Printing Office, 1867.

————. *Fourth Semi-Annual Report on Schools for Freedmen, July 1, 1867*. Washington, D.C.: Government Printing Office, 1867.

————. *Fifth Semi-Annual Report on Schools for Freedmen, Jan. 1, 1867*. Washington, D.C.: Government Printing Office, 1868.

————. *Sixth Semi-Annual Report on Schools for Freedmen, July 1, 1868*. Washington, D.C.: Government Printing Office, 1868.

————. *Eighth Semi-Annual Report on Schools for Freedmen, July 1, 1869*. Washington, D.C.: Government Printing Office, 1869.

American Freedmen's Inquiry Commission Report. In *Report of the Secretary of War*, 38th Cong., 1st sess., 1864, S. Exec. Doc. 53.

Annual Report of the Secretary of War, Nov. 14, 1866. In *Message of the President of the United States and Accompanying Documents*. 39th Cong., 2nd sess., 1866, H. Exec. Doc. 1.

Barnard, Henry. *Special Report of the Commissioner of Education on the Condition and Improvement of Public Schools in the District of Columbia*. 41st Cong., 2nd sess., 1871, H. Exec. Doc. 315.

Bill in Addition to the Several Acts for Establishing the Temporary and Permanent Seat of the Government of the United States. Senate bill 97. 39th Cong., 1st sess., 1866.

Committee on the District of Columbia. *Report*. 40th Cong., 2nd sess., 1868, S. Rept. Com. 131.

Congressional Globe

Congressional Record

Goodwin, Moses B. "History of Schools for the Colored Population in the District of Columbia." Part I of *Special Report of the Commissioner of Education on the Condition and Improvement of Public Schools in the District of Columbia*. 41st Cong., 2nd sess., 1871, H. Exec. Doc. 315.

Historical Sketches of the Charities and Reformatory Institutions in the District of Columbia. 55th Cong., 1st sess., 1898, S. Doc. 185.

Letter of Daniel Breed, Mar. 11, 1864. 38th Cong., 1st sess., 1864, H. Misc. Doc. 48.

Journal of the Senate of the United States of America, 1789–1873. 40th Cong., 3rd sess., 1869.

Kennedy, Joseph C. G. *Population of the United States in 1860; Compiled from the Original Returns of the Eighth Census.* Vol. 1. Washington, D.C.: Government Printing Office, 1864.

Laws of the Corporation of the City of Washington, Passed by the Sixty-sixth Council. Washington: Chronicle Print, 1869.

Memorial of Soldiers in Service of the United States. 40th Cong., 2nd sess., 1869, S. Misc. Doc. 99.

Petition of the National Executive Committee of the Colored People, Apr. 29, 1870. 41st Cong., 2nd sess., 1870, S. Misc. Doc. 130.

Petition of the Citizens of the District of Columbia. 41st Cong., 1st sess., 1869, S. Misc. Doc. 24.

Presidential Message Vetoing Act Transferring Duties of Trustees of Colored Schools of Washington and Georgetown. 40th Cong., 3rd sess., 1869, S. Exec. Doc. 47.

Report of the Board of Metropolitan Police for the Year 1865. 39th Cong., 1st sess., H. Exec. Doc. 1.

Report of the Board of Metropolitan Police for the Year 1866. 39th Cong., 2nd sess., H. Exec. Doc. 1.

Report of the Board of Metropolitan Police for the Year 1867. 40th Cong., 2nd sess., 1867, H. Exec. Doc. 1.

Report of the Board of Metropolitan Police for the Year 1868. 40th Cong., 3rd sess., 1868, H. Exec. Doc. 1.

Report of the Board of Metropolitan Police for the Year 1869. 41st Cong., 2nd sess., H. Exec. Doc. 1.

Report of the Board of Metropolitan Police for the Year 1870. 41st Cong., 3rd sess., 1870, H. Exec. Doc. 1.

Report of the Committee for the District of Columbia. 42nd Cong., 2nd sess., 1872, H. Rept. 72.

Report of the Committee on the District of Columbia, Feb. 24, 1864. 38th Cong., 1st sess., 1864, S. Rept. Com. 17.

Report of the Committee on the Judiciary. 41st Cong., 3rd sess., H. Rept. 22.

Report of the Joint Select Committee on the District of Columbia. 43rd Cong., 1st sess., 1874, S. Rept. 453.

Report of the Operations of the Bureau of Refugees, Freedmen, and Abandoned Lands for the District of Columbia, Embracing the Period from November 1, 1865, to September 30, 1866. Sen. 39A-E4, RG 46. Records of the United States Senate, National Archives and Records Administration.

Report of the Secretary of the Senate. 37th Cong., 2nd sess., 1861, S. Misc. Doc. 66.

Report of the Secretary of the Senate. 37th Cong., 3rd sess., 1862, S. Misc. Doc. 11.

Report of the Secretary of the Senate. 43rd Cong., 2nd sess., 1874, S. Misc. Doc. 74.

Report of the Secretary of the Senate. 44th Cong., 1st sess., 1875, S. Misc. Doc. 1.

Report of the Secretary of War, Part I, Nov. 1867. In *Message of the President of the United States and Accompanying Documents.* 40th Cong., 2nd sess., 1867, H. Exec. Doc. 1.

Report to Accompany Bill S. 511. 41st Cong., 2nd sess., 1870, S. Rept. 29.

Summary Report of the District of Columbia. In *Letter from the Secretary of War.* 39th Cong., 1st sess., 1866, H. Exec. Doc. 70.

U.S. Bureau of the Census. *Historical Statistics of the United States, Colonial Times to 1970.* Bicentennial Edition, Part 1. Washington, D.C., 1975.

United States Senate Catalogue of Graphic Art, with essays by Diane K. Skvarla and Donald A. Ritchie. Prepared by the Office of Senate Curator under the direction of the U.S. Senate Commission on Art. Washington, D.C.: Government Printing Office, 2006.

U.S. Statutes at Large

Walker, Francis A. *The Statistics of the Population of the United States, Embracing the Tables of*

Race, Nationality, Sex, Selected Ages, and Occupations . . . from the Original Returns of the Ninth Census. Vol. 1. Washington, D.C.: Government Printing Office, 1872.

Printed Primary Sources

Adams, Francis Colburn. *Our Little Monarchy: Who Runs It, and What It Costs.* Washington, D.C.: F. A. Fills, 1873.

Adams, Lois Bryan. *Letter from Washington, 1863–1865.* Edited with an introduction by Evelyn Leasher. Detroit: Wayne State University Press, 1999.

Ashon, J. Hubley, ed. *Official Opinions of the Attorneys General of the United States.* Vol. 10. Washington, D.C.: W. H. & O. Morrison, 1868.

Berlin, Ira, Barbara J. Fields, Thavolia Glymph, Joseph P. Reidy, and Leslie S. Rowland, eds. *The Destruction of Slavery.* Series 1, vol. 1, of *Freedom: A Documentary History of Emancipation, 1861–1867.* New York: Cambridge University Press, 1982.

Berlin, Ira, Steven F. Miller, Joseph P. Reidy, and Leslie S. Rowland, eds. *The Wartime Genesis of Free Labor: The Upper South.* Series 1, vol. 2, of *Freedom: A Documentary History of Emancipation, 1861–1867.* New York: Cambridge University Press, 1993.

Berlin, Ira, Joseph P. Reidy, and Leslie S. Rowland, eds. *The Black Military Experience.* Series 2 of *Freedom: A Documentary History of Emancipation, 1861–1867.* New York: Cambridge University Press, 1982.

Bowen, Sayles J. *Message of the Mayor of the City of Washington.* Washington, D.C.: Chronicle Print, [1869].

———. *Message of the Mayor to the Boards of Aldermen and Common Council.* Washington, D.C.: Chronicle Print, 1868.

Boyd's Directory of Washington and Georgetown. Washington, D.C., 1867, 1869, 1870.

Briggs, Emily Edson. *The Olivia Letters.* New York: Neale Publishing, 1906.

Brooks, Noah. *Washington, D.C., in Lincoln's Time: A Memoir of the Civil War Era by the Newspaperman Who Knew Lincoln Best.* Edited by Herbert Mitgang. 1895. Athens: University of Georgia Press, 1989.

Busey, Samuel C. *Personal Reminiscences and Recollections of Forty-six Years' Membership in the Medical Society of the District of Columbia.* Philadelphia: Dornan Printers, 1895.

Callan, John F. *The Military Laws of the United States: Relating to the Army, Volunteers, Militia, and to Bounty Lands and Pensions, from the Foundation of the Government to 3 March 1863.* Philadelphia: G. W. Childs, 1863.

Celebration by the Colored People's Educational Monument Association in Memory of Abraham Lincoln on the Fourth of July, 1865, in the Presidential Grounds, Washington, D.C. McGill and Witherow, 1865.

Chipman, Norton P. *Speech of Hon. Norton P. Chipman of the District of Columbia, June 3, 1872.* Washington, D.C.: F. and J. Rives/Geo. A. Bailey, 1872.

Coffin, Carlton. *Drum-Beat of the Nation: The First Period of the War of the Rebellion from Its Outbreak to the Close of 1862.* New York: Harper, 1888.

Colman, Lucy N. *Reminiscences.* Buffalo, N.Y.: H. L. Green, 1891.

Coombs, J. J. *Address Delivered by J. J. Coombs, Esq., Aug. 19, 1872.* N.p., [1872].

Cox, William Van Zandt. *Public Improvements Secured in the Northern Section of the District of*

Columbia by the Brightwood Avenue Citizens' Association. Washington, D.C.: W. F. Roberts, 1898.

————, ed. *The Unveiling of a Statue to the Memory of Alexander R. Shepherd in Front of the District Building, Washington, D.C., May 3, 1909.* Washington, D.C., 1909.

Dickens, Charles. *American Notes for General Circulation.* 1842. New York: Viking Penguin, 2001.

Douglass, Frederick. *Frederick Douglass on Women's Rights,* edited by Philip S. Foner. Westport, Conn.: Greenwood Press, 1976.

————. *The Life and Times of Frederick Douglass, Written by Himself.* 1881. New York: Carol Publishing Group, 1995.

————. *The Life and Writings of Frederick Douglass.* Edited by Philip S. Foner. Vol. 4. New York: International Publishers, 1955.

Dunning, William Archibald. *Reconstruction: Political and Economic.* New York: Harper, 1907.

Extracts from Letters of Teachers and Superintendents of the New-England Freedmen's Aid Society. Fifth Series. Boston: John Wilson, 1864.

First Annual Report of the National Freedman's Relief Association of the District of Columbia. Washington, D.C.: McGill and Witherow, 1863.

Foner, Philip S., and George E. Walker, eds. *Proceedings of the Black National and State Conventions, 1865–1900.* Philadelphia: Temple University Press, 1986.

————, eds. *Proceedings of the Black State Conventions, 1840–1865.* Vol. 1. Philadelphia: Temple University Press, 1980.

French, Benjamin Brown. *Witness to the Young Republic: A Yankee's Journal, 1828–1870.* Edited by Donald B. Cole and John J. McDonough. Hanover, N.H.: University Press of New England, 1989.

Garnet, Henry Highland. *A Memorial Discourse; by Rev. Henry Highland Garnet.* Philadelphia: Joseph M. Wilson, 1865.

Haviland, Laura S. *A Woman's Life-Work: Labors and Experiences of Laura S. Haviland.* Chicago: C. V. Waite, 1887.

Henry, William Wirt, and Ainsworth Rand Spofford. *Eminent and Representative Men of Virginia and the District of Columbia in the Nineteenth Century.* Madison, Wis.: Brant and Fuller, 1893.

Herbert, Hilary A., et al., eds. *Why the Solid South? Or, Reconstruction and Its Results.* 1890. New York: Negro Universities Press, 1969.

Holmes, James H. *Report on the Condition of the Cause of Woman Suffrage.* Washington, D.C.: Universal Franchise Association, 1868. In *History of Women* Microfilm Collection, no. 8801. New Haven: Research Publications, 1977.

Howard, Oliver Otis. *Autobiography of Oliver Otis Howard.* Vol. 2. New York: Baker and Taylor, 1907.

Johannsen, Robert W., ed. *The Lincoln-Douglas Debates of 1858.* 150th Anniversary Edition. New York: Oxford University Press, 2008.

Johnson, Andrew. *The Papers of Andrew Johnson.* Edited by LeRoy P. Graf et al. Vols. 10 and 11. Knoxville: University of Tennessee Press, 1991, 1992.

Journals of the City Council of Washington. Washington, D.C.: various printers, 1866–70.

Kasson, Caroline Eliot. "An Iowa Woman in Washington, D.C., 1861–1865." *Iowa Journal of History* 52 (January 1954): 61–90.

Keckley, Elizabeth. *Behind the Scenes, or Thirty Years a Slave, and Four Years in the White House.*

1868. Schomburg Library of Black Women Writers edition. New York: Oxford University Press, 1988.

Laws of the Corporation of the City of Washington Passed by the Sixty-fourth Council. Washington, D.C.: Joseph L. Pearson, 1867.

Lincoln, Abraham. *Collected Works of Abraham Lincoln.* Edited by Roy P. Basler. Vol. 5. New Brunswick, N.J.: Rutgers University Press, 1953.

Mackey, Franklin H., ed. *District of Columbia Reports.* Vol. 6. Washington, D.C.: Law Reporter Print, 1889.

Masur, Louis P., ed. *The Real War Will Never Get into the Books: Selections from Writers during the Civil War.* New York: Oxford University Press, 1993.

McPherson, Edward. *The Political History of the United States of America during the Period of Reconstruction.* 1875. New York: Negro Universities Press, 1969.

Moore, William W. *Contraband Suffrage.* Washington, D.C.: J. L. Pearson, [1867].

Page, Thomas Nelson. *The Negro: The Southerner's Problem.* 1904. New York: Johnson Rept. Corp., 1970.

Payne, Daniel A. *Welcome to the Ransomed, or, Duties of the Colored Inhabitants of the District of Columbia.* Baltimore: Bull and Tuttle, 1862.

Pierce, Edward L. *Memoir and Letters of Charles Sumner.* Vol. 4. Boston: Roberts Brothers, 1893.

Proceedings of the Civil Rights Mass-Meeting Held at Lincoln Hall, October 22, 1883. Washington, D.C., 1883.

Proceedings of the Colored National Labor Convention. Washington, D.C.: New Era, 1870.

Proceedings of the Eleventh National Woman's Rights Convention, Held at the Church of the Puritans, New York, May 10, 1866. New York: Robert J. Johnston, 1866.

Reid, Whitelaw. *A Radical View: The "Agate" Dispatches of Whitelaw Reid, 1861–1865.* Vol. 2. Edited by James G. Smart. Memphis, Tenn.: Memphis State University Press, 1976.

Report of the Board of Trustees of Colored Schools of Washington and Georgetown, D.C. Washington, D.C.: McGill and Witherow, 1871.

Ripley, C. Peter, et al., eds. *The United States, 1859–1865.* Vol. 5 of *The Black Abolitionist Papers.* Chapel Hill: University of North Carolina Press, 1992.

Second Annual Report of the Freedmen and Soldiers' Relief Association (Late Contraband Relief Association). Washington, D.C.: Chronicle Print, 1864.

Second Annual Report of the National Freedman's Relief Association of the District of Columbia. Washington, D.C.: McGill and Witherow, 1864.

Second Annual Report of the New England Freedmen's Aid Society. Boston: The Society, 1864.

Siddons, Frederick L. "Municipal Condition of Washington." In *Proceedings of the Second National Conference for Good City Government.* Philadelphia: National Municipal League, 1895.

Sixth Annual Report of the Executive Board of the Friends' Association of Philadelphia and Its Vicinity, for the Relief of Colored Freedmen. Philadelphia: Sherman, 1869.

Stanton, Elizabeth Cady, and Susan B. Anthony. *In the School of Anti-Slavery, 1840–1866.* Vol. 1 of *The Selected Papers of Elizabeth Cady Stanton and Susan B. Anthony.* Edited by Ann D. Gordon. New Brunswick, N.J.: Rutgers University Press, 1997.

———. *Against an Aristocracy of Sex, 1866 to 1873.* Vol. 2 of *The Selected Papers of Elizabeth Cady Stanton and Susan B. Anthony.* Edited by Ann D. Gordon. New Brunswick, N.J.: Rutgers University Press, 1997.

Stanton, Elizabeth Cady, Susan B. Anthony, and Matilda Joslyn Gage, eds. *History of Woman Suffrage*. 4 vols. 1881. New York: Source Book Press, 1970.

Sterling, Dorothy, ed. *We Are Your Sisters: Black Women in the Nineteenth Century*. New York: W. W. Norton, 1984.

Stoddard, William O. *Inside the White House in War Times: Memoirs and Reports of Lincoln's Secretary*. Edited by Michael Burlingame. Lincoln: University of Nebraska Press, 2000.

Sumner, Charles. *Charles Sumner: His Complete Works*. 20 vols. Introduction by George Frisbie Hoar. Boston: Lee and Shepard, 1900.

Truth, Sojourner. *Narrative of Sojourner Truth; a Bondswoman of Olden Time, with a History of Her Labors and Correspondence Drawn from Her "Book of Life."* Edited by Olive Gilbert. Battle Creek, Mich., 1878.

Turner, H. M. "Reminiscences of the Proclamation of Emancipation." In *The Negro in Slavery: War and Peace*. Philadelphia: AME Book Concern, 1913.

Twentieth Annual Report of the Board of Trustees of the Public Schools of the City of Washington. Washington, D.C.: McGill and Witherow, 1865.

Twenty-second Annual Report of the Board of Trustees of the Public Schools of the City of Washington. Washington, D.C.: McGill and Witherow, 1867.

Whitman, Walt. *Complete Prose Works*. Philadelphia: David McKay, 1892.

———. *Specimen Days and Collect*. 1883. Mineola, N.Y.: Dover, 1995.

Willcox, J. K. H. *Suffrage a Right, Not a Privilege*. Washington, D.C.: Universal Franchise Association, 1867. In *History of Women* Microfilm Collection, doc. 8799. New Haven: Research Publications, 1977.

Secondary Sources

Abbott, Richard H. *The Republican Party in the South, 1855–1877: The First Southern Strategy*. Chapel Hill: University of North Carolina Press, 1986.

Alfers, Kenneth G. *Law and Order in the Capital City: A History of the Washington Police, 1800–1886*. George Washington University Studies, no. 5. Washington, D.C.: George Washington University, 1976.

Alldredge, Everett O. *Centennial History of First Congregational United Church of Christ, Washington, D.C., 1865–1965*. Baltimore: Port City Press, 1965.

Allen, William C. *History of Slave Laborers in the Construction of the United States Capitol*. Office of the Architect of the Capitol, June 1, 2005; pdf available at http://clerk.house.gov/art_history/art_artifacts/, accessed 7/16/2008.

Anderson, James D. *The Education of Blacks in the South, 1860–1935*. Chapel Hill: University of North Carolina Press, 1988.

Angell, Stephen Ward. *Bishop Henry McNeal Turner and African-American Religion in the South*. Knoxville: University of Tennessee Press, 1992.

Aptheker, Bettina. *Woman's Legacy: Essays on Race, Sex, and Class in American History*. Amherst: University of Massachusetts Press, 1982.

Arnebeck, Bob. *Through a Fiery Trial: Building Washington, 1790–1900*. Lanham, Md.: Madison Books, 1991.

Arnesen, Eric. *Waterfront Workers of New Orleans: Race, Class, and Politics, 1863–1923*. New York: Oxford University Press, 1991.

Aron, Cindy Sondik. *Ladies and Gentlemen of the Civil Service: Middle-Class Workers in Victorian America*. New York: Oxford University Press, 1987.

Avins, Alfred. "The Civil Rights Act of 1875: Some Reflected Light on the Fourteenth Amendment and Public Accommodations." *Columbia Law Review* 66, no. 5 (May 1966): 873–915.

Barkley Brown, Elsa. "To Catch the Vision of Freedom: Reconstructing Southern Black Women's Political History, 1865–1880." In *African American Women and the Vote, 1837–1965*, edited by Ann D. Gordon et al. Amherst: University of Massachusetts Press, 1997.

———. "Negotiating and Transforming the Public Sphere: African American Political Life in the Transition from Slavery to Freedom." *Public Culture* 7 (Fall 1994): 107–46.

Barkley Brown, Elsa, and Gregg D. Kimball. "Mapping the Terrain of Black Richmond." *Journal of Urban History* 21 (March 1995): 296–346.

Barnard, Job. "Early Days of the Supreme Court of the District of Columbia." *Records of the Columbia Historical Society* 22 (1919): 1–35.

Beauchamp, Tanya Edwards. "Schools for All: Adolf Cluss and Education." In *Adolf Cluss, Architect: From Germany to America*, edited by Alan Lessoff and Christof Mauch. New York: Berghahn Books, 2005.

Beckert, Sven. *The Monied Metropolis: New York City and the Consolidation of the American Bourgeoisie, 1850–1896*. New York: Cambridge University Press, 2001.

Bederman, Gail. *Manliness and Civilization: A Cultural History of Gender and Race in the United States, 1880–1917*. Chicago: University of Chicago Press, 1995.

Belz, Herman. "The Freedmen's Bureau Act of 1865 and the Principle of No Discrimination According to Color." *Civil War History* 21 (Fall 1975): 197–217.

———. "Origins of Negro Suffrage during the Civil War." *Southern Studies: An Interdisciplinary Journal of the South* 17, no. 2 (1978): 115–30.

Benedict, Michael Les. *A Compromise of Principle: Congressional Republicans and Reconstruction, 1863–1869*. New York: Norton, 1974.

———. "Preserving the Constitution: The Conservative Basis of Radical Reconstruction." *Journal of American History* 61, no. 1 (June 1974): 65–90.

Bentley, George R. *A History of the Freedmen's Bureau*. Philadelphia: University of Pennsylvania Press, 1955.

Bercaw, Nancy. *Gendered Freedoms: Race, Rights, and the Politics of the Household in the Mississippi Delta, 1861–1875*. Gainesville: University Press of Florida, 2003.

Berkeley, Kathleen C. "'Colored Ladies Also Contributed': Black Women's Activities from Benevolence to Social Welfare, 1866–1896." In *The Web of Southern Social Relations: Women, Family, and Education*, edited by Walter J. Fraser Jr., R. Frank Saunders Jr., and Jon L. Wakelyn. Athens: University of Georgia Press, 1985.

———. *"Like a Plague of Locusts": From an Antebellum Town to a New South City, Memphis, Tennessee, 1850–1880*. New York: Garland, 1991.

Berlin, Ira. *Many Thousands Gone: The First Two Generations of Slavery in North America*. Cambridge: Harvard University Press, 1998.

———. *Slaves Without Masters: The Free Negro in the Antebellum South*. New York: Pantheon, 1974.

Berlin, Ira, Barbara J. Fields, Steven F. Miller, Joseph P. Reidy, and Leslie S. Rowland. *Slaves No More: Three Essays on Emancipation and the Civil War*. New York: Cambridge University Press, 1992.

Biggleston, William E. *They Stopped in Oberlin: Black Residents and Visitors of the Nineteenth Century*. Oberlin, Ohio: Oberlin College, 2002.

Billings, Elden E. "Social and Economic Conditions in Washington during the Civil War." In *Records of the Columbia Historical Society, 1963–1965*, edited and with an introduction by Francis C. Rosenberger. Washington, D.C.: The Society, 1966.

Blackett, R. J. M. *Beating against the Barriers: Biographical Essays in Nineteenth-Century Afro-American History*. Baton Rouge: Louisiana State University Press, 1986.

Blackmar, Elizabeth. *Manhattan for Rent, 1785–1850*. Ithaca: Cornell University Press, 1989.

Blakley, Allison. "Richard T. Greener and the 'Talented Tenth's' Dilemma." *Journal of Negro History* 59, no. 4 (October 1974): 305–21.

Blassingame, John W. "Before the Ghetto: The Making of the Black Community in Savannah, GA." *Journal of Social History* 6, no. 4 (Summer 1973): 463–88.

———. *Black New Orleans, 1860–1880*. Chicago: University of Chicago Press, 1973.

Blight, David W. *Frederick Douglass' Civil War: Keeping Faith in Jubilee*. Baton Rouge: Louisiana State University Press, 1989.

Bogue, Allan G. *The Congressman's Civil War*. New York: Cambridge University Press, 1989.

Borchert, James. *Alley Life in Washington: Family, Community, Religion, and Folklife in the City, 1850–1970*. Urbana: University of Illinois Press, 1980.

Bowers, Claude G. *The Tragic Era: The Revolution after Lincoln*. New York: Houghton Mifflin, 1929.

Boyd, Willis. "Negro Colonization in the National Crisis, 1860–1870." Ph.D. diss., UCLA, 1953.

Brown, Letitia Woods. *Free Negroes in the District of Columbia, 1790 to 1846*. New York: Oxford University Press, 1972.

Bryan, Wilhelmus B. *A History of the National Capital*. 2 vols. New York: Macmillan, 1916.

Bulkley, John Wells. "The War Hospitals." In *Washington during War Time: A Series of Papers Showing the Military, Political, and Social Phases during 1861–1865*, edited by Marcus Benjamin. Washington, D.C.: Committee on Literature for the Encampment, 1902.

Burg, Robert W. "Amnesty, Civil Rights, and the Meaning of Liberal Republicanism, 1862–1872." *American Nineteenth Century History* 4, no. 3 (Fall 2003): 29–60.

Burin, Eric. *Slavery and the Peculiar Solution: A History of the American Colonization Society*. Gainesville: University Press of Florida, 2005.

Butchart, Ronald E. *Northern Schools, Southern Blacks, and Reconstruction: Freedmen's Education, 1862–1875*. Westport, Conn.: Greenwood, 1980.

Clark, Allen C. "Richard Wallach and the Times of His Mayoralty." *Records of the Columbia Historical Society* 21 (1917): 195–245.

Clark, Olynthus B. "The Bid of the West for the National Capital." *Mississippi Valley Historical Association Proceedings* 3 (1909–10): 214–90.

Clark-Lewis, Elizabeth, ed. *First Freed: Washington, D.C., in the Emancipation Era*. 2nd ed. Washington, D.C.: Howard University Press, 2002.

Clephane, Walter C. "The Local Aspect of Slavery in the District of Columbia." *Records of the Columbia Historical Society* 3 (1900): 224–56.

Cobb, W. Montague. *The First Negro Medical Society: A History of the Medico-Chirurgical Society of the District of Columbia, 1884–1939*. Washington, D.C.: Associated Publishers, 1939.

Cohen, William. *At Freedom's Edge: Black Mobility and the Southern White Quest for Racial Control, 1861–1915*. Baton Rouge: Louisiana State University Press, 1991.

Coleman, Willi. "Architects of a Vision: Black Women and Their Antebellum Quest for Political and Social Equality." In *African American Women and the Vote, 1837–1965*, edited by Ann D. Gordon et al. Amherst: University of Massachusetts Press, 1997.

————. "Black Women and Segregated Public Transportation: Ninety Years of Resistance." In *Black Women in United States History*, edited by Darlene Clark Hine. Brooklyn, N.Y.: Carlson, 1990.

Conlin, Michael F. "The Smithsonian Abolition Lecture Controversy: The Clash of Antislavery Politics with American Science in Wartime Washington." *Civil War History* 46, no. 4 (2000): 300–323.

Cooling, Benjamin Franklin. *Symbol, Sword, and Shield: Defending Washington during the Civil War*. 2nd rev. ed. Shippensburg, Pa.: White Mane, 1991.

Cooper, Frederick, Thomas Holt, and Rebecca Scott. *Beyond Slavery: Explorations of Race, Labor, and Citizenship in Postemancipation Societies*. Chapel Hill: University of North Carolina Press, 2000.

Corrigan, Mary Elizabeth. "A Social Union of Heart and Effort: The African-American Family in the District of Columbia on the Eve of Emancipation." Ph.D. diss., University of Maryland–College Park, 1996.

————. "The Ties That Bind: The Pursuit of Community and Freedom among Slaves and Free Blacks in the District of Columbia, 1800–1860." In *Southern City, National Ambition: The Growth of Early Washington, D.C*, edited by Howard Gillette. Washington, D.C.: American Architectural Foundation and George Washington University Center for Washington Area Studies, 1995.

Cowdrey, Albert E. *A City for the Nation: The Army Engineers and the Building of Washington, D.C., 1790–1967*. Washington, D.C.: Historical Division, Office of Administrative Services, Office of the Chief of Engineers, [1978].

Cox, Lawanda, and John H. Cox. *Politics, Principle, and Prejudice, 1865–1866: Dilemma of Reconstruction America*. New York: Free Press of Glencoe, 1863.

Cromwell, John W. "The First Negro Churches in the District of Columbia." *Journal of Negro History* 7, no. 1 (January 1922): 64–106.

Cullen, Jim. "'I's a Man Now': Gender and African American Men." In *Divided Houses: Gender and the Civil War*, edited by Catherine Clinton and Nina Silber. New York: Oxford University Press, 1992.

Curry, Leonard P. *Blueprint for Modern America: Nonmilitary Legislation of the First Civil War Congress*. Nashville, Tenn.: Vanderbilt University Press, 1968.

Curry, Richard O., ed. *Radicalism, Racism, and Party Realignment: The Border States during Reconstruction*. Baltimore: Johns Hopkins University Press, 1969.

Dabney, Lillian G. *The History of Schools for Negroes in the District of Columbia, 1807–1947*. Washington, D.C.: Catholic University of America Press, 1949.

Dailey, Jane E. *Before Jim Crow: The Politics of Race in Postemancipation Virginia*. Chapel Hill: University of North Carolina Press, 2000.

Dale, Elizabeth. "'Social Equality Does Not Exist among Themselves, nor among Us': Baylies vs. Curry and Civil Rights in Chicago, 1888." *American Historical Review* 102, no. 2 (April 1997): 311–39.

Davis, Hugh. "The Pennsylvania State Equal Rights League and the Northern Black Struggle for Legal Equality, 1864–1877." *Pennsylvania Magazine of History and Biography* 126, no. 4 (2002): 611–34.

Davis, Madison. *A History of the Washington City Post-Office, from 1795 to 1903.* Lancaster, Pa.: New Era Printing, [1902].

DeBoer, Clara Merritt. "The Role of Afro-Americans in the Origin and Work of the American Missionary Association, 1839–1877." Ph.D. diss., Rutgers University, 1973.

Deyle, Steven. *Carry Me Back: The Domestic Slave Trade in American Life.* New York: Oxford University Press, 2005.

Dittmer, John. "The Education of Henry McNeal Turner." In *Black Leaders of the Nineteenth Century,* edited by Leon Litwack and August Meier. Urbana: University of Illinois Press, 1988.

Donald, David. *Charles Sumner and the Rights of Man.* New York: Alfred A. Knopf, 1970.

Douglas, Davison M. *Jim Crow Moves North: The Battle over Northern School Segregation, 1865–1954.* New York: Cambridge University Press, 2005.

Drago, Edmund L. *Black Politicians and Reconstruction in Georgia: A Splendid Failure.* Baton Rouge: Louisiana State University Press, 1982.

Dubler, Ariela R. "In the Shadow of Marriage: Single Women and the Legal Construction of the Family and the State." *Yale Law Journal* 112, no. 7 (May 2003): 1641–1715.

DuBois, Ellen Carol. *Feminism and Suffrage: The Emergence of an Independent Women's Movement in America, 1848–1869.* Ithaca: Cornell University Press, 1978.

———. *Woman Suffrage and Women's Rights.* New York: New York University Press, 1998.

DuBois, Ellen Carol, and Richard Candida Smith, eds. *Elizabeth Cady Stanton, Feminist as Thinker: A Reader in Documents and Essays.* New York: New York University Press, 2007.

Dubois, Laurent. *A Colony of Citizens: Revolution and Slave Emancipation in the French Caribbean, 1787–1804.* Chapel Hill: University of North Carolina Press, 2004.

Eaton, John. *Eulogy on Hon. James Willis Patterson, L.L.D.,* June 14, 1894. Concord, N.H.: Republican Press Association, 1894.

Edwards, Laura F. *Gendered Strife and Confusion: The Political Culture of Reconstruction.* Urbana: University of Illinois Press, 1997.

———. "'The Marriage Covenant Is at the Foundation of All Our Rights': The Legal and Political Implications of Marriage in Postemancipation North Carolina." *Law and History Review* 14, no. 1 (Spring 1996): 81–124.

———. *The People and Their Peace: Legal Culture and the Transformation of Inequality in the Post-Revolutionary South.* Chapel Hill: University of North Carolina Press, 2008.

———. "The Problem of Dependency: African Americans, Labor Relations, and the Law in the Nineteenth-Century South." *Agricultural History* 72, no. 2 (Spring 1998): 313–40.

Einhorn, Robin L. *Property Rules: Political Economy in Chicago, 1833–1872.* Chicago: University of Chicago Press, 1991.

Ethington, Philip J. *The Public City: The Political Construction of Urban Life in San Francisco, 1850–1900.* New York: Cambridge University Press, 1994.

Everly, Elaine C. "The Freedmen's Bureau in the National Capital." Ph.D. diss., George Washington University, 1972.

Farmer, Mary J. "'Because They Are Women': Gender and the Virginia Freedmen's Bureau's 'War on Dependency.'" In *The Freedmen's Bureau and Reconstruction: Reconsiderations*, edited by Paul A. Cimbala and Randall M. Miller. New York: Fordham University Press, 1999.

Farmer-Kaiser, Mary. "'Are They Not in Some Sorts Vagrants?': Gender and the Efforts of the Freedmen's Bureau to Combat Vagrancy in the Reconstruction South." *Georgia Historical Quarterly* 68, no. 1 (Spring 2004): 25–49.

Faulkner, Carol. *Women's Radical Reconstruction: The Freedmen's Aid Movement*. Philadelphia: University of Pennsylvania Press, 2004.

Fehrenbacher, Don E. *The Slaveholding Republic: An Account of the United States Government's Relations to Slavery*. New York: Oxford University Press, 2001.

Fields, Barbara Jeanne. *Slavery and Freedom on the Middle Ground: Maryland during the Nineteenth Century*. New Haven: Yale University Press, 1985.

Finkelman, Paul. "Prelude to the Fourteenth Amendment: Black Legal Rights in the Antebellum North." *Rutgers Law Journal* 17 (1986): 415–82.

Fischer, Roger A. "A Pioneer Protest: The New Orleans Street-Car Controversy of 1867." *Journal of Negro History* 53, no. 3 (July 1968): 219–33.

———. *The Segregation Struggle in Louisiana, 1862–1877*. Urbana: University of Illinois Press, 1974.

Fishel, Leslie H., Jr. "Northern Prejudice and Negro Suffrage, 1865–1870." *Journal of Negro History* 39, no. 1 (January 1954): 8–26.

———. "Repercussions of Reconstruction: The Northern Negro, 1870–1883." *Civil War History* 14, no. 4 (1968): 325–45.

Fitzgerald, Michael W. *The Union League Movement in the Deep South: Politics and Agricultural Change during Reconstruction*. Baton Rouge: Louisiana State University Press, 1989.

———. *Urban Emancipation: Popular Politics in Reconstruction Mobile, 1860–1890*. Baton Rouge: Louisiana State University Press, 2002.

Flack, Horace Edgar. *Adoption of the Fourteenth Amendment*. Baltimore: Johns Hopkins University Press, 1908.

Fleischner, Jennifer. *Mrs. Lincoln and Mrs. Keckly: The Remarkable Story of the Friendship between a First Lady and a Former Slave*. New York: Broadway Books, 2003.

Fletcher, Robert Samuel. *A History of Oberlin College from Its Foundation through the Civil War*. Vol. 2. Oberlin, Ohio: Oberlin College, 1943.

Foner, Eric. *Freedom's Lawmakers: A Directory of Black Officeholders during Reconstruction*. Rev. ed. Baton Rouge: Louisiana State University Press, 1996.

———. *Free Soil, Free Labor, Free Men: The Ideology of the Republican Party before the Civil War*. New York: Oxford University Press, 1970.

———. *Nothing but Freedom: Emancipation and Its Legacy*. Baton Rouge: Louisiana State University Press, 1983.

———. *Reconstruction: America's Unfinished Revolution, 1863–1877*. New York: Harper and Row, 1988.

Foner, Philip S. "The Battle to End Discrimination against Negroes on Philadelphia Streetcars." Part 1: "Background and Beginning of the Battle"; Part 2: "The Victory." *Pennsylvania History* 40, nos. 3 and 4 (1973): 260–90, 354–79.

Forman, James, Jr. "Juries and Race in the Nineteenth Century." *Yale Law Journal* 113, no. 4 (January 2004): 895–938.

Frank, John P., and Robert F. Munro. "The Original Understanding of 'Equal Protection of the Laws.'" *Columbia Law Review* 50, no. 2 (February 1950): 131–69.

Franke, Katherine M. "Becoming a Citizen: Reconstruction Era Regulation of African American Marriages." *Yale Journal of Law and the Humanities* 11 (1999): 251–309.

Frankel, Noralee. *Freedom's Women: Black Women and Families in Civil War Era Mississippi.* Bloomington: Indiana University Press, 1999.

Fredrickson, George M. *Big Enough to Be Inconsistent: Abraham Lincoln Confronts Slavery and Race.* Cambridge: Harvard University Press, 2008.

———. *The Black Image in the White Mind: The Debate on Afro-American Character and Destiny, 1817–1914.* New York: Harper and Row, 1971.

Frey, Sylvia R. *Water from the Rock: Black Resistance in a Revolutionary Age.* Princeton, N.J.: Princeton University Press, 1991.

Frisch, Michael. "The Community Elite and the Emergence of Urban Politics: Springfield, Massachusetts, 1840–1880." In *Nineteenth-Century Cities: Essays in the New Urban History*, edited by Stephan Thernstrom and Richard Sennett. New Haven: Yale University Press, 1969.

Fuke, Richard Paul. "Blacks, Whites, and Guns: Interracial Violence in Post-Emancipation Maryland." *Maryland Historical Magazine* 92 (Fall 1997): 326–47.

———. *Imperfect Equality: African Americans and the Confines of White Racial Attitudes in Post-Emancipation Maryland.* New York: Fordham University Press, 1999.

Furgurson, Ernest B. *Freedom Rising: Washington in the Civil War.* New York: A. A. Knopf, 2004.

Furstenberg, François. "Beyond Freedom and Slavery: Autonomy, Virtue, and Resistance in Early American Political Discourse." *Journal of American History* 89 (March 2003): 1295–1330.

Gatewood, Willard B. *Aristocrats of Color: The Black Elite, 1880–1920.* Bloomington: Indiana University Press, 1990.

Gerber, David A. *Black Ohio and the Color Line, 1860–1915.* Urbana: University of Illinois Press, 1976.

Gibbs, C. R. *Black, Copper, and Bright: The District of Columbia's Black Civil War Regiment.* Silver Spring, Md.: Three Dimensional Publishing, 2002.

Gibson, Florence E. *The Attitudes of the New York Irish toward State and National Affairs, 1848–1892.* New York: Columbia University Press, 1951.

Gillette, Howard, Jr. *Between Justice and Beauty: Race, Planning, and the Failure of Urban Policy in Washington, D.C.* Baltimore: Johns Hopkins University Press, 1995.

———. "Introduction." In *Southern City, National Ambition: The Growth of Early Washington, D.C., 1800–1860*, edited by Howard Gillette Jr. Washington: American Architectural Foundation and George Washington University Center for Washington Area Studies, 1995.

Gillette, William. *Retreat from Reconstruction, 1869–1879.* Baton Rouge: Louisiana State University Press, 1979.

Gilmore, Glenda Elizabeth. *Gender and Jim Crow: Women and the Politics of White Supremacy in North Carolina, 1896–1920.* Chapel Hill: University of North Carolina Press, 1996.

Glaab, Charles N., and Theodore Brown. *A History of Urban America.* New York: Macmillan, 1967.

Glassie, Henry H. "Victorian Homes in Washington." *Records of the Columbia Historical Society* 63–65 (1963–1965): 320–65.

Goffman, Erving. *The Presentation of Self in Everyday Life.* New York: Overlook Press, 1973.

Goldfield, David R. "Antebellum Washington in Context: The Pursuit of Prosperity and Identity." In *Southern City, National Ambition: The Growth of Early Washington, D.C., 1800–1860*, edited by Howard Gillette. Washington, D.C.: American Architectural Foundation and George Washington University Center for Washington Area Studies, 1995.

———. "Pursuing the American Dream: Cities in the Old South." In *The City in Southern History: The Growth of Urban Civilization in the South*, edited by Blaine A. Brownell and David R. Goldfield. Port Washington, N.Y.: Kennikat Press, 1977.

Goldstein, Mark L. "Washington and the Networks of W. W. Corcoran." *Business and Economic History On-Line* 5 (2007). http://www.thebhc.org/publications/BEHonline/2007/beh2007. html. Accessed Dec. 29, 2009.

Goluboff, Risa. *The Lost Promise of Civil Rights*. Cambridge: Harvard University Press, 2007.

Green, Constance McLaughlin. *The Secret City: A History of Race Relations in the Nation's Capital*. Princeton, N.J.: Princeton University Press, 1967.

———. *Washington: A History of the Capital, 1800–1950*. 2 vols. Princeton, N.J.: Princeton University Press, 1962–63.

Green, Elna C. *This Business of Relief: Confronting Poverty in a Southern City, 1740–1940*. Athens: University of Georgia Press, 2003.

Griffith, Ernest S. *A History of American City Government: The Conspicuous Failure, 1870–1900*. New York: Praeger, 1973.

———. *The Modern Development of City Government in the United Kingdom and the United States*. Vol. 1. London: Oxford University Press, 1927.

Griffith, Ernest S., and Charles R. Adrian. *A History of American City Government: The Formation of Traditions, 1775–1870*. Washington, D.C.: University Press of America, 1983.

Grimshaw, William H. *Official History of Freemasonry among the Colored People in North America*. 1903. New York: Negro Universities Press, 1969.

Groves, Paul A. "The Development of a Black Residential Community in Southwest Washington, 1860–1897." *Records of the Columbia Historical Society* 49 (1973–74): 260–75.

Gudmestad, Robert H. *A Troublesome Commerce: The Transformation of the Interstate Slave Trade*. Baton Rouge: Louisiana State University Press, 2003.

Guelzo, Allen C. *Lincoln's Emancipation Proclamation: The End of Slavery in America*. New York: Simon and Schuster, 2004.

Gutman, Herbert G. "The Failure of the Movement by the Unemployed for Public Works in 1873." *Political Science Quarterly* 80 (June 1965): 254–76.

———. "Schools for Freedom: The Post-Emancipation Origins of Afro-American Education." In *Power and Culture: Essays on the American Working Class*, edited by Ira Berlin. New York: Pantheon, 1987.

Hahn, Steven. *A Nation under Our Feet: Black Political Struggles in the Rural South from Slavery to the Great Migration*. Cambridge: Harvard University Press, 2003.

Hahn, Steven, et al., eds. *Land and Labor, 1865*. Series 3, vol. 1, of *Freedom: A Documentary History of Emancipation, 1861–1867*. Chapel Hill: University of North Carolina Press, 2008.

Harris, Alfred G. "The Enforcement of the Fugitive Slave Laws, 1861–1864." *Lincoln Herald* 52, no. 1 (February 1950): 2–16, 43.

———. "Slavery and Emancipation in the District of Columbia, 1801–1862." Ph.D. diss., Ohio State University, 1946.

Harris, Carl Vernon. *Political Power in Birmingham, 1871–1921*. Knoxville: University of Tennessee Press, 1977.

Harris, Leslie M. *In the Shadow of Slavery: African Americans in New York City, 1626–1863*. Chicago: University of Chicago Press, 2003.

Harrison, Robert. "From Biracial Democracy to Direct Rule: The End of Self-Government in the Nation's Capital, 1865–1878." *Journal of Policy History* 18, no. 2 (2006): 241–69.

———. "An Experimental Station for Lawmaking: Congress and the District of Columbia, 1862–1878." *Civil War History* 53, no. 1 (2007): 29–53.

———. "Race, Radicalism, and Reconstruction: Grassroots Republican Politics in Washington, D.C., 1867–1874." *American Nineteenth-Century History* 3, no. 3 (Fall 2002): 73–96.

———. "Welfare and Employment Policies of the Freedmen's Bureau in the District of Columbia." *Journal of Southern History* 72, no. 1 (February 2006): 75–110.

Harrold, Stanley. *Subversives: Antislavery Community in Washington, D.C., 1828–1865*. Baton Rouge: Louisiana State University Press, 2003.

Hartman, Saidiya V. *Scenes of Subjection: Terror, Slavery, and Self-Making in Nineteenth-Century America*. New York: Oxford University Press, 1997.

Higginbotham, Evelyn Brooks. *Righteous Discontent: The Women's Movement in the Black Baptist Church*. Cambridge: Harvard University Press, 1993.

———. *From Strength to Strength: A History of the Shiloh Baptist Church, 1863–1988*. Washington, D.C.: Shiloh Baptist Church, 1989.

Hine, William C. "Black Organized Labor in Reconstruction Charleston." *Labor History* 25 (1984): 504–17.

———. "The 1867 Charleston Streetcar Sit-Ins: A Case of Successful Black Protest." *South Carolina Historical Magazine* 77, no. 2 (April 1977): 110–14.

Hodes, Martha. *White Women, Black Men: Illicit Sex in the Nineteenth-Century South*. New Haven: Yale University Press, 1997.

Holt, Thomas C. *Black over White: Negro Political Leadership in South Carolina during Reconstruction*. Urbana: University of Illinois Press, 1977.

———. "'An Empire over the Mind': Emancipation, Race, and Ideology in the British West Indies and the American South." In *Region, Race, and Reconstruction: Essays in Honor of C. Vann Woodward*, edited by J. Morgan Kousser and James McPherson. New York: Oxford University Press, 1982.

———. "The Essence of the Contract: The Articulation of Race, Gender, and Political Economy in British Emancipation Policy, 1838–1866." In *Beyond Slavery: Explorations of Race, Labor, and Citizenship in Postemancipation Societies*, edited by Frederick Cooper, Thomas C. Holt, and Rebecca J. Scott. Chapel Hill: University of North Carolina Press, 2000.

———. "Race, Race-making, and the Writing of History." *American Historical Review* 100 (February 1995): 1–20.

Holt, Thomas C., Cassandra Smith-Parker, and Rosalyn Terborg-Penn. *A Special Mission: The Story of the Freedmen's Hospital, 1862–1962*. Washington, D.C.: Academic Affairs Division, Howard University, 1975.

Holzman, Robert S. *Stormy Ben Butler*. New York: Macmillan, 1954.

Hood, Clifton. "Changing Perceptions of Public Space on the New York Rapid Transit System." *Journal of Urban History* 22, no. 3 (March 1996): 308–31.

Horton, Lois Elaine. "The Development of Federal Social Policy for Blacks in Washington, D.C., after Emancipation." Ph.D. diss., Brandeis University, 1977.

Horton, Lois E., and James O. Horton. "Race, Occupation, and Literacy in Reconstruction Washington, D.C." In *Toward a New South? Studies in Post–Civil War Southern Communities*, edited by Orville V. Burton and Robert C. McMath Jr. Westport, Conn.: Greenwood Press, 1982.

Hunter, Tera. *To 'Joy My Freedom: Southern Black Women's Lives and Labors after the Civil War*. Cambridge: Harvard University Press, 1997.

Hyman, Harold M., and William M. Wiecek. *Equal Justice under Law: Constitutional Development, 1835–1875*. New York: Harper and Row, 1982.

Indritz, Phineas. "Post Civil War Ordinances Prohibiting Racial Discrimination in the District of Columbia." *Georgetown Law Journal* 42, no. 2 (January 1954): 179–209.

Isenberg, Nancy. *Sex and Citizenship in Antebellum America*. Chapel Hill: University of North Carolina Press, 1998.

Jacob, Kathryn Allamong. *Capital Elites: High Society in Washington, D.C., after the Civil War*. Washington, D.C.: Smithsonian Institution Press, 1995.

———. "'Like Moths to a Candle': The Nouveaux Riches Flock to Washington, 1870–1900." In *Urban Odyssey: A Multicultural History of Washington, D.C.*, edited by Francine Curro Cary. Washington, D.C.: Smithsonian Institution Press, 1996.

Jenkins, Wilbert L. *Seizing the New Day: African Americans in Post–Civil War Charleston*. Bloomington: Indiana University Press, 1998.

Johnson, Franklin. *The Development of State Legislation Concerning the Free Negro*. 1918. Westport, Conn.: Greenwood Press, 1979.

Johnson, Thomas Reed. "The City on the Hill: Race Relations in Washington, D.C., 1865–1885." Ph.D. diss., University of Maryland, 1975.

Johnston, Allan. *Surviving Freedom: The Black Community of Washington, D.C., 1860–1880*. New York: Garland, 1993.

Jones, Beverly W. "Before Montgomery and Greensboro: The Desegregation Movement in the District of Columbia, 1950–1953." *Phylon* 43, no. 2 (1982): 144–54.

Jones, Jacqueline. *Labor of Love, Labor of Sorrow: Black Women, Work, and the Family from Slavery to the Present*. New York: Basic Books, 1985.

———. *Soldiers of Light and Love: Northern Teachers and Georgia Blacks, 1865–1873*. Chapel Hill: University of North Carolina Press, 1980.

Jones, Martha S. *All Bound Up Together: The Woman Question in African American Public Culture, 1830–1900*. Chapel Hill: University of North Carolina Press, 2007.

Jung, Moon-Ho. *Coolies and Cane: Race, Labor, and Sugar in the Age of Emancipation*. Baltimore: Johns Hopkins University Press, 2006.

Kaczorowski, Robert J. "To Begin the Nation Anew: Congress, Citizenship, and Civil Rights after the Civil War." *American Historical Review* 92, no. 1 (February 1987): 45–68.

———. "Revolutionary Constitutionalism in the Era of the Civil War and Reconstruction." *New York University Law Review* 61 (November 1986): 863–940.

Kaestle, Carl F. *Pillars of the Republic: Common Schools and American Society, 1780–1860*. New York: Hill and Wang, 1983.

Keller, Morton. *Affairs of State: Public Life in Late Nineteenth Century America*. Cambridge: Harvard University Press, 1977.

Kelley, Robin D. G. "Congested Terrain: Resistance on Public Transportation." In *Race Rebels: Culture, Politics, and the Black Working Class*. New York: Free Press, 1994.

Kelly, Alfred H. "The Congressional Controversy over School Segregation, 1867–1875." *American Historical Review* 64 (April 1959): 537–46.

Kerber, Linda K. *No Constitutional Right to Be Ladies: Women and the Obligations of Citizenship.* New York: Hill and Wang, 1998.

Kerr, Andrea Moore. *Lucy Stone: Speaking Out for Equality.* New Brunswick, N.J.: Rutgers University Press, 1992.

Kerr, R. W. *History of the Government Printing Office (at Washington, D.C.) with a Brief Records of the Public Printing for a Century, 1789–1881.* 1881. New York: Burt Franklin, 1970.

Kettner, James H. *The Development of American Citizenship, 1608–1870.* Chapel Hill: University of North Carolina Press, 1978.

Keyssar, Alexander. *The Right to Vote: The Contested History of Democracy in the United States.* New York: Basic Books, 2000.

King, LeRoy O., Jr. *100 Years of Capital Traction: The Story of Streetcars in the Nation's Capital.* College Park, Md.: Taylor Publishing Company, 1972.

Klebaner, Benjamin J. "Poor Relief and Public Works during the Depression of 1857." *Historian* 22, no. 3 (1960): 264–79.

Kloppenberg, James. "Premature Requiem: Republicanism in American History." In *The Virtues of Liberalism.* New York: Oxford University Press, 1998.

Kornell, Gary L. "Reconstruction in Nashville, 1867–1869." *Tennessee Historical Quarterly* 30, no. 3 (1971): 277–87.

Kousser, J. Morgan. "Before *Plessy*, before *Brown*: The Development of the Law of Racial Integration in Louisiana and Kansas." In *Toward a Usable Past: Liberty under State Constitutions,* edited by Paul Finkelman and Stephen E. Gottlieb. Athens: University of Georgia Press, 1991.

————. *The Shaping of Southern Politics: Suffrage Restriction and the Establishment of the One-Party South, 1880–1910.* New Haven: Yale University Press, 1974.

————. "'The Supremacy of Equal Rights': The Struggle against Racial Discrimination in Antebellum Massachusetts and the Foundations of the Fourteenth Amendment." *Northwestern University Law Review* 92 (1987–88): 941–1010.

Kurtz, Michael J. "Emancipation in the Federal City." *Civil War History* 24, no. 3 (1978): 250–67.

Lamb, Daniel Smith. *History of the Medical Society of the District of Columbia, 1817–1909.* Washington, D.C.: The Society, 1909.

————. *Howard University Medical Department, Washington, D.C.: A Historical, Biographical, and Statistical Souvenir.* Washington, D.C.: R. Beresford, 1900.

Lapsansky, Emma Jones. "Friends, Wives, and Strivings: Networks and Community Values among Nineteenth-Century Philadelphia Afroamerican Elites." *Pennsylvania Magazine of History and Biography* 108, no. 1 (January 1984): 3–24.

Leech, Margaret. *Reveille in Washington, 1860–1865.* New York: Harper, 1941.

Leonard, Elizabeth D. *Yankee Women: Gender Battles in the Civil War.* New York: W. W. Norton, 1994.

Lessoff, Alan. *The Nation and Its City: Politics, "Corruption," and Progress in Washington, D.C., 1861–1902.* Baltimore: Johns Hopkins University Press, 1994.

Lester, C. Edwards. *Life and Public Services of Charles Sumner.* New York: United States Publishing Company, 1874.

Levey, Jane Freundel. "Segregation in Education: A Basis for Jim Crow in Washington, D.C., 1804–1880." M.A. thesis, George Washington University, 1991.

Lewis, Earl. *In Their Own Interests: Race, Class, and Power in Twentieth-Century Norfolk, Virginia*. Berkeley: University of California Press, 1991.

Lewis, Elsie M. "The Political Mind of the Negro, 1865–1900." *Journal of Southern History* 21, no. 2 (May 1955): 189–202.

Litwack, Leon. *Been in the Storm So Long: The Aftermath of Slavery*. New York: Knopf, 1979.

———. *North of Slavery: The Negro in the Free States, 1790–1860*. Chicago: University of Chicago Press, 1961.

Lofgren, Charles A. *The Plessy Case: A Legal-Historical Interpretation*. New York: Oxford University Press, 1987.

Mabee, Carleton. *Sojourner Truth: Slave, Prophet, Legend*. New York: New York University Press, 1993.

———. "Sojourner Truth Fights Dependence on Government: Moves Freed Slaves Off Welfare in Washington to Jobs in Upstate New York." *Afro-Americans in New York Life and History* 14, no. 1 (January 1990): 7–26.

MacGregor, Morris J. *The Emergence of a Black Catholic Community: St. Augustine's in Washington*. Washington, D.C.: Catholic University of America, 1999.

Mack, Kenneth W. "Law, Society, Identity, and the Making of the Jim Crow South: Travel and Segregation on Tennessee Railroads, 1875–1905." *Law and Social Inquiry* 24 (1999): 377–409.

Mahon, John K. *History of the Militia and National Guard*. New York: Macmillan, 1983.

Maltz, Earl. *Civil Rights, the Constitution, and Congress, 1863–1869*. Lawrence: University Press of Kansas, 1990.

———. "The Civil Rights Act and the *Civil Rights Cases*: Congress, Court, and Constitution." *University of Florida Law Review* 44 (1992): 605–35.

———. "Fourteenth Amendment Concepts in the Antebellum Era." *American Journal of Legal History* 32, no. 4 (October 1988): 305–46.

———. "'Separate but Equal' and the Law of Common Carriers in the Era of the Fourteenth Amendment." *Rutgers Law Journal* 17 (1985–86): 558–68.

Masur, Kate. "The African American Delegation to Abraham Lincoln: A Reappraisal." *Civil War History* 56, no. 2 (June 2010).

———. "New National Era." In *Encyclopedia of African American History, 1619–1895: From the Colonial Period to the Age of Frederick Douglass*, edited by Paul Finkelman. New York: Oxford University Press, 2006.

———. "'A Rare Phenomenon of Philological Vegetation': The Word 'Contraband' and the Meanings of Emancipation in the United States." *Journal of American History* 93 (March 2007): 1050–84.

———. "Reconstructing the Nation's Capital: The Politics of Race and Citizenship in the District of Columbia, 1862–1878." Ph.D. diss., University of Michigan, 2001.

Maury, William M. *Alexander "Boss" Shepherd and the Board of Public Works*. George Washington University Studies, no. 3. Washington, D.C.: George Washington University, 1975.

McAleer, Margaret H. "'The Green Streets of Washington': The Experience of Irish Mechanics in Antebellum Washington." In *Urban Odyssey: A Multicultural History of Washington, D.C.*, edited by Francine Curro Cary. Washington, D.C.: Smithsonian Institution Press, 1996.

McArdle, Walter F. "The Development of the Business Sector in Washington, D.C., 1873–1973." *Records of the Columbia Historical Society* 49 (1973–74): 556–94.

McClintock, Megan J. "The Impact of the Civil War on Nineteenth-Century Marriages." In

Union Soldiers and the Northern Home Front: Wartime Experiences, Postwar Adjustments, edited by Paul A. Cimbala and Randall M. Miller. New York: Fordham University Press, 2002.

McCluskey, Audrey Thomas. "Setting the Standard: Mary Church Terrell's Last Campaign for Social Justice." *Black Scholar* 29, nos. 2–3 (1999): 47–53.

McCurry, Stephanie. *Masters of Small Worlds: Yeoman Households, Gender Relations, and the Political Culture of the Antebellum South Carolina Low Country*. New York: Oxford University Press, 1995.

McFeely, William S. *Frederick Douglass*. New York: Norton, 1991.

McGerr, Michael. *The Decline of Popular Politics: The American North, 1865–1928.* New York: Oxford University Press, 1986.

McKay, Ernest. *Henry Wilson: Practical Radical, a Portrait of a Politician*. Port Washington, N.Y.: Kennikat Press, 1971.

McKitrick, Eric L. *Andrew Johnson and Reconstruction*. Chicago: University of Chicago Press, 1960.

McMillan, Lewis K., Jr. "Anthony Bowen and the Y.M.C.A." *Negro History Bulletin* (April 1958): 159–60.

McPherson, James M. "Abolitionists and the Civil Rights Act of 1875." *Journal of American History* 52, no. 3 (December 1965): 493–510.

———. "Grant or Greeley? The Abolitionist Dilemma in the Election of 1872." *American Historical Review* 71, no. 1 (October 1965): 43–61.

———. *The Negro's Civil War: How American Negroes Felt and Acted during the War for the Union*. New York: Vintage, 1965.

———. *The Struggle for Equality: Abolitionists and the Negro in the Civil War and Reconstruction*. Princeton, N.J.: Princeton University Press, 1964.

Meersman, Roger, and Robert Boyer. "The National Theatre in Washington: Buildings and Audiences, 1835–1972." *Records of the Columbia Historical Society* 71–72 (1971–72): 190–242.

Mehta, Uday S. *Liberalism and Empire: A Study in Nineteenth-Century British Liberal Thought*. Chicago: University of Chicago Press, 1999.

Melder, Keith E. "Angel of Mercy in Washington: Josephine Griffing and the Freedmen, 1864–1872." *Records of the Columbia Historical Society of Washington, D.C.* 45 (1963–65): 243–72.

Miller, Floyd J. *The Search for a Black Nationality: Black Emigration and Colonization, 1787–1863*. Urbana: University of Illinois Press, 1975.

Minter, Patricia Hagler. "The Failure of Freedom: Class, Gender, and the Evolution of Segregated Transit Law in the Nineteenth-Century South." *Chicago-Kent Law Review* 70 (1995): 993–1009.

Moldow, Gloria. *Women Doctors in Gilded-Age Washington: Race, Gender, and Professionalization*. Urbana: University of Illinois Press, 1987.

Monkkonen, Eric H. "The Politics of Municipal Indebtedness and Default, 1850–1936." In *The Politics of Urban Fiscal Policy*, edited by Terrence J. McDonald and Salley K. Ward. Beverly Hills, Calif.: Sage, 1984.

Montgomery, David. *Beyond Equality: Labor and the Radical Republicans, 1862–1872*. New York: Knopf, 1967.

Moore, Jacqueline M. *Leading the Race: The Transformation of the Black Elite in the Nation's Capital, 1880–1920*. Charlottesville: University Press of Virginia, 1999.

Moran, Ella V. Payne. "Anthony Bowen." *Negro History Bulletin* (October 1944): 5–6, 18–21.

Morris, Robert C. *Reading, 'Riting, and Reconstruction: The Education of Freedmen in the South, 1861–1870.* Chicago: University of Chicago Press, 1976.

Moss, Hilary J. "The Tarring and Feathering of Thomas Paul Smith: Common Schools, Revolutionary Memory, and the Crisis of Black Citizenship in Antebellum Boston." *New England Quarterly* 80, no. 2 (2007): 218–41.

Myrdal, Gunnar. *An American Dilemma: The Negro Problem and Modern Democracy.* Vol. 1. New York: Harper, 1944.

Nelson, William E. *The Fourteenth Amendment: From Political Principle to Judicial Doctrine.* Cambridge: Harvard University Press, 1988.

Newman, Louise Michele. *White Women's Rights: The Racial Origins of Feminism in the United States.* New York: Oxford University Press, 1999.

Nieman, Donald G. "The Language of Liberation: African Americans and Equalitarian Constitutionalism, 1830–1950." In *The Constitution, Law, and American Life: Critical Aspects of the Nineteenth-Century Experience,* edited by Donald G. Nieman. Athens: University of Georgia Press, 1992.

———. *To Set the Law in Motion: The Freedmen's Bureau and the Legal Rights of Blacks, 1865–1868.* Millwood, N.Y.: KTO Press, 1979.

Noell, F. Regis, and Margaret Brent Downing. *The Court-House of the District of Columbia.* Washington, D.C.: Judd and Detweiler, 1919.

Norgren, Jill. *Belva Lockwood: The Woman Who Would Be President.* New York: New York University Press, 2007.

Norris, Marjorie M. "An Early Instance of Nonviolence: The Louisville Demonstrations of 1870–1871." *Journal of Southern History* 32, no. 4 (November 1966): 487–504.

Novak, William J. "The American Law of Association: The Legal-Political Construction of Civil Society." *Studies in American Political Development* 15 (Fall 2001): 163–88.

———. "The Legal Transformation of Citizenship in Nineteenth-Century America." In *The Democratic Experiment: New Directions in American Political History,* edited by Meg Jacobs, William J. Novak, and Julian E. Zelizer. Princeton, N.J.: Princeton University Press, 2003.

———. *The People's Welfare: Law and Regulation in Nineteenth-Century America.* Chapel Hill: University of North Carolina Press, 1996.

Oberholtzer, Ellis Paxon. *Jay Cooke: Financier of the Civil War.* Vol. 2. Philadelphia: George W. Jacobs, 1907.

O'Malley, Michael. "Specie and Species: Race and the Money Question in Nineteenth-Century America," with response by Nell Irvin Painter. *American Historical Review* 99, no. 2 (April 1994): 369–408.

Omori, Kazuteru. "Race-Neutral Individualism and Resurgence of the Color Line: Massachusetts Civil Rights Legislation, 1855–1895." *Journal of American Ethnic History* 22, no. 1 (2002): 32–58.

Osher, David Martin. "Soldier Citizens for a Disciplined Nation: Union Conscription and the Construction of the Modern Army." Ph.D. diss., Columbia University, 1992.

Painter, Nell Irvin. "'Social Equality,' Miscegenation, Labor, and Power." In *The Evolution of Southern Culture,* edited by Numan V. Bartley. Athens: University of Georgia Press, 1988.

———. *Sojourner Truth: A Life, a Symbol.* New York: Norton, 1996.

———. "Voices of Suffrage: Sojourner Truth, Frances Watkins Harper, and the Struggle for

Woman Suffrage." In *Votes for Women: The Struggle for Suffrage Revisited*, edited by Jean H. Baker. New York: Oxford University Press, 2002.

Pascoe, Peggy. *What Comes Naturally: Miscegenation Law and the Making of Race in America*. New York: Oxford University Press, 2009.

Pateman, Carole. *The Sexual Contract*. Stanford, Calif.: Stanford University Press, 1988.

Patterson, George W. *James W. Patterson as an Educator*. Concord, N.H.: Republican Press Association, n.d.

Pearson, Henry Greenleaf. *James S. Wadsworth of Geneseo*. New York: Charles Scribner's, 1913.

Penningroth, Dylan C. *The Claims of Kinfolk: African American Property and Community in the Nineteenth-Century South*. Chapel Hill: University of North Carolina Press, 2003.

Perdue, Robert. *The Negro in Savannah, 1865–1900*. New York: Exposition Press, 1973.

Perman, Michael. *Struggle for Mastery: Disfranchisement in the South, 1888–1908*. Chapel Hill: University of North Carolina Press, 2001.

Platt, Harold L. *City Building in the New South: The Growth of Public Services in Houston, Texas, 1830–1910*. Philadelphia: Temple University Press, 1982.

Pocock, J. G. A. "Machiavelli, Harrington, and English Political Ideologies in the Eighteenth Century." *William and Mary Quarterly* 22, no. 4 (October 1965): 549–83.

Powell, Lawrence N. "Centralization and Its Discontents in Reconstruction Louisiana." *Studies in American Political Development* 20 (Fall 2006): 105–31.

———. "Politics of Livelihood: Carpetbaggers in the Deep South." In *Race, Region, and Reconstruction: Essays in Honor of C. Vann Woodward*, edited by J. Morgan Kousser and James McPherson. New York: Oxford University Press, 1982.

Press, John. "South of the Avenue: From Murder Bay to the Federal Triangle." *Records of the Columbia Historical Society* 51 (1984): 51–70.

Preston, Emmett D., Jr. "The Development of Negro Education in the District of Columbia." *Journal of Negro Education* 9, no. 4 (October 1940): 595–603.

———. "The Development of Negro Education in the District of Columbia, 1800–1860." *Journal of Negro Education* 12, no. 2 (Spring 1943): 189–98.

Primus, Richard A. *The American Language of Rights*. New York: Cambridge University Press, 1999.

Proctor, John Clagett. *Washington: Past and Present*. Vol. 1. New York: Lewis Historical Publishing Company, 1930.

Provine, Dorothy. "The Economic Position of the Free Blacks in the District of Columbia, 1800–1860." *Journal of Negro History* 58, no. 1 (January 1973): 61–72.

Quarles, Benjamin. *The Negro in the Civil War*, with new introduction by William S. McFeely. 1953. New York: DeCapo, 1989.

Quigley, David. "'The Proud Name of "Citizen" Has Sunk': Suffrage Reconstruction, Class Formation, and the Tilden Commission of 1877." *American Nineteenth-Century History* 3, no. 2 (Summer 2002): 69–92.

———. *Second Founding: New York City, Reconstruction, and the Making of American Democracy*. New York: Hill and Wang, 2004.

Rabinowitz, Howard N. "The Conflict between Blacks and the Police in the Urban South, 1865–1900." *Historian* 39 (November 1976): 62–76.

———. "Continuity and Change: Southern Urban Development, 1860–1900." In *The City in*

Southern History: The Growth of Urban Civilization in the South, edited by Blaine A. Brownell and David R. Goldfield. Port Washington, N.Y.: Kennikat Press, 1977.

———. "Half a Loaf: The Shift from White to Black Teachers in the Negro Schools of the Urban South, 1865–1890." *Journal of Southern History* 40, no. 4 (1974): 565–94.

———. *Race Relations in the Urban South, 1865–1890*. New York: Oxford University Press, 1978.

———. "From Reconstruction to Redemption in the Urban South." *Journal of Urban History* 2, no. 2 (February 1976): 169–94.

———. "Segregation and Reconstruction." In *The Facts of Reconstruction: Essays in Honor of John Hope Franklin*, edited by Eric Anderson and Alfred A. Moss Jr. Baton Rouge: Louisiana State University Press, 1991.

Rable, George C. *But There Was No Peace: The Role of Violence in the Politics of Reconstruction*. Athens: University of Georgia Press, 1984.

Rachleff, Peter J. *Black Labor in the South: Richmond, Virginia, 1865–1890*. Philadelphia: Temple University Press, 1984.

Rapport, Sara. "The Freedmen's Bureau as a Legal Agent for Black Men and Women in Georgia: 1865–1868." *Georgia Historical Quarterly* 73, no. 1 (Spring 1989): 26–53.

Redkey, Edwin S. "Henry McNeal Turner: Black Chaplain in the Union Army." In *Black Soldiers in Blue: African American Troops in the Civil War Era*, edited by John David Smith. Chapel Hill: University of North Carolina Press, 2002.

Reidy, Joseph P. *From Slavery to Agrarian Capitalism in the Cotton Plantation South: Central Georgia, 1800–1880*. Chapel Hill: University of North Carolina Press, 1992.

Rhodes, Jane. *Mary Ann Shad Cary: The Black Press and Protest in the Nineteenth Century*. Bloomington: Indiana University Press, 1998.

Richardson, Heather Cox. *The Death of Reconstruction: Race, Labor, and Politics in the Post–Civil War North, 1865–1901*. Cambridge: Harvard University Press, 2001.

Riegel, Stephen J. "The Persistent Career of Jim Crow: Lower Federal Courts and the 'Separate but Equal' Doctrine, 1865–1896." *American Journal of Legal History* 28, no. 1 (January 1984): 17–40.

Ritchie, Donald A. *Press Gallery: Congress and the Washington Correspondents*. Cambridge: Harvard University Press, 1991.

Rives, Jeannie Tree. "Old Families and Houses—Greenleaf's Point." *Records of the Columbia Historical Society* 5 (1901): 54–63.

Robinson, Henry S. "Some Aspects of the Free Negro Population in Washington, D.C., 1800–1862." *Maryland Historical Magazine* 64, no. 1 (1969): 43–64.

Rodrigue, John C. *Reconstruction in the Cane Fields: From Slavery to Free Labor in Louisiana's Sugar Parishes, 1862–1880*. Baton Rouge: Louisiana State University Press, 2001.

Rose, Willie Lee. *Rehearsal for Reconstruction: The Port Royal Experiment*. New York: Oxford University Press, 1964.

Rosen, Hannah. "The Rhetoric of Miscegenation and the Reconstruction of Race: Debating Marriage, Sex, and Citizenship in Postemancipation America." In *Gender and Slave Emancipation in the Atlantic World*, edited by Pamela Scully and Diana Patton. Durham, N.C.: Duke University Press, 2005.

———. *Terror in the Heart of Freedom: Citizenship, Sexual Violence, and the Meaning of Race in the Postemancipation South*. Chapel Hill: University of North Carolina Press, 2009.

Rosenberg, Charles E. *The Cholera Years: The United States in 1832, 1849, and 1866*. Chicago: University of Chicago Press, 1962.

Ross, Steven Joseph. "Freed Soil, Freed Labor, Freed Men: John Eaton and the Davis Bend Experiment." *Journal of Southern History* 44, no. 2 (May 1978): 213–32.

Rothman, David J. *The Discovery of the Asylum: Social Order and Disorder in the New Republic*. Boston: Little, Brown, 1971.

Rousey, Dennis C. *Policing the Southern City: New Orleans, 1805–1889*. Baton Rouge: Louisiana State University Press, 1996.

Ruchames, Louis. "Jim Crow Railroads in Massachusetts." *American Quarterly* 8, no. 1 (Spring 1956): 61–75.

Russell, James Michael. *Atlanta, 1847–1890: City Building in the Old South and the New*. Baton Rouge: Louisiana State University Press, 1988.

Ryan, Mary P. *Civic Wars: Democracy and Public Life in the American City during the Nineteenth Century*. Berkeley: University of California Press, 1997.

Sandoval-Strausz, A. K. "Travelers, Strangers, and Jim Crow: Law, Public Accommodations, and Civil Rights in America." *Law and History Review* 23, no. 1 (2005): 53–94.

Saville, Julie. "Rites and Power: Reflections on Slavery, Freedom, and Political Ritual." *Slavery and Abolition* 20, no. 1 (April 1999): 81–102.

———. *The Work of Reconstruction: From Slave to Wage Laborer in South Carolina, 1860–1870*. New York: Cambridge University Press, 1994.

Savitt, Todd L. "Politics in Medicine: The Georgia Freedmen's Bureau and the Organization of Health Care, 1865–1866." *Civil War History* 28, no. 1 (1982): 45–64.

Scheips, Paul J. "Lincoln and the Chiriquí Colonization Project." *Journal of Negro History* 37, no. 4 (October 1952): 418–53.

Schmidt, James D. "'A Full-Fledged Government of Men': Freedmen's Bureau Labor Policy in South Carolina, 1865–1868." In *The Freedmen's Bureau and Reconstruction: Reconsiderations*, edited by Paul A. Cimbala and Randall M. Miller. New York: Fordham University Press, 1999.

Schwalm, Leslie A. *A Hard Fight for We: Women's Transition from Slavery to Freedom in South Carolina*. Urbana: University of Illinois Press, 1997.

Schwartz, Nancy. "H Street: A Neighborhood's Story," Part III, *Voice of the Hill*, March 2003.

Schweninger, Loren. "Black Economic Reconstruction in the South." In *The Facts of Reconstruction: Essays in Honor of John Hope Franklin*, edited by Eric Anderson and Alfred A. Moss Jr. Baton Rouge: Louisiana State University, 1991.

———. *Black Property Owners in the South, 1790–1915*. Rev. ed. Urbana: University of Illinois Press, 1997.

Scobey, David M. *Empire City: The Making and Meaning of the New York City Landscape*. Philadelphia: Temple University Press, 2002.

Scott, Rebecca J. "The Battle over the Child: Child Apprenticeship and the Freedmen's Bureau in North Carolina." *Prologue* (Summer 1978): 101–12.

———. *Degrees of Freedom: Louisiana and Cuba after Slavery*. Cambridge: Harvard University Press, 2005.

———. "Public Rights, Social Equality, and the Conceptual Roots of the *Plessy* Challenge." *University of Michigan Law Review* 106, no. 5 (March 2008): 777–804.

Seibold, George S., comp. *Historical Sketch of Columbia Typographical Union*. Washington, D.C.: National Capital Press, 1915.

Severson, William H. *History of Felix Lodge No. 3, F.A.A.M.* Washington, D.C.: R. L. Pendleton, 1908.

Shaw, Stephanie. "Black Club Women and the Creation of the National Association of Colored Women." *Journal of Women's History* 3 (Fall 1991): 10–25.

Singer, Joseph William. "No Right to Exclude: Public Relations and Private Property." *Northwestern University Law Review* 90 (Summer 1996): 1283–1477.

Sluby, Paul E., Jr. *Asbury: Our Legacy, Our Faith, 1836–1993.* Washington, D.C.: The Church, 1993.

Smith Rosenberg, Carroll. *Religion and the Rise of the American City: The New York City Mission Movement, 1812–1870.* Ithaca: Cornell University Press, 1971.

Spero, Sterling D., and Abram L. Harris. *The Black Worker: A Study of the Negro and the Labor Movement.* New York: Columbia University Press, 1931.

Sproat, John G. *"The Best Men": Liberal Reformers in the Gilded Age.* New York: Oxford University Press, 1968.

Stanley, Amy Dru. *From Bondage to Contract: Wage Labor, Marriage, and the Market in the Age of Slave Emancipation.* New York: Cambridge University Press, 1998.

Stoler, Ann Laura. "Racial Histories and Their Regimes of Truth." *Political Power and Social Theory* 11 (1997): 183–246.

Sullivan, Barry. "Historical Reconstruction, Reconstruction History, and the Proper Scope of Section 1981." *Yale Law Journal* 98 (January 1989): 541–64.

Summers, Mark Wahlgren. *The Era of Good Stealings.* New York: Oxford, 1993.

———. *Railroads, Reconstruction, and the Gospel of Prosperity: Aid under the Radical Republicans, 1865–1877.* Princeton, N.J.: Princeton University Press, 1984.

Sylvester, Richard. *District of Columbia Police: A Retrospect of the Police Organizations of the Cities of Washington and Georgetown and the District of Columbia, with Biographical Sketches, Illustrations, and Historic Cases.* Washington, D.C.: Gibson Bros., 1894.

Talbot, George Foster. "Lot M. Morrill: Sketch of His Life and Public Services." *Collections and Proceedings of the Maine Historical Society* 5 (1891): 225–75.

Taylor, Alrutheus A. *The Negro in the Reconstruction of Virginia.* Washington, D.C.: Association for the Study of Negro Life and History, 1926.

Teaford, Jon C. *The Unheralded Triumph: City Government in America, 1870–1900.* Baltimore: Johns Hopkins University Press, 1984.

Terborg-Penn, Rosalyn. *African American Women in the Struggle for the Vote, 1850–1920.* Bloomington: Indiana University Press, 1998.

Terrell, Mary Church. "History of the High School for Negroes in Washington." *Journal of Negro History* 2 (July 1917): 252–66.

Terry, David Taft. "A Brief Moment in the Sun: The Aftermath of Emancipation in Washington, 1862–1869." In *First Freed: Washington, D.C., in the Emancipation Era,* edited by Elizabeth Clark-Lewis. 2nd ed. Washington, D.C.: Howard University Press, 2002.

Teute, Fredrika J. "'A Wild, Desolate Place': Life on the Margins in Early Washington." In *Southern City, National Ambition: The Growth of Early Washington, D.C.,* edited by Howard Gillette. Washington, D.C.: American Architectural Foundation and George Washington University Center for Washington Area Studies, 1995.

Tindall, William. "A Sketch of Alexander Robey Shepherd." *Records of the Columbia Historical Society* 14 (1911): 49–66.

———. "A Sketch of Mayor Sayles J. Bowen." *Records of the Columbia Historical Society* 18 (1915): 25–43.

———. *Standard History of the City of Washington from a Study of the Original Sources*. Knoxville, Tenn.: H. W. Crew, 1914.

Todd, Frederick P. "The Militia and Volunteers of the District of Columbia, 1783–1820." *Records of the Columbia Historical Society* 50 (1948–50): 379–440.

Tracy, George A., comp. *History of the Typographical Union, Its Beginnings, Progress, and Development, Its Beneficial and Educational Features Together with a Chapter on the Early Organization of Printers*. Indianapolis, Ind.: International Typographical Union, 1913.

Vorenberg, Michael. "Abraham Lincoln and the Politics of Black Colonization." *Journal of the Abraham Lincoln Association* 14, no. 2 (1993): 23–45.

———. "Citizenship and the Thirteenth Amendment: Understanding the Deafening Silence." In *Promises of Liberty: Thirteenth Amendment Abolitionism and Its Contemporary Vitality*, edited by Alexander Tsesis. New York: Columbia University Press, forthcoming.

———. *Final Freedom: The Civil War, the Abolition of Slavery, and the Thirteenth Amendment*. New York: Cambridge University Press, 2001.

———. "Reconstruction as a Constitutional Crisis." In *Reconstructions: New Perspectives on Postbellum America*, edited by Thomas J. Brown. New York: Oxford University Press, 2006.

Walker, Dale L. *Mary Edwards Walker: Above and Beyond*. New York: Tom Doherty Associates, 2005.

Wang, Xi. *The Trial of Democracy: Black Suffrage and Northern Republicans, 1860–1910*. Athens: University of Georgia Press, 1997.

Washington, John E. *They Knew Lincoln*. New York: E. P. Dutton, 1942.

Welke, Barbara Y. *Recasting American Liberty: Gender, Race, Law, and the Railroad Revolution, 1865–1920*. New York: Cambridge University Press, 2001.

———. "When All the Women Were White, and All the Blacks Were Men: Gender, Class, Race, and the Road to Plessy, 1855–1914." *Law and History Review* 13, no. 2 (Autumn 1995): 261–316.

Wesley, Charles H. *Negro Labor in the United States, 1850–1925: A Study in American Economic History*. New York: Vanguard Press, 1927.

Westwood, Howard C. "Getting Justice for the Freedman." *Howard Law Journal* 16, no. 3 (1970–71): 492–537.

Whyte, James H. *The Uncivil War: Washington during the Reconstruction*. New York: Twayne, 1958.

Wiecek, William M. *The Sources of Antislavery Constitutionalism in America, 1760–1848*. Ithaca: Cornell University Press, 1977.

Williams, George W. *History of the Negro Race in America, from 1619 to 1880*. New York: G. P. Putnam's, 1882.

Williams, Heather Andrea. *Self-Taught: African American Education in Slavery and Freedom*. Chapel Hill: University of North Carolina Press, 2005.

Williams, Melvin Roscoe. "Blacks in Washington, D.C., 1860–1870." Ph.D. diss., Johns Hopkins University, 1975.

———. "A Blueprint for Change: The Black Community in Washington, D.C., 1860–1870." *Records of the Columbia Historical Society* 48 (1971–72): 359–93.

Wilson, Kirt H. *The Reconstruction Desegregation Debate: The Politics of Equality and the Rhetoric of Place, 1870–1875*. East Lansing: Michigan State University Press, 2002.

Wrenn, Lynette Boney. *Crisis and Commission Government in Memphis: Elite Rule in a Gilded Age City*. Knoxville: University of Tennessee Press, 1998.

Wright, George C. *Life behind a Veil: Blacks in Louisville, Kentucky, 1865–1930*. Baton Rouge: Louisiana State University Press, 1985.

Yearley, Clifton K. *The Money Machines: The Breakdown and Reform of Governmental and Party Finance in the North, 1860–1920*. Albany: State University of New York Press, 1970.

Young, J. Russell, and James L. Feeney. *The Metropolitan Police Department: Official Illustrated History*. Washington, D.C.: Lawrence Publishing Co., 1905.

Zipf, Karin L. *Labor of Innocents: Forced Apprenticeship in North Carolina, 1715–1919*. Baton Rouge: Louisiana State University Press, 2005.

Acknowledgments

It is humbling to think of all the people and institutions that helped me write this book. First, I feel obliged to thank and honor the people I have written about, in particular the black residents of Washington of the 1860s and 1870s. I hope I have managed to say something truthful and useful about the world they inhabited and the aspirations they held dear. I am also deeply indebted to historians of Washington who came before me and whose work, both published and unpublished, charted the territory and therefore made this book possible.

If I am a historian today, it is because of the company I kept at the University of Michigan, where I was lucky to be part of a wonderful cohort of faculty and students in history and related fields. I am particularly grateful to June Howard and George J. Sánchez for ushering me into the American Culture Program and for their dedication to making it an extraordinary place for graduate study. Elsa Barkley Brown inspired me and believed in me while at the same time asking the hardest questions. Terrence McDonald taught a superb course on American liberalism in history and historiography and became a provocative interlocutor and staunch supporter. Other faculty also encouraged and guided me, and I especially thank Frances Aparicio, Sandra Gunning, Kristen Hass, Earl Lewis, Michele Mitchell, Hannah Rosen, David Scobey, Richard Cándida Smith, Carroll Smith-Rosenberg, and Ann Stoler. For affirming that scholarship and friendship could be knit together, and for moments of transcendence that included popping popcorn in a graduate seminar on poststructuralism, I warmly thank fellow former Ann Arbor-ites Kimberly Alidio, Adrian Burgos, Barbara Burglund, Doris Dixon, Paul Eiss, Libby Garland, Tom Guglielmo, Daryl Maeda, April Mayes, John McKiernan-González, Aims McGuinness, Karen R. Miller, Natalia Molina, Michele Morales, David Pedersen, Anna Pegler-Gordon, and Alexander Shashko.

When I decided to write about Washington, Howard Gillette, James Horton, Lois Horton, Alan Lessoff, and James A. Miller welcomed me warmly into the fold. Mary Beth Corrigan became a friend and colleague, and Michele Gates-Moresi and Don Bramen became writing partners. I am thankful for the good counsel of U.S. Senate Historian Donald Ritchie; Felicia Bell, Lauren Borchard, and Donald Kennon of the U.S. Capitol Historical Society; and Rodney Ross, Joseph Schwarz, and Reginald Washington at the National Archives. I owe a special debt to Robert Ellis of the National Archives, who has developed a remarkable knowledge of the District of Columbia court records and who always had the time to answer an email or investigate a question. I also thank archivists and special collections staff at the Library of Congress, Howard University, Haverford College, the University of Rochester, Cornell University, Columbia University, and the Washingtoniana Division of the District of Columbia Public Library.

As I finished graduate school, Jack Censer and many others welcomed me into George Mason University's History Department as a J. N. G. Finley fellow. There, I was lucky to cross paths with Roy Rosenzweig and Lawrence Levine, two giants in the field of U.S. history who have since passed away. Roy and Larry were both masters of bringing people together, telling stories, and advising young historians. They remain sources of inspiration as I think about what kind of professor I want to be, and what kind of human being.

At the University of Maryland's Freedmen and Southern Society Project, Steve Miller and Leslie Rowland taught me new ways of doing history. The project's intensive focus on the social history of emancipation and its commitment to deep archival research reshaped how I understood my own work and pushed me in new directions. At Maryland, I also had the terrific fortune to meet Ira Berlin, who incisively critiqued an early draft of this manuscript and who has remained a source of support and good counsel.

The critical engagement of many others, whether in casual conversation or more formal settings, improved this book and made my life much more fun and interesting. Tyler Anbinder and Sonya Michel offered guidance at an early stage, and Jill Grinberg helped me envision the manuscript as a book. Robert Self's assessment at a critical moment gave me confidence to press on. Jane Dailey and Laura Edwards, both of whose first books were touchstones for me, offered important encouragement. Leslie Rowland, Pauline Maier, and Michael Vorenberg all asked big questions that pushed me to dig deeper and still have me wondering. For inspiring comments, critiques, and conversations, I am also grateful to Ronald Butchart, Margot Canaday, Jay Cook, David Chang, Matthew Gilmore, Joanna Grisinger, Dan Hamilton, Lois Horton, Martha Jones, Tony Kaye, Paul Kramer, Lisa Levenstein, Marya McQuirter, Michele Mitchell, Hilary Moss, John Rodrigue, Manisha Sinha, Christopher W. Schmidt, James D. Schmidt, Christopher Schmidt-Nowara, Rebecca Scott, Stephen Siegel, James Brewer Stewart, Lisa Tetrault, and Barbara Welke. Brian Kelly introduced me to the illustration of black Washingtonians with Charles Sumner's casket.

For opportunities to present my research and to benefit from the insights of commentators and audiences, I thank the American Bar Foundation's Legal History Seminar, the Urban History Seminar at the Chicago Historical Society, the Newberry Library's Labor History Seminar, the U.S. Capitol Historical Society, Marquette University's Legacies of Lincoln conference, Howard University's conference on Emancipation and Race in the Age of Lincoln, the George and Ann Richards Civil War Era Center at Penn State, the University of Wisconsin's Nineteenth-Century American Studies Seminar, the Social History Workshop at the University of Chicago, the Urban Studies Seminar at George Washington University, the Atlantic Emancipations Conference at the McNeil Center for Early American Studies, the American Historical Association, the Organization of American Historians, the Social Science History Association, the American Society for Legal History, and the American Studies Association.

ACKNOWLEDGMENTS

Time and money are crucial to most research enterprises, and this one surely required both. I had generous funding during graduate school from University of Michigan's Rackham Graduate School; Institute for Research on Women and Gender; College of Literature, Science, and the Arts; and Michigan Society of Fellows. A postdoctoral fellowship at the Library of Congress's John W. Kluge Center allowed me to broaden my research. While I was there, Mary Lou Reker was a wonderful presence, and Sarah Wilkes, then a master's student at George Washington University, helped me pore through newspapers on microfilm. A faculty fellowship from the National Endowment for the Humanities in 2007–8 provided me with a crucial year to write the book. Quality childcare has also been essential, and for this I thank the teachers at my sons' schools and also Martha Avila, an indispensable and wonderful caregiver.

At Northwestern University, colleagues welcomed me in countless ways. Three chairs of the History Department—Sarah Maza, Nancy MacLean, and Peter Hayes—offered guidance and support, and the dean's office granted me a year of leave to write. Dwight McBride and Darlene Clark Hine, successive chairs of the Department of African American Studies, brought me on board and encouraged both my teaching and research. I owe a colossal debt to Dylan Penningroth, a warm friend, wise counselor, and astute and patient reader. I am also especially grateful to Henry Binford for wonderful conversations about urban history and to Susan J. Pearson, whose insights have considerably improved this book and whose friendship has been a beacon. For advice and smiles, I also thank Northwestern colleagues Michael Allen, Josef Barton, Martha Biondi, T. H. Breen, Sherwin Bryant, Geraldo Cadava, Peter Carroll, Lane Fenrich, Brodwyn Fischer, Benjamin Frommer, Jonathon Glassman, Regina Grafe, Elizabeth Shakman Hurd, Tessie Liu, Melissa Macauley, Edward Muir, Mónica Russell y Rodríguez, David Schoenbrun, Michael Sherry, Julia Stern, Ivy Wilson, and Ji-Yeon Yuh.

Others at Northwestern also had a hand in this work. Staff in the History Department, particularly Paula Blaskovits and Susan Hall, helped me understand the institution. Amy Odenthal, a history and education major, had tremendous instincts for historical research and remarkable patience before a microfilm reader. Elizabeth Kacel provided library help; Andrew Warne worked on the bibliography; and Anastasia Polda and Keeanga Taylor asked terrific questions in an independent study on the legal history of equality. Victoria Zahrobsky, Liz Fraser, and the rest of the Inter-Library Loan Department coordinated an onslaught of obscure materials and were inordinately patient with me. Chieko Maene, who repeatedly assured me that she is not a cartographer, produced beautiful maps and handled my geographical neuroses with aplomb.

I thank Kate Torrey at the University of North Carolina Press for taking an early interest in this project and Chuck Grench for shepherding it into the fold. Paul Betz, Katy O'Brien, and Heidi Perov answered innumerable questions and kept things moving forward, and Dorothea Anderson copyedited with great humanity.

Several scholars read the manuscript in its penultimate form. For wrestling with a lengthy document written by someone who was neither a colleague nor a student, and for their intelligent, probing, and sensitive comments, I humbly thank Jane Dailey, Greg

Downs, Laura Edwards, Stephen Kantrowitz, and Michael Vorenberg, as well as Michael Fitzgerald and Michael Perman, who read the manuscript for the press. This book benefited enormously from the input of all these accomplished historians, and I am profoundly grateful for the time they took and the thought they committed to my work. While I have undoubtedly left some questions unanswered and some criticisms unaddressed, I hope they will be pleased with the result.

For life-affirming friendships whose strength, I hope, is undiminished by distance or time or the demands of our busy lives, I thank John Audley and Andrea Durbin, Alicia Gámez, Libby Garland, Lisa Levenstein, Daryl Maeda, Kate Diana, Melani McAlister, and Koritha Mitchell. All have been pillars of support and fonts of humor and wisdom; my gratitude is boundless.

In the most basic sense, my family made this book possible. I thank my parents for moving our family to Oak Park, Illinois, for sending me to public school, and for caring about equality and inequality. Writing this book, I have enjoyed the support and encouragement of my mother, Ann Masur, and my brother, Ben, as well as my extended family and family-in-law: Lucy Lieberfeld, Lawrence Lieberfeld and Ruth Turner, Herschel Bornstein, Steffi Masur, Howard and Elise Masur, Sandy Masur and Scott Spector, Ann and Ed Peck, Michael Slevin, Jonathan Slevin, and Katherine and the late Joseph Slevin. I have dedicated this book to my grandma, Eva Bornstein, whose passion for life and love for her family got me started and will always sustain me.

I have asked a great deal of my own little family unit. My sons, Isaac and Milo, and my stepson, Nik, often wondered whether this mysterious "book" would ever materialize. I thank them for being the terrific people that they are, and for their questions, their laughter, and their forbearance. Peter Slevin—expert in deadlines, clotheslines, and last lines—believed in me and in the life we could build together. He read the manuscript, took care of the kids, and cultivated patience (with an edge). My partner, my friend, my love, thank you.

Index

from slavery, 29; and fugitive slave laws, 30; and freedpeople, 31, 32–34, 131, 148, 150–51, 262; and emigration, 35, 36, 37–38; and black public schools, 80, 83, 85; and Kate Brown incident, 88; and Emancipation Day parade, 89; and access to Executive Mansion, 99; and petition for enfranchisement, 117, 132, 133–34; and African American men's enfranchisement, 131, 133; and Sayles J. Bowen, 157; and public accommodations, 160–61, 225, 230, 231–32, 260; and public school integration, 177; and Wilbur, 184; and consolidation of governance of Washington, D.C., 200–201; and territorial government of Washington, D.C., 215, 248; and Sumner, 215–16, 226; white criticism of, 228, 255; and real estate holdings, 233–35

Black man's party, 240–45

Black militia units, 89, 118, 120, 121–24

Black political activism: public demonstrations, 7, 8, 15–16, 48, 86, 125, 262; individual protests, 7, 86; and upstart claims, 7–8, 23, 88–89, 96–97, 99, 118, 260, 262; and African American churches, 8, 48, 146–47, 156; and public school integration, 85, 167–71, 177, 188, 189, 238, 239–40, 241, 245; and African American men's enfranchisement, 131–34, 145–46, 172, 178, 259; and social equality, 138, 227–28; and black public schools, 146–47, 156–57; independence from white political leaders, 146–47, 242–46, 247; and political equality, 147; and freedpeople/black elite alliance, 148, 150–51; and trade unions, 151–52, 163, 171; and disagreements, 158, 171, 189, 239, 240, 241; resistance to, 159; and woman suffrage, 181–82; and consolidation of governance of Washington, D.C., 200; and Citizens Association, 219; interpretations of, 222, 255; and Washington, D.C. improvements, 223–24; and public accommodations, 225, 231, 261; and racial caste, 225, 231–32. *See also* Republican Party

Black private schools: and arson, 21; and black teachers, 20–21, 54, 77, 79–80, 83;

statistics on, 34; as foundation of black public schools, 54, 79–80, 81, 156; in first ward, 132; and African American men's enfranchisement, 134

Black public schools: establishment of, 25–26; autonomy of, 26, 54, 80–82, 156; Interior Department's authority over, 26, 77, 80–82, 84, 148, 156, 157, 239; and Freedmen's Bureau, 54, 60, 65–66, 71; black private schools as foundation of, 54, 79–80, 81, 156; and property values, 56, 57; and abilities of freedchildren, 66, 67, 82; and black teachers, 77, 80, 82–83; and missionary schools, 77, 80, 83; white opposition to, 78; and white northern teachers, 80, 81, 82, 83; and high school, 83, 84, 239, 245, 306 (n. 59); children served by, 83–84; and black political activism, 146–47, 156–57; and Sayles J. Bowen, 153, 156–57; proposed consolidation of black and white school boards of, 156–58, 188, 189, 190; and territorial government of Washington, D.C., 215, 239, 244. *See also* Board of Trustees of Colored Schools

Black soldiers: and equal access to streetcars, 7, 15, 23, 44, 101, 107, 111, 263; rights and privileges of, 11; African American church support for, 32; recruitment of, 42–43; and citizenship status, 42–43, 47–48; undermining slavery, 44; demands for respect, 45–47, 49; and unequal pay, 47; and Emancipation Day celebrations, 120; and African American men's enfranchisement, 133, 134

Black teachers: and black private schools, 20–21, 54, 77, 79–80, 83; discrimination against, 54, 82; and missionary schools, 65, 82; and black public schools, 77, 80, 82–83; and public school integration, 84, 171, 189; and Sayles J. Bowen, 153

Black veterans, militias formed by, 89, 118, 123, 124, 125

Black Washingtonians: diversity of, 7, 19, 146, 262; individual protests of, 7, 86; autonomous institutions of, 8; and black emigration, 13–15, 25, 31, 35–39; and racial equality debates, 15–16; population of, 19,

25, 28, 55, 69, 113, 262; and black codes, 19–20; and migration of fugitive slaves, 27–29, 31; and fugitive slave laws, 29, 30–31; and freedpeople's relief societies, 31, 32–33; and Emancipation Proclamation, 41; and military officials, 47; and independent black schools, 54; and Interior Department, 77, 80–81; and control of public schools, 80–82, 156; political factions among, 81, 247; and pride in black public schools, 84; and culture of protest, 88–89; and access to previously excluded spaces, 90; and legal equality, 112; and defining civil rights, 118; and Civil Rights Act, 120; and African American men's enfranchisement, 131–34; and municipal elections, 146; debate on public schools, 156–57; and public school integration, 177, 189; and consolidation of governance of Washington, D.C., 200

Bland, Allen M., 123–24, 125

Board of Trustees of Colored Schools: and Interior Department, 26, 148; petitions for appointment of candidates, 77, 80, 81; and taxes, 79; and school building construction, 80; first African American member of, 80, 148; and Sayles J. Bowen, 80, 153; and black teachers, 82–83; and level of schooling, 84, 156; proposed consolidation of, 156–58, 188, 189, 190; school integration opponent appointed to, 232, 239, 244. *See also* Black public schools

Borchert, James, 237

Boston, Mass., 84

Boswell, Frederick A., 153–54

Bowen, Anthony, 150, 157, 160, 205–6

Bowen, Sayles J.: on abolitionist speakers, 23; and freedpeople's relief programs, 63, 153; and Board of Trustees of Colored Schools, 80, 153; and black public schools, 153, 156–57; and Republican Party, 153, 158, 173, 178, 204–5; as mayor of Washington, D.C., 153–58, 162–63, 172, 173, 178, 196, 197, 198, 201–4, 205, 206, 208, 218, 221, 261; and public works improvements, 154, 173; and public school integration, 162–63; and appointment of African Americans, 172; and

public works employment, 178; and black men's enfranchisement, 290 (n. 12)

Boyle, Cornelius T., 79

Breed, Daniel, 80

Brooks, John H., 239, 240, 241

Brown, Emma V., 41, 82, 83, 153, 160

Brown, George T., 92, 98

Brown, John, 33

Brown, J. Sayles, 152

Brown, Kate, 87–88, 98, 116, 125, 262

Browne, Andrew K., 53, 116, 165, 257, 259

Businessmen: and governance of Washington, D.C., 12, 195–96, 200, 214, 219–20, 256, 262; and Washington, D.C. improvements, 219–20, 256; and defining of citizenship, 221; and real estate, 233, 235; and Shepherd, 258

Butler, Benjamin, 186

Butler, Louisa, 166, 167, 184–85

Camp Barker, 41, 44, 47

Capitol: building of, 19; equal access to, 20, 49, 91–93, 95–100, 262; and martial law of Civil War, 22; and upstart claims, 88, 89; dynamics of race and power in, 97; service positions for African Americans in, 97–98; as public space, 104; and Emancipation Day celebrations, 120

Carpenter, Matthew, 191, 192

Carroll, Charlotte, 79–80, 83

Carroll, David, 79–80

Cartter, David, 187–88, 197, 273 (n. 44)

Caste, 66, 168, 170, 225, 231–32, 261, 305 (n. 42)

Catholics, 78, 99, 191

Central America and black colonization, 35, 36, 37

Central Market, 114

Century Magazine, 258

Chamberlain, Silas S., 51–52, 53

Charleston, S.C., 150, 221

Chase, Thomas W., 239, 245, 247

Chautauquan, 258

Chicago, Ill., 195

Chicago Tribune, 140, 161–62, 227

Child rearing, 50, 53, 60, 63–65, 86

Child support, 51

Chipman, Norton P., 217, 306 (n. 58)

Chiriquí region, Panama, and black colonization, 36, 37, 38

Cholera epidemic, 57, 58

Christian Recorder: and fugitives from slavery, 29; and stereotypes of freedpeople, 31; and freedpeople's relief programs, 34, 41; and black delegation to Lincoln, 38–39; and assertive attitudes of African Americans, 42; and black soldiers, 43, 47; and equal access to streetcars, 45

Circuit Court of the District of Columbia, 28, 30

Citizen, 219

Citizens Association of the District of Columbia, 219–20, 221, 223, 224, 254

Citizenship: as legal concept, 3; benefits and obligations of, 5; as local status, 5, 16, 21, 34–35, 119, 220–21, 255; and Fourteenth Amendment, 5, 119, 187, 221; as national status, 5, 119, 220; and stewardship, 5–6; in antebellum period, 5–6, 119; hierarchical understandings of, 6; and privileges, 6–7, 50, 262; blacks' insistence on, 8; preparing freedpeople for, 11, 50, 60, 86, 216; and meaning of freedom, 15–16; race not posing barrier to, 41; and black soldiers, 42–43, 47–48; Republican Party support for, 50, 118; and respectability, 53, 97; and freedmen's barracks housing, 71; pedagogy of, 71; and black public schools, 77; and common schools, 77; and equal access, 91; birthright, 119; and Civil Rights Act, 120, 123, 221; and militia service, 122–23, 130; and voting rights, 182, 183, 185, 186, 187; defining of, 221, 254, 262, 264; African Americans' claiming of, 254–55

Citizens movements, 10, 176–77, 196–97, 198, 208, 215, 219–21. *See also* Taxpayer status

City directory, 10

Civil equality: Republican Party support for, 9, 10; and laws, 9, 10, 11; defining of, 9, 31, 90, 112, 117, 118, 136; and public demonstrations, 48; political equality separated from, 118, 120, 145; and black militias, 125; and African American men's enfranchisement, 130; social equality distinguished from, 260. *See also* Civil rights; Civil Rights Act of 1866; Civil Rights Act of 1875

Civilization: and uplift of freedpeople, 11, 15, 52–53, 54, 60, 61, 64, 65, 66, 67–68, 72, 75, 77, 85–86, 198, 254–55, 264, 276 (n. 2), 278 (n. 26); African Americans' supposed lack of, 90, 190–91, 252; and woman suffrage, 175, 182–83; hierarchies of, 182–83, 252

Civil rights: and Reconstruction, 4–5; defining of, 8, 89, 90, 118, 119–20, 125, 130, 145, 173, 260, 261, 265; and voting rights, 9, 119, 120; and Kate Brown incident, 88; and Republican Party, 89, 90, 117–18, 119, 120, 265; and contracts, 89, 119, 152; and law enforcement, 89–90; extent of, 90; and common law tradition, 100; and public accommodations, 107, 119; ambiguities of, 117–26; and discrimination, 119, 152; and jury service, 119, 120, 130; and African American men's enfranchisement, 137

Civil Rights Act of 1866: and illegality of racially discriminatory statutes, 75; and streetcar access, 112; and defining of civil rights, 118–20, 145, 173, 260, 289 (n. 105); and defining of citizenship, 120, 123, 221; and federal government/states relationship, 120; opposition to, 121; and white violence, 123; and militia laws, 124; voting rights excluded from, 126; northern support for, 141; and public accommodations, 161

Civil Rights Act of 1875, 164–65, 193–94, 215–16, 224, 225–28, 230–31, 242, 243, 255, 260

Civil Rights Cases (1883), 230–31, 259–60

Civil War: and egalitarianism, 6; and fugitive migrants to Washington, D.C., 11; and black colonization, 13–15; and racial equality debates, 15–16; Washington, D.C. as military garrison during, 22; and citizenship, 119; patriotism of, 151

Clapp, Almon M., 163

Class issues. *See* Black elite; Citizens movements; Labor rights; Poor whites; Strike of day laborers; Taxpayer status;

District of Columbia Emancipation Act, 15, 25, 28, 29, 35, 41

District of Columbia Supreme Court, 30, 56, 79, 154, 187, 216, 218, 230

Doolittle, James R., 103

Douglas, Stephen, 8

Douglass, Charles, 91, 160

Douglass, Frederick: and black emigration, 35, 38; and freedpeople's capabilities, 39; and Thirteenth Amendment, 91; and Lincoln, 104, 105; attack on, 118; auto-biographies of, 125; and woman suffrage, 181, 187; and *New Era*, 200, 247; and territorial government of Washington, D.C., 217, 247; and public accommodations, 226; and Sumner, 229; and Sumner's civil rights bill, 242; and Republican Party, 248; and social equality, 260

Douglass, Frederick, Jr., 200, 239, 247

Douglass, Lewis, 163, 200, 239

Downing, George T.: and Kate Brown, 88, 98; and public school integration, 170, 189; and woman suffrage, 182, 183–84; and public accommodations, 227–28

Dred Scott v. Sandford (1857), 41, 119, 122

Dunning, William Archibald, 259

Duvall, George W., 29–30

Eaton, John, 60, 64–65

Ebenezer Chapel (Georgetown), 32

Economic issues: and Freedmen's Bureau, 63, 75, 76; and African Americans' boycott of businesses, 132; and African American men's enfranchisement, 135–36, 138, 150, 197, 219; and trade unions, 150; and freedpeople/black elite alliance, 150–51; and fairness for freedpeople, 153; and corruption of electorate, 176–77; and consolidation of governance of Washington, D.C., 195, 197–98, 207; and day laborers' strike, 209; and territorial government of Washington, D.C., 214–15, 246; and Washington, D.C. improvements, 219–20; and commission government of Washington, D.C., 258. *See also* Crash of 1873

Emancipation: and Congress, 15, 24–25, 95, 192, 262; and racial equality debates, 15, 263; and black elite, 21; and imprisonment of fugitives from slavery, 24; and municipal government, 55; and neediness of freedpeople, 58; and involuntary apprenticeship of African American children, 75; and African American men's enfranchisement, 134; woman suffrage in context of, 174; challenges of, 256

Emancipation Day celebrations, 45, 89, 118, 120–21

Emancipation Proclamation, 30, 41

Emery, Matthew, 205, 206–7

Emigration: and Lincoln, 13–14, 15, 31, 36–37; and black Washingtonians, 13–15, 25, 31, 35–39; Washington, D.C. as center of debate on, 25; and federal government, 39, 41

Employment: and black codes, 20; and discrimination, 20, 152; for freedpeople, 52, 59–60, 61, 62–63, 68, 70, 71, 76, 152; and African American men's enfranchisement, 133. *See also* Public works employment

Enforcement Acts, 213

Enlightenment, 4, 7, 131

Enslaved people: and equality, 4; as black Washingtonians, 19; conditions of, 65, 72. *See also* Freedpeople; Fugitives from slavery; Slavery

Equality: and Reconstruction policies, 3–5, 7; and public policy, 4, 7; types of, 5; meanings of, 7, 228; expansive vision of, 7–8; Lincoln's conceptual categories of, 8; and woman suffrage, 174, 188. *See also* Civil equality; Legal equality; Political equality; Racial equality; Social equality

Equal Rights League, 216, 240–43, 244, 245, 246, 255

Ethnicity: and civilizational hierarchies, 181, 182–83, 191; and Republican Party, 204, 216; and lobbying for ethnic interests, 243. *See also* German Republicans; Irish immigrants

Evening Star: and African American men's enfranchisement, 135, 136, 140, 197, 252; and public works improvements, 154; and public accommodations, 162; and public

of, 63, 75, 76; and freedwomen, 63–64, 73–74; and northern migration of freedpeople, 68–69; and marriage, 71–74; and claims to rights, 72–73, 76, 263; and reunification of freed families, 75–76; and Sojourner Truth's streetcar protest, 108; and white violence, 114, 115; legal defense program, 116; and black militia regiment, 118; Andrew Johnson's veto of renewal of, 118

Freedom: defining of, 3–4, 15–16, 40, 50, 131, 262; of black Washingtonians, 19; and self-reliance, 62

Freedpeople: freedom of, 3–4, 50; political equality of, 9; and civilizational uplift, 11, 15, 52–53, 54, 60, 61, 64, 65, 66, 67–68, 72, 75, 77, 85–86, 198, 254–55, 264, 276 (n. 2); and citizenship preparation, 11, 50, 60, 86, 216; and fugitive slave laws, 30; and black elite, 31, 32–34, 131, 148, 150–51, 262; stereotypes of, 31, 152, 197–98, 222–23, 251–53; and aid from African American churches, 31–34, 41; and relief societies, 31–34, 41, 52, 54, 60, 61, 63, 65, 67, 80, 153, 184; and colonization, 35, 36; protection from exploitation, 38; supposed capabilities of, 39, 176, 251–52, 255; and marriage, 51, 71–74, 75, 76–77, 85, 263; barracks housing for, 51–52, 53, 60, 69–74, 76, 85, 86, 113, 114, 115; employment for, 52, 59–60, 61, 62–63, 68, 70, 71, 76, 152; comportment of, 52–53, 198; neighborhoods of, 57–59, 69, 70; reuniting with family, 65, 68, 74–75, 263; responses to Freedmen's Bureau agents, 68–69, 76–77, 85; and parents' rights to children, 76; Sojourner Truth's work with, 107; migration to South, 176; and African American men's enfranchisement, 176, 197; and capacity to vote, 198, 216, 219, 222, 253; and territorial government of Washington, D.C., 237. See also Fugitives from slavery

Freeman, John, 204

Freemasons, 21, 48, 120

Fugitives from slavery: migration to Washington, D.C., 7, 11, 15, 22, 23, 27–28, 30, 31–32, 54–55; and Maryland, 23, 24, 27, 28, 29–30; imprisonment of, 24–25; and law enforcement, 28–29; and African American churches, 31, 34; and black colonization, 35; and black private schools, 79–80. See also Freedpeople

Fugitive slave laws: enforcement of, 15, 23, 24, 28–29, 30; legal decisions on, 29–30; Congress's voiding of, 30, 48

Gage, Frances, 93, 144

Gaines, Daniel Webster, 167

Gaines, Frank, 223

Gaines, Minnie, 165–67, 220, 257

Garnet, Henry Highland, 49, 91, 93, 121

Gender: and freedom, 4; and respectability, 93; and segregation by sex, 93, 95, 103, 106, 111; and sexual hierarchies, 109, 140, 144, 145, 166, 221. See also Woman suffrage; Women

Georgetown, D.C.: and District of Columbia, 17, 18; and free blacks, 20; and black public schools, 26; antebellum public schools of, 78; and African American men's enfranchisement, 132, 134–35; election with African American men voting, 147; and consolidation of governance, 194, 195

German Republicans, 204, 216, 243

Gilbert, Olive, 107–8

Gleason, Albert, 210

Government Hospital for the Insane, 167

Government Printing Office, 113, 114, 163

Grant, Ulysses S.: and police, 113; and Emancipation Day celebrations, 120; and racial equality, 131, 242; and appointment of African Americans, 158, 160; inauguration of, 158–59; and public school integration, 170; and corruption, 175; and consolidation of governance of Washington, D.C., 178, 207; and Irish Republicans, 203; and Republican Party, 205; and territorial government of Washington, D.C., 215, 217, 218, 224, 233, 246, 248, 259; waning support for, 220, 238, 250; and Liberal Republican movement, 226; and Sumner, 226–27; and black political activism, 246, 247

Greeley, Horace, 205

Green, J. W., 222, 223

Greener, Richard T., 239, 244, 246–47, 248

Grice, Caroline, 51, 52

Grice, Hannah, 51–52, 53, 70, 71

Griffing, Josephine, 107, 146, 166–67, 174–75, 180–81, 184, 186–87, 206

Grow, Galusha, 92–93

Hahn, Steven, 35

Haiti, 35, 36, 143, 204, 243, 252

Hall, Andrew, 29–30

Hamer, J. P., 34

Hamlin, Hannibal, 92

Handy, James A., 147–48

Harlan, James, 80, 197

Harlan, John Marshall, 260

Harper's Weekly, 140–41, 252

Harrold, Stanley, 19

Hatton, George, 45, 171, 202–3, 205, 206, 209–10, 219, 223, 301 (n. 72)

Haviland, Laura, 108

Henderson, Alexander, 151, 152, 293 (n. 61)

Herbert, Hilary, 259

Hibernia Engine House, 185

Himber, Henry, 209, 210

Hinton, Thomas H. C., 42, 45, 47

Hotels: equal access to, 100, 112, 161, 162, 190, 192, 225, 227; racial exclusion and segregation in, 230

Housekeeping: and equality, 50; and Freedmen's Bureau, 52, 53, 60, 86; Sojourner Truth on, 61, 107

Howard, Charles H., 60, 68–69, 70, 72–74, 76

Howard, Oliver O., 60, 67, 83, 121–22, 123, 199, 219, 291 (n. 26)

Howard, Sophia, 76

Howard University, 83, 114, 160, 192, 226, 261

Howard University Law School, 83

Howard University Medical School, 43, 83, 164

Immigrants, 20, 78, 175, 183. *See also* Irish immigrants

Independent Reform Republican movement, 178, 203, 204, 205, 206, 209

Individual rights: theories of, 4, 5, 6, 7, 263, 264; status merged with, 7, 8, 264; preparing freedpeople for, 60; and common carriers, 100, 106; and respectability, 111, 141; and

African American men's enfranchisement, 131; development and protection of, 142–43, 144; and Republican Party, 174, 179; and woman suffrage, 174, 179; and citizenship, 221; and public accommodations, 231

Industrial schools for freedwomen, 63–64, 65, 70, 71, 86

Ingle, James, 165–66

Interior Department: and black public schools, 26, 77, 80–82, 84, 148, 156, 157, 239; and freedpeople, 56; and Seventh Street corridor, 114

Irish immigrants: relationship to African Americans, 20, 113–14, 117, 204; and public works employment, 151, 201; and Republican Party, 178, 203–4, 216, 243; capability of voting, 254, 263

Israel AME Church: and freedpeople's relief programs, 31, 32; and Emancipation Proclamation, 41; and black soldiers, 42, 43; and public demonstrations, 48; and black political activism, 132, 147; and black public schools, 157–58

Israel Lyceum, 32, 33

Jacobs, Harriet, 82, 184

Jim Crow system and black public schools, 54

Johnson, Andrew: and 1865 celebration of July 4, 99; and police, 113; and Republican Party, 117–18, 119; lenient policy toward former Confederates, 118, 126, 141; and African American men's enfranchisement, 120, 127, 130, 135, 139, 140, 145, 153; and Emancipation Day celebration, 121; and black militias, 123, 124; and black public schools, 157; and racial discrimination in laws, 159; and political appointments, 160

Johnson, Harriet, 182

Johnson, Henry, 91, 95, 239, 240

Johnson, Jerome, 241

Johnson, John D., 35–36, 38

Johnson, John T., 223, 241, 246

Johnson, Reverdy, 103–4, 105, 110, 136, 144

Johnston, Allan, 28

John Wesley AME Zion Church, 34

Jones, Alfred, 80

Julian, George A., 186

Jury service: for African American men, 1, 158, 159, 192, 262; and political equality, 9; and civil rights, 119, 120, 130; and African American men's enfranchisement, 127; and Gaines case, 166–67; for women, 166–67; law banning discrimination in, 228

Justices of the peace, African Americans as, 159

Kaczorowski, Robert J., 119

Keckly, Elizabeth, 32, 33, 273 (n. 51)

Kelley, William, 134

Kendall Green, 113

Kentucky, 146

Ketchum, Agnes, 160

Kilbourn, Hallet, 233

Kimball, John, 51–52, 74, 82

King, Charles, 80

Ku Klux Klan, 213

Labor rights, 151, 152, 208–9, 210, 212, 231, 232, 265. *See also* Trade unions

Lamon, Ward, 24, 29–30

Land access and freedpeople, 3–4

Land reform, 231

Langston, John Mercer, 160, 217, 226, 242, 293 (n. 64)

Latta, James, 233

Law enforcement: and equal rights, 7–8; and black codes, 20; and fugitives from slavery, 28–29; and legal equality, 89, 112; and civil rights, 89–90; discrimination in, 115, 116–17, 159; and public accommodations, 230; and crime rates, 300–301 (n. 59). *See also* Police

Laws: and racial discrimination, 6, 8, 9, 10, 26–27, 159, 262; and upstart claims, 7; and civil equality, 9, 10, 11; fugitive slave laws, 15, 23, 24, 28–30, 48; state laws, 119, 186, 187–88, 190, 225, 226, 265; militia laws, 124; banning discrimination, 158, 160–62, 172, 216, 224–25, 230, 261. *See also specific laws*

Lee, Margaret Noble, 258

Legal equality: and radical Republicans, 23, 73, 265; defining of, 27, 89, 105, 112, 130, 131, 136, 138, 164–65, 171, 224, 227, 228,

255, 259–61, 264, 265; and freedpeople's circumstances as former slaves, 73, 75; and public school integration, 85, 170–71; and discrimination, 105–6, 110, 112, 152, 255; and criminal law, 112, 116; and public accommodations, 129, 130, 259–60; and women's rights, 179–80; opponents of, 241; institutionalization of, 255

Legal proceedings: discrimination in, 9, 25, 26, 27, 112, 116, 255; and civil rights, 89

Lessoff, Alan, 207, 220

Levy Court, 18, 194

Lewis, Elsie M., 225

Liberal Republicans, 205, 226, 227, 228, 252

Liberator, 104

Liberia and black colonization, 35–36, 38

Liberty and freedom, 4

Lincoln, Abraham: and conceptual categories of equality, 8; and black emigration, 13–14, 15, 31, 36–37; and black delegation, 13–15, 21, 31, 35, 36–39, 240; and fugitive slave laws, 24; and District of Columbia Emancipation Act, 25; and black soldiers, 43; and Catholic Sabbath schools' fund-raiser, 99; and social occasions, 104–5; and birthright citizenship, 119; and Emancipation Day celebrations, 121; rally in memory of, 131; and restrictions on African American men's enfranchisement, 139

Lincoln Cooperative Building and Deposit Association, 153

Lincoln Radical Republican Laboring Association, 151

Lincoln Reserves, 121, 123–24

Lippincott's Magazine, 238

Literacy: and disfranchisement, 10; and African American men's enfranchisement, 139, 222; and voting rights, 179, 180

Lloyd, Thomas E., 135

Low, Eliza, 75–76

Low, Harriet, 76

MacArthur, Arthur, 230

Marriage: of freedpeople, 51, 71–74, 75, 76–77, 85, 263, 281–82 (n. 68); and African American men's enfranchisement, 127, 129;

Navy Yard, 163

Neighborhoods, 55, 56, 57, 113–15, 132–33, 167–68, 233–34, 235, 237

New Era, 200–201, 208

Newman, Charlie, 184

Newman, Emma, 184

New National Era, 223, 229, 239

New National Era and Citizen, 239–40, 243, 244, 245, 246–47

New Orleans, La., 123, 221

Newton, Alonzo E., 168

New York City: draft riots of, 47; black northerners from, 65; and consolidated governance, 195, 215; citizens movement, 221; political reform in, 253–54, 263

New York Herald, 140, 195

New York Independent, 228

New York Stock Exchange, 246

New York Times, 185, 244, 260

New York Tribune, 185, 248

New York World, 33, 172, 197

Night schools for freedpeople, 65

Norfolk, Va., 123

Normal schools, 83, 239, 241, 245, 247

North and northerners: citizenship in antebellum period, 6; black northern speakers in Washington, D.C., 33, 38; black northerners against colonization, 35–36; and freedpeople's relief societies, 52, 54, 60, 63, 65, 80; black northern teachers, 65; schools for freedpeople established by, 65; and common schools, 77; white northern teachers, 80, 81, 82, 83; and public school integration, 84–85, 190; and meaning of civil rights, 89; and African American men's enfranchisement, 131, 140, 141; black northerners as political leaders, 160; municipal government in, 176; and public accommodations, 225; black northerners in Republican Party, 244; urban reform movements in, 263

Northern Market, 46

Novak, William, 57

Odd Fellows, Grand United Order of, 48, 120, 161

Olin, Abraham B., 273 (n. 44)

Omnibuses, 45

Owner, William, 93, 95–96, 121, 126

Patent Office, 114, 150

Patriot, 211, 223

Patterson, James W., 78, 189–91, 193

Patterson, Mary Jane, 306 (n. 59)

Payne, Daniel, 31

Pearl (schooner), 20

Pennsylvania Avenue, 17, 18, 43, 99, 154, 217

Perry, Rufus, 61–62

Petitions: and defining equality, 7; for appointment of Board of Trustees of Colored Schools candidates, 77, 80, 81; and African American men's enfranchisement, 117, 132, 133–34

Philadelphia, Pa., 65, 195

Piatt, Donn, 252

Police: discrimination against African Americans, 7, 112, 114, 115, 116–17, 159; and black codes, 20, 21; and fugitives from slavery, 24; indifference toward blacks, 41–42; and assaults on black soldiers, 46; and protection of property, 57–58, 117; and freedpeople's neighborhoods, 57–59, 70; cooperation with Freedmen's Bureau, 58–59; treatment of African American women, 87–88; and legal equality, 89; and street-level politics, 89–90; working conditions of, 112–13; African Americans' confrontations with, 125; supervision of election, 147; African Americans as, 159; and African Americans as justices of the peace, 159; and day laborers' strike, 209, 211. *See also* Law enforcement

Political appointments for African Americans, 158, 160, 172

Political equality: and Lincoln, 8; of freedpeople, 9; civil equality separated from, 118, 120, 145; and black militias, 125; and social equality, 129, 137–38, 166, 192; and African American men's enfranchisement, 130, 137, 147, 192; defining of, 136, 138, 159; and jury service, 166; and woman suffrage, 175; opposition to, 251

Quartermaster of the Military Department, 113, 114

Quasi-public places: equal access to, 6, 44, 48, 89, 104, 167, 192, 193; segregation in, 6, 44, 48, 89, 230; and respectability, 90; and social equality, 129, 227

Rabinowitz, Howard, 177

Race, determination of, 170

Race-based solidarity, 33

Race war rhetoric: and African American men's enfranchisement, 145, 148; and Republican Party, 204, 216, 242, 243

Racial deference: rituals of, 117, 125, 230; and African American men's enfranchisement, 137; and public works employment, 152; white expectations of, 228–29

Racial difference: theories of, 52, 86, 137, 176, 227, 264; and racial traits, 66–67

Racial discrimination: supposed cultural deficiencies of freedpeople, 53, 61, 66, 67–68; and public accommodations, 90, 109; and African American men's enfranchisement, 137, 138, 140, 143, 183; and jury service, 159; and civilizational hierarchies, 182–83, 252, 264; and public school integration, 188–89, 191, 193; and citizenship, 221

Racial equality: and abolition of slavery, 2; defining of, 3, 7, 8, 9–10, 11, 129, 130, 148, 159, 162, 171, 241, 244, 255, 265; and emancipation, 15, 263; and Republican Party, 15, 177, 198, 216, 233, 255–56; Civil War debates on, 15–16; congressional debates on, 16, 26–27, 262; Augusta as activist for, 43; and black associations, 49; and public school integration, 84; consensus vision of, 89; Sayles J. Bowen as activist for, 154–55; and corruption, 175; limits of, 212, 227, 261; and citizenship, 221; acceptance of formal racial equality, 255

Racial uplift: black elite's commitment to, 32–33, 61–62, 81–82, 151, 231–32; and racial discrimination, 53, 66–68, 193, 198–99, 216–17, 222, 264

Racism: avoiding explicit language of, 10, 53,

110, 175, 177, 254; and black colonization, 36; Lincoln charged with, 36; and woman suffrage, 175; government's role in, 193; intransigence of, 256; and historiography of Reconstruction, 259

Radical Republicans: and civil equality, 9; and legal equality, 23, 73, 265; resistance to, 73, 173; and Kate Brown incident, 88; and social equality, 137–38, 192; and African American men's enfranchisement, 139, 140, 158, 192; and Sayles J. Bowen, 153; egalitarian reform in Washington, D.C., 179, 262; and woman suffrage, 185, 186; and nondiscrimination principles, 193; and governance of Washington, D.C., 196, 207, 213, 257; and race as arbitrary category, 242; and emancipation, 262

Railroads: equal access to, 1, 87–88, 98, 100, 101–2, 130, 138, 190; and separate accommodations, 103; segregation on, 106; and class issues, 106, 125; and antidiscrimination provisions, 107

Reconstruction: and civil rights, 4–5; and status, 5; unrest during, 89, 212–13; and racial equality, 90, 242, 261; and public accommodations, 101, 261; Andrew Johnson's opposition to, 118; Republican Party unity on, 118–19; and voting rights, 178; and consolidation of governance of Washington, D.C., 194; waning support for, 217, 220, 224, 238, 250, 257; and defining of citizenship, 221; and African American men's enfranchisement, 259; and individual rights, 263

Reconstruction Acts of 1867, 112, 146

Reconstruction policies: and equality, 3–5, 7; conflict over, 11, 16, 118–19, 212–13, 225–26; and civilization of freedpeople, 53; debates on, 118; and Republican Party, 126; and African American men's enfranchisement, 139, 238, 251–52; and corruption, 175; and Fifteenth Amendment, 205; excesses of, 237; and South, 262

Redemption, 177, 213, 216, 262

Reid, Whitelaw, 109–10

Republican Party: and African American men's

246–51, 261, 262; and Republican Central Committee, 239, 245; and black political activism, 247, 248; reputation of, 258; and corruption, 259

Shiner, Isaac, 245

Shiner, Michael, 245

Simms, John, 32

Simms, John A., 223

Simon, Charles, 117

Slade, William, 34

Slaveholders' republic, 135

Slaveowners: compensation of, 25; reclaiming fugitives from slavery, 28, 29; sexual dominion over enslaved women, 65, 72; holding freedchildren as apprentices, 75–76

Slave patrols, 27

Slavery: abolition of, 1, 2, 3–4, 6, 7, 11, 25, 48, 91, 121, 140, 171, 193; and American principles, 12; congressional debates on, 19; in Washington, D.C., 19–20, 21, 23, 25, 27, 140; black soldiers undermining, 44; remnants of, 44–45, 48, 161, 230; barbarism of, 52, 60, 72, 85, 191; and habits of freedpeople, 52, 66, 72, 219, 264; legacy of, 52, 75, 78, 85, 105–6, 125, 189, 242, 255; recognition of freedpeople's relationships during, 72–73, 74; effects on African Americans, 73, 139, 176, 255; reunification of slave families, 75–76; laws and customs replacing, 89; violence of, 90; and racial deference, 125; status hierarchies of, 142–43; and party alignments, 205. See also Enslaved people; Freedpeople; Fugitives from slavery

Slave trade, 19

Smalls, Robert, 33

Smith, James McCune, 49, 91

Smithsonian lecture series, 23

Social, Civil, and Statistical Association (SCSA), 34–38, 39

Social equality: and Lincoln, 8, 104–5; and public school integration, 9, 190, 191–93, 194; ambiguity in, 9–10, 261; and African American men's enfranchisement, 127, 129, 130, 134, 136–37, 140, 172; and private spaces, 127, 129, 130, 136, 192–93, 225, 227, 261, 265; and political equality, 129, 137–38,

166, 192; defining of, 136, 137–38, 171–72, 173, 177, 192, 212, 216, 227, 260, 261; and public accommodations, 160–62, 230–31; civil equality distinguished from, 260; and segregation, 261

Social mobility for African Americans, 225, 231, 232

Soldiers and Sailors Union, 163

South: and disfranchisement, 10, 259; and black emigration, 35; and public schools, 78; antebellum laws forbidding African American education, 79; and black preparatory high schools, 83; and streetcar access, 112; white violence in, 123; and Fourteenth Amendment, 141; and African American men's enfranchisement, 145, 146, 176–77, 180, 183, 238, 252, 259; urban crisis in, 176–77; and trade unions, 181; and public school integration, 189, 190, 191; and infrastructure improvements, 215; and public accommodations, 225; and Reconstruction policies, 262

South Carolina, 252

Spencer, George E., 11, 256

Spurgin, William F., 58–59

Stanton, Edwin M., 123–24, 168

Stanton, Elizabeth Cady, 143, 166, 175, 178–79, 180, 181, 182–84

Starkweather, Henry H., 224, 248

State laws: racially discriminatory language prohibited in, 119, 226, 265; and woman suffrage, 186, 187–88; and public school integration, 190; and public accommodations, 225

States: and voting requirements, 56; and slave marriages, 72; and involuntary apprenticeship of African American children, 75; and private institutions, 265. See also Federal government/states relationship

Status: and voting rights, 5, 263; and civic associations, 5, 21, 48, 129; in relation to individual rights, 5–6, 7, 8, 9, 23, 142–43, 220–21, 263–65; of white women, 6, 95; of soldiers, 42, 44–46, 48, 111; domestic uplift as foundation for, 53, 86; of militiamen,

termination of self-government in, 1, 10, 11, 250, 253, 255, 256, 257, 258, 259; governance of, 1–2, 3, 7, 12, 18, 19–20, 22, 26, 135, 145–46, 165, 177–78, 185–86, 193, 194–207, 216, 217, 221, 224, 237, 240, 249–50, 251, 253, 254, 257, 258, 259; citizenship issues in, 3; as federal territory, 10, 12, 178, 187, 199–200, 207; establishment of, 16–18; development of, 19; urbanization in, 19; slavery in, 19–20, 21, 23, 25, 27, 140; as military garrison during Civil War, 22; and political changes of Civil War, 23; ratio of blacks to whites in, 28; black northerners visiting, 33; as crucible of equality, 49; housing reform efforts in, 59; as focal point for freedmen's aid, 60; population of, 69, 112–13; marriage law in, 73–74; public schools in, 78, 83; and public school integration, 84, 85, 191, 194, 207, 238, 239; and federal government ties, 90, 91, 256, 258; and business licenses, 105, 161; and African American men's enfranchisement, 131, 134–36, 146, 147, 148, 172, 176, 177–78, 196; and public works improvements, 151, 154, 162, 176, 177–78, 201–3, 206, 208, 213, 214, 215, 217–19, 221–24, 232, 233, 238, 249, 251; and woman suffrage, 174, 177, 179, 185–86, 188, 207; and movement to consolidate governance, 177–78, 188, 194–207, 208, 210, 211, 213, 217, 218, 219–20, 223, 254; Board of Public Works, 207, 210, 211, 215, 217, 218, 219, 224, 233, 237, 249, 252; and day laborers' strike, 208–11; and territorial government, 214, 215–21, 223–24, 230, 232–33, 235, 237–41, 244–45, 246, 247–53, 255, 257, 259, 261, 262; and real estate market, 233–35, 237–38, 249, 258; and economic crash of 1873, 246. *See also* Black Washingtonians; Police; White Washingtonians

Washington, George, 17
Washington and Alexandria Railroad, 101
Washington Board of Trade, 195–96, 198
Washington City: and District of Columbia, 17, 18; and free blacks, 20; antiemancipation resolution of, 25; and black public schools,

26; antebellum public schools in, 78; and consolidation of governance, 194, 195
Washington County, 17, 18, 194
Weeden, John C., 108
Wesley Zion Church (7th ward), 147
West, Marcellus, 202, 210, 230, 260
Western territories and universal manhood suffrage, 145–46
White as variegated category, 243–44
White children, public schools for, 78, 168
White elite: and racial equality, 10, 255; and black codes, 20; and hostility toward freedpeople, 55, 56, 264; and public schools, 78–79, 84; hostility toward black private schools, 79; and African American men's enfranchisement, 135–36, 145, 199, 253; and governance of Washington, D.C., 196, 199, 207, 217, 251, 254, 257, 258; and Washington, D.C. improvements, 219–20, 233; and urban problems, 238, 258
White lawyers, 30
White men: suffrage of, 4, 6, 18; militia service duty for, 6
White northern teachers and black public schools, 80, 81, 82, 83
White supremacy, 137, 198–99, 259
White violence: and Emancipation Proclamation, 41, 42; and recruitment of black soldiers, 43–44; and black soldiers' demands for respect, 45–46, 47; and military officials, 46–47; and New York City draft riots, 47; and freedpeople, 69; and streetcars, 107, 115; and Swampoodle neighborhood, 113–14; and Seventh Street neighborhood, 114–15; and African American men's enfranchisement, 117; and black militia units, 123; in South, 123; and Ku Klux Klan, 213
White Washingtonians: hostility toward blacks, 16, 20, 44; associations of, 21; and black associations, 48; and Metropolitan Police, 113; and African American men's enfranchisement, 134–35, 196
White Woman's Intelligent Franchise Association, 180
White women: status of, 6, 95; African

Americans as threat to, 55, 129, 138, 140, 183, 228–29; on industrial schools, 63–64; and attendance in Congress, 93, 95–98, 228; and streetcars, 108, 109–10, 228; and suffrage movement, 175, 179, 180, 184

White working-class population: and Swampoodle, 113; and African American men's enfranchisement, 136; and African American laborers, 155; and day laborers' strike, 209, 210, 211; and Washington, D.C. improvements, 232; capability of voting, 254, 263

Whitman, Walt, 17

Wilbur, Julia: and freedpeople, 61; and Kate Brown, 88; and attendance at Congress, 93, 96; and racial tensions, 118, 123; and Republican Party, 126; and election with African American men voting, 148; and presidential appointment of African Americans, 160; and separate accommodations, 161; and Gaines case, 167; and public school integration, 170; and woman suffrage, 184–85, 187

Willey, Waitman T., 102, 143

Williams, Joseph E., 35, 36

Wilson, Henry, 24–27, 105, 131

Wilson, James, 134

Wilson, William J., 82

Wirtz, Henry, 217

Wisewell Barracks, 114, 115

Witnesses and racial discrimination, 25, 27

Woman suffrage: and racial equality, 3; and universal rights, 4; and African American men's enfranchisement, 11, 174–75, 180–81, 183–84, 262; congressional debates on, 131, 143–45, 174, 177, 179, 185–86; and Republican Party, 139, 143, 144, 145, 262; lack of political urgency for, 144–45; schism in movement, 175, 180, 181, 183; and corruption of electorate, 175–76, 188, 264; paradoxes of, 178–88; and women as wage labor, 179; New Departure argument, 186–87; and privileges, 263–64

Women: women's rights, 6, 179–80. *See also* African American women; Gender; White women; Woman suffrage

Woodhull, Victoria, 186

Workingmen's associations. *See* Labor rights; Public works employment; Trade Unions

Wylie, Andrew, 56, 57, 218, 273 (n. 44)

YMCA, 150